CHARLES F SCHAEFFER

Annotations on Matthew Part 2

Copyright © 2019 by Charles F Schaeffer

Copyright 2019 Just and Sinner. All rights reserved. The original text is in public domain, but regarding this updated edition, besides brief quotations, none of this book shall be reproduced without permission.

Permission inquiries may be sent to JustandSinner@yahoo.com

Just & Sinner

Ithaca, NY 14850

www.JSPublishing.org

First edition

ISBN: 9780692427194

This book was professionally typeset on Reedsy. Find out more at reedsy.com

Contents

Original Publishing Info	iv
Matthew 16	1
Matthew 17	23
Matthew 18	43
Matthew 19	72
Matthew 20	102
Matthew 21	130
Matthew 22	165
Matthew 23	195
Matthew 24	223
Matthew 25	274
Matthew 26	304
Matthew 27	372
Matthew 28	416
Appendix	432

Original Publishing Info

ANNOTATIONS
on the
GOSPEL ACCORDING TO ST. MATTHEW
by
CHARLES F. SCHAEFFER, D.D.
Formerly Professor of Theology, in Capital University. Columbus, O., and in the Theological Seminary of the General Synod, Gettysburg, Pa.; and Chairman of the Theological Faculty in the Lutheran Theological Seminary, Philadelphia, Pa.
Part I.—Matthew 1.–15
Part II.—Matthew 16.–28
New York
The Christian Literature Co.
MDCCCXCV
Copyright, 1895,
by
THE CHRISTIAN LITERATURE CO.
THE LUTHERAN COMMENTARY
a plain exposition of the
Holy Scriptures of the New Testament
by
scholars of the lutheran church in america
edited by
HENRY EYSTER JACOBS

Vol. I. & II

1

Matthew 16

¹ And the Pharisees and Sadducees came, and tempting him asked him to shew them a sign from heaven.

A. "The Jews require a sign," said Paul (1 Cor. 1:22), alluding to their dulness in apprehending divine truth, and their carnal desire after mere outward manifestations of divine power. They require signs of Christ at least thrice; first, John 2:18; second, above, 12:38, ff.; here we have the third. The Pharisees as a body always manifest hostility to the Saviour's holy doctrine. The individuals who appear here, undoubtedly form a different group from those who are presented on the previous occasion (ch. 12); the locality, the accompanying discourses, etc., are different; the Sadducees here unite with them, and the request now either assumes a new form, or is repeated with a distinct specification—the sign must come **from heaven.—B. Tempting** (see 4:1, D.); the word is here used as in 19:3; 22:18, and John 8:6). In the latter passage the word is explained by the additional clause: "that they might have (= be enabled) to accuse Him."

The sense then is: They subjected Him to a trial or test, which, as they maliciously hoped, He could not successfully endure.—**C. A sign, etc.** (see the ann. to 12:38, D.).

2, 3 But he answered and said unto them, When it is evening, ye say, *It will be* fair weather: for the heaven is red. And in the morning, *It will be* foul weather to-day: for the heaven is red and lowering. Ye know how to discern the face of the heaven; but ye cannot *discern* the signs of the times?

A. He answered, etc. The Lord alludes, as on an earlier occasion (Luke 12:54–56), to the well-known diligence with which the Jews observed the prognostics of fair or foul weather. The sense is: Do ye allege that ye cannot yet decide whether My works prove that I am of God? (John 10:38; 14:11). But ye regard the sky as furnishing indications of the weather which is at hand; can ye not then judge with similar accuracy from My past works or *signs* that the kingdom of God is come unto you = that the Messiah, exercising divine power, "standeth among you" already? (John 1:26). See a similar illustration, 24:32, 33.—**Lowering** = *gloomy;* the same word is rendered *sad* (Mark 10:22).—**B. Discern** = *judge of, decide on,* as the original word sometimes means (e. g. 1 Cor. 6:5). The wise men (2:2) exhibited far more religious intelligence.—**C. The face of the heaven** = the aspect, that is, the visible expanse, resembling an extended surface (comp. "face of the earth," Gen. 11:4, 8; Luke 21:35).—**D. The signs of the times** = the signs already given, indicating the times of the Messiah. These distinguishing signs are, for instance, the fulfilment of the ancient prophecies respecting the birth of Christ (2:4–6), the preaching of His forerunner (3:3, ff.; 11:4–15), the giving of the light of the Gospel (4:14 ff.), the miracles wrought by Christ (11:4, 5).

⁴ An evil and adulterous generation seeketh after a sign; and there shall be no sign given unto it, but the sign of Jonah. And he left them, and departed.

As the demands of the Jews proceeded from presumption and hatred to Christ, and not from a spirit of honest inquiry, He refuses to comply, and dismisses them with the same answer which He had given to others on the previous occasion (see above, 12:39), where the terms are explained.—**He left them** (comp. Tit. 3:10).

⁵ And the disciples came to the other side, and forgot to take bread.

A. The other side = of the sea of Galilee.—**B. Forgot, etc.** Possibly the Lord, at the close of the foregoing conversation, had hastened their departure; "one loaf" (Mark 8:14) alone remained of their former stock of provisions.

⁶ And Jesus said unto them, Take heed and beware of the leaven of the Pharisees and Sadducees.

A. Jesus said = in allusion to the malice and hypocrisy which these men, who preferred their own wisdom to God's truth, had betrayed during the last conversation. **Take heed, etc.** So, too, Paul frequently admonishes Timothy and Titus to be on their guard and watch strictly over the preservation of "sound doctrine" (1 Tim. 1:10; 2 Tim. 1:13; 4:3; Tit. 1:9, 13; 2:1, 2).—**B. Leaven.** An image of any influence acting powerfully but noiselessly on the mind and heart. In 13:33, B., above, it illustrates the power of divine grace over the soul. Here it exemplifies the powerful but corrupting influence of religious errors on the minds and hearts of the thoughtless and ignorant (see below, ver. 12). A false doctrine, like "a little leaven" (1 Cor. 5:6; Gal. 5:9), may vitiate an individual's whole system of faith, and operate disastrously on his soul.

⁷ And they reasoned among themselves, saying, We took no bread.

Reasoned = reflected, as in Luke 1:29; they sought after the Lord's object in uttering the words. The disciples at first misunderstood Him, as the words were probably addressed to them without any preliminary remark, and were an abrupt expression of the Lord's grief mentioned in Mark 8:12. Their slowness of heart (Luke 24:25) in understanding and believing, had only recently been rebuked (15:16). They imagine, in their ignorance of their Master's spiritual meaning, that He said: Even as the Jews do not eat with Gentiles (Acts 11:2, 3), so I now command you, My disciples, when ye need food, not to eat bread in company with the Pharisees and Sadducees.

⁸ And Jesus perceiving it, said, O ye of little faith, why reason ye among yourselves, because ye have no bread?

A. O ye ... faith (see 6:30, C.).—**B. Why reason, etc.** = why do ye apprehend that ye will suffer from the want of food, even if your carnal interpretation of my words were correct?

⁹, ¹⁰ Do ye not yet perceive, neither remember the five loaves of the five thousand, and how many baskets ye took up? Neither the seven loaves of the four thousand, and how many baskets ye took up?

The sense is: When, on two occasions recently (14:15 ff.; 15:32 ff.) no food could be obtained by human means, did I not each time supply the wants of thousands? Can you still think that any serious inconvenience will result from your want of a supply of food? For **loaves** (see 26:26, B.).

¹¹ How is it that ye do not perceive that I spake not to you concerning bread? But beware of the leaven of the Pharisees

and Sadducees?

How is it, etc. = Why are ye so slow in understanding that the leaven to which I refer is an image only of spiritual things? (Comp. 15:16).

¹² Then understood they how that he bade them not beware of the leaven of bread, but of the teaching of the Pharisees and Sadducees.

A. Then = when His rebuke recalls their wandering thoughts.—**B. Teaching, etc.** The word *teaching,* includes not only precepts, articles of faith, etc., but also, as in 7:28, C., the general spirit, tendency, or genius of any particular system of faith ("leaven," ver. 6); see 2 John, ver. 9, 10; Rev. 2:14, 15, 24, and above, 15:3. According to Luke 12:1, the characteristic feature of the religion of the Pharisees, was its insincerity or "hypocrisy;" (see below, ch. 23:3, B.). The Lord's words here, therefore, imply: Be upright, humble and earnest in serving God, and beware of everything that characterizes the sectarian doctrines of the Pharisees, as distinct from the spiritual truths which they read to you in the synagogue (23:1–3).

¹³ Now when Jesus came into the parts of Cesarea Philippi, he asked his disciples, saying, Who do men say that the Son of man is?

A. Parts, vicinity, region of, as above, 15:21, B.—**B. Cesarea Philippi.** In the northern part of Palestine, an ancient city named Paneas (now called by the Arabs *Bânèâs*), was situated at the southern base of Mount Hermon. The tetrarch Philip (Luke 3:1) rebuilt it, and in honor of the emperor Tiberius (who, like Augustus, Luke 2:1; Claudius, Acts 11:28; Nero, Acts 25:8, and other Roman emperors, bore the title of Caesar, Luke 20:22; John 19:12), gave it the name of

Cesarea = Cesar's city, imperial city. It was called *Philip's* (= Philippi) Cesarea, in order to distinguish it from another city of the same name on the Mediterranean Sea, often mentioned in the Acts, e. g. 8:40; 9:30; 10:1, where the Roman procurators usually resided (Acts 23:23, 24, 33; 25:1; see below, 27:2, B.).—**C. He asked his disciples** = to whose faith in Him He desires to give greater distinctness and power, as ver. 15 shows, and whose future official character as His apostles and the founders of the Church, He now proposed to explain more fully as the close of His labors approached. The conversation occurred "by the way" (Mark 8:27), after the Lord had been "alone praying" (Luke 9:18).—**D. Who do men** = that are neither My disciples nor My declared enemies, etc.; the sense is: Who am I, according to the popular opinion, I, who so often (for instance, 8:20; 9:6; 10:23) term Myself the Son of man? (See 8:20, B.). The question, in another form, still recurs to the believer in his daily self-examination: What is Christ to *me?* Is He indeed precious to my soul? (1 Pet. 2:7).

[14] And they said, Some *say* John the Baptist; some, Elijah; and others, Jeremiah, or one of the prophets.

A. John the Baptist (14:2, B.; John 1:20).—**B. Elijah.** Many Jews, misinterpreting the words in Malachi 4:5, supposed that this prophet could re-appear on earth as the immediate forerunner of the Messiah (see 11:14, B. and 17:10).—**C. Jeremiah, etc.** Others of the Jews, with no better authority than that of idle legends, supposed that Jeremiah would be the herald of the Messiah; others, again, believed that some one of the prophets of the O. T. not specified by name, would hold the office. Such opinions of the ignorant and unreflecting present, among other grave errors, these two: first, that a deceased prophet would return to the earth at the coming of the Messiah, and, secondly, that Jesus was not Himself the Messiah, but, at most, only His forerunner. "Our reason, without the light and grace of revelation, will not enable us to receive Christ according to the true faith. They who believe that Christ is in nothing higher than a holy man and wise teacher, or than 'one of the prophets,' still walk in darkness, and do not truly know Him." (John 17:3).—Luther.

¹⁵ He saith unto them, But who say ye that I am?

The conversation was commenced by the Lord in order to reach the present point = a solemn, direct and sincere confession of faith on the part of the disciples (comp. 22:42).—**Ye** = all the disciples, for "this question, the reply to it of Peter, or the confession of faith, and the following declaration of Christ, concern all the disciples alike, and not Peter alone."—Luther.

¹⁶ And Simon Peter answered and said, Thou art the Christ, the Son of the living God.

A. Answered = in the name of all, for Christ had asked the question of all (comp. John 6:69).—**B. The Christ** = the Messiah Himself (see the explanation of the term, 1:1, B., and comp. 26:63).—**C. The Son** = not merely the Son of man, possessing a human nature, but also the Son of God = divine (see 3:17, B. and 8:29, C., **D. Living God.** The term *living*, repeatedly and emphatically applied to God (Acts 14:15; 2 Cor. 3:3; Hebr. 3:12; 10:31; Rev. 7:2), belongs to Him alone, inasmuch as He who always was, and always will be, and who alone "hath life in Himself" (John 5:26), is the source of all life. The idols or gods of the heathen "are nothing in the world" (1 Cor. 8:4), and the life of men and angels depends on His will (comp. 26:63, D.). The sense is: We believe that Thou art not only the promised Messiah, our Deliverer from sin and death, but also that Thou art the eternal and only begotten Son of God (John 1:14, 18), our only Lord and King.

¹⁷ And Jesus answered and said unto him, Blessed art thou, Simon Barjona: for flesh and blood hath not revealed it unto thee, but my Father which is in heaven.

A. Blessed = very happy, highly favored (see 5:3, B.).—**B. Bar-jona** = son of Jonas (see John 1:42; 21:16). The word *bar*, a Chaldee term often occurring in Jewish names (e. g. Acts 4:36, signifies *son*).—**C. Flesh and blood.** This expression in Eph. 6:12, and especially in Gal. 1:16, referring to the distinguishing attributes of man in his present state (see 1 Cor. 15:50), evidently designates that which is *human* = feeble, transitory, etc., as contra-distinguished from the divine perfections. It is hence here equivalent to the terms: feeble human reason or wisdom, imperfect human knowledge, skill, etc.—**D. Hath not ... heaven.** These deep truths respecting Christ's nature or person, His atoning work, etc., can be known only from revelation through grace (Matt. 11:27; 1 Cor. 2:10; 12:3; Gal. 1:15, 16; 1 John 4:2). "I cannot by my own reason or strength believe in Jesus Christ my Lord, or come to Him; but the Holy Spirit hath called me through the Gospel, etc."—Luther's *Explanation of the Creed.*—The Saviour terms Peter **blessed** for a twofold reason: first, because the Father condescended to reveal such momentous and life-giving truths to him, and, secondly, because Peter himself had followed the guidance of divine grace, and received the truth with a believing, trusting and joyful heart, not like the "devils who also believe and tremble" (James 2:19).

¹⁸ And I also say unto thee, That thou art Peter, and upon this rock I will build my church; and the gates of Hades shall not prevail against it.

A. And I ... thee = Thy confession of faith is so prompt, sound and sincere, that I will now reveal the nature of thy future apostolic commission. From this period, also (ver. 21), the Lord began to speak plainly of His approaching sufferings and death.—**B. Thou art Peter** = remember thy surname of **Peter.** The Lord alludes to an earlier occasion (John 1:42), when He gave to Simon the name of Cephas or Kephas. This word means *stone,* or, rather, *rock,* and the Hebrew form of the word (*Keph,* plur. *Kephim;* Syr. and Chal. *Kepha*) is so translated in Job 30:6; Jer. 4:29. (When the word *rock* in Greek stands as the name of Simon, it has the form *Petros,* the final syllable being a masculine termination; but when it is to be understood in the sense of *rock,* as in this verse, and in Matt. 7:24; Rom. 9:33; 1 Cor. 10:4, the last syllable usually has the Greek feminine form, namely, *petra.*) It is worthy of observation that Mark, Luke and John omit these words entirely; this circumstance plainly shows that they did not find in them the sense which the Papists ascribe to the passage in their vain attempt to justify the pernicious doctrine respecting the primacy of the Pope.—**C. And upon this rock** (Greek, *petra,* not *Petros*—thus indicating that the *rock* is not Peter *himself*). A **rock** is a familiar image indicating power, stability, security (Ps. 27:5). Hence God is called a *rock* (Deut. 32:4; 2 Sam. 22:2; Ps. 18:2); thus, too, David calls the Lord *the rock of his salvation* (Ps. 89:26; 2 Sam. 22:47). Now, in view of such scriptural language, and also of the superstructure, namely, the Church of Christ, which is to be built upon the rock, it is already evident that a feeble mortal cannot possibly constitute such an enduring foundation.—**D. I will build my church.** After the Church had been actually organized, the name *church*, was repeatedly employed in the Acts, the Epistles and the Revelation; it occurs only in one other verse in the four Gospels, namely, Matt. 18:17. In the latter passage the Lord evidently refers to the Church as a visible organization, that is, consisting of members publicly known and recognized as such. In this sense the Church, when rightly constituted, consists of all believers among whom the Gospel is preached in its purity, and the holy Sacraments are administered according to the Gospel. Among these believers, however, "tares" (13:25, 38), that is, hypocrites and false Christians, may exist, for God alone knows the heart. In the present passage, on the other hand, the Lord appears to speak of the Church, as it is designed to exist on earth, consisting of true believers and saints alone. These, whose faith, hopes and internal light and glory, cannot be seen with the eye (comp. Col. 1:13) constitute the invisible Church, and of them it is said: "The Lord knoweth them that are His" (2 Tim. 2:19). It is further styled: "a glorious church, etc." (Eph. 5:27). This Church, in its spiritual and holy character, in which light, life and peace dwell (Rom. 14:17), and which Christ in various parables terms *the kingdom of God* (see Excursus I.), is the church to which reference is made in the present text. The word **build** indicates the image, originally derived from the holy temple, of an edifice constructed of suitable materials, and established on a firm foundation; the image often occurs (1 Cor. 3:9, ff.; 2 Cor. 6:16; Eph. 2:20; 1 Peter 2:5). Now, since the whole constitutes, according to the character of the invisible church, as just described, a spiritual building, and is, indeed called "a spiritual house" in 1 Peter 2:5, it is evident again (as in ann. C. above) that the foundation cannot be any one living man, like Peter, but must be of a spiritual and divine nature. Further, that foundation is declared in Eph. 2:20; Rev. 21:14, to be, or to consist of, "the apostles and prophets" whose holy doctrines and preaching alone gave them rank and importance; they again are all supported by Jesus Christ, He Himself being the "chief corner stone" (1 Peter 2:6), the "author and finisher of our faith" (Hebr. 12:2). But these apostles and prophets have long since passed away, while the doctrine which they taught by inspiration, and by which they edified or built up the church (Eph. 4:11, 12) remains forever; therefore the foundation can be only the life-giving *doctrine* (John 6:63), which proceeds from, and which conducts to, a crucified Redeemer; it is this doctrine which constituted the great topic of apostolic preaching (Acts 4:12; 1 Cor. 2:2; 3:11), namely: *Jesus Christ, the Son of God, is the Christ or Messiah.* The *rock* which supports the church can be nothing else than the fundamental doctrine (1 Cor. 2:2) that Christ came into the world to save lost sinners by shedding His blood for the remission of sins.—E. **And the gates, etc.** For the explanation of the word **Hades,** see above (11:23, B.). Here it designates specially the kingdom of Satan. As in the case of the church above, so, too, its opposite, or Satan's kingdom, is compared to a vast edifice, strongly fortified; the strength of the gates placed at the entrance may be assumed to correspond to the strength of the edifice itself. Hence **gates,** as in Job 38:17, are an image of strength or power. **Prevail,** as in Luke 23:23, = overcome, overpower. The sense then is: All the malice and the power which Satan who "had the power of death" (Hebr. 2:14) exercises in opposing the growth and success of the church (Matt. 13:19, 27, 28; Eph. 6:16) shall be finally prostrated and overcome (1 Cor. 15:54, 55; Col. 2:15; 2 Tim. 1:10; Hebr. 2:14), and Christ, the Head of the Church (Eph. 2:22) shall finally put all His enemies under His feet (1 Cor. 15:25, 26).

^{19} And I will give unto thee the keys of the kingdom of heaven: and whatsoever thou shalt bind on earth shall be bound in heaven: and whatsoever thou shalt loose on earth shall be loosed in heaven.

A. And ... thee. The time when this promise of giving the keys was fulfilled, doubtless coincided both with that in which the Lord "breathed" on His disciples (John 20:22, 23), and with that in which the disciples were "baptized with the Holy Ghost," and "received power" (Acts 1:5, 8; Luke 24:49), that is, on the day of Pentecost (Acts 2:1, ff.). Peter is specially addressed because he had spoken in the name of the other apostles. No rights or privileges are here granted to him exclusively. So, too, the command to feed the Lord's lambs—sheep (= preach the Gospel, etc.) in John 21:15–17, applied to all the other apostles also. Indeed, the commission here given to him, is afterwards extended in equal fulness and power to all the other apostles, and to the Church generally, in ch. 18:18, 19; John 20:23. (See also Gal. 2:9; Eph. 2:20; Rev. 21:14, and in reference to Paul, Rom. 1:14; 1 Cor. 9:16; 2 Cor. 11:5; 12:11). Peter accordingly never claims higher rank, authority or privileges than his fellow-disciples, the other "pillars" of the Church (Gal. 2:9), exercised (comp. Acts 15:6–23; 1 Pet. 2:5, 6; 5:1). Hence it is obvious that the Romish pope's claims of supremacy as Peter's successor, which rest mainly on this passage, proceed from impious pride and unbelief alone.—**B. The keys ... heaven.** The *kingdom of heaven,* as explained in ver. 18, D., above, is the Church of Christ viewed as the congregation of true believers or saints. Now he who was authorized to carry the key of a building, was invested with authority both to admit and also to exclude (see Isai. 22:22). The Pharisees and lawyers (= interpreters of the law) took away the key of knowledge, as the Lord declares (Luke 11:52; Matt. 23:13), when they restrained the people from listening to Christ, believing in Him, and obtaining salvation. Here the **keys** represent a certain authority to admit or exclude in reference to the Church of Christ, and this authority seems to indicate an official act that follows the regular preaching of the Gospel, in place of being simply that preaching itself (see ann. to 18:18). According to John 20:23, when the Lord gave the same commission to all the apostles, He breathed on them, and communicated to them the Holy Ghost. By virtue of this gift (with which compare the gift of "discerning of spirits," 1 Cor. 12:10), the apostles were enabled to distinguish between true believers and hypocrites. See an illustration in the case of Ananias and Sapphira (Acts, ch. 5); Paul, in 2 Cor. 2:6, 10, forgives certain individual whom he had *bound* (= excommunicated and punished), (1 Cor. 5:3–5; see also 1 Tim. 1:20). To sincere believers they declared the divine forgiveness of sins (Eph. 4:32; James 5:15; 1 John 2:12). To the ungodly and hypocritical they denied Christian privileges and mercies. The office of the keys is now explained by many as referring to the exercise of church discipline (the excommunication, restoration, etc., of members) as distinct from the ordinary act of preaching the Gospel (see below, 18:18).—**C. Whatsoever, etc.** This promise is repeated, and its application extended to all other disciples of the Lord (see below, 18:18, 19).—**Bind.** For this figurative term a literal phrase is substituted in John 20:23, namely, "whose soever sins ye retain," that is, whom ye refuse to absolve and whom ye declare to be impenitent. For an illustration see Acts 8:20–23.—**D. On earth** = in the visible church on earth.—**E. Shall ... heaven** = your sentence, dictated by the Holy Ghost, will be equivalent to a divine judgment. For an illustration see Acts 15:25, 28.—**F. Loose** = "whose soever sins ye remit" (John 20:23), and whom ye admit to church-fellowship, by virtue of the authority now given to you, and in conformity to the divine will. For an illustration see Acts 8:14–17.—**G. Shall ... heaven** = such shall receive the divine pardon of his sins. The keys (or the office of administering discipline and imparting the promises of the Gospel respecting the divine forgiveness in the case of a penitent believer), even though the gift of "discerning of spirits" no longer exists on earth, still belong to the Church, to which they were subsequently given (see below, Matt. 18:15–20). But while the apostles themselves could virtually remit and retain sins, in consequence of their inspired knowledge, the Church at present can grant only a conditional absolution, that is, can declare to individuals the forgiveness of their sins only when they are truly penitent and sincerely exercise faith in Christ. The sentence is always ratified by the Searcher of hearts in the case of those who truly believe that their sins are forgiven for Christ's sake (see below, 18:18).

[20] Then charged he the disciples that they should tell no man that he was the Christ.

A. The Christ = the Messiah (see ver. 16).—**B.** The strict (Luke 9:21) prohibition here mentioned differs in its main purpose from the one explained above (8:4, A.). Like the one mentioned below (17:9), it referred to the danger of producing an undue political excitement among the Jews before the Lord's "hour was come" (John 13:1; 17:1). The people did not yet understand the spiritual nature of the Messiah's kingdom (see John 18:36), and the premature public announcement that Jesus was the true Messiah would have led to disastrous tumults. These did afterwards occur, when several impostors respectively claimed that august title. After Christ's resurrection, this temporary prohibition was changed into the command: "Go ye into all the world, etc." (Mark 16:15).

21 From that time began Jesus to shew unto his disciples, how that he must go unto Jerusalem, and suffer many things of the elders and chief priests and scribes, and be killed, and the third day be raised up.

A. From that time = not before, but now, when the knowledge and confidence of the disciples had been so far matured as to lead to an unequivocal and unhesitating expression of their faith that the lowly Jesus was the Lord of all (see ver. 16, ff.).—**B. Began Jesus to shew, etc.** Some religious truths cannot be properly comprehended without previous exercise of the heart and mind in religious doctrine (comp. Mark 4:33; 1 Cor. 3:1, 2; Hebr. 6:1, ff.). So, too, if the disciples had been informed of the awful mode in which Christ was to die, before they were qualified to understand the gracious purpose of God in permitting it (Acts 4:27, 28; 5:30, 31), they would not have been able "to bear" (John 16:12) = to *support* or comprehend it. But now, His divine words and acts had so enlightened and strengthened them, that the mournful prophecy, even if not immediately fully comprehended, would at least not cause them to "go back and walk no more with Him" (John 6:66).—**C. How He must.** The Greek word, often rendered **must**, as in 24:6; 26:54, is as often translated *ought* (Luke 24:26), but also *behooved* (Luke 24:46), *was needful* (Acts 15:5). It indicates at times some kind of obligation, and specially, that which proceeds from a divine arrangement, purpose, etc. as in John 3:14; 20:9; Acts 4:12; 14:22. It was "according to Scriptures" (1 Cor. 15:3, 4) that Christ died and rose again (see Matt. 26:54; Luke 24:27, 44). The first promise of a Redeemer occurs Gen. 3:15; subsequently, very striking prophecies respecting His sufferings, death and resurrection are found (see Ps. 22; Isai. 50:6; ch. 53; Hosea 6:2; Zech. 12:10; and Ps. 16:10 compared with Acts 2:24, 27). Now, as the "gifts and calling of God are without repentance" (Rom. 11:29) = as God neither regrets nor forgets His promises, the fulfilment of the divine promises rendered it needful ("must") that, in accordance with them the Lord Jesus, who "was foreordained before the foundation of the world" (1 Peter 1:20; Eph. 1:4; Rev. 13:8) should suffer, die, and rise again (see 20:22, C.). The same Greek word sometimes indicates that which is *natural, proper, meet* (Luke 15:32; Acts 23:11), sometimes the *certainty* of future events, as in Matt. 24:6; 1 Cor. 15:53.—**D. Elders ... scribes** = the Sanhedrim.—**E. Raised again.** The glory which succeeded the shame of the cross is also revealed (Luke 24:26).—**F. The third day.** The Lord here supplies His disciples with an infallible test of His divine mission. If Christ should not be raised on the third day, their faith was vain (1 Cor. 15:17); but if He did rise on the third day, that resurrection became a sure foundation of faith (Acts 2:32), for thereby He was declared to be the Son of God (Rom. 1:4).

[22] And Peter took him, and began to rebuke him, saying,

Be it far from thee, Lord: this shall never be unto thee.

A. Took Him = *grasped Him* with His hand, or, possibly, *took Him aside.* Peter was deeply moved by the thought that his adored Master should consent to suffer such a death.—**B. To rebuke** = to speak earnestly to Him, or, *charged* Him, as the same word is translated in 12:16, or, *expostulated* with Him, as in Luke 17:3, "rebuke."—**C. Be ... from thee.** Some suppose the phrase to correspond to one in Hebrew, which is an exclamation of abhorrence, nearly equivalent in sense to: *Away with that!* If it is interpreted in the Greek sense, it is equivalent to: *God be merciful to thee!* = May God preserve thee from such an end! The former interpretation is more probably the correct one.—**D. This shall, etc.** = this *must not* take place. (The Greek double negative with a future tense or adv. subj. often involves the thought that the event mentioned *shall not,* must not by any means occur.) The warmth of Peter's affection for his Master, and the impetuosity of his character betray him into declarations which pointedly contradict the divine will and purpose as announced by the Lord in ver. 21. He did not yet understand the sublime truth that Christ was to become a perfect Saviour by suffering, and then be crowned with glory and honor (Hebr. 2:9, 10). Compare with his present imperfect views, his own later declarations (1 Peter 2:21, ff.; 3:18, ff.).

23 But he turned and said unto Peter, Get thee behind me, Satan: thou art a stumbling block unto me: for thou mindest not the things of God, but the things of men.

A. But He (Jesus) **turned** = away from Peter. Even sentiments of pure friendship and love must be controlled by wisdom, and submit readily to the divine will.—**B. Get ... Satan.** The same phrase, indicating the utmost abhorrence, was employed once before by the Lord (Luke 4:8; see Matt. 4:10, A.). For the word **Satan** see 4:1, E. The sentiment which Peter expressed, however affectionate it might be, was not inspired by faith in God's wisdom and love, nor by a child-like submission to the divine will; hence it was "sin" (Rom. 14:23). For, all the thoughts and feelings of man which come in conflict with the divine purpose and will, proceed ultimately from Satan himself (Acts 5:3; 26:18). As Satan "hindered "Paul in his labors (1 Thess. 2:18), so he here attempts to hinder Christ = to discourage Him by means of the entreaties of a friend. While he seeks to influence Peter who is a friend of Jesus, he is again "transformed into an angel of light" (2 Cor. 11:14). Christ, by whose revelations the apostles ceased to be "ignorant of Satan's devices" (2 Cor. 2:11), appears to allude to the temptation described in ch. 4, and reveals to Peter, *by addressing Satan directly,* that the unclean spirit had instigated him to speak as he did. When afterwards Satan again exercised his power, he prevailed; for the love of money and the dishonesty of Judas had opened an avenue for him (John 12:6; Luke 22:3).—C. **Thou art a stumbling block unto Me.** The sense is: If I listened to thy fair words, as Eve once listened to the same subtle tempter (Gen., ch. 3), and did not now repel him, I would stumble in the path of duty. By dissuading Me from exposing My life, thou puttest an *occasion to fall,* in My way (Rom. 14:13). We may easily commit sins in thought, word or deed, the true source and character of which we heedlessly omit to consider, but which are very grievous sins in the eyes of God.—D. **Thou mindest.** The original term here employed is translated *to be minded* (Rom. 15:5; Gal. 5:10), and frequently designates the general disposition or character of the mind (Phil. 2:5; 3:19). Thus in 1 Cor. 13:11, where it also occurs: "I *understood* as a child," it is equivalent to: I had the sentiments or feelings of a child. The same word, with the same construction, occurs in Rom. 8:5, "they do *mind*" = *are intent on, governed by*. This last passage shows that the sense here is: Thy thoughts and sentiments, as now expressed, are not "of God" = according to God's will, but "of men" = such as erring, unwise and carnal men entertain; it was not the divine Spirit, but human nature influenced by Satan, that prompted those words.

24-25 Then said Jesus unto his disciples, If any man would come after me, let him deny himself, and take up his cross, and follow me.—For whosoever would save his life shall lose it: and whosoever shall lose his life for my sake shall find it.

A. Then said Jesus. He repeats the solemn words which He had pronounced on a former occasion (10:38, 39), with a special reference to Peter's state of mind, although speaking "to all" the disciples (Luke 9:23). The sense then is: Not only shall I suffer persecution and death, but ye also, if ye remain My followers, must expect a similar lot (*the fellowship of My sufferings*, Phil. 3:10).—**If any man will** = *is willing*, as in John 5:35, *desires* to come, etc. The opposite will or purpose is mentioned in John 5:40. Man is not introduced into heaven by force; his own will, wishes and desires to escape from the wrath to come, and his own conviction of his need of a Saviour must conduct him to Christ. Such a disposition is wrought in all who do not resist the Divine Spirit.—**B. Let him deny himself.** The phrase: *deny himself* is equivalent to: *not to know himself* = *not* to regard at all his personal feelings or wishes (comp. Matt. 26:34, 74). It implies here not only the control and suppression of all ungodly lusts (Tit. 2:12), but also the willing sacrifice of all our natural affections in the service of God (Matt. 10:37; 19:29), like that of Abraham (Gen. ch. 22), and a prompt submission to the will of God.

²⁶ For what shall a man be profited, if he shall gain the whole world, and forfeit his life? or what shall a man give in exchange for his life?

A. Life (see above, 10:39, A. and B.).—**B. The whole world** = all temporal riches, power and pleasures (comp. 1 John 2:15–17; Matt. 4:8, 9; John 18:36; James 4:4).—**C. Lose his life** = be consigned to eternal torment after death.—**D. Give in exchange for** = with what can he purchase back and deliver his life or soul. The original word signifies *that which is exchanged against any thing an equivalent, a price paid.* The sense is: Does man possess any means for saving his soul, when he has forfeited it by becoming the servant of sin? What will he ultimately gain, if, in the hope of "enjoying the pleasures of sin for a season" (Hebr. 11:25), he thereby incurs as a punishment the eternal loss of his soul. No price can redeem the sinner except that which Christ paid (1 Cor. 6:20), namely his blood (1 Pet. 1:18, 19).

²⁷ For the Son of man shall come in the glory of his Father with his angels; and then shall he render unto every man according to his deeds.

A. For ... come. The future coming of the Lord, for the purpose of judging man, is more fully described in ch. 24:27–31, and 25:31–46. It is here revealed for the purpose of cheering the disciples, whom the prospect of earthly trials had greatly moved (see 2 Thess. 1:7, ff.; 2:1). He, to whom the divine office of judging the world belongs (John 5:22), will come as the Son of man = His human and divine nature are united inseparably and forever.—**B. In the glory of his**

Father = revealed in His divine glory (Matt. 25:31; John 1:14), which He had with the Father before the world was (John 17:5).—**C. With his angels,** as in Matt. 24:30, 31; 25:31 (see above, 13:39, C.).—**D. Render** = pay (20:8 and 18:28); *render* (22:21), that is, make a corresponding return. The doctrine of a future state of retribution for the just and unjust is here announced.—**Deeds,** lit.*working, doing,* corresponding to *labor* in 1 Cor. 3:8. The term expresses the controlling good or evil tendency of the heart of the individual, as revealed in the conduct.

²⁸ Verily I say unto you, There be some of them that stand here which shall in no wise taste of death, till they see the Son of man coming in his kingdom.

A. Verily (see 5:18, A.). The intermediate thought between this verse and the former, indicating that cheering and consolatory words will follow, appears to be: Yea, even before that last great day of judgment, ye who are faithful shall see an illustration of My power and truth.—**B. There be** (= are) **... here.** As the Lord and His disciples appear to be alone (ver. 20, 21, 24) during this conversation, the sense must be that while Judas would no longer be alive (27:5) at this particular coming of the Lord ("some"), others of their number (John, Peter, etc.) would live to see that event.—**C. Taste of death.** This phrase, under the image of drinking from a cup, alludes to the "pains of death" (Acts 2:24), and is equivalent to: *shall not pass through the struggle* which attends the separation of body and soul. The image was familiarly employed in the east (John 8:52; Hebr. 2:9).—**D. Till they see, etc.** After the Lord had, in the foregoing verse, alluded to His second or final visible coming, He adds the comforting assurance, that before that event occurs, even during the lifetime of the disciples (of all except Judas, Acts 2:1) He would, at an *intermediate* coming powerfully manifest to them His invisible presence; the same promise, in a still more distinct form, is repeated in John 14:18, 26. That this coming or manifestation of the truth, the power, the grace and the invisible presence of the Lord occurred on the day of Pentecost, when He came not visibly, but **in His kingdom** (= founded His Church) and was revealed and acknowledged as its heavenly Head and King (Acts 2:33–36), has been more fully stated above (10:23, B., where see the annotation).

2

Matthew 17

¹ And after six days Jesus taketh with him Peter, and James, and John his brother, and bringeth them up into a high mountain apart.

A. After six days. An interval of six days occurred between the one on which the Lord uttered the words at the close of the foregoing chapter, and the one on which the event next recorded, occurred. In Luke 9:28 these two days are added, and hence arises the expression: "about an eight days" = a week.—**B. Peter, and James, and John.** Of the twelve, these three alone witnessed the restoration to life of the daughter of Jairus (Mark 5:37). In Gethsemane, they alone accompanied Him to the spot where an angel strengthened Him (Matt. 26:37; Luke 22:43, 44). Here, again, they alone are permitted to be "eyewitnesses of His majesty" (2 Peter 1:16–18). It is remarkable that these three also received peculiar and significant surnames: the first, that of *Peter* (John 1:42, and see above, 16:18; the other two, that of *Boanerges,* Mark 3:16, 17). **C. A high mountain,** called by Peter (2 Peter 1:18) "the holy mount" on account of the solemn occurrence which took place on it, as here described. An ancient tradition specifies mount Tabor in Galilee as the locality, apparently without other reasons than those which passages like Judges 4:6; Ps. 89:12; Jer. 46:18, might suggest. Tabor, which was not an unoccupied spot at this period, had already been the site of a city more than two centuries before Christ. As the Lord had previously visited the vicinity of Cæsarea Philippi (16:13), others suppose that one of the lofty eminences of the ridge of Hermon near that city, was the spot.

² And he was transfigured before them; and his face did shine as the sun, and his garments became white as the light.

Transfigured. Paul twice employs the same Greek word (Rom. 12:2, and 2 Cor. 3:18, "transformed") in reference to the spiritual change which occurs in the renewed man. Luke says (9:29): "the fashion (= external appearance, manner) of his countenance was altered," indicating that His ordinary human appearance had been changed.—**His face did shine as the sun** = with overpowering brilliance; a supernatural, shining whiteness (Mark 9:3), or effulgence appeared through and over His raiment (= His garments, 5:40, B.), from which the light *flashed out like lightning,* which is the sense of Luke's word "glistering" (comp. Matt. 28:3, B.). The light was probably the same which Paul beheld when Jesus appeared to him from heaven (Acts 26:13, ff.). These appearances are called in Luke (9:31, 32), "his glory" and "majesty" (= greatness, glory). If we compare Peter's description of the Lord's "honour and glory" on that occasion (2 Peter 1:17) with the Lord's own reference to "the glory" which he had in heaven before the creation of the world (John 17:5), then, the term *transfiguration,* in the sense of *glorification,* seems to indicate that the splendor of His divine nature (the form of God, Phil. 2:6), which was usually covered by 'the veil, that is to say, his flesh" (Heb. 10:20), on this occasion shone forth in fulness.

³ And, behold, there appeared unto them Moses and Elijah talking with him.

A. There appeared. So, too, the Scriptures repeatedly, mention the appearance of angels, who assumed a visible form, and uttered audible words (e. g. Gen. 16:7; Judges 13:3, ff. Luke, ch. 1; ch. 2).—**B. Moses and Elijah.** Both of these men had been removed from this world in a mysterious manner (Deut. 34:5, 6; 2 Kings 2:11); both, too, had visions of the glory of God never granted to other mortals (Ex. 23:18, ff., and 34:6, ff.; 1 Kings 19:11, ff.). "The law was *given* by (= through the instrumentality of) Moses" (John 1:17), 1500 years before Christ. It was *restored* to its authority by Elijah (900 years before Christ) at a period of general iniquity and idolatry. It was *fulfilled* by Christ (Matt. 5:17). In Malachi 4:4, 5, where both are mentioned, Moses appears as the representative of the law, while Elijah, the representative of the order of the prophets, already appears as a type of Christ's forerunner (Matt. 11:14). Both faithfully labored in the work of sustaining the old covenant, which opened the way for the second or better covenant. The Scriptures, however, do not fully reveal the special purpose for which God sent *them* on this occasion, rather than the prophet Samuel, in whom the prophetic office first appeared in its fully-developed form, or King David, etc. "Here God teaches, by the reappearance of the men that those whom we call *dead* are not dead, and that the death of believers is really an ascent and removal to a brighter and happier existence in the light of God's presence."—Luther.—**C. Talking with Him** = with Jesus, concerning His "decease (= departure from life, as in 2 Peter 1:15), which He was to accomplish at Jerusalem" (Luke 9:31). Nothing further is revealed respecting the subject or design of this conversation, except its general reference to the atoning death of the Lord.

⁴ And Peter answered, and said unto Jesus, Lord it is good for us to be here: if thou will, I will make here three tabernacles; one for thee, and one for Moses, and one for Elijah.

A. Then answered = proceeded, began to speak (see 11:25, C.) Peter did not speak until he saw that Moses and Elijah were beginning to recede (Luke 9:33.)—**B. And said, etc.;** the parallel passages add: "not knowing what he said" (Luke 9:33) "for they were sore afraid" (Mark 9:6). It appears from these remarks that, as we might expect, the heavenly vision dazzled and overwhelmed Peter; the moment was not one which allowed a man of his ardent temperament to indulge calmly in reflections. At the same time, his, first alarm was tempered by the hallowed brightness and the quiet of the scene, and subsided when he ascertained the character of the holy messengers. Soothed and cheered, even before his varied emotions allowed him to think calmly, he uttered his feelings at once; his words indicate that although his mind was still confused, the whole impression now made on his feelings was delightful.—**C. Lord ... here** = O let me remain in the presence of Thyself as Thou now appearest in Thy glory, and in the presence of the glory of Moses and Elijah.—**D. Let us ... Elias.** The Greek word, which is always rendered **tabernacle** in the New Test., except in Luke 16:9, and the compound word in Acts 18:3, indicates any *tent* or booth as in Heb. 11:9; it specially designates in some cases (Acts 7:44; Heb. 8:5; 9:2, 3, 8, 21) the sacred tent, in which the ark was kept before the temple was built; see Exod. ch. 25, etc. The phrase: to *make* or *pitch a tent* implies *remaining, abiding, dwelling* (Gen. 12:8; 26:17; 1 Chron. 15:1). Peter's words, therefore, uttered while he was still bewildered and not fully conscious of their precise import ("not knowing what he said" Luke) mean: Call them back, O Lord; we will give them a home. His true feeling may be thus expressed: I desire evermore to enjoy the bliss which this moment of Thy communion with these holy men affords me. If Peter, while in the flesh, could, by a special gift such as seems to be here exercised, at once identify Moses and Elias, whose features he had never previously seen, much more will "the spirits of just men made perfect" (Heb. 12:23), with "bodies fashioned like unto the glorious body" of Christ (Phil. 3:21), in heaven recognize there both beloved friends who died in the Lord, and also all who before their day, like Enoch, Noah, (Gen. 5:22; 6:9), walked with God on earth.

⁵ While he was yet speaking, behold a bright cloud overshadowed them: and behold, a voice out of the cloud, saying, This is my beloved Son, in whom I am well pleased; hear ye him.

A. While ... speaking = and Moses and Elijah were still in view, but receding.—**B. A bright cloud** = not an ordinary dark cloud, but a brightness or splendor resembling a mass of light. It was, possibly, that divine light which still shone on the face of Moses when he came down from the mount (Ex. 34:29–35), conveying to us a faint idea of that unapproachable light in which God dwells (1 Tim. 6:16).—**C.**

Overshadowed them = Moses and Elijah "entered into the cloud" (Luke 9:34), but not the three disciples, nor Jesus, to whom the voice came out from the cloud (2 Pet. 1:17). The brightness of the cloud, called the "the excellent glory" (2 Pet. 1:17), *concealed* them from the view of the three disciples, in a blaze of light.—**D. A voice, etc.** Once before, the Father had audibly pronounced these words (see above, 3:17); His voice was afterwards heard a third time (John 12:28). On this occasion the words **hear ye Him** are added, in reference to the prophecy which Moses uttered (Deut. 18:15; Acts 3:22). Such language, never applied even to an angel (Hebr. 1:5), much less to Moses and Elias, taught the disciples the immeasurable distance between all creatures and Him who is the "mediator of a better covenant" (Hebr. 8:6), and "by whom all things were made" (John 1:3). That these sublime revelations were given to Peter and the other two disciples for the confirmation of their faith, appears from 2 Pet. 1:16–18. But all the divine objects of this wonderful occcurrence are not made known. While some interpreters are disposed to regard it as intended primarily for Moses and Elias, who had, like the angels (1 Pet. 1:12), desired to "look into" the mysteries of redeeming love, others believe that it was somewhat similar to the angel's visit described in Luke 22:43, in so far that this communication of "honor and glory" to the Lord Jesus (2 Pet. 1:17) was intended to "strengthen" Him in the sufferings which were now rapidly approaching. But such conjectures, which often conflict with each other, are of little practical value (see ver. 3, C.).

⁶ And when the disciples heard it, they fell on their face, and were sore afraid.

The disciples were overpowered by the divine voice; they

seem, like John in Rev. 1:17, to have fallen into a swoon (comp. Dan. 10:8–10, and Acts 9:4).—**Sore afraid** = in the utmost fear. The old English word *sore* (here = *very much,* 18:31, or, *exceedingly,* as in 19:25), originally indicating *pain* or sorrow, came in time to signify, like the German *schr,* intensity, or *a high degree.*

⁷ And Jesus came and touched them and said, Arise, and be not afraid.

He restored them to consciousness, strengthened them anew by His life-giving touch and words of tender love.

⁸ And lifting up their eyes, they saw no one, save Jesus only.

The celestial light and the visitors had vanished, and Jesus appeared in His usual humble form.

⁹ And as they were coming down from the mountain, Jesus commanded them, saying, Tell the vision to no man, until the Son of man be risen from the dead.

A. Vision = persons and things *seen* by them (Mark 9:9), equivalent to *the sight,* as the same word is rendered in Acts 7:31. In a different sense the same word sometimes indicates not realities beheld with the bodily eyes as in this instance, but objects presented to the mind alone or the spiritual eye, as in Acts 9:12; 11:5—**Risen;** the resurrection of the Lord had already been revealed (16:21).—**C. To no man, etc.** The reasons for which this prohibition is pronounced, may have to some extent coincided with those stated above (16:20, B.). The words in Luke 9:36 indicate that these three disciples withheld the knowledge of these facts temporarily even from the other nine. The Lord's injunction also tested the self-control and obedient spirit of the former.

¹⁰ And his disciples asked him, saying, Why then say the scribes that Elijah must first come?

The three disciples, alluding to the prohibition in ver. 9, say: If Elijah is to come first (= before thee), only in this private manner, as he has now appeared on the mount, and if even this coming is to be temporarily concealed, why then does Malachi (ch. 3:1; 4:5) speak of his coming first (= before the Messiah) in such a manner that the scribes explain it of a public event, known to all? (see 11:14, A.; 16:14, B.). Will he perhaps come once more? The popular error of the age of supposing that Elijah the Tishbite (1 Kings 17:1) would himself appear as the forerunner of the Messiah, was not of recent origin. The Greek translation of the O. T. called the Septuagint (which was in existence two centuries before the birth of Christ) had actually substituted the name *Tishbite* for the word *prophet* after the name Elijah in Malachi 4:5. This version, which was held in high esteem by the Jews, seemed to confirm the teaching of the scribes.

[11] And he answered and said, Elijah indeed cometh, and shall restore all things.

A. Elijah indeed cometh = the words of the prophet contain a declaration which is strictly true; the public appearance of the Elijah mentioned by him, that is, of John "in the spirit and power of Elijah" (Luke 1:17), does precede my own (11:14, B.).—**B. Shall restore all things.** This future tense here simply implies that when the prophet spoke, the event still belonged to futurity, as above, in 11:14, "for to come." These words express the substance of Mal. 4:6, which passage is again explained by the angel (Luke 1:17) as descriptive of the office of one who, by restoring the bonds of affection and love which had been broken by sin, "makes ready a people prepared for the Lord." It is possible that the prophetic description of the restoration of concord between fathers and children ultimately refers to the work of the Saviour, by whom we receive "the adoption of sons" (Gal. 4:5). John's preaching of repentance and the coming of the kingdom of heaven (Matt. 3:2), together with the witness which he bore of the Messiah (John 1:15–36), constituted the preparation of the great work of **restoring** (= *replacing in their former state, as the word is also used in 12:13*), **all things** = leading fallen man back to God.

¹² But I say unto you, That Elijah is come already, and they knew him not, but did unto him whatsoever they listed. Even so shall the Son of man also suffer of them.

A. Elijah is come already = John the Baptist, called Elijah, because he came in "the spirit and power of Elijah" (Luke 1:17; see the ann. to 11:14, B.). This authoritative declaration of the Lord that the fulfilment of the prophetic words has already occurred, conclusively shows that the opinion of a few interpreters who still expect a coming of Elijah is as unfounded, as the opinion would be that, according to Jer. 30:9, King David himself will again appear on earth, while David's *Son* (Matt. 1:1) is there evidently meant.—**B. They knew ... listed.** Like the chief priests and scribes, who did not recognize and believe in John's divine mission (21:32), Herod and Herodias imprisoned and then beheaded him (see ann. to 11:13, and 14:10).—**Listed** = *would, desired, pleased,* etc. God suffered all these, in His overruling Providence "to walk in their own ways" (Acts 14:16), but "for all these things will bring them into judgment" (Eccl. 11:9).—**C. Likewise, etc.** = similar injustice, and a similar surrender of myself to "the will" of my enemies (Luke 23:25), will characterize my lot (see 16:21, and ver. 22, 23, below).

¹³ Then understood the disciples that he spake unto them

of John the Baptist.

Understood = that Malachi (3:1; 4:6) referred to John the Baptist, as indeed the Lord had, on a foregoing occasion, explained (11:10).

¹⁴ And when they were come to the multitude, there came to him a man, kneeling to him, and saying.

A. And when = on the day after the transfiguration (Luke 9:37), which had probably occurred during the preceding night.—**B. To the multitude** = which, including certain cavilling scribes, surrounded the other disciples, whom he was seeking (Mark 9:14, 16).—**C. Kneeling** = in the deepest distress, occasioned by the sufferings of his "only child" (Luke 9:38), appealing to Jesus, his last hope.

¹⁵ Lord, have mercy on my son; for he is epileptic, and suffereth grievously: for ofttimes he falleth into the fire, and ofttimes into the water.

A. Lord (see 8:2, C.).—**B. Epileptic,** lit. very nearly, *moonstruck.* As the father added that the child had a "dumb spirit" (Mark 9:17), the term *lunatic* does not mean, on the one hand, simply that the child was insane, nor, on the other, that the case was one of ordinary epilepsy.—**C. For, etc.** The father proceeds to narrate that the unclean spirit suddenly produced convulsions in the child, and hurled him sometimes on the burning coals in the house, sometimes into the cistern, and that the sufferer, foaming and gnashing with his teeth (Mark 9:18), and bruised by his violent falls, was scarcely relieved from one fit, before another was produced (Luke 9:39).

¹⁶ And I brought him to thy disciples, and they could not cure him.

Could not = *were not able,* as the Greek word is often

translated (e. g. 3:9; 9:28). The disciples afterwards (ver. 19), themselves desire to know the cause that prevented them from exerting successfully the power to heal, which they had previously recieved (10:1).

¹⁷ And Jesus answered and said, O faithless and perverse generation, how long shall I be with you? how long shall I bear with you? bring him hither to me.

A. Faithless ... generation. As English usage has fixed on the word *faith* as the noun corresponding to the verb *to believe*, instead of the conjugate or allied word *belief*, various inconveniences have arisen. Thus when in the English N. T. Abraham is called *faithful* (Gal. 3:9), the word does not indicate simply that he was reliable or exhibited fidelity, but means *believing* (= exercising a living faith), as the same word is rendered in John 20:27; 1 Tim. 6:2. So here, as in John 20:27, the original word translated *faithless*, does not mean *false, perfidious*, but *unbelieving*, as it is translated in 1 Cor. 7:14; Tit. 1:15. The word **perverse** (in which the Lord alludes to the song of Moses, (Deut. 32:5, 20, as also Paul does, Phil. 2:15), originally designates, like both the Hebrew and the Greek corresponding words, that which is *twisted, turned aside* from the right way, as the English word *wrong* comes from *wring* = to twist, wrest; it then figuratively describes men who are *perverse* = misguided by an evil influence, which is the meaning here.—**Generation**, here = race, kind, class of men (for the word see 24:34).—**B. How long ... bear with.** The song of Moses (Deut., ch. 32), mentioned above, strikingly illustrates these words. Religious sloth prevents a ready understanding of divine truth; here, as often elsewhere, such a slow progress in the acquisition of divine knowledge, is rebuked (John 14:9; Hebr. 5:12). But to whom are these words of rebuke addressed? First, to the father, whose faith, according to the parallel passage (Mark 9:23, 24, "if thou canst, etc."), like that of the nobleman addressed in John 4:48, was weak, and then to the disciples, whose "unbelief" the Lord mentions Himself in ver. 20. The sense is: After so many evidences of the divine character of My mission, is your faith still so feeble, that ye cannot prevail in a contest with unclean spirit?—**C. Bring, etc.** The words are addressed to the father (Luke 9:41), who, in his eagerness, had advanced to meet the Lord.

¹⁸ And Jesus rebuked him; and the devil went out from him: and the boy was cured from that hour.

A. Mark relates (9:20–27), that at this moment a frightful scene was presented by a new attack of the spirit; the paroxysm was so violent that ultimately the child was completely exhausted, and seemed to the spectators to be dead. The Saviour's delay in affording relief is, according to the circumstantial narrative of Mark, to be traced to the weak faith of the father.—**B. Rebuked the devil,** lit. *him,* the spirit (Mark 9:25; Luke 9:42); the same word: **rebuked,** occurs in 8:26. The Lord's words are preserved in Mark 8:25.—**C. The child, etc.** Jesus took the child by the hand (Mark), and delivered him to his father (Luke) in health and vigor, forever free from a similar affliction (Mark 9:25).

¹⁹ Then came the disciples to Jesus apart, and said, why could not we cast it out?

The disciples, grieved and humbled in consequence both of their failure to expel the evil spirit, and of the rebuke which the Lord had administered, approach the latter in the house, in the absence of the spectators (Mark 9:28); they confess their unworthiness, and humbly solicit instruction respecting their future conduct.

[20] And he saith unto them, Because of your little faith: for verily I say unto you, If ye have faith as a grain of mustard seed, ye shall say unto this mountain, Remove hence to yonder place; and it shall remove; and nothing shall be impossible unto you.

A. Because of your little faith. Moses, who was on other occasions so "faithful" (Heb. 3:5), greatly displeased God at Meribah by one act of unbelief and rebellion, when, for a moment, he doubted that God would give him power to perform a promised miracle, (Numb. 20:7–12; 27:14; Ps. 106:32, 33). Now the disciples who had in many cases expelled evil spirits, like the "other seventy" (Luke 10:1, 17), were at that time already embarrassed and discouraged, in the absence of their Master, by the scoffs and insults of the scribes (Mark 9:16). When, in this dejected frame of mind, against which they should have struggled, they behold the epileptic, it is possible that the unusually frightful convulsions of the child, which no spectator could behold unmoved, and which indicated the presence of a spirit "more wicked" (12:45) than others, so powerfully affected them as men, that the flesh prevailed at last over the spirit; at the moment they feared that they could not control such awful powers of darkness. Like Moses they failed to rely implicitly on divine truth and power. As Peter walked safely on the water till, for a moment he looked away from Jesus and glanced at the mighty waves, then yielded to a carnal fear and began to sink (14:30), so here the disciples looked more at Satan's rage than at Christ's power, and now their faith failed. They did not "stir up the gift of God which was in them" (2 Tim. 1:6), namely, of "the working of miracles" (1

Cor. 12:10). So too, it is recorded (26:56), that, with all their faith and their love to their Master, when the multitude came to take Him with swords, they "all forsook Him and fled." They doubted whether they were invested with sufficient power to expel the spirit, and their doubt marred their faith. Why cannot we all now, as individuals, became personnally familiar with the delightful religious experience of Paul as described in Gal. 2:19, 20; Phil. 4:13, and entertain his joyful and unclouded hopes (2 Tim. 4:8)? Why cannot the Church of Christ, to which the work of missions is assigned, "subdue kingdoms, etc.," as other believers have done (Heb. 11:33, ff.)? Alas! the Lord's answer is: "Because of your little faith."—**B. Faith ... mustard seed;** for *mustard seed* (see 13:31, C.). The sense is: A degree of faith in the divine appointment of yourselves as apostles which is apparently low as compared with the effects to be wrought through you. Hence the mustard seed and mountain are contrasted (comp. Mark 16:17; John 14:12). But the Lord also means such a faith which, like the mustard seed, expands continually in beauty and power.—**C. This mountain;** the Lord pointed to the mountain from which He had recently come down (ver. 9).—**D. Nothing ... you** = which, with true wisdom and in a spirit of faith, ye desire to do for the glory of God. True faith always has a revealed object; the believer cannot err, while his faith clings to that object. The Lord thrice addressed language like that occurring in this verse to His apostles (21:21; Luke 17:6). In all these cases the sense appears to be: Ye now have faith in Me; nevertheless, it is not sufficient for your future course as founders of the Church to believe that I am the Son of God. You must entertain an unclouded and thorough conviction and faith ("and doubt not" 21:21) that through your personal labors and word, confirmed with signs following (Mark 16:20), the kingdom of heaven, so long ago promised by the prophets, will be established, and that God will never fail to fit you for your work. When you have such a faith, although it may still correspond in the degree of its power to the feeble nature of man ("as a grain of mustard seed,") you will, in *that* faith, unhesitatingly attempt any miracle ("greater works than these" which I do, John 14:12), and you will always find such works possible, being wrought by divine power in answer to your believing prayers (comp. James 5:14–18). The mention of the removal of the **mountain** indicates that an enlightened faith finds no impossibilities in the path of duty which God has prescribed.

[The Revised Version, in accordance with the most reliable Greek text. omits verse 21.]

22, 23 And while they abode in Galilee, Jesus said unto them, The Son of man shall be delivered up into the hands of men:—And they shall kill him, and the third day he shall be raised up. And they were exceeding sorry.

During this temporary abode of the Lord in Galilee (Mark 9:30) previously to His last journey to Jerusalem, when His "time came" (John 7:2–10), He again (16:21) refers to the subject of His death and resurrection The disciples, who still did not understand "that saying" (Mark 9:32), retained only a general and painful impression that great distress awaited Him and them, and "were exceeding sorry." **Shall be delivered up** = is to be *betrayed* or *delivered* over. The word so translated, here alludes to Judas (10:4), occurs also in 20:18, 19; in 27:2 it is applied to the act of transferring the Lord to the heathen governor (see also 26:15, B.). The Greek word here represented by **shall**, often describes events as being simply near at hand, hence rendered *will* (2:13); *to come* (Luke 3:7); *at the point of* (John 4:47); *about to* (Acts 5:35); *coming on* (Acts 27:33),—**into the hands of men** = subjected to any treatment which their cruelty may suggest, as, for instance, 26:57, ff., 67; 27:26–30; Luke 23:6–11, **raised up** (16:21).

²⁴ And when they were come to Capernaum, they that received the half-shekel came to Peter, and said. Doth not your master pay the half-shekel?

A. Capernaum (see 4:13, B.). As the Lord "dwelt" here = was a resident of this place, rather than of any other (4:13, B.), the collectors of this particular district naturally make the inquiry contained in this verse.—**B. The half = shekel** = the "atonement money" of Ex. 30:11–16. The Greek word here rendered half-shekel is *didrachma* (plural); this coin, for which no corresponding English name exists, was a *double drachma*. The Attic (Greek) silver coin which bore the latter name (translated "piece of silver" in Luke 15:8) was nearly equal to 15:1–2 cents, but was current among the Romans as equal to their *denarius*, which was worth about 14 cents, and is always called *penny* (plural, *pence*), in the English N. T. (Matt. 18:28; 20:2, and see ann. to 22:19, B.). The Jewish piece of money called a *shekel* and often mentioned in the O. T. (c. g. Lev. 27:25), was worth very nearly 56 cents, so that two drachmas (which are one didrachmon) were nearly equivalent to half a shekel, or about 28 cents. Four of these Greek drachmas were equal to another Greek or Attic silver coin called a *stater*, mentioned below, ver. 27, D. Hence the latter was also equal to one Jewish shekel. Indeed, the silver stater was on this account often called a tetradrachmon = a piece of four drachmas. (The "pieces of silver" mentioned in Matt. 26:15; Acts 19:19, are called *argurion* in the original, which means *silver,* as Acts 3:6, or *money* in general, as in Matt. 25:18, and also the common Jewish shekel in particular Matt. 26:15 and 27:9; Acts 19:19 comp. with Zech. 11:12 and Numb. 7:13, 14, where the word *shekel* is implied. The *tribute-money* mentioned in Matt. 22:19 = money of the tribute, bears in the original the general name of *nomisma,* which is equivalent to *current money* or *coin;* the *penny* also mentioned there is the denarius.) Now, according to Exod. 30:11–16; 2 Kings 12:4; 2 Chron. 24:6, every Jewish male adult was required at the numbering of the people to contribute to the ordinary expenses of the public worship (animals for the sacrifices, incense, etc.) the sum of half a shekel = two drachmas, or about 28 cents, which subsequently acquired the character of an annual payment (comp. 21:12, D.). A Greek stater was, accordingly, sufficient to pay for two persons (see ver. 27 below). It is doubtless this personal tax (called in the original a double drachma = 28 cents = half-shekel) which the collectors mention in the present verse, and not any civil impost claimed by the government. Possibly, foreign Jews paid the amount at their annual visits to the temple (21:12, D.). The value of ancient coins is variously estimated by modern writers; the computations given above accordingly present merely an approximation to the truth. Modern investigations have led to the opinion that silver was ten times as valuable in the days of our Lord as it is at present (comp. 20:2, B.). For *talent* (see 18:24, B.), and for *farthing* (see ann. to 5:25, 26; 10:9, 29).—**C. Doth not, etc.** As this payment was for a religious purpose, and could not be enforced by the civil law, it was easily, and probably, often evaded (2 Chron. 24:6) by those whom religious principles did not control. To such principles the collectors doubtless refer; their language differs widely from that of Roman publicans who were authorized by law to collect the taxes from all without regard to their inclinations. **Your master,** lit. *teacher (see* 8:19, B.).

²⁵ He saith, Yea. And when he came into the house, Jesus spake first to him, saying, What thinkest thou, Simon? the kings of the earth, from whom do they receive toll or tribute? from their sons, or from strangers?

A. He saith, Yea. The other disciples were probably not present (see 18:1, A.). Peter somewhat rashly admits that an obligation to observe all the points of the laws of Moses necessarily lies on Jesus, forgetting that He who is "Lord of the sabbath" (Mark 2:28), and" greater than the temple" (Matt. 12:6), cannot really be bound by laws designed for fallen men alone.—**B. Jesus spake first.** Before Peter, on entering the house, could state the case, the Lord, who knew all things (John 16:30; 21:17), Himself brings it forward.—**C. What thinkest, etc.—toll** = taxes paid on goods (Rom. 13:7),—**tribute** = capitation or poll-tax paid by each person whose name and real estate were inscribed in the census (Matt. 22:17),—**strangers** = people other than royal children, namely, subjects, not blood-relations of the king. The Greek word is not the one so translated in 27:7; Acts 17:21, but the one rendered *another man, other men, others,* in Luke 16:12; Rom. 14:4; 2 Cor. 10:15; Hebr. 9:25. The sense of the question is: Do the sons of a king in earthly monarchies contribute to the support of the state and the royal honor, or does this duty devolve exclusively on the subjects who are of inferior rank?

²⁶ And when he said, From strangers, Jesus said unto him,

Therefore the sons are free.

Therefore ... free = Thou hast rightly answered; but that answer shows that thy reply to the collectors betrayed a forgetfulness of my true nature and character. As the Son of God, I can, according to the same principle, claim exemption from the duty of supporting the temple erected to the honor of my Father, "the great King" (Matt. 5:35).—**Sons.**—The general principle which is applicable to *all* the sons of earthly king, is applied in this case to the *only-begotten* Son of God. On the other hand, Christ "was found in fashion as a man" (Phil. 2:8), and "was made under the law" = subject to it as a man, solely for the purpose of "redeeming" men (Gal. 4:4, 5).

27 But lest we cause them to stumble, go thou to the sea, and cast a hook, and take up the fish that first cometh up; and when thou hast opened his mouth, thou shalt find a shekel: that take, and give unto them for me and thee.

A. Lest ... stumble = lest we should furnish an occasion to fall, by apparently giving a bad example (an example of avarice, contempt of religion, etc.), if we refuse to sustain the service of the temple, since they do not know, or believe in, my true character. The whole is illustrated by Rom. 14:21.—**B. Go thou ... mouth.** Possibly the disciple who carried the purse was absent (John 12:6; 13:29); no money was at hand, and yet it was needed. The resources of the divine Redeemer never fail. While He works a miracle which demonstrated His possession of divine knowledge and power, as the Son of God, He still connects with it a command to the fisherman (4:18) that He should proceed to the sea of Galilee which was near, and perform all that He is able to accomplish.—**C. A shekel.** The original gives the name of the silver coin, *stater,* which, as explained above (ver. 24, B). was very nearly equal in value to one shekel, and thus paid for two persons. There was an Attic gold coin, also called a *stater,* which varied at different periods in weight and value, and is not here meant.—**E. That take.** Possibly these words were spoken after the brief interval during which Peter went for the fish and returned with the coin.—**F. For me and thee.** The Lord desired that no reproach should attach to the disciple as if the latter disregarded the claims of religion.

3

Matthew 18

¹ In that hour came the disciples unto Jesus, saying, Who then is greatest in the kingdom of heaven?

A. In that hour = when Peter, after paying the piece of money, 17:27, had returned to the house, and, with the other disciples, who had been absent, stood before the Lord (Mark 9:33, 35).—**B. Came ... saying.** They had previously (and doubtless with undue warmth, Mark 9:33, 50; Luke 9:16), debated the question which now follows.—**C. Who ... heaven?** The Lord Himself assigns a very high position to His disciples (19:28) as the original heralds of the cross, but He did not invest them with temporal or political power. At this period, however, they still erroneously supposed that He would establish an earthly kingdom, and that those to whom He might assign offices in it, would respectively differ in rank, power and dignity; (see an illustration in 20:21). At a latter period they understood its true nature as described in Rom. 14:17.

² And he called to him a little child, and set him in the midst of them.

A. And ... child = doubtless a well-known and beloved young member of the family dwelling in the house; the scene is in Capernaum (Mark 9:33). The act of the Saviour, as described in Mark 9:36, "taking him in his arms," indicates that the child was still of the most tender age, while its modest and obedient conduct, when the Lord called it, indicates that it had already passed the earliest period of infancy.—**B. And set, etc.** = as a visible and therefore more impressive illustration of the following lesson. Such a mode of teaching by a symbolical action prevailed in the east (see 10:14, C., and comp. John 13:4–14; Acts 21:11, and 2 Kings 13:17; 2 Chron. 18:10; Ezek. 12:3–11).

³ And said, Verily I say unto you, Except ye turn, and become as little children, ye shall in no wise enter into the kingdom of heaven.

A. Verily ... you. The Lord claims the most earnest attention ("verily") to His words, for He intends to teach two solemn lessons: first, that His kingdom is a *spiritual* kingdom (John 18:36; Rom. 14:7), and, secondly, that none are admitted into it except those who, like Himself, are meek and lowly in heart (11:29). For **verily**, see 5:18, A.—**B. Turn.** The original word, in its spiritual sense, designates a *turning* or *changing* "from darkness to light, etc." (Acts 26:18; 11:21; James 5:20). Here the Lord specially declares that without a change to entirely opposite views and feelings, such a deep humility before God, His hearers can have "neither part nor lot" (Acts 8:21) in the kingdom of heaven.—**C. Become ... children** = like this little child (ver. 4). That child was gazing in modest silence at the Lord and His disciples; if was too young to comprehend and covet earthly power and fame; it was conscious that it could not control adults, and was willing to be controlled. The child's freedom from ambition or a thirst for fame, its unassuming, modest, ingenuous spirit, its ready submission and trustfulness, were some of the traits which fitted it to be an image of an humble, obedient and loving follower of Christ (comp. 1 Cor. 14:20). Such traits alone, and not its sinful nature, its ignorance, etc., are here intended, even as the coming of the thief in the night only in *some* features (the unexpectedness of his visit, according to Rev. 3:3) resembles that of the day of the Lord (see. above, 7:6, A.). Original sin, or corruption of heart, adheres even to the little child, according to John 3:6; Eph. 2:3). The true greatness or dignity of man, therefore, is not derived from any personal quality or act, but from the circumstance that he is an object of divine pity and redeeming love (ver. 11). They who really acquire such greatness are those who most of all abase themselves before God (ver. 4), and give the honor to God alone.—**D. Ye shall, etc.** To Nicodemus Christ said: "Ye must be born again" (John 3:3, 5, 7). So, too, He announces here to His disciples and to all men, that no one can become a child of God without becoming a new creature (Gal. 6:15). The unregenerate soul is incapable of entering the kingdom of God (Rom. 6:6; Eph. 4:22; Col. 3:9).

⁴ Whosoever therefore shall humble himself as this little child, the same is the greatest in the kingdom of heaven.

A. Whoever ... child = whosoever shall be unassuming (*humble,* in the same sense in which the word occurs in 1 Pet. 5:5), and as little occupied in thought and feeling with the objects of human ambition as this child now is, and who has attained to that state by penitence and faith, the same is, etc.—**B. The same, etc.** = such a discipline shall, in strict accordance with the degree of his humility and heavenly-mindedness, be "counted worthy of (= fit for) the kingdom of God" (2 Thess. 1:5).

⁵ And whoso shall receive one such little child in my name receiveth me.

The circumstances lead the Saviour to repeat the truths which he had uttered on a previous occasion (see 10:40–42, and comp. Mark 9:41). The sense is: If ye desire to be My true disciples, and to extend My kingdom on earth, ye must seek to acquire such a spirit of humility. When ye feel most deeply that ye yourselves are "but dust and ashes" (Gen. 18:27), and when ye "count all things but loss for the excellency of the knowledge" (Phil. 3:8) of Me, your Lord, *then* have ye obtained your true rank, and then shall ye bring the blessings of the Gospel to those who receive you (comp. *receive* in Acts 21:17). This Gospel must be preached and received "in My name" = I am its Author; it is authoritative because it comes from Me, and I dwell with the humble alone (comp. Isai. 57:15, and see below, 20:26, B.). The whole tenor of the words proves that no office in the Christian Church, whatever its name may be, essentially confers a higher rank than that which all other believers possess in the eyes of God, and that no motive which inclines an individual to seek such an office, can be acceptable, unless that motive flow from a disinterested and holy source (comp. 1 Tim. 3:1).

⁶ But whoso shall cause one of these little ones which believe on me to stumble, it is profitable for him that a great millstone should be hanged about his neck, and *that* he should be sunk in the depth of the sea.

A. Cause to stumble = give them an occasion to fall, tempt, mislead or corrupt them (see above, 5:29, 30). The Lord here impressively sets forth the deep guilt of those who, by their levity or bad example or other conduct, teach the young to adopt evil practices, or lead them from the path of duty. "Even well-meaning persons, when governed by a zeal without knowledge, may cause many to stumble, that is, lead them off from the way of life and truth. So Gregory, who taught the doctrine of purgatory, and Francis, Benedict and Dominic, who filled the world with monasteries and convents, perverted many souls by pretending to find a new and shorter road to heaven."—Luther.—**B. Little ones.** This expression first occurs in 10:42, which see; it is repeated below (ver. 10 and 14). It appears to be here employed as a descriptive name of all who receive Christ in humility and faith, and of whom little children are an image, according to ver. 3, C. Little children are, however, included in the phrase, for they, too, may be converted and become believers at a very early age. Hence, their spiritual wants claim the deep and active interest and care of parents, pastors, teachers and all believers.—**C. Great millstone.** The grinding of grain was usually performed by two females (Exod. 11:5; Matt. 24:41) by means of handmills; the lower stone, on which the upper revolved, was not turned. Mills of the largest kind were usually turned by asses; the upper millstone or *rider* was, in this case, very large and heavy (Rev. 18:21), and is the one which the original here indicates.—**D. Were hanged, etc.** The allusion is to the mode of inflicting capital punishment by submersion in the sea, The whole phrase, which is proverbial in its character. was usually intended, in its popular use, to represent the particular evil which the speaker believes to be so great, that even inevitable death, in any frightful form, is less terrible. The sense here is: No evil which the offender endured previously to the commission of this sin, could inflict such an injury on him as this sin does. The Lord Himself, by employing the phrase, indicates the awfulness of the guilt and punishment of those who through thoughtlessness, covetousness or malice, tempt an humble believer to sin against God.

⁷ Woe unto the world because of occasions of stumbling! for it must needs be that the occasions come; but woe to that man through whom the occasion cometh!

A. Woe (see 11:21, A.), occasions of stumbling (see 5:29, 30). The Lord here, as in Luke 19:41, mourns over the miseries to which man ("the world") is now exposed; these proceed from the temptations to sin to which men originally yielded (Gen. ch. 3). Hence, no individual who feels the power of the truth, can consider the subject of the future salvation of himself and of others, with any other feeling except that of deep concern.—**B. For ... come.** The *necessity* here expressed, as also in Luke 14:18; Heb. 7:12; Jude, ver. 3; 2 Cor. 9:5; Phil. 2:25, is simply to be so understood that the circumstances of the particular case easily lead to, or point out, such a result, while man is a free agent. Temptations to sin *must needs* occur in a world lying in wickedness (1 John 5:19), the Saviour says, in allusion to the corrupt nature of man, for "every imagination of the thought of his heart is only evil continually" (Gen. 6:5; 8:21), and the tree must needs yield fruit corresponding to its nature (comp. 1 Cor. 11:19).—**C. But woe to, etc.** The sense is: Inasmuch as God has been pleased to afford all necessary means and opportunities to man to overcome the power of sin by His grace, we are fully responsible for all our acts as much as Judas was (26:24), and "must give account" of ourselves to God (Rom. 14:12).

⁸, ⁹ And if thy hand or thy foot causeth thee to stumble, cut

it off, and cast it from thee: it is good for thee to enter into life maimed or halt, rather than having two hands or two feet to be cast into the eternal fire. And if thine eye causeth thee to stumble, pluck it out, and cast it from thee: it is good for thee to enter into life with one eye, rather than having two eyes to be cast into the hell of fire.

A. And if, etc. So far the Lord had spoken of temptations and snares which *others* place in the way of the believer. But, before He dismisses the subject, He glances once more into man's heart, in order to reveal anew its deceitfulness; the temptation may proceed directly from *man's own heart,* and lead to his eternal ruin. The Lord therefore repeats the doctrine which He had taught already in the Sermon on the Mount (5:29, 30).—**B. Halt** = *lame.* The sense is: If thou, in place of denying thyself (cutting off the hand, 5:29, 30), dost gratify the lusts of thy heart, the eternal loss of thy soul will be a greater evil than the temporary gratification of thy carnal will, was an enjoyment (comp. Luke 16:25).—**C. Eternal fire.** The original word is found very frequently in the N. T. It occurs specially in combination with the word *life,* when the blessedness of heaven is meant, as in 19:16; John 3:15, 16, 36; Rom. 2:7, and frequently, elsewhere. It is also placed in combination with words designating the punishments in the world to come, as Matt. 25:41; Mark 3:29; 2 Thess. 1:9; Jude, ver. 7. Even as the blessedness of the redeemed in heaven will be endless, so, too, the punishments of the lost in hell will be endless (see 25:41, B.).—**D. The hell of fire.** The same expression occurs above (5:22, G.), where see the explanation.

[10] See that ye despise not one of these little ones; for I say unto you, That in heaven their angels do always behold the

face of my Father which is in heaven.

A. See that ... ones. When the Lord here resumes the subject already introduced in ver. 6 ("little ones"), He designs to reveal in the words: "their angels, etc." a truth to the disciples, the remembrance of which shall ever give them a deep interest in the spiritual welfare of the most humble and obscure believer.—**Despise** = *think lightly of, not care for,* as too insignificant or mean (comp. the same word in Rom. 2:4).—**B. In heaven their angels, etc.** Inasmuch as oriental monarchs usually admitted none to their presence except persons of great distinction, the privilege of daily beholding his face (= approaching near to him), indicated the possession of high rank (see 1 Kings 10:8; 2 Kings 25:19, margin; Esther 1:14). The allusion in the text to this usage, like the corresponding words of the angel Gabriel (Luke 1:19), implies, first, that there are degrees of rank, or at least distinctions in office, among the angels, not further explained in the Scriptures (see Eph. 1:21; 3:10; Col. 1:16; 1 Peter 3:22); and, secondly, that the angels of "these little ones" hold the highest rank or office. The Scriptures repeatedly teach that angels are employed by the Creator in executing His will, and that they are specially engaged in the service of God when they protect believers (see Ps. 34:7; 91:11; Dan. 10:13, 21; 12:1; Hebr. 1:14, and for illustrations, Acts 5:19; 12:7). Neither the present passage, nor any other found in the Scriptures, expressly teaches that *each* believer is *always* attended by an invisible tutelary or guardian angel. Not only is such a view contradicted in the present passage by the declaration that these angels, when not sent on a special mission, are "always" in heaven (see Acts 12:10), but also by the well-known doctrine that the omnipresent God does not, like an earthly monarch, really need the aid of any creature while He protects His people. The sense of the present passage, therefore, which is explained by no other in the Scriptures containing the phrase "their angels," probably is the following: When God is pleased to employ an angel in conferring a special favor on any of His people, He commissions one of the highest rank, and thus shows us the deep interest which we should feel in the salvation of the soul of every believer, without regard to age, sex, temporal rank or condition.

[Verse 11 of the A. V. is omitted in the Revised Version.]

¹² How think ye? if any man have a hundred sheep, and one of them be gone astray, doth he not leave the ninety and nine, and go unto the mountains, and seek that which goeth astray?

The sense is: If a man, who is evil, can sometimes show pity and love, how much more compassionate and tender may you believe the God of love to be! (Comp. 7:11). The illustration which now follows (and is found also in Luke 15:3, ff.) refers only to the point that a lost sheep may be remembered, be pitied, and be patiently sought, even when it is "gone astray." The **ninety and nine,** like the "servants of the householder" (13:27), are introduced simply to complete the narrative, viewed as a parable. They are an image neither of the proportion between the numbers of the lost and saved, nor any class or portion of human beings who never fell from God, for "all have sinned" (Rom. 3:23). Neither does God, as it would otherwise appear, ever temporarily abandon the care of His faithful people because they are faithful—an inference which manifestly involves an error. It is possible, however, that by the one lost sheep the Saviour represents the entire human race, the world (John 3:16; 1 John 4:14), and by the ninety-nine sheep the angels, of whom He had just spoken, who never fell into sin, and who rejoice (Luke 15:10), when the lost one is found by divine grace, and now unites with them in praising God. (See above, 9:13, E.).

¹³ And if so be that he find it, verily I say unto you, he rejoiceth over it more than over the ninety and nine which have not gone astray.

A. If [it should] **so be ... it** = not every lost sinner is necessarily found, that is, repents and is saved. The "calling and election" belong to all who hear the Gospel, but are not "made sure" (= firm, efficacious), unless man "gives diligence" in complying with the Gospel terms of salvation (2 Peter 1:10).—**B. He rejoiceth, etc.** The motives and feelings of the unjust Judge mentioned in Luke 18:1–8, were by no means images of the divine purposes; nevertheless, they furnished an affecting illustration of the divine willingness to listen to the believer's prayers. So, too, in the present case, the rejoicing of the owner of the sheep, who seems in his delight to forget the ninety-nine, simply indicates the divine pleasure with which the conversion, sanctification and salvation of man are beheld (Ezek. 18:23; Ps. 147:11). The image is taken from human emotions. The undisturbed possession of property allows the feelings to be calm; a loss creates anxiety and pain; the act of finding produces a pleasing excitement, a positive enjoyment. This is the point of the comparison = the positive pleasure of God in the conversion and salvation of a lost sinner.

¹⁴ Even so it is not the will of your Father which is in heaven, that one of these little ones should perish.

The Saviour here declares the divine will in reference to

"these little ones," of whom He had just spoken (ver. 6 and 10). On the general subject, the apostles teach that the gracious purposes of God (who is "not willing that any should perish, but that all should come to repentance," 2 Peter 3:9; 1 Tim. 2:4), contemplated the salvation of all men (Tit. 2:11) who are willing to become "little ones," and to believe (John 5:40; comp. Ezek. 18:23; 33:11). Hence the object of the mission of Christ is announced to be: "that the world through Him might be saved" (John 3:17).

¹⁵ And if thy brother sin against thee, go, show him his fault between thee and him alone: if he hear thee, thou hast gained thy brother.

A. And if. After the Lord had cautioned his disciples, and commanded that they should neither give offence to others (ver. 6), nor yield to internal temptations to sin (ver. 8), He proceeds to a third point—the course which the believer is to follow when *he* is *himself the* offended or injured party. He presupposes that no genuine disciple will avenge himself (Rom. 12:19), and prescribes the modes in which an offender may be reclaimed, and fraternal love be restored. As the following words prospectively refer to the Church (ver. 17), viewed as an organized body, the offender is here described as a "brother" = a member of the Church of Christ. The love to which he is entitled, is enkindled by the believer's experience of God's forgiving love to himself (5:44, 45; John 13:34; Eph. 4:32; 1 John 4; 11, 20, 21.—**B. Sin against.** A **brother,** a Christian by profession, commits, not a trivial offence, but a *sin* when he, in any manner, does wrong to another, for he "transgresses" (1 John 3:4) the "royal law (James 2:8).—**C. Go, show ... alone** = the *first* step of the injured party. The latter, bearing in mind the words in 6:14, 15, shall not immediately complain openly, and needlessly bring reproach on the Christian name; he shall, with a suffering, hoping and enduring love (1 Cor. 14:4, 7), remember that while the offender is an *erring* brother, he is still a *brother* (comp. Lev. 19:17, 18). A private interview, voluntarily sought and conducted by the injured party in a forgiving, holy spirit ("speaking the truth in love" Eph. 4:15), while candidly exposing the offender's fault to him, may soften him, convince him of his sin, and induce him to seek the forgiveness not only of his brother, but also of his God.—The word translated **show** (= expostulate) often signifies to *convince* another of his error (Tit. 1:9), *reprove* or admonish (Luke 3:19), *disclose* or make manifest (John 3:20; Eph. 5:11).—**D. Thou hast, etc.** = either, thou hast regained his love which he had withdrawn, or, rather, as ver. 14 and 17 indicate, thou hast won him back for Christ and salvation (1 John 3:8, 15, Comp. 1 Cor. 9:19–22; James 5:20).

¹⁶ But if he hear thee not, take with thee one or two more, that at the mouth of two witnesses or three every word may be established.

A. Take with, etc. = the *second* step of the injured party. **One or two more;** this is a general allusion to the Mosaic law (such as Paul also makes in 2 Cor. 13:1), namely to Deut. 19:15. In the next phrase: **two or three,** the offended party is counted with the power, "one or two," the precise number, however, not being material.—**Witnesses** = not in the sense of witnesses who testify an oath before a public tribunal. These individuals rather resemble *arbitrators* of acknowledges good judgment and character, who, without an official appointment, but with the consent of both parties, *bear witness* (= give their opinion) respecting the merits of the case. The Lord, even at this stage, desires that unnecessary notoriety should be avoided.—**B. Every word** (= case, matter) **etc;** the words are quoted from Deut. 19:15, where it is declared that thus "the *matter* shall be established" (comp. 2 Cor. 13:1). The Greek term, generally translated *word,* occasionally means a *matter, affair* or *thing,* and is so translated in Luke 2:15; Acts 5:32; here it *is = matter in dispute.* This is in conformity to the usage of the corresponding Hebrew term, which often means *word,* but also sometimes *thing,* as in Gen. 15:1; 20:10, and is applied to a disputed question, and translated *matter* (Exod. 18:16).—**Established** = settled, determined.—The sense is: These umpires, who are themselves believers and disinterested brethren, shall conscientiously examine the case and pronounce their judgment respecting the course which the offender should pursue. The Lord requires the injured party to be well satisfied, by a severe self-examination, before any steps are taken, that he is not in reality himself the offending party.

[17] And if he refuse to hear them, tell it unto the church: and if he refuse to hear the church also, let him be unto thee as the Gentile and the publican.

A. Refuse to hear thee, The form of the Greek word translated *refuse to hear,* suggests as a translation the word *mishear,* which is not in general use; the first syllable, as in *misdirect, misapply,* etc., would indicate an *error* or a *wrong.* Hence, a wilful or contumacious rejection of the decision of the "witnesses" (which is assumed to be made in an enlightened, disinterested and holy spirit), is indicated, as equivalent to disobedience.—**B. Tell ... church** = the *third* step of the injured party. The word **church** is not usually employed in the N. T. in the sense of *synagogue,* and yet here evidently designates an organized or visible society of worshippers (see above 16:18, D. and 16:19, G.). Hence, the Lord, who now gives a rule which is of perpetual validity, speaks by way of anticipation of a Christian congregation established in any spot, and constituting a representative of the general Christian Church. The two parties are assumed to be persons who have made an open confession of their faith in Christ. The Lord does not prescribe the precise mode of obtaining the sense of the church, indicating that such details, like the number, names or specific duties of church officers, should be subsequently arranged by the Christian wisdom of His people, as the circumstances might require or dictate (comp. Acts 6:3).—**C. Let him ... publican** = let him no longer be counted as a fellow-Christian, but be as one of those who are "without" the pale of the church, not Christians (see 1 Cor. 5:12; Col. 4:5; 1 Thess. 4:12; 1 Tim. 3:7; Rev. 22:15). The heathen or Gentile (Eph. 2:11, 12), and the **publican** (see 5:46, C.), were regarded as aliens and outcasts. The Lord, in using this proverbial language (in the original "**the** Gentile"), not only implies that the obstinate offender betrays an entire want of Christian knowledge, faith and love (Rom. 15:2), but he also commissions his people, for the sake of the purity and peace of the Church, to refrain from having any ecclesiastical fellowship with him. Nevertheless, while the Church thus administers justice always in love, its duty to endeavor to reclaim the offender never ceases, even as the wandering sheep (ver. 12), never ceases to be an object of pity to the Good Shepherd himself. The principles which are to guide the Church in administering discipline, the occasions, the mode, the treatment of penitent offenders, etc., are further developed in Rom. 16:17; 2 Thess. 3:6, 14; 2 Tim. ch. 3; Tit. 3:10; 1 Cor. ch. 5, comp. with 2 Cor. 2:5–8; 7:12, and 6:14; Gal. 6:1.

18 Verily I say unto you, what things soever ye shall bind on earth shall be bound in heaven: and what things soever ye shall lose on earth shall be loosed in heaven.

These words had previously been addressed to Peter individually; (see above, 16:19). Here, where they are repeated, the whole tenor of the discourse indicates that the same authority, power or office is now extended to Christ's believing people, or the Church generally, as ver. 17 shows. Hence, as the Lord implies that His people will not be abandoned to their own erring wisdom, but be guided in their deliberations by the Holy Spirit, such heavenly wisdom will reveal itself in two or three devout believers as fully as if the whole company of believers were assembled. It is evident, as the following words also imply, that, in addition to faith, very thorough religious knowledge and the utmost purity of heart are essential features in the Christian character of Church members. The whole tenor of the verse indicates that some special action, distinct from the preaching of the Gospel, is here described by the words **bind** and **loose.** Now as verses 15:17 contain rules of church discipline which are of perpetual force, and as ver. 19:20, are regarded as conferring privileges and blessings on the Church which have by no means been withdrawn since the age of the apostles, it may be assumed that this 18th or intermediate verse also contains a commission which still exists in the church, namely, the exercise of the power of the keys (see 16:19, B.), or the right to grant or withhold absolution (John 20:23). Not one of the errors which the

Romish Church attempts to sustain by this passage, such as auricular confession (implying a rigid enumeration of sins before a priest), penance, works of satisfaction and merit, etc., is indicated in the least degree. Nevertheless, the words clearly refer to an ecclesiastical course, or indicate some act which implies a previous preaching or teaching of the Gospel as a distinct procedure, and as the ground or the justification of the binding or loosing. When the apostle says: "Confess your sins, etc." (James 5:16), he refers to a confession which members of the Church make under circumstances which he regards as familiarly known to his readers. The present text may then be understood as declaring that if a person, properly authorized and competent to "try the spirits" (1 John 4:1), confer with a sincerely penitent sinner, and, after receiving a satisfactory statement respecting his penitence and faith, declare his sins to be forgiven (which is only the application in a special case of the Saviour's gracious words in Mark 16:16), such forgiveness or absolution, when received in faith, shall be esteemed as sanctioned by the Lord. Now, as God alone can actually forgive sins, that exercise of the "loosing key" ("remit," John 20:23), in a case in which the "binding key" ("retain") should have been applied, namely, in the case of an impenitent or hypocritical person, will not secure the divine forgiveness. As the exercise of "the power of the keys," led to gross abuses, during the general reign of popery, on the part of the clergy, who alone exercised it as a special right; as it is, moreover, attended with difficulties of a peculiar nature when it assumes the form of an absolution of a penitent, and as it is not enjoined in this verse as indispensable to the existence and healthy growth of the Church, it has, as a formal act of confession and absolution in the case of individuals, been discontinued by large numbers of Protestants, while it is retained with many enormous and dangerous abuses by the papists. In place of the declaration announcing the forgiveness of God to an individual who is a believer, a general statement of the divine terms of forgiveness is deemed by many as sufficient, and the private and personal application is left to the conscience of the individual. In some cases the "power of the keys" is viewed as nothing more than the right of a congregation to receive, suspend or exclude individuals in accordance with their confession and conduct (16:19, B.)

¹⁹ Again I say unto you, that if two of you shall agree on earth as touching anything that they shall ask, it shall be done for them of my Father which is in heaven.

A. If two ... earth. The privileges of believers are here still further enlarged. If any two Christians, who seek to acquire the character described in Eph. 1:17–19, unite in opinion and feeling on any point connected not only with church discipline, but with the religious life generally ("anything"), and then bring their petitions to the throne of grace, their prayers shall be heard = "it shall be done, etc.," (comp. 1 John 5:14, 15). The words **agree as touching, etc.,** indicates that the consultation must be conducted in a spirit of Christian love in order to give efficacy to the prayer which succeeds it.—**Again** = further, besides, as in 4:8; 5:33; 13:44.—**B. Touching ... done.** The same conditions on which the fulfilment of the promise in 7:7, B. and C. depends, apply also here. The Lord addresses the words to those who are enlightened and genuine believers.—**Touching** = with respect to, concerning. If prayer ought to be "made for all men," according to 1 Tim. 2:1, then one of its subjects must be the repentance of the erring brother whose case has just been described.—**C. In heaven;** this term answers to the former: "on earth," teaching how "nigh the Lord is unto all them that call upon him" (Ps. 145:18).

[20] For where two or three are gathered together in my name, there am I in the midst of them.

A. For ... together = come together, meet for any such a special religious purpose (consultation, ver. 19, mutual encouragement, study of the divine word and will, prayer), and are "of one heart and one soul" (Acts 4:32). Any informal, private meeting ("two or three"), not disturbing, but rather promoting the harmony and godliness of the Church, may be understood. The connection obviously shows that no meeting or gathering of a few members held in opposition to the Church, or governed by a schismatic spirit, can be meant.—**B. In My name.** The original slightly varies from the phrase so rendered in John 14:13, 14; 16:24, and might be rendered: *unto* My name." Possibly there is an allusion to those passages (mentioned in 6:9, E.), in which the *name* of God indicates His divine *presence*. This verse, accordingly, very impressively represents these two or three believers as enjoying at all times the inestimable privilege of coming *unto* the very presence of the Lord. That divine presence is also found by the individual in the closet, where the Saviour specially commands us to seek it when we pray (6:6).—**C. There am, etc.** = as they, whose hearts are purified by faith (Acts 15:9; 2 Pet. 1:4), are "made perfect in one" (John 17:20–23), I am therefore in them, directing them in their consultations (ver. 19), teaching them by my Spirit how, and for what, they ought to pray (Rom. 8:26), and I will "fulfil all their petitions" (Ps. 20:5), for I myself am with them. Comp.

the phrase: God, Christ, *with* His people, (Matt. 28:20; John 3:2; Acts 18:10; 2 Tim. 4:17). It is Jesus of Nazareth who speaks here; but it is only divine power which can fulfil such a promise. Consequently, by virtue of the inseparable union of the divine and the human nature in Christ, the attributes of the former are also now by communication in possession of the latter, for the Person of Christ is *one* only.

²¹ Then came Peter and said to him, Lord, how oft shall my brother sin against me, and I forgive him? until seven times?

Peter ventures to refer to a point which he appears to think that the Lord had omitted to explain in ver. 15, as well as in 5:44; 6:14, 15. The Jewish teachers held very probably at that time already the doctrine which was afterwards introduced into their writings, that a man was not required to extend forgiveness to an offender who repeated the offence more than three times. Does his Master—Peter questions, sanction that rule, or ought the act of forgiving to be repeated more frequently, until, for instance, the number *seven* had been reached, and only afterwards be succeeded by retaliation? (The number **seven,** after Gen. 2:2, is very frequently introduced in the laws of Moses, in connection with the sacred times, the sacrifices, purifications, etc.; hence it was invested with a religious character (comp. 25:1, C.). This fact possibly led to the choice of the *seven* men in Acts 6:3).

²² Jesus saith unto him, I say not unto thee, until seven times: but, until seventy times seven.

The whole character of the language in this verse clearly shows the sense to be, that Christian love does not jealously count, weigh or measure its good deeds, but flows on in a full stream, placing no limit to its action. In all cases the offender has a claim on the indulgence and forgiveness of the believer (Eph. 4:32; Rom. 12:9; Deut. 32:36), even if there is, according to ver. 17, a limit beyond which the *Church* cannot consistently and safely retain him in her communion. When Lamech arrogantly and impiously spoke of being "avenged seventy and sevenfold" (Gen. 4:24), he meant, by the accumulation of the numbers, his thirst for revenge could never be appeased. To this ungodly spirit the Saviour opposes the spirit of His religion; by a similar repetition of the number *seven* (seven, multiplied by seventy) he indicates that the limit can never be reached beyond which wrath and vengeance become lawful. When He repeats the injunction in Luke 17:4, the number *seven* seems to be used proverbially as a designation of an indefinite but very large number of occasions, as in the passages mentioned in 12:43–45, A.). The sense then is: Multiply the number which thou hast specified by ten times the amount, and then multiply again, without coming to an end.

[23] Therefore is the kingdom of heaven likened unto a certain king, which would make a reckoning with his servants.

A. Therefore = In this respect, or, in reference to the reasons of the law enjoining unlimited forgiveness. The Lord enforces the lesson taught here (and in 6:14, 15) by pronouncing the parable of the Unmerciful Servant; it is intended to show, in view of the divine spirit of forgiving love, on the one hand, the folly and wickedness of the man who yields to an unforgiving spirit, and, on the other, the destruction to which that spirit necessarily leads (see below, ver. 35). It teaches, further (ver. 24, 25), that no sinner can offer from his own resources (wisdom, strength, etc.) a sufficient atonement to Him who is "King for ever and ever" (Ps. 10:16), and impresses the lesson, that, as our continued enjoyment of life and liberty proceeds from grace alone, it would be an unpardonable act to avail ourselves of our present privileges for the purpose of indulging in malice and revenge.—**B. The kingdom ... unto** = the divine course of action, as revealed in the work of the Messiah, and the acts expected of men, resemble the following circumstances—the course pursued by a certain king, etc. (comp. 13:24, B.). The willingness of God to forgive the humble suppliant is here described, as an example for man. "The civil government, which ought to punish criminals (Rom. 13:3, 4) for the sake of public order and safety, is not here intended; in the Christian Church on earth, on the contrary, the law of forgiveness and mercy must always prevail."—Luther.—**C. Take account** = investigate the amount which the servants respectively owed (comp. 25:19). Every human being owes a heavy debt to divine justice (comp. 6:12, A., B.). The law of God, revealed in His word, daily takes account of us, and teaches us to consider the amount of our debt to Him."—Luther.—**D. His servants** = the officers of state (stewards, treasurers, etc.), like those mentioned in Gen. 41:37, 38; 1 Sam. 18:22; 2 Sam. 20:24; 1 Kings 4:6; 9:22; 18:3; 2 Kings 18:18; 1 Chron. 27:25 (comp. 14:2, A.). If the most eminent of God's creatures must expect to "give account to Him that is ready to judge the quick (= the living) and the dead" (1 Pet. 4:5), no individual can hope to escape. No mountains nor hills (Luke 23:30; Hos. 10:8; Isai. 2:19) can hide us from "Him with whom we have to do" (Heb. 4:13).

24 And when he had begun to reckon, one was brought unto him, which owed him ten thousand talents.

A. One ... him. Christ here deems one case to be sufficient for the purpose of showing the deep guilt of man, from which he cannot cleanse himself by any human means.—**B. Ten ... talents.** There is some uncertainty respecting the actual amount of this sum of money, when stated in terms belonging to modern currency. The *Hebrew* **talent** mentioned in Exod. 38:24, ff., and elsewhere, was equivalent to 3,000 shekels (for which see above, 17:24, B.), estimated by some to be equal to = $1680. The Attic or *Greek* talent of silver is valued at nearly $1000 (see 25:15, A.). Others assign a still higher value to it. Among the ancient Hebrews, before coined money was known, the precious metals circulated according to their weight; hence we read of talents of gold (2 Sam. 12:30) and of silver (2 Kings 5:23). The whole amount of the talents mentioned in the text, if they were of silver, must, according to the lowest calculation have been between ten and fifteen millions of dollars; if talents of gold were understood, the amount would be enormously increased. The Greeks and Hebrews had no single or uncompounded words which, like the English word *million,* expressed more than 10,000. The former frequently used the word here found in the original, not only for ten thousand, but also in order to designate a number that was indefinitely large, like the word *myriad,* which is derived from it (comp. the Hebrew usage in Deut. 33:2, 17; Ps. 3:6, and Dan. 7:10; Ps. 68:17). The Lord evidently intends, in the case of the treasurer of a king who is a defaulter, to specify a sum of money too vast in amount to be ever paid by an individual. Man cannot "answer God one of a thousand" (Job 9:3). "Who can understand his errors?" (Ps. 19:12. See Rom. 3:19).

[25] But forasmuch as he had not wherewith to pay, his lord commanded him to be sold, and his wife, and children, and all that he had, and payment to be made.

A. Had not = wherewith to pay, had no means to pay. The law conferred many advantages on the Jew (Rom. 3:1, 2, 20), but it could not impart righteousness to man (Rom. 8:3).—**B. His lord ... had** = The Jews retained the oriental practice of selling a debtor and the members of his family as bond-servants, when the debt was not paid (2 Kings 4; 1; Nehem. 5:5); but by a merciful provision of the divine law, such bondage invariably ceased on the arrival of the year of jubilee (Lev. 25:39–55; in Deut. 15:12) the seventh year was fixed as the limit of bondage.—**C. And payment, etc.** The Lord historically introduces the well-known practice, for the purpose of showing that even as the sale of a whole family with all its goods could never produce a sum equivalent to the one mentioned above, so man can never by any works or sacrifices or sufferings sufficiently atone to God for his grievous sins (see Rom. 6:23). If, therefore, divine justice rigidly exacted payment from the sinner himself, and a divine Redeemer had not appeared (Tit. 3:4, 5; 1 Pet. 1:18), no way of salvation would be open to man (Acts 4:12). "Here lies one of the dangers of popery, that it holds a doctrine according to which men can free themselves from their guilt by their own merits and works of satisfaction; whereas, the only way to obtain forgiveness of sin is—to look to Christ in penitence and faith, and, with the publican, to pray: God be merciful to me a sinner. (Luke 18:13)."—Luther.

²⁶ The servant therefore fell down, and worshipped him, saying, Lord, have patience with me, and I will pay thee all.

A. The servant ... worshipped Him = besought Him, as in the margin of the English Bible; lit. *prostrated himself* (see 3:2, D).—**B. Have patience, etc.** = grant me more time. Even if this servant had the *will* to pay the immense amount, whence would he obtain the *means?* If the strictest obedience of man to the divine will is only a partial discharge of a debt never fully paid and cancelled, whence are our means to be derived for satisfying divine justice, in view of our many acts of disobedience? (Comp. Luke 17:10). Obedience in one case, while it entitles no man to a reward, and simply preserves from punishment, does not even before a human tribunal make amends for an act of disobedience in another case.

²⁷ And the Lord of that servant, being moved with compassion, released him, and forgave him the debt.

A. Moved with compassion; the Hebrew phrase rendered in Gen. 43:30, "his bowels did yearn," indicates very strong and tender emotions, and hence often described the depth and power of divine pity and compassion (Deut. 13:17; Ps. 25:6; 40:11). The usage of the corresponding Greek word is the same here and elsewhere in the N. T. (Matt. 9:36; 14:14; 15:22; 18:27; 20:34; Phil. 1:8; 2:1). The tenderness and greatness of divine pity or the riches of God's goodness (Rom. 2:4), are here designed to be set forth, which resulted in the mission of a Saviour (John 3:16). Without *His* redeeming work our salvation would have been an event inconsistent with the divine character, and therefore impossible (Rom. 3:23–26).—**B. Loosed him** = released him from the hands of the officers of justice (ver. 25, 30), who had already seized him as a dishonest debtor. Although the sentence of death, eternal death, is not yet executed (Eccl. 8:11), it is already pronounced (Rom. 1:18; John 3:36), and will be executed in our case, if we are not "quickened" (Eph. 2:1, 5) in Christ, who alone can "blot out the handwriting of ordinances that was against us" (Col. 2:13, 14).—**C. Forgave**

the debt = *remitted it,* as the same word is rendered in John 20:23, or *cancelled* it. A different Greek word in Luke 7:42, similarly translated, indicates a similar gracious act (Comp. the phrase: "blotting out sins," Isai, 44:22; Acts 3:19). "When the trembling sinner fears that he is too guilty to be forgiven, let him in faith remember that the power and love of God are infinite, and that the believer is now bought and redeemed by Christ, and let him be comforted by these words. The law condemns and 'worketh wrath' (Rom. 4:15 and ch. 7), but grace in Christ forgives."—Luther. At this point, the parable, which illustrated forgiving love in its actual results, does not introduce the whole system of the Christian faith, such as the Atonement, etc. Neither does it intend to describe the divine attributes precisely; no changes of opinion and purpose such as this king exhibits occur in the immutable God (Rom. 11:29).

28 But that servant went out, and found one of his fellowservants, which owed him a hundred pence: and he laid hold on him, and took *him* by the throat, saying, Pay what thou owest.

A. But ... fellow-servants. The Lord here recognizes the fact that man may at times have reason to complain of wrongs done to him by his fellow-man, such offences being viewed as "debts" (see 6:12, A.). Still, no injury which can possibly be inflicted on us by another, equals in enormity the guilt which we have contracted by our own sins against God, as the comparatively small debt now specified, is intended to teach.—**B. A hundred pence** = about fourteen dollars in our currency (see 17:24, B.). The Lord uses round numbers, or, in modern language, compares *tens* and *millions,* when He designs to teach the lesson just stated under A.—**C. Laid**

hands, etc. Compare this violent and cruel conduct (the sternness, throttling, etc.), with the king's compassion and bounty (ver. 27). The contrast places the selfishness and wickedness of an unforgiving spirit in a very strong light. Even independently of a view of the divine mercy, the apostle Paul admonishes us that the consciousness of our own imperfections and sins should teach us to deal gently with others (Tit. 3:2, 3; Gal. 6:1).

²⁹ So his fellow servant fell down and besought him, saying, Have patience with me, and I will pay Thee.

This debtor, who does not deny his indebtedness, represents the penitent brother who has injured us. In view of the small amount of the debt, which a reasonable indulgence on the part of the creditor would have enabled the debtor to pay (indicating the comparatively slight injury which others can ever do to us), no excuse remains for feelings or acts that betray an unforgiving or avengeful spirit.

³⁰ And he would not: but went and cast him into prison, till he should pay that which was due.

Here are revealed the wisdom and justice of God in withholding forgiveness from the unpenitent and unbelieving. What impression had the king's grace made on the first servant? What honor would God gain, or what advantage would the sinner himself derive, if "faith, which worketh by love" (Gal. 5:6), were not the condition on which God will grant pardon? A pardoned but impenitent sinner would then exhibit only increased arrogance and impiety. (Imprisonment, as a punishment for debt or for crime, was not recognized by the laws of Moses, but had been introduced among the Jews after the Babylonish Captivity, Ezra 7:26; comp. 5:25, B.).

³¹ So when his fellowservants saw what was done, they were exceeding sorry, and came and told unto their lord all that was done.

This portion of the parable, which exhibits the grief of believers when one of their number betrays an unholy spirit, as well as the connection of the whole (ver. 15) indicates that the Lord here refers chiefly to the conduct of members of his church (comp. Eph. 4:32)—"of the househould of God" (Eph. 2:19). On the other occasions *all* men are declared to be objects of forgiving love (6:14, 15), even as "the Lord over all" died for all (Rom. 10:12; 11:32; 2 Cor. 5:14; 1 Tim. 2:6; Hebr. 2:9; 8:11). While the earthly king needs information, the all-seeing God knows all the sin of man's heart and life, without the intervention of men or angels. When, therefore, "prayer was made without ceasing of (= by) the church unto God" for the persecuted apostle Peter (Acts 12:5), or is now made in any case, believers do not design to communicate information to God, but to entreat Him to grant relief, as well as to obtain new strength and faith themselves.

³² Then his lord called him unto him, and saith to him, Thou wicked servant, I forgave thee all that debt, because thou besoughtest me:

Men may stifle the voice of conscience and spurn the authority of God's word, but such evasions will not in the end shield them from divine wrath. "Can any hide himself in secret places, that I shall not see him? saith the Lord." (Jerem. 23:24; comp. Ps. 139:1–12).—**Thou wicked, etc.** = wicked, as thy unforgiving spirit, which my mercy did not move, proves that to be. The language shows that the divine forgiveness of sins is conditional, that is, it does not take effect without corresponding sentiments, and a corresponding course of conduct on the part of man; (see 6:14, 15).

³³ Shouldest not thou also have had mercy on thy fellowservant, even as I had mercy on thee?

"And he was speechless" (Matt. 22:12). If the impenitent should attempt to justify themselves on the day of judgment (comp. 25:44), they will be judged out of their own mouth (Luke 19:22), and proved to be "without excuse" (Rom. 1:20). "Behold, it is written before me" (Isai. 65:6, and comp. Mal. 3:16; Rev. 20:12).

³⁴ And his lord was wroth, and delivered him to the tormentors, till he should pay all that was due.

A. Wroth = indignant, angry, as the word is rendered in Luke 14:21; see 2:16, B. The king's wrath is an image of the divine sentence of condemnation.—**B. Tormentors.** The word probably designates the jailer and his assistants, who, according to the Roman law, bound insolvent debtors with fetters and cords, and sometimes secured prisoners by making their "feet fast in the stocks" (Acts 16:24). The sufferings of those who were exposed to the rapacity and cruelty of a Roman jailer (chains, foul air, dampness, darkness, scourging, hunger, vermin, etc.), were proverbially not less than actual torture. "Eternal damnation" (ver. 8; Mark 3:29.) will consist not simply in the exclusion from heaven, but also in positive punishments (25:46).—**C. Till he should, etc.** As it was obvious that this cruel servant never could pay "all" that he owed (ver. 24. B.), the sentence virtually subjected him to perpetual imprisonment—an image of the endless punishments of the wicked; (25:46; see above, 5:26, and comp. James 2:13). The "great gulf" which separates the lost in the eternal world from heaven, can never be passed

(Luke 16:26). The problem which reflecting men in all ages felt unable to solve by human wisdom was: "How can man be justified with God?" (Job 25:4). No man could open the sealed book in which that deep mystery was explained (Rev. 5:2, ff.), until the Lamb of God appeared, took away the sin of the world (John 11:29), and made an atonement (Rom. 5:11). God was revealed as both "just and the justifier of him which believeth in Jesus" (3:26).

35 So shall also my heavenly Father do unto you, if ye forgive not every one his brother from your hearts.

A. So likewise; the whole scope or purpose of the parable, or the lesson which it is intended to convey, is stated here; the Saviour teaches that he who does not "from his heart" forgive an offending brother, is destitute of love; that want of love betrays an unrenewed, unbelieving heart; such an impenitent sinner, inasmuch as he rejects the only means of salvation which are accessible, will necessarily be lost forever (see Rom. 2:3–9.)—**B. From your hearts.** A similar phrase occurs in 22:37; Rom. 6:17; it corresponds to the English word *heartily,* in the sense of *sincerely,* promptly, with good will.—**C. Trespasses** (see 6:12, A).—"God has given us sufficient evidences that our sins shall be forgiven, namely, the word of the Gospel, Baptism, the Lord's Supper, and the Holy Spirit, in our hearts. But it now becomes necessary for us to give evidence that we have truly and actually *received* the forgiveness of our sins. *That* evidence is furnished by us when every one of us from his heart forgives his brother's trespasses."—Luther.

4

Matthew 19

¹ And it came to pass when Jesus had finished these words, he departed from Galilee, and came into the borders of Judæa beyond Jordan.

A. He departed = commencing His last journey from Galilee to Jerusalem (20:17; 21:1), where death awaited Him. Matthew appears to have selected such incidents and discourses connected with this journey, as illustrate the true character of the Christian, of which the former chapter had also treated.—**These words** (comp. 26:1).—**B. Beyond Jordan** = He did not, as on a former occasion, when He travelled in an opposite direction (John 4:3, 4), take the direct road leading through Samaria, but passed over to the eastern side of the Jordan, and travelled through Peræa; this region was separated by the river from Judea.—**Into the coasts** = remaining in the vicinity of the Jordan.

² And great multitudes followed him: and he healed them there.

Such was frequently the case (comp. 4:25; 8:1; 12:15).

³ And there came unto him Pharisees, tempting him, and saying: Is it lawful *for a man* to put away his wife for every cause?

A. Pharisees—B. Tempting Him = with an evil design, that they might entangle Him, as in 22:15. They knew that He had established principles respecting divorces (5:31, 32), which, if uttered by Him publicly in Peræa, might, as they hoped, induce the ruler of that country, Herod Antipas, to slay Him, as he had previously slain John the Baptist (14:1–10); for **tempt** (see 4:1, D.).—**C. Is it lawful, &c.** = Does the law of Moses, when properly interpreted, permit or not permit a man, etc.? One party of the Jews, loosely interpreting Deut. 24:1, maintained that even a trivial cause, such as a mere caprice, would justify a man who repudiated his lawful wife; another, and the stricter party held that such an act could be justified only by very gross offences and immoralities on the part of the wife. The former party relied on the authority of Hillel, the latter on that of Shammai, two Jewish teachers of great distinction. Rabbi Hillel, who died ten years after the birth of Christ, was the grandfather of Paul's teacher Gamaliel (Acts 22:3). The Lord had decided the question in the Sermon on the Mount (see above, 5:31, 32), but here assigns certain reasons which explain that decision; He rejects the authority of all mere human teachers, and at once appeals to the written Word.

⁴ And he answered and said; Have ye not read, that he which made *them* from the beginning made them male and female?

The passage quoted occurs in Gen. 1:27, 28. The sense here is: Why do ye ask? Did not the Creator distinctly teach by the creation of a single pair, namely, one man and one woman, and by the nature of the marriage-blessing which He bestowed at the time, that a *permanent* union of the two individuals, during the whole of their natural life, was intended, serving as an example for all succeeding cases of marriage?—**Male and female;** the Greek indicates a single individual of each sex.

⁵ And said, For this cause shall a man leave his father and mother, and shall cleave to his wife: and the twain shall become one flesh?

These words were spoken by Adam (Gen. 2:24) in allusion to the divine act of forming the first woman of a portion of Adam's body. The Saviour quoted them as words spoken by the Creator, for the reason that Adam, who had at that time no knowledge of his own respecting the divine will and the law of marriage, repeats these words only after God had first pronounced them. The sense is: The marriage tie shall be firm and indissoluble, as long as both parties live; even the tie of nature existing between parents and children, which we instinctively regard as sacred, shall sooner be ruptured than the sacred tie which unites man and wife. Hence these two (**twain,** 5:41, B.), shall constitute in this respect only one person in the eyes of God (comp., Eph. 5:28–31.

⁶ So that they are no more twain, but one flesh. What therefore God hath joined together, let no man put asunder.

Since God has declared that the husband and wife shall remain inseparably united, let not men, who are mere creatures of the dust, arrogantly and impiously annul such a union either directly or indirectly by human laws. The words embody the general principle:—Let no man in any case contravene a divine appointment (comp. Acts 10:15; Numb. 23:8).—**Joined together,** lit. *yoked together* = joined as one pair having the same duties and interests.

⁷ They say unto him, Why then did Moses command to give a bill of divorcement, and to put *her* away?

(See 5:31, B.). Moses did not recommend, much less did he *command* divorces as these Pharisees appear to say, implying that either Christ disputed the authority of the revered lawgiver, or else that Moses must have erred, which none could assert. Moses simply placed restrictions by this command on the custom of divorcing, by requiring certain writings, during the preparation of which time would be won for consultation and the reconciliation of the parties. Thus, too, the ancient Oriental usages connected with vows (Deut. 23:21, 22) and the "revenger of blood" (Numb. ch. 35; Deut. 4:41, ff.), were tolerated by Moses, but new and definite limits and restrictions were prescribed. Things that are lawful (= allowed by the law), are not necessarily expedient or edifying (1 Cor. 6:12; 10:23).

⁸ He saith unto them, Moses for your hardness of heart suffered you to put away your wives: but from the beginning it hath not been so.

A. Moses ... hearts (see 5:31, B.).—**B. But from the beginning** = of the creation (10:6), when Adam and Eve were created. The first man who departed from the divine order by introducing polygamy was the wicked Lamech, a murderer, and the descendant of the murderer Cain (Gen. 4:18, 23).

⁹ And I say unto you, Whosoever shall put away his wife, except for fornication, and shall marry another, committeth adultery: and he that marrieth her when she is put away committeth adultery.

The Lord repeats the declaration which He had already

made in the Sermon on the Mount (5:32). It appears from Mark 10:10, that at this point the narrative of Matthew introduces the substance of a private conversation of the Lord with the disciples.

¹⁰ The disciples say unto him, If the case of the man is so with his wife, it is not expedient to marry.

A. His disciples ... him = after returning to the house, when they were alone with the Lord (Mark 10:10). At a later period the Corinthians asked counsel of Paul respecting the subject of marriage (1 Cor. 7:1). "The present distress" mentioned in ver. 26, 28, 29, as well as the other circumstances to which he alludes in the same chapter, refer to the trials of Christians in his day, their expulsion by persecutors from their homes, their poverty, the violent rending asunder of the family circle, etc. He does not represent celibacy as a duty of religion, neither does he even remotely imply that it is a more holy state than that of marriage; on the contrary, he regards the latter as a divinely instituted state, the ties of which are sacred and "honorable in all" (Hebr. 13:4). Accordingly, several of the other apostles were accompanied by their wives in their missionary journeys (1 Cor. 9:5). But Paul himself remained unmarried, and in the distressing circumstances of the times, and in view of his peculiar duties, was, in consequence of his freedom from family ties, more free in his peculiar apostolic work. The Lord on the present occasion gives liberty to each individual to enter the married state or to refrain, requiring him, however, in either case, to act conscientiously and in the fear of God.—**B. If the case.** The word here translated **case** is rendered *cause* in ver. 3, and *accusation* in 27:37; Acts 25:18. The sense is: If only such a cause, accusation or charge (that is, the guilt contracted in the eyes of God by lewdness) can justify a man in divorcing his wife, then, etc.—**C. It is not expedient.** The disciples indirectly ask the question: What course shall *we* pursue? The Lord replies in the next verses that marriage of itself, like celibacy, neither fits nor unfits an individual for the kingdom of heaven. He teaches that marriage, like personal liberty or bondage (Matt. 22:30; 1 Cor. 7:20, 21), or like national distinctions and those of race and sex (Gal. 3:28; Col. 3:11; 1 Cor. 7:17), which are of a terrestrial character, of themselves neither facilitates nor impedes any individual's entrance into the Church and the heavenly kingdom. All such circumstances may promote, and they may hinder our growth in grace, according to the spirit and principles which influence us.

[11] But he said unto them, All men cannot receive this saying, but they to whom it is given.

Receive = *contain,* as the same word is rendered in John 2:6; 21:25; either word will often answer, as in Mark 2:2. The sense here is:—receive it into, or give place to it, with respect to the mind and judgment, that is, comprehend a truth, and *contain* it. The word translated **saying,** here seems to mean *subject* or *matter* as in Mark 1:45; Acts 8:21; 15:6, or *topic, thing,* as in Matt. 21:24; Luke 1:4. The phrase: **All men cannot,** as the use of the same Greek negative in some other passages shows (24:22; Luke 1:37; Rom. 3:20; 1 Cor. 1:29) is probably = *no one can.* The sense of the whole then is: As men are not naturally enlightened and sanctified, they cannot of themselves select holy principles of action, and adopt a strictly wise and holy course of conduct; such grace is the gift of God (1 Cor. 7:7). That such is the sense, appears from the concluding words of the following verse, which resembles the proverb: He that hath ears, etc. (see 11:15).

¹² For there are eunuchs, which were so born from their mother's womb: and there are eunuchs, which were made eunuchs by men: and there are eunuchs, which made themselves eunuchs for the kingdom of heaven's sake. He that is able to receive it, let him receive it.

A. The Lord now answers the indirect question of the disciples (ver. 10, B.), by showing that the state which is the opposite of marriage, namely, celibacy, does not necessarily possess merit in the eyes of God (who rather declared that it was "not good," Gen. 2:18), and that it does not invariably facilitate the performance of the duties of religion. The popish views of celibacy, as of a pre-eminently holy state, are not sanctioned by the divine Word. As Shimei was not literally a servant of Solomon, but nevertheless, according to custom, applied that name to himself as a man subject to the king's authority (1 Kings 2:38), so the **eunuchs** here mentioned doubtless receive that name in a figurative sense.—**B. There are, etc.** Certain mental conditions, such as those of idiots, etc., unfit an individual for the duties of domestic life; accordingly, some (the *first* class), in consequence of their personal condition, exhibit this inaptitude. Thus, too, the man who "had an infirmity thirty and eight years" (John 5:5–7), appears to have been alone in the world. Some (the *second* class) encounter, in consequence of direct or indirect constraint or compulsion on the part of others, insurmountable obstacles which necessarily prevent them from forming the ties of marriage. Thus, too, according to laws established in some cases, soldiers serving in a monarch's army, prisoners, etc., are in such a situation. A *third* class ("there are eunuchs, etc.") consists of the special cases of those who, like Paul (1 Cor. 7:7, 8, 26), and possibly some other apostles, or like many missionaries, contract no ties of this description, and establish no home of their own, in order that they may be at liberty to labor for the Gospel ("for the kingdom of heaven's sake"), and abide in any place without neglecting family duties.—**C. He that is, etc.** (comp. 11:15). The Lord here desires that every individual should primarily be guided by holy principles; if he believes that peculiar circumstances connected with the propagation of the Gospel in the world, or the growth of grace in his own soul, indicate that he should assume no marriage ties, he may refrain. Even in this case, no necessity is imposed on him by a divine command—such a decision is his voluntary act, as the Lord twice implies by the words: "have made themselves, etc.", and "let him receive it."

[13] Then were there brought unto him little children, that he should lay his hands on them, and pray: and the disciples rebuked them.

A. Then. This word does not necessarily imply that the event now related occurred immediately after the foregoing conversation; it is often an indefinite and general reference to a period of time which may be of greater or less duration (comp. 2:16; 3:5; 9:14) and is accordingly rendered: From that time in 4:17; 16:21. Luke places the occurrence in a different connection (18:14, ff.), while Matthew, who had just related the Saviour's decisions respecting marriage and divorce, now proceeds to place other relations of domestic life in a Christian light, by describing the Saviour's love of little children. Luke (18:15) calls these children *babes,* the term applied to children immediately after birth (Luke 2:12, 16; Acts 7:19; 1 Pet. 2:2). The parents who brought them, were, doubtless, believers, who already understood the nature of the spiritual blessings which Christ could confer.—**B. Lay his hands ... pray** = invoke a blessing during the act. This is the sense of the word "touch" in Mark 10:13. It was a Jewish practice to bring little children to venerated religious teachers for such a purpose. For illustrations of the imposition of hands as a religious act (see Gen. 48:14; Numb. 27:18; Acts 6:6; 18:18; 19:6; 2 Tim. 1:6).—**C. The disciples, etc.**; they had not yet acquired a true and religious view of childhood, of its spiritual wants and capacities, etc., and appear to have regarded the act of the parents simply as an intrusion on their revered master (comp. 20:31). Their mistaken zeal displeased him greatly (Mark 10:14), and led him to speak specially of the claims of childhood on the attention and aid of adults. At a later period, when the disciples were more fully enlightened (John 14:26; 16:12, 13), they gladly declared to the Jews: "The promise is unto you, *and to your children, etc.*" (Acts 2:39). They had then obtained a better understanding of Holy Baptism, which was not merely substituted for circumcision, as an initiatory rite (Col. 2:11, 12), but which also, as one of the means of grace, greatly enlarged those privileges and blessings which had been conferred on the Jewish child by circumcision (see 20:22, C.).

¹⁴ But Jesus said, Suffer the little children, and forbid them not, to come unto me; for of such is the kingdom of heaven.

A. Suffer. The original word, precisely as in 15:14, and John 12:7, signifies: *Let these* parents and children *alone*,—**forbid** = *hinder, prevent,* as in Acts 8:36. The act of the parents (ver. 13), is regarded as the act of the children = let them (the children, as indicated by the Greek) come unto me (Mark 10:14). The Lord implies that the deprivation of His blessing would be an actual loss to these children, for, otherwise, His act of blessing would be a mere formality. Much more is the deprivation of the Holy Sacrament of Baptism, which is the "washing of regeneration" (Tit. 3:5; John 3:5) a severe loss to an infant.—**B. Of such, etc.** These words, which were spoken at a place and a time entirely different from those in which the occurrences described in 18:1, ff. took place, refer to these little children themselves, in this sense:—The kingdom of heaven and its spiritual blessings as imparted in the Church of Christ, are not adapted to, and designed for adults alone, but for *such* little children also (see 28:19, B.). They too may be sanctified by divine power and grace (1 Cor. 7:14), and be received into the bosom of the Church; to such privileges no adult has a better title than an infant, since all are alike unworthy. The solemn duty of parents to bring their children to the Lord in Holy Baptism, and teach them the way of salvation at the earliest age, is here affectingly and impressively declared. "Infant Baptism," says Alford on Mark 10:14, "is the normal pattern of all Baptism; none can enter God's kingdom, except as an infant."

¹⁵ And he laid his hands on them, and departed thence.

Mark says (10:16), "He took them up in His arms, put His hands upon them, and blessed them." The Saviour's act of blessing can surely not be viewed as a mere ceremony, devoid of value and power, although as in Baptism, no visible results at once appeared. The precise nature of that blessing it is impossible to define; that it, however, was a positive blessing, actually conferring certain divine gifts, is unquestionable. The operations of the divine Spirit are mighty, although our senses perceive them not (Col. 1:29; Hebr. 13:21). His blessing is still imparted by Him to little children who are brought to Him in Holy Baptism, "working in them mightily" (Col. 1:29) that which is well-pleasing in His sight. Although those little children were too young (ver. 13, A.) to be fully conscious of the value of the Saviour's blessing, it was not the less real and efficacious on that account. So, too, the blessed influences of Holy Baptism are not hindered by the infant's inability to comprehend the nature of that Sacrament. An illustration may be found in the case of an orphan child, whose inheritance is secured by legal processes the efficacy of which it is too young to understand. But as the seed, though it possesses vitality, may still bear no fruit (Matt. 13:3, ff.), so the blessing granted in Baptism to the infant must be secured, developed and enlarged by subsequent wholesome instructions from the word of life; otherwise, that blessing may be lost.

¹⁶ And, behold, one came to him, and said, Master, what good thing shall I do, that I may have eternal life?

A. Behold; this introductory word (see 1:20, B.), directs the reader's attention to the very important lessons respecting the nature of the sovereign good, the snares of riches, etc., which the occurrence affords.—**B. One came** = young (ver. 20), very wealthy (ver. 22), and holding a high position, being a ruler (Luke 18:18), either, like the one mentioned in 9:18, or, possibly, a member of the Sanhedrin (comp. Luke 24:20; John 7:26). Mark relates (10:17) that he "kneeled to Christ," whom he eagerly sought. This act, when connected with the two circumstances that Jesus "loved him" (Mark 10:21), and that the young man was "sorrowful" (ver. 22, below), shows that he interrogated the Saviour not from malicious motives, but with a sincere desire to learn.—**C. Master** (= **teacher,** in the original; see 8:19, B.), etc. [Both Mark and Luke say, "Good Master."] There were Jews in the days of Christ, of an earnest frame of mind, who desired to inherit spiritual and eternal joys (John 5:39). The religious teachers of the day had, however, reduced the true worship of God to a mere external observance of the letter of the law, and disregarded the worship which a believing and loving heart alone can render to God. These dangerous errors the Lord often lamented (9:36) and exposed (ch. 5–7; 9:14, ff.; ch. 15, and comp. John 3:5; 4:22, 23). Of various fundamental principles of religion, this young man, with all his respectability, amiable disposition, sincerity and zeal, was totally ignorant. His question betrayed two fatal errors in particular, which he cherished; the first was his opinion that a man could earn or merit everlasting life (which is mentioned in Dan. 12:2), by his own acts ("what good thing" in addition to ordinary religious duties shall I *do* = perform, work); the second was the very low standard by which he estimated genuine *goodness,* in the sense of true virtue or holiness, not knowing that faith alone can give a proper character to works (Rom. ch. 4). He accordingly applied the word **good** to any outward work that seemed to conform to the letter of the law, and to any religious teacher who appeared to observe the moral law. Here, he assumed that Christ was a mere mortal, an imperfect creature, like all other teachers. It is common even in our day among those who deny the divinity of Christ to compliment him with the terms: "Wise teacher," Loving Jesus," "Noble, exalted man," etc. As Christ commanded the unclean spirit which called Him "the Holy One of God" to be silent (Mark 1:25,

34, with which compare Acts 16:17, 18), because He would not receive testimony from such a source, so here he declines to be called "*Good* Master," when that appellation proceeds from low views of His Person and Work, and withholds Him the divine honor which is due to Him even as to the Father (John 5:23); it reduces Him to the rank of a merely wise and virtuous *human being,* instead of recognizing the Father in Him (John 14:9), and showing acknowledging that He alone was without sin (for His sinlessness, see 1:16, C.).

[17] And he said unto him, Why askest thou me concerning that which is good? One, there is who is good: but if thou wouldest enter into life, keep the commandments.*

A. Why askest ... good = Before thou canst expect to *do* actions which are good, thou must rightly understand the exalted nature of that *goodness* which alone is acceptable in the eyes of God. Thou callest Me *good,* and yet thinkest that I am like any other man, of whom it is said, as thou knowest, that "the imagination of his heart is evil from his youth" (Gen. 8:21). Hast thou ever reflected properly on the true nature of goodness as it is revealed in the character of the perfect and infinite God, or inquired whether, in *such a sense,* any mortal can possess that attribute? The precision with which the Lord here fixes the meaning of the term proceeds from His perception of the young man's total misapprehension of the nature of purity and holiness. When He Himself at other times speaks of good and evil men (5:45, C.; 12:35), he regards the former as only comparatively good, in the popular sense of the word. But when the title *good* is applied to himself, he desires that it should be applied to him not as a mere man, but as the God-Man. The truth that God alone is good is strikingly expressed in the English and German names,

God, Gott, which coincide ultimately with the words *good, gut.*—**B. But if, etc,** The Lord Jesus, who sees the sincerity as well as the ignorance of the young man, designs to expose His Pharisaic errors in all their folly, and thus prepare the way for the entrance into his heart of pure Gospel truth. The sense is:—Thy question answers itself; the good thing which thou desirest to know, must naturally be the keeping, in accordance with the divine purpose, of all, and not of a part only of the commandments which God, the sovereign good, has given. "If a man do them, he shall live in them" (Lev. 18:5). *Hast* thou done—*canst* thou do, them with a perfect heart? Art thou not, after all thy efforts, only an "unprofitable servant"? (Luke 17:10).

18, 19 He saith unto him, Which? And Jesus said, Thou shalt not kill, Thou shalt not commit adultery, Thou shalt not steal, Thou shalt not bear false witness,—Honour thy father and thy mother: and, Thou shalt love thy neighbour as thyself.

A. Which? The young man already becomes conscious of the power of the searching words of Christ; he feels the insufficiency of the Pharisaic religious lessons, for these had not yet indicated a sure and satisfactory principle of holy living (see 5:19, A.).—**B. Jesus said, etc.** By this general reference to the Decalogue or Ten Commandments (Exod., ch. 20), which were written on the "two tables of the testimony" (Exod. 32:15), the Lord indicates the moral law in its whole extent. He had on former occasions (5:21, 27; 15:4) illustrated their true meaning and spirit. He now adds from Lev. 19:18 the words: Thou shalt love, etc. (see 5:43, C.), for the purpose of showing to the young man, who was not a hypocrite, but was, nevertheless, ignorant and self-righteous, that obedience to God consists not simply in outward acts, but also in pure and kindly emotions of the heart (see ann. to 25:35, 36). The phrase: **as thyself,** is equivalent to: with the same sincerity and uniformity with which thou laborest for thy own welfare. When a similar answer was given by the Lord to a less earnest inquirer (Luke 10:28), the sense is nearly the same = This do, love God with all thy heart, etc., if thou canst! But thou canst not do this by thy own strength. (See Paul's language in Rom. 3:20; 8:7; Gal. 2:16)

20 The young man saith unto him, All these things have I observed: what lack I yet?

A. All these, etc. There is no reason to doubt the truth of the young man's assertion that he had led a moral life (had not been an idolater, adulterer, etc). But he again betrays very low views of true religion, and gross ignorance of the state of his heart. He looked to the letter of the law alone, and was not aware that, according to the Lord's solemn declarations, even if he were no actual thief or murderer according to the common interpretation of the law, he might still be "in danger of hell-fire" (Matt. 5:21–32). So Paul was zealous and "blameless" as a Jew, but found such "righteousness" (Phil., ch. 3) to be "as filthy rags" (Isai. 64:6). The Ten Commandments may be kept according to the letter, and yet be violated in their spirit. Had this young man kept, for instance, the Commandment: "Thou shalt not kill," as it is explained in 1 John 3:15? Did his good works all proceed from a principle of love to God? (Matt. 22:37, 38). Had he not, on the contrary, always misinterpreted the last commandment, which the Lord had quoted from Lev. 19:18—the law of love? Its true Gospel meaning is found in 5:43, ff.; 22:39, 40; Rom. 13:8–10; Gal. 5:14; James 2:8.—**B. What lack I yet?** = Have I not yet fulfilled all my duty to God? What *is* my spiritual want which yet remains, as Thou impliest by Thy words and looks, and which my heart now begins to feel? This dawning of light in the young man's soul, which indistinctly revealed to him his spiritual poverty, and now awakened a desire to find God, explains the words in Mark 10:21: "Jesus beholding him, loved him" = was greatly pleased with the feeble effort made by the young man, and felt great pity for him. But divine love is not always returned on the part of men. God loved and pitied the world (John 3:16); but he who scorns that love, and will not believe in Christ, is guilty of self-destruction. To *lack* = *to want* or need; a deficiency is implied. The original word is translated *to be in want* in Luke 15:14; *fall short* (Rom. 3:23; Hebr. 4:1); *come behind* (1 Cor. 1:7); *to be in want* (Phil. 4:12); *being destitute* (Hebr. 11:37). The Lord, in His remarkable treatment of this case, designed to teach the young man that mere morality or freedom from vice, and the outward observance of the precepts of virtue, could not atone for other sins of the heart and life, which polluted every child of fallen Adam (John 3:6); such morality, therefore, cannot give true peace to an awakened conscience (Hebr. 9:9; 10:2). Such peace can flow from faith in the crucified Redeemer and His atoning work alone (Hebr. 9:14; 10:19–22). The knowledge and cordial acceptance of this evangelical truth, to which the Lord refers in the words: "follow me" (ver. 21), constituted the "one thing" (Mark) which he yet lacked. To this point the Lord designs to conduct the young man by unveiling to him the true state of his heart.

²¹ Jesus said unto him, If thou wouldest be perfect, go, sell that thou hast, and give to the poor, and thou shalt have treasure in heaven: and come, follow me.

A. If ... perfect = if thou desirest to acquire a holy character which is really "perfect and complete" (Col. 4:12), that is, in which no essential feature is lacking. For **perfect,** see 5:48. The Lord here begins with the First Commandment (Exod. 20:2, 3) as a test = Hast thou no other gods whom thou dost worship, such as Mammon? Examine thy heart. Absolute perfection is not attainable in this life (Phil. 3:12–14).—**B. Go ... hast** = Dost thou believe that thou canst by thy own wisdom and strength acquire the faith and love of the heart which essentially constitute obedience to God? The Lord issues a command suited to this special case, and not one intended in a literal sense for universal application to all the members of a Christian community. *Buyers* as well as *sellers* or vendors can be, and are required to be, genuine followers of Christ. Indeed, such a sacrifice of property, merely as an outward act, is of no value, according to Paul (1 Cor. 13:3), and is, accordingly, never made, in any passage of Scripture, an universal duty. The popish vows of poverty taken by monks and nuns, is merely a part of their mechanical religion, which, like that of the Samaritans, teaches them to worship "they know not what" (John 4:22). The command is, rather, designed to unveil to the young man the hidden "plague of his own heart" (1 Kings 8:38). To him God had not been known as the highest or sovereign good (ver. 17); it appears that his desires and care really referred rather to the preservation and increase of his wealth, than to his growth in divine knowledge and the love of God. But the disastrous influences of such a state of feeling are strikingly taught in Matt. 13:22; 1 Tim. 6:9; James 5:1, ff.). The sense then is: Pluck out thy right eye (5:29); deny thyself; cease to serve mammon (6:24), and transfer all thy love to God. Art thou prepared to give evidence of thy sincerity and earnestness of purpose by selling all, etc.?—**that thou hast** = *thy property*, as the original word implies here as well as in 25:14; Luke 8:3; 12:15, 33.—**C. Give to the poor.** When these words were pronounced, the Christian Church was not yet organized, and the importance and necessity of the various benevolent and Churchly activities in Missions, Bible distributions, Institutions of Christian learning etc., of modern times were not distinctly known and felt; consequently, the only form in which pecuniary resources could be consecrated to works of love, consisted in the aid granted to the indigent (comp. 26:11, A.; Acts 2:45; 4:34, 35; 6:1).—**D. Thou shalt ... heaven** = God in heaven will regard thy disinterested love to man with favor, and impart rich blessing to thy soul (see 5:12, B., and 6:20, A.).—**E. Come and follow me** = If thou wilt have eternal life (ver. 16), thou must withdraw all thy love from the world (Luke 12:33; 14:33), and "count all things but loss for the excellency of the knowledge" (Phil. 3:8) of *Me*, as thy Saviour. Come unto Me and take My yoke upon thee (11:28, 29), for I alone "am the way, and the truth, and the life, etc." (John 14:6). I will guide thee to heaven (comp. 4:19, A.).

²² But when the young man heard the saying, he went away sorrowful: for he was one that had great possessions.

The young man was sorrowful, because he now learned that his wealth, which was his idol (Col. 3:5), might ensnare him, and that his love of mammon must be crushed. The struggle in his soul, the lusting of the flesh and of the spirit against each other, the necessity of crucifying the former (Gal. 5:17, 24)—such were the causes of his grief. If he had consecrated himself to Christ, the acquisition of the "true riches" (Luke 16:11) would have soothed his grief, as in the case of Paul (Phil. 4:11–13). But he **went away** from Christ! That young man has long since passed to the eternal world; the sacred history does not record the result, whether he finally returned to Christ, or whether "the deceitfulness of riches choked the word" (13:22) and ultimately led to the eternal loss of his soul, as the deep emotion with which the Saviour speaks, leads us to fear.

²³ And Jesus said unto his disciples, Verily I say unto you, it is hard for a rich man to enter into the kingdom of heaven.

A. Then said Jesus = after looking around Him (Mark 10:23), and evidently much affected Himself by the departure of the young man at that solemn moment of his life. The subject was so important, the possible loss of the soul of that retreating young man was an event so awful, that the Lord imparted further instructions to His deeply moved heavens.—**B. Verily** (5:18, A.).—**C. Hard for a rich man.** The Lord means that the struggle between the corrupt love of mammon and the conscience will terminate in the victory of the flesh, thus preventing the acquisition of a heavenly mind and the salvation of the soul, unless the rich man earnestly and faithfully seek the aid of the divine grace (see Rom. 8:5–8; 1 Cor. 2:12–14). The disciples, as we learn from Mark 10:24, were astonished at His words, and erroneously supposed that he considered the possession of riches in itself as being a hindrance to salvation. The Lord therefore explained His meaning to be, that the difficulty arose not from a man's mere possession of riches, but from his inclination to put *his trust* in them (Mark. 10:24; comp. the word *trust* in 27:43; Hebr. 2:13), in place of making God his only source of enjoyment and peace. Such friendship of the world necessarily excludes from "the kingdom of heaven," that is, from all communion with God (James. 4:4). Comp. the two parables concerning rich men whose worldly-mindedness, not whose wealth, caused their ruin (Luke 12:15, ff. and 16:19, ff.). Indeed, the poor rather than the rich seem to have originally embraced the religion of Christ (James 2:5). Still, we find among the earliest Christian converts several wealthy persons, such as Zaccheus (Luke 19:2), and the "rich man," Joseph of Arimathea (Matt. 27:57).

24 And again I say unto you, It is easier for a camel to go through a needle's eye, than for a rich man to enter the kingdom of God.

A. And again (see 18:19, A.).—**B. It is easier, etc.** It is obvious that, as in the analogous passage (Jerem. 13:23, the terms **camel** (for which see 3:4, A. and 23:24, B.) and **needle's eye,** indicate not simply a high degree of difficulty, but literally an absolute impossibility. Hence no interpretation which, by a slight change of the original Greek word (*kamilon* for *kamelon*), would furnish the translation *rope, cable* in place of *camel,* or which refers to a small door or wicket placed in the large gate of a city wall, can really evade that impossibility. The proverbial language of the Orientals here employed, can indicate nothing else than an actual impossibility; sometimes the figure of an elephant is employed in place of that of a camel. The latter is often an image of a disproportionably large object (as in 23:24). It has one or two humps on the back, and its limbs are very long. "There is nothing graceful or sprightly in any camel, old or young; all is misshapen, ungainly and awkward. The camel is a silly, timid, gregarious, heavy, sullen animal. It eats and drinks little, and its sure-footedness is another important quality of this 'ship of the desert,' having a broad, awkward foot adapted to the arid sands and gravelly soil."—Robinson: Bibl. Res. ii. 209. The sense here is, not that a rich man necessarily finds it impossible to live and die as a genuine disciple of Christ, if he retains his wealth. The history of many wealthy Christians who have been faithful stewards of the Lord, refuted such an interpretation. But the lesson taught, is the following: God has made the love of Himself the first and great duty of man (Matt. 22:37, 38, comp. with Deut. 6:5; 10:12); hence, any frame of mind or state of feeling that gives to mammon the honor which God claims, utterly unfits a man for the acceptable worship of God on earth, and for the enjoyment of His presence in heaven. According to the proverb of the camel, such a man cannot possibly approach God at any time in an acceptable manner (see 6:24).

25 And when the disciples heard *it,* they were astonished exceedingly, saying, Who then can be saved?

The disciples were already conscious of the corruption of the human heart and its opposition to God, but they had never before beheld the consequences of human depravity so clearly as in this solemn moment. They felt the weight of "the body of this death," and the weakness of the law (its inability to subdue the sinful affections and lusts of men (Rom. 7:24; 8:3), and they now perceived the following mournful truth: that, in view of the fact stated in Gen. 6:5 and 8:21, and the truth that "a man is not justified by the works of the law" (Gal. 2:16), as the Lord had just taught the young man, no man, whether rich or poor ("who then" = who at all) can be saved by his own personal efforts. The phrase: **astonished, exceedingly,** describes the consternation produced in the disciples by these new views, and the deep anxiety with which they gazed at one another (Mark 10:26), all uttering the language of despair: Who then can be saved?

²⁶ And Jesus looking upon *them* said to them, With men this is impossible; but with God all things are possible.

A. But. The Greek word is here equivalent to *And,* as in ver. 28, where it is so translated (see 5:1, A.).—**B. Looking upon them** = fixed His eyes upon them earnestly, with all that fulness of compassion displayed on other occasions (Matt. 9:36; Luke 19:41), and here expressed by the soothing appellation: "Children" = my beloved disciples (Mark 10:24). The Lord taught many a solemn lesson by a glance or a look (Luke 22:61).—**C. With men, etc.** "The Lord means: I do not speak of the rich only, but of *all* men, who are induced by the influence of Original Sin to trust (Mark 10:24) in worldly possessions rather than to love and to confide in God; none can save themselves. The grace of God alone can renew man's heart, and fit him for heaven."—Luther. Accordingly, the Lord pronounces that the conclusion which the distressed disciples had reached, is correct—it *is* impossible for man to change his own corrupt nature, for "who can bring a clean thing out of an unclean? not one" (Job 14:4). But—adds he with overflowing love—the infinitely wise, mighty and merciful God can accomplish this great work of man's salvation; it is wrought by "sending His own Son" (Rom. 8:3), renewing man's nature (Tit. 3:5), and making Christ unto man "wisdom, and righteousness, and sanctification, and redemption" (1 Cor. 1:30; Rom. 6:23). Man's salvation is solely a work of God's grace (Eph. 2:8; Acts 11:18).

²⁷ Then answered Peter and said unto him, So we have left all, and followed thee; what then shall we have?

The encouraging words which the Lord had just pronounced: With God, etc., did not yet calm the fears of the disciples who deeply felt their own unworthiness. Nevertheless, they had really done more by **forsaking all** (4:18–22; Luke 5:11), than the young man whose case had awakened their painful doubts respecting themselves. What was then their own relation to the kingdom of God? Could they *hope,* or must *they fear* and *despair?* Hence Peter's question follows. The original words, literally translated, are: What then shall be to (for) us? = What will then be our lot? The sense is: If we have shown greater love and devotion than this young man has done, can we hope that *we* shall be saved? The Lord's answer, which is full of encouragement, implies that Peter asked, not in a mercenary spirit, after the amount of the reward, but rather in much anxiety, greatly fearing that he and his fellow-disciples had not sufficiently manifested the sincerity of their attachment to the Lord.

^{28} And Jesus said unto them, Verily I say unto you, That ye which have followed me, in the regeneration when the Son of man shall sit on the throne of his glory, ye also shall sit upon twelve thrones, judging the twelve tribes of Israel.

A. Three points in this remarkably full and and comprehensive answer of the Lord, claim attention: first, He promises a beautiful reward in ver. 28, to His disciples, and gives them the comforting assurance that they are sincere and accepted followers, so that their prospects are far more cheering than those of the young man who had just departed. Secondly, in ver. 29, He extends His promise, which now adds "everlasting life," to all others, who, like the disciples, shall renounce the world, and follow Him. But, thirdly, He utters a solemn warning in ver. 30, illustrated by the parable which succeeds, and intended to suppress all human pride and vain-glory both in the disciples and in all other Christians: if God grants a reward to the faithful, that reward is reckoned of *grace* and not of *debt* (see Paul's explanation in Rom. 4:4, 16). **B. Verily ... followed me;** the comma which should be placed after the words: *followed me,* is inaccurately omitted in some editions of the English N. T., and, in that case, the sense of the passage becomes confused. The true order of the words is: Ye which (= who) have followed Me, shall sit, in the regeneration when the Son of Man shall sit in the throne of His glory, even ye (shall sit) upon twelve, etc. Their sacrifices in a pecuniary respect, had probably been somewhat limited, but still were not altogether trivial, as the facts in Mark 1:20; Luke 5:11, 29 seem to show. Certainly they had the *will* to leave all for Christ, and this holy disposition the Lord regards with favor.—**C. In the regeneration.** The Lord gives a double promise; the one in ver. 28 refers to this world ("in this time," Mark 10:30, as in 1 Tim. 4:8; comp. Deut. 4:40; 5:33; Ps. 37:4); the other, which is extended to" every one that, etc., (including the disciples), and refers to "everlasting life" ("in the world to come," Mark) is expressed in the next verse. Hence the term **regeneration,** as applied to the apostles, must describe a time or period which *precedes* the second or final coming of Christ to judgment, when the redeemed enter into life eternal, (25:46). The Greek word translated *regeneration,* and found only in one other passage of the N. T. (Tit. 3:5), strictly signifies a *second* or new *birth;* it is then applied to any important change or improvement of condition, in the sense of *renewal, renovation, or restoration of a former and happier state.* Thus in Tit. 3:5, (where the word refers to the actual beginning of spiritual life only, and not to an advanced degree of Christian holiness, which is rather its result), the grace imparted as a new germ or principle of spiritual life through Holy Baptism, is viewed as a regeneration = the establishment of a new and happier state. So, too, Josephus (Antiq. 11:3–9) calls the re-occupation of the Holy Land by the Jews after the Babylonian Captivity and their new liberty, a restoration or "regeneration" of the country, using the same Greek word, and applying it, as the Lord does in this verse, to a new and happier state of man *in this life*. Now the Lord describes that future age of the Church on earth as one of great blessedness, when "all shall know Him, from the least to the greatest" (Hebr. 8:11), according to the predictions of the prophets Jeremiah (31:34) and Isaiah (54:13). The world shall be given to the apostles as their field of labor, and "all the earth," in which the darkness and misery of heathenism still prevail, "shall worship God" (Ps. 66:4). Then shall all Gentiles hear the preaching of the Gospel, and men in every nation, as Peter declared (Acts 10:35), that fear God and work righteousness, shall be accepted with him. When this kingdom is given to the Son of man, and "the heathen have become His inheritance" (Ps. 2:8), "all people, nations and languages shall serve Him" (Dan. 7:13, 14). To that blessed period when the light of the Gospel shall shine in all the earth and no longer be confined within the narrow limits of Palestine and the neighboring regions, the Lord had already distinctly referred on a former occasion (see above, 8:11). The banner of the cross shall be displayed in lands that were once covered with gross darkness (Isai. 60:2; Luke 1:79); "the sun of righteousness shall arise with healing in his wings" (Mal. 4:2), and "the ends of the earth" (Isai. 45:22) shall hear the Gospel call to repentance and faith in Christ. This new impulse given to mankind by the Gospel, and the happy state which shall follow, is here described by the Lord as a *regeneration* of the world. When Jews and Gentiles shall be "made one" in Christ (Eph. 2:14), Paul emphatically terms that result "life from the dead" (Rom. 11:15). Other analogous terms, also descriptive of the happy state of the world, when the Messiah shall be known and owned in every land, occur in the N. T., such as "times of refreshing," "times of restitution" (*apokatastasis*) Acts 3:19, 21; the time of the Gospel dispensation is "the time of reformation" (Hebr. 9:10) predicted in Isai. 65:17; 66:22; Hag. 2:6; Hebr. 12:26.—**D. When the Son ... glory** = when Christ shall be acknowledged in every land as Lord and King (Matt. 22:44, B.; Phil. 2:10, 11).—**Throne of his glory** = His glorious throne, indicating power and honor, as in 1 Sam. 2:8, where the phrase also implies an authority generally acknowledged. The figurative expression **shall sit** (= seating himself) **on the throne,** indicates, as in Ps. 29:10, the general and *peaceful acknowledgment* of Christ's divine glory, which "we see not yet" (Hebr. 2:8), but which will appear when "all flesh shall see the salvation of God" (Luke 3:6). (The Saviour's sitting "upon the throne of His glory" in 25:31 refers to a later period; it is there expressly distinguished by the words: "when the Son of man shall *come*" from the period of time here meant, and refers to His second or visible coming to judgment. That different events of this class are described in similar terms, appears from 10:23, B).—**E. Ye also ... of Israel.** The circumstance that Judas, who had once been "numbered with" the apostles, as one of the Twelve (Acts 1:17), was afterwards "lost" (John 17:12), and the fact that the Ten tribes which had been carried to Assyria never returned (2 Kings 17:23), both show that the Lord here speaks figuratively only, and in general terms.

The number **twelve** expressed among the Jews the idea of completeness and totality (see 10:1, A.). The sense is, that the company of the disciples, to whom a special office had been given, should be divinely sustained in their honorable work, and exercise, long after their death, a controlling religious (but not political, 18:1, C.) influence on all Christian nations. All Christendom, that is, the spiritual Israel, the "Israel of God" (Gal. 6:16; Rom. 2:28, 29), viewed here as a whole, is designated by the term used to describe the totality of "Israel after the flesh" (1 Cor. 10:18). Thus Christians or believers are "the children of Abraham" (Gal. 3:7), and are probably "the twelve tribes" mentioned in James 1:1, = the "strangers scattered, etc.," in 1 Pet. 1:1.—The **thrones** (here an image of power and authority) refer to the high character, peculiar work and undisputed authority in the Church of the apostles, upon whose labors, as upon a foundation, the Church was built (Eph. 2:20; Rev. 21:14). No passage of Scripture teaches that the apostles will have authority over the redeemed in heaven, while, on the other hand, passages descriptive of their superior or ministerial authority in the Church on earth abound in the N. T., for instance, Rom. 1:5; 11:13; 1 Cor. 12:28; 2 Cor. 12:12. The same truth is involved in the word **judging**, which alludes to the peculiar office of the men of whom the book of Judges treats, who are also termed *saviours* in Nehem. 9:27, or *deliverers;* comp. Judges 3:9, margin. They exercised not only judicial, but also executive and even kingly powers (1 Sam. 8:5) as rulers who had no earthly superiors. See Luke 22:29, 30, where similar highly figurative language occurs, referring apparently to the fact that the principles of the Gospel which they preached would decide on the admission of others into heaven, or their rejection, in accordance with their faith and conduct; (see 26:29). The authority with which the apostles were invested, and which adhered exclusively to their official character on earth, and to their inspired writings which constitute the permanent rule of faith of the Christian Church, was derived from the appointment of Christ alone. These revelations of the efficacy and success of the future labors of the disciples, to which no limits in time are assigned (comp. 28:20), are made to them on this occasion for the purpose of comforting their hearts and assuring them of their Master's love. The general sense then is, that a part of their reward will consist in the privilege of being honored instruments of God, in promoting the divine glory and the happiness of man.

²⁹ And every one that hath left houses, or brothers, or sisters, or father, or mother, or children, or lands, for my name's sake, shall receive a hundredfold, and shall inherit eternal life.

A. The Lord had hitherto spoken of the reward "now in this time," Mark 10:30 (= world), which should be given to His faithful disciples, as far as it consisted in the success in this world of their personal labors. Their future reward "in the world to come" (Mark) = everlasting life, is now mentioned as one in which others shall share.—**B. Every one** = who truly consecrates himself to God shall be saved, without reference (according to the Lord's mode of calculating the value of the widow's two mites, Mark 12:43), to the visible or outward amount of his works, as a rich or poor, influential or obscure, learned or unlearned, old or young disciple (2 Tim. 4:8). "She hath done *what she could*" (Mark 14; 8.)—**C.** That hath ... **name's sake.** The Lord had on a former occasion (10:37, 38), illustrated the nature of self-denial viewed as the necessary result of Christian faith. Here He again refers to such witnesses of self-denial. He teaches by the phrase: **for my name's sake** (for which see 10:22, B.) that such renunciation of every tie formed by nature or affection is expected, when no choice remains between fidelity to him and his religious duty ("and the Gospel's sake," Mark 10:29) on the one hand, or the sacrifice of every earthly comfort and advantage, on the other. The sense of the whole passage, according to 1 Cor. 7:29–31, then is: No claim which others possess on our love can justify any act of unfaithfulness to Christ (see 10:37).—**D. Shall receive a hundredfold** = already in this present life, according to Mark 10:30; Luke 18:30; "with persecutions," is an addition found in Mark. The sense is explained by passage like 1 Cor. 3:22; 2 Cor. 6:10; 1 Tim. 6:6, and Matt. ch. 10, all of which refer to the abundant gifts of grace and to God's protecting care of His faithful people. "Much food is in the tillage of the poor," (Prov. 13:23). The followers of Christ are strengthened in their "light affliction" (2 Cor. 4:17), by their faith and their hope of future glory and peace.—**A hundredfold** (13:8, B.) = their eternal gain shall be far greater than their temporal loss (comp. 1 Chron. 21:3.)—**E. And shall inherit, etc.** = shall find eternal rest and joy in heaven (Rev. 21:4). For the force of the word life, see 7:13, 14, ann.

³⁰ But many shall be last *that are* first; and first that are last.

The experience of believers teaches that when they do not strictly watch over their hearts, the great value and abundance of their spiritual privileges and graces may, by a perversion of "that which is good" (Rom. 7:13) tempt them to "be exalted above measure" (2 Cor. 12:7). The Saviour desires to preserve His disciples, whose honorable position

He has just described, from indulging in pride and vainglory. Hence He pronounces these words now, repeats them immediately afterwards (20:16), and elsewhere recurs to them, (Luke 13:30). The general sense, which will be made more apparent by the examination of the parable (see 20:6, A.), which is immediately added, is:—Great differences in the advantages bestowed on men are found, such as priority in the time of the calling of an individual, the abundance of the gifts of divine grace, the choice of the Jewish nation as the people of God, and "children of the covenant" (Acts 3:25), the number of the years and the amount of the labors in the Christian Church which believers have been able to give to God's service, etc. These are all circumstances which, as they do not confer personal merit, seeing that all the wisdom and strength displayed, were imparted by God, cannot entitle to a special reward. The disciples are, it is true, the "first" when the Saviour called; yet others may arise in the Church, after their day, whose faith, love and humility, will be so deep, that even apostles cannot take rank before them. Accordingly, St. Paul makes no distinction between his own reward and that of "all them" that are true believers (2 Tim. 4:8). This verse and the following parable contain, therefore, very solemn warnings against spiritual pride.

5

Matthew 20

¹ For the kingdom of heaven is like unto a man that is a householder, which went out early in the morning to hire laborers into his vineyard.

A. For. This introductory word indicates that the parable which immediately succeeds, is very intimately connected with the conversation recorded at the close of the foregoing chapter, and should not have been separated from that conversation by those who divided the text into chapters and verses. The previous words of the Lord (see above, 19:30, ann.) had contained a solemn warning against that spiritual pride or religious self-complacency which may arise in Christians (comp. 2 Cor. 12:7), unless they strictly watch, and are specially sustained by divine grace in such a temptation. It is the main purpose of the parable to teach that no amount of labors in the service of God, nor any long period of time devoted to that service, nor any result produced by human instrumentality, can impart to any man a right and title to the gifts of God, before whom even the most faithful continue to be "unprofitable servants" (Luke 17:10); this principle applies alike to all men (Rom. 4:2–5). The parable refers first to Peter and the disciples ("ye which have, etc.," 19:28), teaching them that while their fidelity shall be rewarded, priority in the time of their call, and important results of their labors, do not *entitle* them to a higher reward than others may receive, who are called after the age of the apostles, but who exhibit equal faith and love. Paul was called after all the other apostles; yet he labored more abundantly than they all (1 Cor. 15:8–10). Then, secondly, the Lord refers to all His other followers, whom He had already mentioned ("and every one, etc.," 19:29), teaching them that while the Jews were indeed the people originally chosen by God (Deut. 4:31–38; 14:2; Acts 3:25, 26; Rom. 9:4), other nations should, at a later period, also receive a divine call, and constitute a peculiar people, to whom even greater privileges should be granted in the Christian Church than those which the mere descendants of Abraham had ever enjoyed (1 Pet. 1:11, 12; Hebr. 8:6). The circumstance that the original founders of such nations had once been pagan should not operate injuriously on later generations that accepted the divine call in a spirit of faith and obedience (comp. 1 Pet. 2:3–10). The foregoing words (19:30), when spoken in the connection in which they appear in Luke 13:30, clearly show that they describe God as judging men, not according to the relations of time or personal labor, but according to the nature of their faith in Christ.—**B. The kingdom of heaven** (see Excursus I., vol. I.). Here the term refers generally to the service of God, who is viewed as the sole and eternal Lawgiver and Ruler of all; it does not represent the Christian Church exclusively, nor the Christian dispensation as contra-distinguished from the old covenant, nor eternal blessedness, but, in a wide sense, comprehends all the past manifestations of God's desire to render men happy by attaching them to His special service.—C. **Is like unto** (see 13:24, B., and 18:23, B.).—D. **Householder** = owner of the estate, head of the family, as in 10:25; 13:27. This person, whose title implies that he has the right and power to administer his property and affairs according to his own will, is an image of the divine and uncontrolled Lord and Creator of all things, in so far as he illustrates the divine mode of conferring undeserved blessings. It is, however, to be observed, that comparisons made in a parable between God and any created object, can refer only to particular points of resemblance. Such a point here is the similarity in the amount of the portion allotted to different classes of persons. Minor circumstances are simply introduced, like the drapery of a picture for the purpose of completing the narrative, and do not necessarily represent spiritual things (compare the equal numbers of the wise and foolish virgins, Matt. 25:2; the wine and oil employed by the Good Samaritan, Luke 10:34). So here the householder is simply a human being, and the men whom he hires, are, in this respect, his equals, originally owing him neither allegiance nor labor, whereas, precisely the opposite is the case in the relations existing between the Head and the members of the kingdom of heaven. Such circumstances have as little a necessary connection with the main design of the parable as the spectator finds between a book or table or chair painted on the canvas and the portrait of a person who is presented to his views.—E. **To hire laborers.** God has assigned a work to each individual on earth—it is the promotion of the divine honor (Luke 17:7–10). This householder's **early** call to the laborers doubtless illustrates the divine commands which were issued as soon as human beings existed, and which direct them to "walk with God" (Gen. 5:22; 6:9; 17:1). He **hires** = engages to pay wages for temporary services, according to usage in earthly transactions. The spiritual meaning may be found in the words: "He first loved us" (1 John, 4:10, 19) = God seeks us out, with a view to bless us. No man *earns* a reward for serving God, to whom He already *owes* all that he is, and has, and can do (1 Cor. 4:7; James 1:17, and comp. John 15:16). Nevertheless, God will, in His bounty, abundantly reward the obedient and faithful (Gal. 6:9), which truth alone is here shadowed forth. **The laborers** represent men in general, who are all commanded to serve God.—F. **Vineyard.** Such enclosures, in which grape-vines were cultivated, were very numerous in Palestine in ancient times (see 21:33, C.). The vineyard, the vine, grapes, etc., are frequently employed in Scripture as images or figures of the mercies of God (Deut. 32:32; Ps. 80:8–15; Isai. 5:1–7; Jer. 12:10; comp. 21:28, 33, C.). Israel is called a vine in Jer. 2:21, and Christ applies the name to Himself in John 15:1. The vineyard, in this case, as an image of the kingdom of heaven, represents the service of God on earth during the whole extent of time, from the original call given to man to enter that service ("early in the morning") to the end of the world ("when even was come," v. 8). The vineyard or field of the apostles was *the world* (13:38), that is, the human race which was to be brought back to God. The vineyard of each individual is the work assigned to him by the Lord in reference to his own soul, the good of others, and the glory of God. The Lord purposely omits to specify the *kind* of work (digging, trimming the vines, etc.), inasmuch as the Christian's work, whether it be the preaching of the Gospel, or the giving of a cup of cold water to the thirsty (Matt. 10:42), will, in either case, find a reward when performed in faith; but in both cases it gives "nothing to glory of" (see 1 Cor. 9:16, 17).

² And when he had agreed with the labourers for a penny a day, he sent them into his vineyard.

A. When ... agreed. Fallen man is "condemned already," and under the divine wrath (John 3:18, 36). Nevertheless, God offered to us terms of pardon and salvation even "when we were enemies" (Rom. 5:8, 10). These terms are set forth in the Scriptures as consisting in repentance of our sins and faith in the crucified Redeemer (Acts 20:21; Hebr. 11:6; 2 Pet. 3:9). Inasmuch as he will introduce none into heaven who retain rebellious hearts, these terms must be humbly and voluntarily embraced by man (Ezek. 18:31; 33:11). In so far the course of God resembles that of the householder, that He makes His will known, and affords to men the means and opportunities to accede to them. The old covenant was made through Moses (Exod. 19:5; Deut. 5:2); the new, through Christ (John 1:17; Rom. 5:1; Hebr. 12:18–24). The latter is the *better* covenant (Hebr. 8:6–13; 2 Cor. 3:4–11.—**B. Penny a day** = *by the day*, or, *for that day*. No special meaning is to be attached to the precise sum (= 14 cents; see 17:24, B.). The penny cannot here be an image of eternal life, for certainly the gift of eternal life would never be followed by such murmuring as we hear in ver. 11. It may, possibly, represent those gifts which God's grace bestows in this life, such as the great privileges granted to Jews and Christians respectively. The penny or *denarius* was the usual amount paid at that time for one day's labor, and constituted the ordinary daily pay of the Roman soldier. It was of much greater value than 14 cents are in modern currency, that is, it could pay for a larger quantity of food, and may be assumed to be fully equal to the amount now paid for daily labor, since the discovery of gold and silver in America and elsewhere in modern times has diminished the value of those metals. The best authorities maintain that silver at the period when Christ appeared, was ten times as valuable as it is at present; the penny was therefore really equivalent to 40. Hence the "two pence" advanced by the good Samaritan (Luke 10:35) constituted a liberal provision. The **day** is here the portion of time devoted to manual labor, "from even unto even" (Levit. 23:32).

³ And he went out about the third hour, and saw others standing in the market place idle;

A. The different hours here mentioned cannot be satisfactorily explained as indicating specific eras in the history of revealed religion, such as the ages respectively of Adam, Noah, Abraham, Moses, etc., neither can they exclusively refer to the childhood, youth, etc., of the individual. They appear to indicate in general successive divine calls or communications of divine knowledge made "at sundry times and in divers manners" (Hebr. 1:1). These began historically with Adam, continued through the age of the patriarchs (Abraham, etc.), and were maintained, after that of Moses, through the whole later period of prophecy, during which full streams of religious knowledge continually flowed from heaven. The final revelation, which completes the measure of divine truth that was to be imparted, consists in the Christian religion (Hebr. 1:2). Its lessons, calls and blessings, proceed from Palestine, extended to Europe, have already reached many nations of the earth, and will continue to expand until "all the earth shall be full of the knowledge of the Lord" (Isai. 11:9). At the same time, the calls of God to the individual are similarly made in the early life of the latter, and are afterwards continually repeated; impenitence, when obstinately maintained, consequently, results in an ever accumulating weight of guilt.—**B. Third hour.** The natural day, or the period intervening between sunrise and sunset, was divided by the Jews, according to a practice borrowed from the Chaldeans, into twelve hours (John 11:9); the length of the latter varied at different seasons, as the longest day in Palestine consists, according to our mode of reckoning time, of 14 hours and 12 minutes, the shortest of 9 hours and 48 minutes; an hour in June corresponded in length to one in December, as 14 is related to 10. (*K. v. Raumer: Palestina*, p. 89). It is usually assumed that the first Jewish hour began, upon an average, at our 6 o'clock, and that the third hour accordingly closed at our 9 o'clock; but, strictly speaking, it extended from our 8 o'clock to 9 o'clock only at the vernal and autumnal equinoxes, and came earlier or later at other seasons. During this hour Peter pronouncod the words recorded in Acts 2:15. For the *watches of the night* (see 14:25, A.), and for the Roman division of the civil day (see 27:45, A.).—**C. Market place.** As large numbers of persons assembled in the "public place" (for which see 11:16, 17, B.), not merely for business purposes, but also for pastime, conversation, etc. (comp. Acts 17:17), unemployed laborers found employers there more readily than elsewhere.

⁴ And to them he said, Go ye also into the vineyard; and whatsoever is right I will give you. And they went their way.

A. Go ... vineyard. God permits no man to be idle; in His service all can find employment; the debts which we owe to our own souls, and to God, like those which we owe to our neighbor (Rom. 13:8), are never fully paid.—**B. Whatsoever is right** = *righteous, just,* as the word is usually translated. Strictly speaking, their wages would amount to three-fourths of the sum promised to the first laborers. But, on the one hand, a mercenary spirit is inconsistent with that genuine love to God, which teaches man to submit all his affairs to divine wisdom and goodness, and, on the other the "free gift" of justification (Rom. 5:15), is bestowed by a "God who is rich in mercy" (Eph. 2:4), and who "giveth to all men liberally" (James 1:5).

⁵ Again he went out about the sixth and the ninth hour, and did likewise.

These hours correspond in general terms to our midday or 12 o'clock, and 3 o'clock, P. M.; see ver. 3, B.

⁶ And about the eleventh hour he went out, and found others standing and he saith unto them, Why stand ye here all the day idle?

A. Eleventh hour = about the time when the last one of the twelve parts of the day commenced. The Parables, like many of the brief sayings of Christ, are capable of being variously applied, and have been aptly compared to polished diamonds which sparkle in every direction Still, it is important to distinguish between the true, original sense of a scriptural passage, and any special or practical application which may be made of it in the experience of an individual. The aged or dying sinner who sincerely repents and believes, may be said to have found God at the eleventh hour; nevertheless, this parable originally and directly refers to a different circumstance, as the words in 19:27–30 show. It is not intended to set forth the value of a death-bed repentance; such an event, when it really does occur, will gratify experienced and aged Christians, and certainly not extort from them the murmurs which proceed in (ver. 11) from the laborers who were first hired. The Saviour rather refers to the following circumstance: The Jewish nation was called at an early period, while all Gentiles were suffered for centuries "to walk in their own ways" (Acts 14:16). The Jews ultimately adopted the belief that they alone, as Abraham's descendants, would share in the blessings of the Messiah's kingdom, while the heathen should remain outcasts. Even the early Christians, who were converted from Judaism, with great difficulty learned to understand that Gentiles might become Christians, and be admitted to every privilege conferred an Abraham's descendants, without having previously observed the laws of Moses (Acts 11:1–4). Thus the Jews "were filled with wrath," when the Lord alluded to the divine mercy granted to Gentiles (Luke 4:25–28), and Paul describes the truth as a mystery to the Jews for many ages "that the Gentiles should be fellow-heirs, etc." (Eph. 4:4–6). This jealousy is described under the figure of the murmurs mentioned in ver. 11, and is again presented in the conduct and language of the Prodigal's elder brother (Luke 15:25–30). Hence, the calling of the Gentiles at a late period of the world, as described in Rom. ch. 11, is doubtless indicated by the act of hiring the laborers at the eleventh hour, as the primary spiritual sense (comp. the ann. to 19:30).—**B. Idle** = not actively engaged in the service of the true God. The Scriptures represent idleness or sloth in God's service as wicked and ruinous (Matt. 25:26; Prov.

24:30–34). Man is the servant either of God, or of sin and death (Rom. 6:16). The *idleness* of the Gentile nations, with all its horrible features and deadly influence, is described in Rom. ch. 1.

⁷ They say unto him, Because no man hath hired us, He saith unto them, Go ye also into the vineyard.

A. No ... hired us. The language is such as laborers in similar circumstances would employ, simply shadowing forth the historical fact mentioned in Deut. 4:32–34, that the Gentile world had never yet received such direct calls as those which had reached the Jewish nation. The Gentiles possessed no knowledge of Christ and His atoning work; neither had they any knowledge of the divine purpose of receiving them into the Messiah's Church (Rom. 16:25, 26; Col. 1:27). But, on the other hand, they had lost the knowledge of the true God by their own fault: the unutterable wretchedness which resulted (Eph. 2:11, 12), continued until the coming of Christ (Acts 14:16; 17:30; Rom. 1:28; 11:8–32). If the Gentiles who had refrained from serving God, in consequence of ignorance, voluntarily maintained by them are declared by divine authority to be "without excuse" (Rom. 1:20), can any excuse be found for the impenitence or religious sloth of a single individual who dwells in a land in which the light of the Gospel shines?

⁸ And when even was come, the Lord of the vineyard saith unto his steward, Call the labourers, and pay them their hire, beginning from the last unto the first.

A. When even was come = the appointed time for paying wages, according to Deut. 24:15. The close of the season of labor, is, according to some interpreters, an image of the end of the world, and of the judgment which succeeds. According to another, and far more consistent, interpretation, founded on the circumstances that the murmurs mentioned in ver. 11, occurred among the Jews chiefly in the age of Christ (ver. 6, A.), the **even** (= evening) is here introduced as a natural feature in the narrative, and simply indicates the time when the mystery of the calling of the Gentiles was fully revealed, that is, after the ascension of Christ, at the beginning of the apostolic age, according to Eph. 3:4–6.—**B. Steward.** In two other passages, (Luke 8:3; Gal. 4:2), stewards (*epitropoi*) are mentioned; in the latter, the Greek word is equivalent to *guardians;* in the former case, Herod's steward was an officer who superintended the revenues of the king. The other *stewards* mentioned in the English N. T. bear a different Greek name (*oikonomoi*) equivalent to *house-manager, overseer.* Persons of the former class, whose well-known ability and fidelity secured such an appointment, even when they were not simply confidential *servants* (see 24:45, B.), nevertheless held a rank which was far inferior to that of their employers. It is hence not probable that the steward in this verse is an image of Christ, the "son over his own house" (Hebr. 3:6). This steward does not here pronounce a judgment on the conduct of the individuals, and exercises no authority of his own, but is simply introduced for the purpose of completing the narrative, like the servants in 13:27, and the host in Luke 10:35. On the other hand, Christ will hereafter judge the living and the dead (Matt. 16:27; 25:31, ff; John 5:22–27; Acts 10:42; 17:31; 2 Cor. 5:10), and He will execute judgment according to His own divine authority and wisdom.—**C. Beginning, etc.** Our Lord adopts this order in the parable, for the purpose of giving more prominence in the latter part of it to the fact that the first laborers received no more than the last.

⁹ And when they came that *were hired* about the eleventh hour, they received every man a penny.

These laborers receive far more than they had earned; this circumstance illustrates the scriptural doctrine that no man can ever earn or deserve the grace of God (Gen. 32:10; Luke 17:10; Rom. 3:24). "Here we learn from the circumstance that the same amount is paid for unequal periods of labor, that God will not deal with us according to our merits or works, but will grant to every believer, whether he have wrought much or little, *the same penny,* that is, His Son, Jesus Christ, and through Him forgiveness, the gifts of the Holy Spirit, and eternal life. The penny is promised by divine grace, in order that all may labor with diligence, fidelity and hope; but it is not intended to be an equivalent for work that is done—it exceeds the merits of all."—Luther. If God, in His infinite love, gives to the most unworthy of true believers, first, Jesus Christ on earth, and then, heaven hereafter ("all things are yours," 1 Cor. 3:21, 22; Rom. 8:32), what more can He give to others?

¹⁰ And when the first came, they supposed that they would receive more; and they likewise received every man a penny.

A. The first ... more. They inferred that if those who had wrought only one hour, received full pay, they would themselves receive more than the stipulated amount. Their error consisted in regarding not only the penny but also any additional payment as wages earned by them, not as a gift proceeding from the bounty of the householder. The Lord here presents a view of the mercenary and self-righteous spirit of the Jews (comp. 18:11, 12). It was an ostentatious (Matt. 23:5), and hypocritical spirit (Matt. 23:25–27), and hence could not receive the divine approbation. The lesson which the Lord appears to teach is this:—If ye Jews expect to earn or deserve divine blessings, be assured that all your expectations, founded on your outward righteousness, will be disappointed; you will fail to obtain grace; divine bounty will be extended to the meek and contrite alone. Your works of the law, wrought in a mercenary spirit, attract no divine favor.—**B. They likewise, etc.** "There are various ranks in the world, kings and peasants, rich and poor. But in the kingdom of God, the prince and the beggar, the bond and the free, meet on equal terms, and are alike. They have the same Gospel and Sacraments, the same Saviour and God. Do thy duty on earth with a cheerful heart, in whatever condition thou mayest be. Though thou shouldst not be a prince, yet, if thou art a Christian, what more canst thou desire?"—Luther, (comp. 1 Pet. 2:9; Rev. 1:6; 5:10).

^{11, 12} And when they received it, they murmured against the householder, Saying, These last have spent *but* one hour, and thou hast made them equal unto us, which have borne the burden of the day and the scorching heat.

A. Murmured = expressed their discontent in a low sullen voice.—**B. The householder.** The same Greek term occurs again in 10:25; 21:33; 24:43.—**C. Burden ... heat.** The labor performed in the hot season during the day (Gen. 31:40), is compared by them to a heavy burden. These men represent the Jews, who believed that the subjection of their nation for many centuries to the heavy yoke of the law (Acts 15:10), gave them a better title to the blessings of the Messiah's kingdom than the Gentiles could ever acquire.

¹³ But he answered and said to one of them, Friend, I do thee no wrong: didst not thou agree with me for a penny?

A. One of them = represented as expressing his feelings more loudly and boldly than the others.—**B. Friend.** The same mode of address (in Greek: *hetairos*) occurs in 22:12; 26:50, and merely designates one with whom an association of any kind (here that of employer and the person employed) had existed for a longer or shorter time. It is sometimes equivalent to *comrade,* as in 11:16, B. Another Greek word (*philos*), also translated *friend* (e. g. Luke 7:6; 11:6; 14:10), usually gives more prominence to the personal attachment of the parties. The word in the text is not used ironically, but simply implies that the householder is calm, courteous, and firm in dispensing his gifts.—**C. No wrong.** As the first laborers originally contracted for full wages, and did not view the transaction as a special favor, but as one that gave the householder an equivalent for his money, so the self-righteous Jews regarded the religious services which they and their fathers had rendered (worship, sacrifices, prayers, alms, fasting), as meritorious. They forgot that they were not independent of God, like laborers who may meet an employer as his fellow-citizens and equals, but that they were, on the contrary, most solemnly bound, as God's creatures, to live for His honor and service alone. Hence the Saviour implies in this verse: If ye Jews convert the covenant of your fathers with God into a covenant of works, then abide by the terms which you have yourselves preferred (Rom. 10:5; Exod. 19:5, 6; Lev. 18:5). Now, as ye do not keep that covenant by fulfilling the law, but have all sinned (Rom. 3:9, 10), do not complain when you find that God, who has "concluded all in unbelief" (Rom. 11:32), extends His mercy to Gentiles who *do* repent and believe (Gal. 3:22). Men are not saved by their works (Eph. 2:8), otherwise "grace is no more grace"

(Rom. 11:5). If ye desire salvation, seek it as a *gift* of God (Rom. 6:23), and do not think that it can ever be claimed as a *right*.—**D. Didst not, etc.** = has God ever failed to keep His promise, when ye obeyed Him?

¹⁴ Take up that which is thine, and go thy way: It is my will to give unto this last, even as unto thee.

A. Take ... thine = if ye and your fathers have worshipped God according to the ceremonial law, while the Gentiles have worshipped idols, did you not also enjoy far greater privileges and blessings than those Gentiles found? (Rom. 3:1, ff.; 9:4, 5; Eph. 2:11, 12).—**B. Go thy way.** The language implies that God is not governed by human passions, but is unalterably and eternally just. The sentence which His infinite wisdom has once pronounced, will never be revoked.—**C. I will give, etc.** "I have known Christians who had received the Lord Jesus in faith only a few months or years before their death; nevertheless, they died in faith, and they are now in heaven. I have myself already labored in the service of God more than twenty years; yet I cannot hope to receive more than they who labored only one hour in the vineyard."—Luther.—**This last** = man, who represents the group that entered at the eleventh hour.

¹⁵ Is it not lawful for me to do what I will with mine own? or is thine eye evil, because I am good?

A. Is it ... own? = if God, in His infinite mercy, is pleased to admit believing Gentiles to all the privileges and blessings of the Messiah's kingdom on earth, as well as believing Jews, has He not the authority to do so? (Rom. 9:24–33).—**With mine own** = in my affairs, which depend on my will alone.—**B. Is thine eye, etc.** In Mark 7:22; Deut. 15:9; Prov. 23:6; 28:22, as well as here, the phrase: "an evil eye" (which in Matt. 6:23

has the general sense of *bad, false, wicked*) specially indicates the feeling of envy, as betrayed in the eye or countenance of one who sees with vexation the happiness of another. The first *evil eye* was that of Cain (Gen. 4:5). "The blessed angels might murmur and be envious on seeing that their Lord 'took not on Him the nature of angels' (Hebr. 2:16), but the nature of men, who were even God's enemies (Rom. 5:10). But, on the contrary, they praise God who is good to men, and say: 'Glory to God, etc.' (Luke 2:14)."—Luther.

16 So the last shall be first, and the first last.

A. So the ... last. The former verse contained words spoken by the householder; here, the Lord speaks in His own person. The repetition of these words (which occur in 19:30, where see the ann.) with a slight variation that does not affect the sense, shows that the whole parable is intended to illustrate them. The last laborers called were *first* in the sense that they received a comparatively larger amount of money for their hour than the others. The sense, as explained above, coincides with that of the words in Rom. 11:25, in which Paul describes the Gentiles, who are called long after the Jews, as "coming in," or accepting the Gospel before them. "*The first shall be the last*—such words teach thee to cast off all arrogance and self-righteousness, even if thou thinkest that thou hast equalled an Abraham, David, Peter or Paul; for others may reach a higher degree of humility and faith than thou hast. *The last shall be the first*—such words teach thee to hope and not despair, even if thou believest that thou hast sinned like Pilate, Herod, Sodom and Gomorrah."—Luther. [For exposition of "Many be called," etc., see 22:14].

17 And as Jesus was going up to Jerusalem, he took the twelve disciples apart, and in the way he said unto them,

A. Going up = ascending to the higher region of country in which the city was situated (comp. Luke 2:4; Acts 18:22; 2 Sam. 19:34; Ps. 122:1, 4). This journey to Jerusalem (19:1) for the purpose of keeping the feast, was performed by every Jew, according to Exod. 23:14; Deut. 16:16. The disciples, who dreaded the power and hatred of the Lord's enemies in that city, reluctantly followed (Mark 10:32; John 11:7, 8, 16). His sufferings and death were incurred voluntarily (comp. Isai. 50:6 and John 10:18).—**B. Took, etc.** Possibly the locality is the one mentioned in John 11:54. The city there named, Ephraim, was not far distant from Bethel (2 Chron. 13:19), and not far from Jericho whither the Lord afterwards came (ver. 29). The words that He spoke were intended for the disciples alone.

¹⁸ Behold we go up to Jerusalem; and the Son of man shall be delivered unto the chief priests and scribes: and they shall condemn him to death.

A. Behold, etc. (See *ann.* to 16:21). Several particulars not introduced in that passage, nor in 17:22, 23, are here added.—**B. Son of man** (see 8:20, B.), **delivered** 17:22.—**C. Chief priests—scribes** = the leaders of the Jews;—**shall** (will) **condemn—death** (26:66).

¹⁹ And shall deliver him unto the Gentiles to mock, and to scourge, and to crucify; and the third day he shall be raised up.

Gentiles = heathens (4:15, 16, A.). Here the Roman governor, Pilate, and his soldiers are specially indicated (Acts 4:27),—**mock** (see 2:16, A.). The allusion is to scenes like those described in 27:29,—**scourge** (27:26; see 10:17, C.),—**crucify** (see 27:22, B.). The Lord had previously spoken of the cross (10:38; 16:24); but on this occasion he first reveals that such an awful death as that of crucifixion would be His portion,—**the third day, etc.** (16:21, F.).

[20] Then came to him the mother of the sons of Zebedee with her sons, worshipping *him,* and asking a certain thing of him.

A. Then. As the Lord and His disciples had been previously alone (ver. 17), this word indicates that the present occurrence took place after he had joined a company of Jews who were also proceeding to Jerusalem, in order to keep the feast.—**B. The mother, etc.** Zebedee, who is mentioned in 4:21, may have died soon after the circumstances there described, and that event have been indicated by terming his widow "the mother of, etc." The **sons** are the two disciples James and John (see 10:2, and comp. Mark 10:35). The name of their mother, the wife of Zebedee, was Salome, as a comparison of Matthew 27:56 with Mark 15:40; 16:1, shows. She appears to have been the sister of the Virgin Mary (see 13:55, C.); and she was one of the faithful women who "followed the Lord and ministered unto Him" (Mark 15:40, 41). Her two sons and Peter had already been distinguished by their Master above the other disciples (see 17:1, B.), and one of them, John, was specially known as "the beloved disciple" (John 13:23) indicating a deep love to Christ on his own part, which urged him to seek perpetual communion with his Master. He and his brother, like others, at this period still erroneously believed "that the kingdom of God should immediately appear" (Luke 19:11) = that a temporal kingdom of the Messiah should be established, and they feared any interruption of their continual personal intercourse with the Lord. At the same time, while they reveal genuine confidence in Christ and in the success of His cause, a carnal ambition may have been aroused in their souls. They thought of Jonathan and Abner, each of whom was seated in a place of honor, at the right and left hand of Saul, according to ancient traditions (*Josephus,* Antiq. 6, 11, 9); in such cases no pre-eminence in honor belonged to the right hand (Prov. 3:16; see 22:44, B.; 25:33 and 26:64, C.). The two sons, anxious to acquire a similar distinction in the new temporal kingdom, unite with their mother (comp. v. 24 and Mark 10:35) who had with others now joined them (and to whom they had probably communicated the promise in 19:28) in addressing the present petition to the Lord (see 8:5, C.). It differs widely from the modest terms in which Solomon was addressed by his mother (1 Kings 2:20),—**worshipping** (see 2:2, D.). "The Bible records instances of the faith of believers and saints, as an example for us; it also describes their weaknesses and sins as a warning. If even *they* betray such infirmities, how earnestly should we pray to God that we, whose faith is still weaker, may be graciously strengthened and preserved from being led into temptation."—Luther.

21 And he said unto her, What wouldest thou? She saith unto him, Command that these my two sons may sit, one on thy right hand, and one on thy left hand, in thy kingdom.

A. What wouldest thou? = that I should give Thee. The Lord deals very gently with Salome and her sons; for, while they betrayed much ignorance, they exhibited neither malice nor unbelief, but sincere faith and confidence in His power.—**B. Grant etc.,** see above, v. 20, **B.—sit on Thy ... left;** (see ver. 20, B. and ch. 22:44, B.).

22 But Jesus answered and said, ye know not what ye ask. Are ye able to drink the cup that I am about to drink? They say unto him, We are able.

A. Ye know not, etc. = ye little know that ye cannot be glorified and reign with Me, without having first suffered and died with Me (Rom. 8:17; 2 Tim. 2:11, 12). Ye know not (= little think) that those who shall first occupy positions on My right and left hand, will be two thieves (27:38), nailed to two crosses, and suffering a death of agony and infamy! Even now we know not what we should pray for *as we ought,* unless the Spirit helpeth our infirmities (Rom. 8:26).—**B. Cup.** The scriptural image of a full cup admits of a twofold application, representing a very high degree either of joy and prosperity (Ps. 16:5; 23:5), or of merited or unmerited pain and sorrow (Ps. 11:6; Isai. 51:17, 22; Jer. 49:12). It is here introduced by the Lord in the latter sense, as an image of the bitterness of grief which He foreknew that He would endure in Gethsemane (comp. Matt. 26:39). "Stier rightly observes that this answer of our Lord contains in it the kernel of the doctrines of the two Sacraments."—Alford. [Stier's words are: "What our Lord says contains the kernel and germ of all the apostolic doctrine, as expressed, for example, in Rom. 6, and gives the inmost signification of the two sacraments of His Church by which it is incorporated and united with Him (1 Cor. 12:13). In our case, indeed, it is in inverted order. Christ alone began by His absolutely drinking of the cup, before that cup became baptism to Him. We must first enter with the fellowship of His baptism, before we can have the right to drink of His cup. Let all false dogmatical teaching which satisfies itself with the formal imputation of the sufferings of Christ without a real entering into fellowship with Him, ask how it can dispose of the Redeemer's former saying about *His* cross being intended for all."]

"If the adoption of the Christian faith secured wealth and

honor for every Christian, all men would eagerly proclaim themselves the disciples of Christ, and yet retain those evil hearts which unfit them for heaven. But now the trials of our faith purify the soul (1 Peter 1:7; 4:12, 13; 2 Cor. 4:7). They do not imply wrath on the part of God, but parental love (Hebr. 12:6). Christ, our example, even in His deepest afflictions (Hebr. 5:7–9), remained God's beloved Son."—Luther.—**C. We are able.** John and James now came forward themselves, after Salome (ver. 20, B.), had commenced the conversation, while an undue self-reliance, perhaps amounting to rashness and vain-glory, appears in their answer (as also in the case mentioned in 26:35), they must have correctly understood the Saviour's words, to a certain extent at least, as He had repeatedly (ver. 18; 16:21), referred to His approaching sufferings and death. This sincerity and firm resolution, inspired by faith, may be seen in their subsequent conduct, which, after the first alarm (Matt. 26:56), exhibited neither any shrinking nor any feebleness of purpose (comp. John 18:15; 19:26; Rev. 1:9, for John; Acts 12:1, 2 for James; and Acts 5:40 for both).

²³ He saith unto them, My cup indeed ye shall drink: but to sit on my right hand, and on *my* left hand, is not mine to give, but *it is for them* for whom it hath been prepared of my Father.

A. Ye shall ... with—"ye are they which have continued with me in My temptations; and I appoint unto you a kingdom" (Luke 22:28, 29). The sense is: **I** know full well that ye will be faithful, and I do promise you an entrance, *after much tribulation* and persecution (Acts 14:22; 2 Tim. 3:12), into My kingdom (comp. 1 Peter 1:6, 7; 5:10).—**B. But to sit, etc.** The Lord has not revealed the precise condition in heaven of any individual. Hence, the same John, when more fully enlightened, said: "It doth not yet appear what we shall be" (1 John 3:2). Fallen man could not now endure a vision of that heavenly glory which believers shall enjoy (Col. 3:3, 4; Rom. 8:24, 25). Hence the terms: **To sit, etc.,** are to be figuratively understood (comp. a somewhat similar figure in 19:28, E. and 8:11). As the Lord had on several previous occasions (16:27; John 5:22, 27), declared that He was invested with all power and authority as the Judge of men, He cannot here refer, in the words: "it is not mine to give," to any subordination or inferiority of rank or person (comp. John 5:23), but rather means: to give *indiscriminately*, as the connection shows. The words in Italics in the English Test.: "it is for," are unnecessarily inserted by the translators. The translation here should be: "is not mine to give save to them for whom, etc.," or, "Is mine to give to none except to, etc." The object ("it") which "hath been prepared," is not so much the kingdom mentioned in ver. 21 and below in 25:34, as rather the *appointment* to such positions on His right and left. The Greek word for **prepared,** as in Mark 1:3; 14:16; Luke 1:17; 2 Tim. 2:21, sometimes signifies: *to make ready* or *fit for, to adapt to*. Now "the high and holy place" in which God dwells (Isai. 57:15), and into which "there shall in no wise enter anything that defileth" (Rev. 21:27) is prepared or suited for those alone who are holy (Hebr. 12:14), as indeed all the gracious gifts of God are prepared for and suited to none but such as "love Him" (1 Cor. 2:9). The sense of the whole, then, is:—The decision on My part to give the privilege of occupying a near position to Me in heaven, depends not on a petition proceeding from ignorance or ambition, and therefore made "amiss" (James

4:3), but on the faith, the holiness and love (Eph. 1:4) of those who ask. To such alone the kingdom is adapted; "the Father seeketh such to worship Him." (John 4:23). First "be thou faithful unto death and (then) I will give thee a crown of life" (Rev. 2:10).

²⁴ And when the ten heard *it,* they were moved with indignation, concerning the two brethren.

The ten other disciples were *much displeased* (as the same Greek word is rendered in the authorized version (Mark 10:14, 41), that two of their number desired stations of higher rank than their own. Even in the holy presence of the Saviour, as Matthew here humbly confesses, improper feelings (ambition, jealousy) are still betrayed by the disciples; their subsequent conduct was eminently disinterested and holy. What is man without the renewing and sanctifying grace of God?

²⁵ But Jesus called them unto him, and said, Ye know that the rulers of the Gentiles lord it over them, and their great ones exercise authority over them.

A. But Jesus ... said = desirous to suppress at once such exhibitions of feeling, by the power of the truth.—**B. Rulers**—who possess supreme authority.—**C. Their great ones** = governors appointed by royal authority, high officers of state, etc. In the absence of all constitutional law, such ancient rulers were often at liberty to indulge their own caprices and passions without restraint. The sense of the whole is: Do ye believe that My kingdom will exhibit the imperfect forms of government which prevail among men, or that the pride, ambition, selfishness and wantonness of power which blind and corrupt heathen rulers often manifest, shall be tolerated in it?—**Gentiles** = *nations,* in the sense of *nations ignorant of the* true God (see 4:15, 16).

²⁶ Not so shall it be among you; but whosoever would become great among you shall be your minister.

A. Not … you = do ye not yet understand that My kingdom is one of love and peace (Rom. 14:17). And will ye not receive the lesson that ye are not designed to be earthly rulers, but only instruments in establishing a spiritual kingdom? (1 Cor. 3:5–7; 2 Cor. 1:24; 1 Peter 5:3).—**B. But whosoever, etc.** A **minister,** according to the original Greek word, is a personal attendant, or one who, as in Rom. 15:25, renders services to another (comp. 4:11, B. and 25:44). It is translated *servant* in 22:13 and 23:11. The Lord here repeats the lesson which is found above in 18:4, B. The subsequent allusion (ver. 28), to His own redeeming work, which love prompted Him to perform, furnishes the additional admonition: True greatness in My kingdom consists in a resemblance to me (18:5); but I manifest a love which in its exercise submits willingly to shame and suffering. Ye are most of all remote from a high position in My kingdom, when ye betray a want of humility and love (11:29).

²⁷ And whosoever would be first among you shall be your servant:

Servant. The original Greek word, involving generally the idea of servitude or the very lowest position [bondsman] is here more emphatic than that of *minister,* and is applied to Christ in Phil. 2:7. It was sometimes applied to bondmen and slaves (1 Cor. 7:21; 12:13; Gal. 3:28; Philem. ver. 16. It is the name which Paul (Rom. 1:1), Peter (2 Peter 1:1), James (1:1), Jude (*ver.* 1) and John (Rev. (1:1), familiarly apply to themselves in their relation to Christ their Lord and Master: in a similar sense it belongs to all Christians. The spirit of the whole is set forth in the words of Paul in Phil. 2:3.—**Chief,** as in Acts 28:7, = *first,* as the word is usually translated.

²⁸ Even as the Son of man came not to be ministered unto, but to minister, and to give his life a ransom for many.

A. Son of man (8:20, B.).—**B. Came ... unto**—not for His own advantage, not for the purpose of indulging a selfish ambition.—**C. But to minister** = to *save* (see above, ver. 26, B.). The Lord alludes to the deep humiliation and the vicarious death to which love and pity prompted Him to subject Himself (John 10:18).—**D. To give his life** = to die. For the word life (*psyche*) see 10:39, A. and B., and comp. Luke 22:19; Gal. 1:4; 2:20.—**E. A ransom.** The Greek word is the term originally applied to a sum of money paid for the release of any prisoner or captive from bondage, and is equivalent to: *money that sets loose;* it is here figuratively applied to the "price" of our redemption (1 Cor. 6:20; 7:23; comp. Exod. 30:12; in Num. 35:31, 32), the corresponding Hebrew term is rendered *satisfaction*. After the fall of man, he became the servant of sin, or was in bondage, subject to sin and death (Rom. 3:9; 6:12–23; 7:14; Hebr. 2:15). The "price of redemption" (Lev. 25:51) consisted of "the precious blood of Christ" (1 Peter 1:18, 19; 2:21). Inasmuch as Christ died *for us,* that is, in our place, or as our substitute, when He atoned on the cross (Rom. 5:11), the Scriptures uniformly teach that His sufferings and death were *vicarious* (= endured in the place of others): see Isai. ch. 53; John 1:29; 10:11; Rom. ch. 5; ch. 8:32; 1 Cor. 15:3; 2 Cor. 5:14, 15; Eph. 1:7; 5:2; 1 Tim. 2:6; Tit. 2:14; Hebr. 9:12; 1 Peter 2:24; 3:18.—**F. For many** = for all men, according to 1 Tim. 2:3, 4. When the *one* Saviour (Rom. 5:19) is contrasted with those for whom He died, they are in some passages called the *many,* as in 26:28; Hebr. 9:28. In other passages these *many* individuals are declared to be *all* men (2 Cor. 5:14; 1 Tim. 2:6; Hebr. 2:9; 1 John 2:2). Thus, too, those who in contradistinction from *one* = Adam, are called *many* in Rom. 5:15, are immediately afterwards (ver. 18) declared to be "all men." Hence, in the succeeding verse, the 19th, the atonement of Christ is declared to be sufficient for as *many* as were made sinners by Adam's disobedience = *all* men. At the same time, the solemn truth is revealed that many for whom Christ died will perish, because they continue to be workers of iniquity (Luke 13:24–30; 1 Cor. 8:11). "There are people who do not, it is true, expect to gain salvation by their own works, and who do not deny Christ; but they are so much occupied with the world, that in heart and life they forget the Saviour. Thus they also fail to seek and find pardon and salvation." Luther. The affecting illustrations of true humility and love which the Saviour furnished in His own Person, and which unequivocally declared that the empty honors of the world were not to be found in His kingdom, were designed to constitute subjects for deep reflection and self-examination on the part of the disciples, who now remain silent.

²⁹ And as they went out from Jericho, a great multitude followed him.

A. And ... went out. Mark (10:46, ff.), and Luke (18:15) refer to one blind man only (see above, 8:28, B.). Matthew mentions a second who was also healed during the Saviour's presence in the vicinity of Jericho. Such instances frequently occurred (see 9:27). Matthew and Mark represent the miracle as wrought after the Lord's departure from the city, while Luke describes one which had occurred before His entrance into it. Hence it is probable that one of the two, whose name Luke does not give, was first healed, and that Bartimeus, encouraged by this circumstance, applied to the Lord as He left the city. Matthew groups the two miracles together, as the precise time of each was of no importance to the reader.—**B. Jericho,** called by the Arabs *Eriha,* is, at present a mean village of scarcely 200 inhabitants (Robinson: Bibl. Res. I. 552). The ancient city lay six miles west from the Jordan, and was more then twice that distance from Jerusalem, towards the northeast; between the two cities lay a dreary wilderness. (For notices of this "city of palm-trees" Deut. 34:3, see Josh. ch. 2–ch. 6; 1 Kings 16:34; 2 Kings 2:18, ff., and Luke 19:1, ff.). The **multitude** probably consisted in part at least of Jews who were proceeding to Jerusalem in order to keep the passover there (ver. 20, A.).

30 And, behold, two blind men sitting by the wayside, when they heard that Jesus was passing by, cried out, saying, Lord, have mercy on us, thou Son of David.

See ver. 29, A.—**Thou Son, etc.** (see ann. to 9:27).

31 And the multitude rebuked them, that they should hold their peace: but they cried out the more saying, Lord, have mercy on us, thou Son of David.

A. Rebuked them = probably annoyed by such loud appeals for help, which, as they vainly believed, the Lord could not, or would not, afford,—**that they should** = in order that they might. *To hold one's peace,* is an old English phrase equivalent to the words, *to be silent,* which is simply the sense of the Greek word here used, as well as in 26:63.—**B. They cried the more** = thus furnishing evidence of their earnestness and of their faith.

32 And Jesus stood still, and called them, and said, What will ye that I should do unto you?

The Lord desires to call attention by His question to the greatness of the calamity of the men, and, consequently, the greatness of the power revealed in the instantaneous relief which He designed to grant. Of their own faith they had given unequivocal proof (Luke 18:42); hence He says substantially: Ask whatsoever ye will, and ye shall receive it.

[33] They say unto him, Lord, that our eyes may be opened.

They ask for no temporal honors or profits, but only relief from their greatest burden. Our prayers should refer to those personal wants which most of all distress the soul.

[34] And Jesus, being moved with compassion, touched their eyes: and straightway they received their sight, and followed him.

A. And ... compassion = as always, and most of all in reference to man's spiritual evils (see 9:36, B.).—**B. Touched their eyes** (comp. 8:3, 15; Mark 7:33; Luke 7:14; 22:51). The Lord indicated His special purpose by the act of touching, and doubtless also designed to aid the faith of the men, and thus produce most fully the proper frame of mind.—**C. And followed** = as an instructive example to all, to renounce the world and follow through life our divine Benefactor and Redeemer.

6

Matthew 21

¹ And when they drew nigh unto Jerusalem, and came unto Bethphage, unto the Mount of Olives, then Jesus sent two disciples.

Mount of Olives = Olivet, 2 Sam. 15:30, called by the Arabs Jebel-et-Tur, on the east or north-east of Jerusalem, and separated from it by the brook Cedron (John 18:1). It rises to the height of 2,397 feet above the level of the Mediterranean Sea; it is about one mile in length, stretching from north to south. This eminence commands a wide prospect, and, in particular, enables a spectator to take a full view, not only of the temple (Mark 13:3), but also of every part of the city (Zech. 14:4). It was distant from Jerusalem "a sabbath-day's journey," Acts 1:12 = somewhat less than an English mile ("five furlongs," Jos. *Antiq.* 20, 8, 6); according to others, seven furlongs and a half. The Jews assigned a distance of 2000 cubits (6:27, B.) to a sabbath day's journey, by combining, after their manner, Exod. 16:29 with Num. 35:5). The name was derived from the extensive plantations of olive trees which in ancient times covered the western side.—**Olives** are produced by a tree which the Jews cultivated with great care, and valued on account of its fruit (Jer. 11:16), the rich oil which the olives furnished (Judges 9:9), its wood (1 Kings 6:23, 31), and the great age to which it attained (Ps. 52:8). The wild olive-tree is mentioned in Rom. 11:17, ff.—**Bethphage** was a village at the foot of the mount, not far from Bethany, mentioned below, ver. 17, but no traces of it in modern times have been discovered. For **Jerusalem** (see 4:5, C.). The names of the **two disciples** are not given; a commission of the same general nature was afterwards given to Peter and John (Luke 22:8).

² Saying unto them, Go into the village that is over against you, and straightway ye shall find an ass tied, and a colt with her: loose *them,* and bring *them* unto me.

A. The village = Bethphage, which was in sight. **Straightway** = immediately, "as soon as ye be entered into it" (Mark 11:2).—**B. An ass ... colt.** The oriental nations assigned a very high value to the ass (Gen. 12:16; 24:35; Job. 1:3), which is said to have been of a more stately and handsome appearance than the ignoble animal of the same kind found in countries lying further north. It was not employed simply by poor persons, but, like the mule (1 Kings 1:33), was preferred to horses for riding by men of the highest rank (Judges 5:10; 2 Sam. 17:23; 1 Kings 13:13); the ass-colt is mentioned in such a sense in Judg. 10:4; 12:14. The use of horses, which were pre-eminently employed for war purposes (Jer. 8:6; Job. 39:19–25) was discountenanced among the Jews (Deut. 17:16; Josh. 11:6; Isai. 2:6, 7; 31:1), doubtless with a view to discourage the development of a military spirit among the chosen people. When the time had arrived for giving a visible manifestation of the royal character and dignity of the Prince of Peace (Isai. 9:6), He accordingly chose the ass for riding, so that He might really appear to the world, as He had been prefigured by Melchizedek, namely, as the King of *peace* (Hebr. 7:2; Gen. 14:18; see below, ver. 5, C.). Of the two animals here mentioned, the Saviour chose the colt, "whereon yet never man sat" (Luke 19:30), as the conception of purity or fitness for sacred uses was specially connected in the minds of ancient Jews and Gentiles with an animal that had not yet performed any labor (Numb. 19:2; Deut. 21:3; 1 Sam. 6:7). The ass was not separated from the colt, but simply permitted to follow, without being employed.—**Loose** = *unite*.

³ And if any one say aught unto you, ye shall say, The Lord hath need of them: and straightway he will send them.

A. If—aught = should inquire concerning your purpose or authority. Probably the owners, mentioned in Luke 19:33, are meant. No one of the four evangelists had space to describe in detail (John 21:25) the many individuals who received Christ as the Messiah (see for instance, John 2:23). Thus Matthew and Mark never mention Lazarus and his two sisters, all of whom the Lord tenderly loved (John 11:5). So, too, the man described in 26:18, B., was unquestionably a believer, but his name is not once recorded (Mark 14:13; Luke 22:10). Joseph of Arimathea, although a disciple, is not mentioned until after the death of the Lord (Matt. 27:57; John 19:38). Here again persons are incidentally introduced, whose names, like those of many others, have not been preserved. **Aught** = anything.—**B. The Lord, etc.** = they know Me, believe in Me, and will readily submit to any expression of My will. "*The Lord*" appears to have been the simple but expressive name by which the Saviour's disciples frequently indicated Him in contra-distinction from all other superiors (John 20:2; 21:7). Whenever well-founded appeals are made to us to employ a part of our means in acts of benevolence, let us remember the words: "The Lord hath need of them," and think on Matt. 25:40, 45.

⁴ Now this is come to pass, that it might be fulfilled which was spoken by the prophet, saying,

A. All this is come to pass = so ordered by the Lord. **B. That ... fulfilled** (see 1:22, A.). Matthew gratefully refers to the unchangeableness of the divine purposes; the prophetic promise, which was so cheering to the souls of ancient believers, is literally fulfilled. When this fulfilment subsequently became distinct to the minds of the disciples (John 12:16), it was a new testimony to them that the precious promises of God were all fulfilled in Christ.

⁵ Tell ye the daughter of Zion, Behold, thy king cometh unto thee, meek, and riding upon an ass, and upon a colt the foal of an ass.

A. The introductory words occur in Isai. 62:11; the remainder of the verse is found in Zech. 9:9; the two passages are combined by Matthew as they refer to the same event.—**Tell ye** = all ye that dwell on earth. The prophet regards the Saviour's advent as a matter of the deepest interest to the whole world which He came to redeem, and represents all nations as congratulating the favored city.—**B. Daughter of Zion.** The city of Jerusalem lay on several hills or mounts; the temple was erected on Mount Moriah, while the site of David's house, and of the royal residence of his successors was Mount Zion (2 Sam. 5:7–9; 1 Kings 7:1). The entire city frequently received the name of the latter

(Ps. 9:11; 87:2, 3; 102:13, 16; 110:2). Then, by an oriental figure of speech, kingdoms, cities, etc., were personified or represented as females (comp. Isai. 47:1; Jer. 46:11; Ps. 45:12). Hence Jerusalem, the city built on Zion, is called the *daughter* of Zion in 2 Kings 19:21, and very frequently in the prophetic writings, as, Isai. 1:8 (comp. 8:12, A.). Finally, this name of the holy city is figuratively employed in the widest sense, as a designation of the entire people of Israel, as in Zeph. 3:14.—**C. Behold ... cometh.** When the prophet Zechariah uttered these words, more than 500 years before the events to which they refer, the period of the restoration of the captive Jews to their land had arrived (Ezra 5:1; Zech. 1:1); but their condition was miserable in the extreme. They are cheered by this promise of the advent of the Messiah, the true "King of Israel" (John 1:49).—"Thy King, thy Deliverer cometh to thee—not to others only, but to *thee*. Thou didst not seek Him, but He seeks thee; He first loved thee" (1 John 4:19).—Luther.—**D. Meek;** the original Hebrew term, which properly applies to any lowly condition (poverty, Deut. 24:12), also describes the feeling of humility as opposed to that of pride (Ps. 18:27), "afflicted—high looks." Thus, it acquires, as in the present text, the sense of *lowly in heart* (comp. 5:5, A.; 11:29). "The Lord comes to thee in meekness, not as He came to Adam (Gen. 3:9), not as He came to Cain (Gen. 4:9), not as He came on Mount Sinai (Hebr. 12:18–24)."—Luther.—**E. Sitting, etc.** The Messiah's humility is seen in His choice of the ass, in place of the symbols of war, namely, the "chariot, horse and battle-bow" to which He afterwards refers (Zech. 9:10). He adds: "He shall speak peace unto the heathen," and concludes this portion of his prophecy with a magnificent description of the power and glory of the Messiah's kingdom. "It is true that the means of grace, the Word, Baptism, and the Lord's Supper, seem to be very insignificant and even mean, compared with the spiritual gifts which they confer. But let not thy carnal eyes deceive thee. Here, Christ rides on a borrowed ass, and soon afterwards suffers an ignominious death. Nevertheless, this despised Nazarene conquers sin, death and hell. Do not trust to thine eyes, but believe with thy heart."—Luther.—**F. And a colt, etc.** This language and that which is used in ver. 7 ("thereon," lit, *on them* = both of the animals), does not mean that the Lord rode alternately on the ass and the colt; He employed the latter alone (see ver. 2, B. and John 12:15). The prophet, whose words assume the form of Hebrew poetry called *Parallelism* (15:8, C.), first says in general, "upon an ass," and then, in the following clause, more particularly: "a colt, etc.;" comp. "mighty men," and "men of war" in Joel 2:7. The language, in ver. 7. conforms to a Hebrew idiom which at times employs the plural number where the reader himself can understand that only *one* object is really meant (comp. Gen. 8:4) "upon (one of) the mountains" (Job 21:32), "grave," in the Hebrew *graves* (see margin; Judges 12:7), where the words "one of" are supplied by the translators, but omitted in Gen. 19:29, "cities in (one of) the which." The same expression occurs when a general remark is made, with no intention to describe special cases, as below in 27:44; so the mention of the "prophets" in Acts 13:40 refers to Hab. 1:5, and the "secret chambers" in Matt. 24:26 can mean only one at a time. So, too, only one man offered the Lord a sponge filled with vinegar (Matt. 27:48; Mark 15:36) the general fact only is stated thus in John 19:29, "*they* filled a sponge."

[6] And the disciples went, and did even as Jesus appointed

them.

They are the two disciples to whom reference is made in ver. 1.

⁷ And brought the ass, and the colt, and put on them their garments; and he sat thereon.

A. Ass—colt—thereon, lit. *on them,* that is, on the colt; see above, ver. 5, F.—**B. Clothes,** lit. *cloaks,* "garments," as the same word is rendered in the next verse = outer garments, the *himation* mentioned in 5:40, B., which was frequently laid aside (comp. Acts 7:58; 12:8). The disciples, after the ancient oriental mode, placed articles of clothing instead of a saddle, on the colt, before they rendered their services to their Master in mounting.

⁸ And the most part of the multitude spread their garments in the way, and others cut branches from the trees, and spread them in the way.

A. A ... multitude of Jewish travellers, who went to Jerusalem, as John states (12:12) in order to keep the passover (see above 20:17, A. and 20, A.).—**B. Spread their garments** (ver. 7, B.) = according to the oriental custom, a mark of honor (comp. 2 Kings 9:13.—**C. Branches** = of palm-trees (John 12:13). Branches of these trees were carried in the hand and strewed in the way in seasons of rejoicing (Lev. 23:40), after any victory (Rev. 7:9), and, as here, in welcoming a monarch. "When you confess Christ openly and in truth, when you sustain the order and honor of His Church, and when you consecrate your property, honor and life to His service and to the propagation of His Gospel, then you, too, 'spread your garments in His way,' and give Him a fitting welcome."—Luther.

⁹ And the multitudes that went before him, and that

followed, cried, saying, Hosanna to the son of David: Blessed is he that cometh in the name of the Lord; Hosanna in the highest.

A. Multitudes—before—followed. Besides the fifteen "Songs of degrees" (Ps. 120–134), others also, including Ps. 118, were sung by the Jews on their periodical journeys to Jerusalem, at the times of the great yearly festivals, and during the celebration. In the present case different portions of Ps. 118 appear to have been alternately sung, after the manner of responses, as in Exod. 15:20, 21; 1 Sam. 18:7, by different groups of the same company; thus those who "went before" may have sung the words: "Hosanna ... David;" then those "that followed" responded: "Blessed ... highest."—**B. Hosanna.** This word is simply the Greek form of the Hebrew term occurring in Ps. 118:25, and signifying: "Save now, or, more fully: "Succor—help (thine Anointed, the Son of David), we pray." The former part of the word is the root of the name *Jesus* (1:21); the last syllable, *na,* is a particle expressive of an entreaty = *do now,* or, *we beseech;* it is omitted in the original in 2 Sam. 14:4; 2 Kings 6:26, where the former part of the word is rendered: "Help!" margin, *Save.* The Hebrew is probably written here and in Mark 11:9; John 12:13, in order to point the more distinctly to the song of holy exultation, forming the 118th Psalm,—Son of David (see 1:1, C.).—**C. Blessed ... Lord** (Ps. 118:26). This passage was appropriately repeated on the occasion of the visit of the pilgrims to the house of God. Here, however, it is obviously applied by them specially to the Lord Jesus, and in the sense that, as the Messiah, He is entitled to such a welcome. The immediate cause of this unusual joy is explained in John 12:17, 18. These strangers, who had often heard of Jesus (Matt. 4:24; 9:26), were now in the vicinity of the spot where Lazarus had been restored to life (see ver. 1, and John 11:1). The rapid circulation of these tidings, and the circumstance that the author of the miracle was present, produced extraordinary excitement among the people; they now believed that the promised Messiah or King, "the Son of David" (1:1, C.), had at length visited His people. **Cometh ... Lord** = cometh to bring prosperity in accordance with the divine will (see below, 23:39, A.).—**D. In the highest.** The same phrase occurs in Luke 2:14. A somewhat similar phrase in Job 16:19 ("on high," in the margin: "in the high places," corresponding to the word "heaven," in the former part of the verse), as well as in Isai. 57:15 ("high place") and Ps. 18:16 ("from above" = from the high place) refers to God dwelling *above* us, in heaven. It is a recognition of His exalted nature, whence also He is said to be "most high" (Ps. 92:8; comp. Ps. 56:2), "Thou Most High." The present phrase, which was doubtless used by different individuals in different combinations, is therefore equivalent to: *in heaven* (comp. Hebr. 1:3; 8:1). The whole is a prayer which, in accordance with Mark 11:10 and Luke 19:38, may be thus expressed: "O Thou that dwelleth in the place of heavenly glory, help, save us now by the coming of the Messiah's kingdom."

[10] And when he was come into Jerusalem, all the city was stirred, saying, Who is this?

Stirred = agitated, convulsed; the inhabitants eagerly inquired after the name of Him who, like a king, was welcomed by the acclamations of the multitude. The same word is rendered *quake* in 28:4; tremble in Hebr. 12:26, and also describes an earthquake (Matt. 27:51). The word (like "troubled," 2:3), does not here seem to indicate rapture, but rather a hostile feeling.

¹¹ And the multitudes said, This is the prophet Jesus, from Nazareth of Galilee.

The multitude, which had saluted the Lord as the Messiah (ver. 9), appears to have been at once subdued and discouraged by the wondering ignorance ("who is this?"), stupid amazement and unbelief of the citizens which the Lord deeply deplored (23:37). The rulers or leading classes had already rejected him with scorn (John 7:48). The fickle multitudes, which had so shortly before welcomed him as the Messiah, swayed like a reed, now style the Lord simply "the prophet," as if they, somewhat contemptuously perhaps (see 2:23, C., and John 7:52), wished to say: It is the well-known Galilean prophet (but see 26:69, C., 71, E.). Their next cry was: "Crucify Him, crucify Him (Luke 23:21; Matt. 27:20, 22. **Nazareth** (2:23, A.).

¹² And Jesus entered into the temple of God, and cast out all them that sold and bought in the temple, and overthrew the tables of the moneychangers, and the seats of them that sold the doves.

A. The temple = here, not the "holiest of all" (Hebr. 9:3; Exod. 26:33), called *naos* (see 4:5, E.), but the external courts, and specially the "great court" (2 Chron. 4:9), named by later writers "the court of the Gentiles," beyond which Gentiles, who had not become fully incorporated with the Jewish people, were not permitted to advance. Here the Lord walked (as recorded in John 10:23), and the lame man was healed by Peter (Acts 3:11; see Matt. 26:55, C.). It was intended to be a place for the meditation and prayers of devout men of pagan birth, who had renounced the practice of idolatry. But, with the permission of the ungodly Jewish authorities, it was converted, particularly during the great festivals, into a noisy market or place of business; this abuse, which arrogantly set aside the privileges of the Gentiles ("nations," Mark 11:17), seems to have arisen arisen after the return of the Jews from Babylon. A wall surrounded the second or inner court; within this second court was the third or most sacred enclosure, which none but the priests were allowed to enter; in it stood the *naos* or temple itself, with a small court before it, where the great altar was placed.—**B. Cast out.** Once before (John 2:13–17), at the commencement of His public ministry, the Lord had corrected the gross abuse by which devout or inquiring Gentiles were robbed of their appropriate place of worship. The conversion of that spot into a market was so flagrant a violation, not only of decency, but also of the sanctity of the temple itself, that any devout and earnest man whom a holy zeal (John 2:17) like that of Phinehas animated (Numb. 25:7, 11), or a prophet such as Jesus was believed to be (ver. 11), possessed sufficient authority to expel the intruders. But the countenance of the Lord no doubt also assumed an expression of majesty and divine power which silenced at once all opposition to His will; it wrought powerfully on the men who afterwards came to seize Him (John 18:6). The Pharisees, although much mortified, could not consistently censure the Lord, whose conduct was a severe condemnation of their unfaithfulness, but they secretly resolved to destroy Him (Mark 11:18).—**C. Sold and bought** = cattle, sheep and goats (Lev. 1:2, 10; John 2:14), which the foreign Jews desired to offer as sacrifices, but which they should have procured elsewhere.—**D. Money-changers ... doves.** The annual payment demanded of each Jew, and intended to meet the expenses of the temple service, was half a shekel, or about 28 cents (see 17:24, B.). Jews from a distance who had not paid the amount, and brought only foreign money with them, applied to the money-changers, who furnished them with Jewish or sacred coins, which alone could be offered (Exod. 30:13, and see above, 17:24). The **doves** that were exposed for sale were purchased by poor persons whose means did not allow them to present a more costly sacrifice (Lev. 1:14; 5:7; 12:8; 14:21, 22).

¹³ And he saith unto them, It is written, My house shall be called a house of prayer; but ye make it a den of robbers.

A. And said = explained and justified His apparently stern conduct.—**B. My house ... prayer.** The Lord (who had come to His temple, Mal. 3:1), quotes the concluding words of Isai. 56:7, in which divine compassion is promised to the Gentiles, whom the Jews had virtually expelled from the spot assigned to them. Solomon's language in 1 Kings 8:22–53, indicates that he regarded the temple as specially the place for "prayer and supplication."—**My house**; in the prophetic passage, these words allude to God as "*dwelling* between the cherubim" (Ps. 80:1; Exod. 25:17–22; 40:34; Numb. 7:89; 1 Sam. 4:4; 1 Kings 8:10, 11).—**C. But ye have, etc.** The Lord refers to the words in Jer. 7:11; the impiety of the Jews, as described there in ver. 9, is solemnly rebuked. The application is specially intended for the traders, whose sordid love of gain and dishonest practices in disposing of their merchandise, were revealed to the Lord's eye. As the priests, who had the charge of the sacred edifice and all that lay within its precincts, tolerated this traffic, it is quite probable that they privately received a portion of the gains (comp. 1 Sam. 2:12–17). "Shall we wonder at these abuses among the Jews? But has not the Pope been guilty of still greater enormities? Does he not pretend to sell the pardon of your sins for money? Has he not converted the Lord's Supper into a sacrifice for the living and the dead? Do not he and the priests, for the sake of getting money, profane all that is holy?"—Luther.

^{14} And the blind and the lame came to him in the temple; and he healed them.

The power of the Lord was revealed by new miracles which He wrought as additional evidences of His divine authority; the effect on the Pharisees is related in John 11:47.

^{15} But when the chief priests and the scribes saw the wonderful things that he did, and the children that were crying in the temple and saying, Hosanna to the Son of David; they were moved with indignation.

A. Wonderful things = not only the miracles mentioned in ver. 14, but also the unexpected expulsion of the traders from the temple (ver. 12), whose intrusion the highest authorities had tolerated.—**B. The children, etc.** = repeating cheerfully the words which they had heard the multitude utter (ver. 9). The Jews ordinarily encouraged their children to take an active part in the rejoicings usual at the annual feasts (comp. Exod. 12:26, 27; 13:8, 14; Deut. 6:20).—**Moved with indignation** (= much displeased, Mark 10:41) on seeing that Christ, who so frequently opposed their iniquity, received honor.

^{16} And said unto him, Hearest thou what these are saying? And Jesus saith unto them, Yea; did ye never read, Out of the mouths of babes and sucklings thou hast perfected praise?

A. Hearest ... say? = why dost thou permit thyself to be saluted by ignorant children with a title belonging to the Messiah alone?—**B. Yea** = their language is by no means unsuitable, but is strictly true and appropriate.—**C. Have**

ye, etc. The words occur in Ps. 8:2; according to 1 Cor. 15:27; Eph. 1:22 and Hebr. 2, 6, 7, the whole Psalm refers to the Messiah, who, in His unsullied human nature, and in His "dominion" over the visible creation (ver. 6–8; comp. with Gen. 1:26, 28) exhibited the purity and power which Adam lost after his fall, but which reappeared with new splendor in Christ. The psalmist poetically describes in the words quoted, the instinctive admiration with which even the youngest children gaze at times on the heavenly bodies mentioned in ver. 3; he regards it as a fitting tribute paid to the majesty of the Creator. Even more acceptably—proceeds Christ—may these children, possessing the intelligence of a riper age, and incited by the example of the adults around them, pay a tribute of praise to the truth of God in sending the promised Son of David. **Perfected** = *established,* or, *constituted.* **Praise** = the glory proceeding from, or identified with, the manifestation of the "strength" mentioned in Ps. 8:2.

¹⁷ And he left them, and went forth out of the city to Bethany; and lodged there.

Bethany was a village near Bethphage mentioned in ver. I, "about fifteen furlongs" (= somewhat less than two miles) south-east from Jerusalem (John 11:18), lying, probably, upon the eastern slope of the Mount of Olives, a mile or more below the summit of the ridge (see 28:16, A.). It was the place of residence of Lazarus (John 11:1), to whom the modern Arabic name of *el-'Aziriyeh* is said to refer. Simon the leper (Matt. 26:6), and doubtless others who knew and believed in Christ, also dwelt in this place; here Christ accordingly, together with the twelve (Mark 11:11), passed the night. It is at present a poor village, containing about twenty families.

¹⁸ Now in the morning as he returned to the city, he hungered.

He hungered (see 8:24, B.), having, doubtless, as in Mark 1:35, engaged in private devotion at a very early hour, and then proceeded to the city. The later Jews did not ordinarily break their fast (Acts 2:15) until the first hour of prayer in the morning, that is, the "third hour" (20:3, B.), our nine o'clock, when the daily morning sacrifice was offered (Exod. 29:39; Numb. 28:4; 2 Kings 16:15).

¹⁹ And seeing a fig tree by the wayside, he came to it, and found nothing thereon, but leaves only, and he saith unto it, Let there be no fruit from thee henceforward forever. And immediately the fig tree withered away.

A. A fig tree = among many others planted as usual at the wayside, that stood nearer to Him (Mark 11:13), but probably were not yet furnished with leaves. The fig tree, which abounded in Palestine, furnished a favorite and wholesome article of food (1 Sam. 25:18). The first specimens were exhibited to the Israelites by the spies who had been sent to search the land (Numb. 13:23). Of the several species, the early fig, which was most esteemed (Jerem. 24:2; Hos. 9:10), ripened before the close of June, when the previous winter had been mild; the *foliage* was developed only *after* the fruit had been formed, and was, accordingly, an indication that the latter was nearly ripe. On the day when the occurrence here mentioned took place, the figs had not yet been gathered, as "the time of figs (= fig-gathering) was not yet." This expression in Mark 11:13 strictly corresponds to the one occurring below (ver. 34), where "the time of the fruit" is the time, not of *ripening* but of *gathering;* so, too, the *harvest* is the *time* or season of the wheat in the field (comp. Job 5:26), and the vintage is the time or season of the grapes (Hos. 2:9). Under these circumstances any passenger, on seeing such early leaves, might reasonably expect to find figs on the tree. The absence of fruit in this instance accordingly proved that the tree was barren; it was thus an image of the hypocrite whose leaves (= professions) only promise or pretend that fruit (= religious principle, faith) has already been formed. The privilege which a Jew enjoyed to enter his neighbor's vineyard or grain-field and eat (see 12:1, D.) would amply justify him in plucking fruit from trees standing on the public road, where they were often found. The meaning of the name *Bethphage* is *house of figs,* referring doubtless to the abundance of the fruit in the vicinity.—**B. And said unto it, Let, etc.** The conduct of the Lord, who here speaks calmly but with sadness, receives its fullest explanation from the events which immediately preceded it, specially the exhibition of the malice of the chief priests and scribes mentioned in ver. 15, from whom a very different course could have been expected. Filled with grief, and viewing the approaching ruin of these unholy and hypocritical men, who claimed to be precisely the most devout of all, the Lord expresses His inmost thoughts by the act now described. The same truth is set forth in Hebr. 6:8. We have here, accordingly, a *parable in action* (as in Acts 21:11), strikingly resembling the parable in *words* concerning the fig tree that cumbered the ground (Luke 13:6–9), and inculcating the same general lesson. The fig tree was fitted to furnish abundant fruit of great excellence; so, too, God had richly endowed His people with spiritual gifts (Rom. 3:1, 2; 9:4, 5). But after many centuries of divine forbearance, the Lord Jesus found "a crooked and perverse nation" (Phil. 2:15) whose Pharisaic spirit, so severely rebuked in the Sermon on the Mount (ch. 5, ch. 7 and in ch. 23), rather dishonored than glorified the divine name. In this instance the promise made by the leaves = the presence of good fruit, was delusive; so the outward Pharisaic sanctity of the nation concealed hearts that were destitute of faith and love, the weightier matters of the law (23:23). The ruin of the barren nation is impressively illustrated by the doom pronounced on the fig tree. It **immediately** = *straightway,* as the same Greek word is often translated, withered *away* = *dried up* (as the word is rendered in Rev. 16:12). The occurrence took place in the presence of the disciples without being clearly understood by them, and hence the Lord afterwards revealed the event which it foreshadowed, in plainer terms, in ch. 24:2.

[20] And when the disciples saw it, they marvelled, saying, How did the fig tree immediately wither away?

Saw it = the next morning (Mark 11:20); **marvelled** = *wondered,* as in 8:10; the withered leaves were falling fast, and the whole trunk was evidently dead.

[21] And Jesus answered and said unto them, Verily I say unto you, If ye have faith, and doubt not, ye shall not only do what is done to the fig tree, but even if ye shall say unto this mountain, Be thou taken up and cast into the sea; it shall be done.

A. Jesus answered = by repeating the words already found in ch. 17:20 above (which see), and now pointing to one of the mounts visible at the time, possibly Olivet (ver. 1).—**B. And doubt not.** The original word, frequently translated *doubt* (Acts 10:20; Rom. 14:23), primarily means to *separate, dissolve,* etc., and then is applied to any internal difference or contrariety of thought and feeling; thus it is rendered wavered in Rom. 4:20; it sometimes indicates a contest between opposing forces, and specially the trials to which faith is subjected. Hence it describes an uncertainty, a hesitation, or a fluctuating state of mind, a weak faith—all which is the opposite of that clear, confident and serene frame in which the true believer must appear before God.—**C. It shall be done** (see above, 17:20, D.). As the disciples do not appear on the present occasion to perceive the deep import of the fig tree (ver. 19, B.), the Lord confines His remarks to the subject of faith, which in the case of the disciples was not yet fully enlightened and clear.

22 And all things, whatsoever ye shall ask in prayer, believing, ye shall receive.

Comp. 7:7, C.—**Believing** = praying in faith, as the only genuine mode of prayer, that is, exhibiting due submission to divine wisdom, and unshrinking trust in God.

23 And when he was come into the temple, the chief priests and the elders of the people came unto him as he was teaching, and said, By what authority doest thou these things? and who gave thee this authority?

A. Temple = one of the courts (ver. 12, A.) in which He walked (Mark 11:27), conversed and taught.—**B. Chief priests.** These are accompanied by the scribes (Luke 20:1) and Pharisees (ver. 45, below). Hence, as members of the Sanhedrim, they probably address Christ in an official capacity, as they claimed a certain right founded on passages like Deut. 13:1–5; 18:20–22, and exercised in Acts 4:7, to investigate the character and acts of men who professed to be prophets, and "gave signs or wonders." In the present case these persons would have gladly adopted harsher measures than such an official inquiry, if they had not personally feared the consequences (ver. 46, below).—**C. By what authority,**

etc.?** Of these two questions the former means: "What character and office dost Thou, who art neither a Levite nor a scribe, claim to possess, while Thou doest these things = the expulsion of the traders, and the miracles?" (ver. 15, A.)?. The second means: "If Thou claimest to be a prophet, who has conferred such power on Thee? = Hast Thou the divine sanction?" The object of these persons is obvious. While they assume that Christ cannot in any case claim to be more than a mere human being, they hope to extort from Him a declaration that He is more, namely, the Messiah; in that case they could present Him to the Roman governor (Luke 20:20) as a dangerous person. Or, He might declare that He was the Son of God: now, that declaration had on two former occasions (John 5:17, 18; 10:30–33) converted the popular favor into jealousy and madness; this result they now hoped to produce. Such a declaration, indeed, which the Lord's enemies represented as equivalent to blasphemy, constituted afterwards the ground on which He was condemned to death (26:63–66).

²⁴ **And Jesus answered and said unto them, I also will ask you one question, which if ye tell me, I likewise will tell you by what authority I do these things.**

Among Jewish disputants the right was conceded to him to whom a question was directed, to reply by proposing another in his turn. The Lord by no means here evades the question, but simply demands justice; before these persons came to Him, they should have decided positively and distinctly in the case of His forerunner John. He never failed to give an answer when an honest inquirer really needed information. But at the present period, when He had furnished the strongest proofs of His divine nature and mission (John

3:2; 9:16, 33; 10:37, 38; 15:24; Acts 2:22), the allegation of these men that they needed evidence of His authority could proceed from wilful ignorance or malice alone. The dignity and uprightness of the Lord, accordingly, did not suffer Him to connive at such a mock-trial by pretending to make a formal defence. At the same time the wisdom of the Lord uttered words in ver. 25, which substantially answered the two questions directly and fully. The sense here is: If you really desire information, your own knowledge and recent events will furnish it, as I will show by merely referring to John the Baptist (comp. ver. 25, B.).—**One question**, Greek, *word* = one simple declaration from you, indicating the source of *his* authority, will be sufficient.

²⁵ The baptism of John, whence was it? from heaven, or from men? And they reasoned with themselves, saying, If we shall say, From heaven; he will say unto us, Why then did ye not believe him?

A. The ... John = whence had John derived his authority? The word **baptism** here stands for the office, preaching, baptizing, and mission in general of John, as in Acts 10:37; so the word *crown* (Prov. 27:24) indicates the power and glory of a king; so, too, *the cross* is sometimes only another name for the whole Gospel concerning the way of salvation (1 Cor. 1:17, 18; Gal. 5:11).—**B. Whence ... men?** = was He an impostor, influenced by human and unholy purposes ("of men," Acts 5:38), or was He truly a prophet "sent from God?" (John 1:6; comp. Matt., ch. 3).—**From heaven** = *from God*, as in John 3:27; Luke 15:18. The meaning is: Ye well know in your own hearts that he was divinely authorized; ye also know his testimony concerning Me (John 1:15, 29; 5:33). As God's messenger, and as speaking God's words (John 3:34), his testimony proves that I Myself have divine authority when I teach and work miracles.—**C. They reasoned,** lit. *calculated,* when they perceived the dilemma in which they were now placed, which of the only two possible answers would least expose them to shame, for they could not now hope to retire without deep humiliation. They had not looked for so direct a question which the spectators expected men in their position to be at any moment prepared to answer distinctly, and which, nevertheless, while it was undoubtedly appropriate, most effectually exposed their wickedness of heart.—**D. If we shall, etc.** = if we admit the divine mission of John, we must also admit the divine mission of Jesus, as all men know that John unequivocally bore witness to His divine authority. These persons confess among themselves their wicked rejection of John which Luke relates (7:30).

[26] But if we shall say, From men; we fear the multitude; for all hold John as a prophet.

The deep impression which John's preaching had produced on the public mind rendered it unsafe even for the highest personages (e. g. Herod, 14:5) to reject him openly as an impostor; they would, in the eyes of the people, who regarded John as "a prophet indeed" (Mark 11:32), at once have assumed an attitude of direct rebellion against God Himself, and have incurred great personal danger (Luke 20:6).

[27] And they answered Jesus, and said, We know not. He also said unto them, Neither tell I you by what authority I do these things.

A. We know not = these men could have scarcely suffered a more mortifying exposure. "He taketh the wise in their own craftiness" (1 Cor. 3:19; Job 5:13). They were the acknowledged religious teachers of the people; yet they confess that in the case of John, who was undeniably a messenger of God, they had not had sufficient knowledge or capacity or interest to ascertain whether he were an impostor or a true prophet. And they pretended to teach others the true worship of God!—**B. He also said, etc.** = then cease to act as My judges in a matter respecting which, by your own confession, you are unfit to form a sound judgment; you know not, as you now yourselves admit, the first principles of religion. Your malice would not be converted into faith, even if I gave you an answer (comp. Luke 16:31). These men appear to have still lingered in the presence of the Lord (ver. 45), but not to have ventured to question Him again (see ver. 41).

28 But what think ye? A man had two sons; and he came to the first, and said, Son, go work to-day in the vineyard.

A. But ... ye? = I will ask you another question which you *can* answer: Is there, or is there not, a distinction to be made between profession and practice? I will state a case. The parable of the Two Sons illustrates that distinction in the result, while it represents both of the sons as originally destitute of proper sentiments.—**B. Two sons** = all men, the creatures of God, who is the *Father* of all (Mal. 2:10). The connection, especially in ver. 32, shows that Christ here arranges the people of His day into two classes: first, the publicans and other despised and vicious persons, who had never pretended to be servants of God, but many of whom nevertheless repented on hearing the message of John (Luke 3:10, 11; 7:29), and of Christ (Luke 7:37; 15:1); these are represented by the "first" son introduced here; secondly, the hypocritical Pharisees, scribes, etc., who, in a self-righteous spirit, rejected both John (Luke 7:30) and Christ; these are represented by the other son.—**C. Go work, etc.** (see 20:1, E. and F.). All men everywhere are commanded to repent (Acts 17:30). "I must work ... while it is day" (John 9:4; see also Hebr. 3:7, ff.).

²⁹ And he answered and said, I will not; but afterward he repented himself, and went.

The conduct of the impenitent indicates the spirit from which such words proceed as those of Pharaoh: "Who is the Lord, that I should obey his voice?" (Exod. 5:2). The present case, however, is one in which such impiety is followed by deep and genuine repentance. To the humble and contrite sinner, who sincerely repents and exercises faith, words of encouragement were addressed already by the prophets (Isai. 1:18; Ezek. 18:27, 28), and these are confirmed by the numerous invitations of the Gospel to lost sinners to repent and be saved.—**Repented** = obtained altered views and feelings; the original word occurs again in 27:3, B.

³⁰ And he came to the second, and said likewise. And he answered and said, I *go,* sir; and went not.

The second = corresponding in some measure to the elder son in Luke 15:25. The conduct of the Pharisees and other self-righteous persons is here described, who *say,* "Lord, Lord," but *do not* the will of God (7:21, D., and see 15:8).—**Said likewise.** Inasmuch as "all have sinned" (Rom. 3:23), Paul testified alike, "both to the Jews, and also to the Greeks, repentance toward God, and faith toward our Lord Jesus Christ" (Acts 20:21). He said, **I go,** and **went not** = "they say, and do not" (23:3).

³¹ Whether of the twain did the will of his father? They

say, The first. Jesus saith unto them. Verily I say unto you. That the publicans and the harlots go into the kingdom of God before you.

A. Whether ... twain = which of the two (5:41).—**B. They say** = the same persons who are introduced in ver. 23, or, possibly, other hearers such as those mentioned in ver. 41.—**C. Verily, etc.** = ye, who are governed by Pharisaic pride, regard these classes of people as vile and unclean, but ye do not perceive that ye too are vile and unclean (comp. Luke 18:9–14); now I say unto you, that if they (and Gentiles also, 8:11, 12, and ver. 41, C. below) repent of their sins in sincerity, they shall inherit all the blessings of the Messiah's kingdom. But your impenitence and unbelief will necessarily exclude you altogether, unless you follow ("go—before you") their example, and also turn to God. The unholy persons here mentioned did not pretend that they were righteous, but were conscious of the necessity of repentance and an entire moral change; whereas, the Jewish prejudices of those whom the Lord here addresses, led them to believe that they were already righteous, and thus they permitted no sorrow for sin to enter their souls.

32 For John came unto you in the way of righteousness, and ye believed him not; but the publicans and the harlots believed him: and ye, when ye saw it, did not even repent yourselves afterwards, that ye might believe him.

A. For. The Lord now explains the cause of this rejection of one class, and of the gracious acceptance of the other, in order to illustrate two points of Christian doctrine: first, that all men are sinners (Gal. 3:22), and subject to divine wrath (Rom. 5:8, 9; Eph. 2:3); and, secondly, the necessity and power of faith, which alone can justify (Phil. 3:9).—**B. The way of**

righteousness. The particular habits of thinking, feeling and acting, or the manner of life, as controlled by any leading doctrine or general principle, is sometimes compared to a *way* or *road* leading in a certain direction (Prov. 11:20; 16:31); hence the Christian religion, which is pre-eminently the *way* to righteousness and heaven, receives this general name; for instance, in Acts 9:2; 19:9, 23; 2 Peter 2:21 (comp. also "way of God," below, 22:16, E.). The sense is: John the Baptist taught both by his precepts and by his example the true way of becoming righteous and of pleasing God.—**C. Ye believed him not** = in consequence of your unbelief, ye failed to take the only way that leads to life.—**D. But ... believed him** = repented, sought after pardon in penitence and faith, and therefore were accepted (comp. Rom. 2:5–11).—**E. Saw it** = he repentance and faith of such persons, which should have awakened your conscience.—**F. Not even repent, etc.** = you heard him proclaim the wrath to come (3:7), but you did not "come to yourselves" (Luke 15:17), and in "godly sorrow" (2 Cor. 7:10) appear as penitent believers before God. The construction in the original, like a similar one in Acts 7:19 ("that they"), indicates *believing* as intimately connected with a genuine *repenting*, that is, when the sinner is convinced in his heart of his guilt and danger, he seeks for deliverance, and the same divine grace which awakened him, now conducts him to a saving faith in the atonement of Christ.

33 Hear another parable: There was a man that was a householder which planted a vineyard, and set a hedge about it, and digged a winepress in it, and built a tower, and let it out to husbandmen, and went into another country.

A. Hear ... parable = illustrative of the history of the kingdom of God (ver. 43). That kingdom, in its purest form, consists in the holy communion between God and His creatures (see Excursus I. vol I.). The revelations of God under the old and the new covenant were designed to restore that holy communion between God and fallen men. The Jews ungratefully and wickedly resisted the gracious purposes of God, and, after slaying many prophets (23:31), filled the measure of their guilt by crucifying and slaying (Acts 2:23) the Son of God (Hebr. 1:1, 2). They subsequently rejected the preaching of the apostles also (Acts 13:46); ultimately, the believing Gentiles, "the nations that knew not God" (Isai. 55:5), became pre-eminently the people of God (Rom. 9:24–33, and comp. ver. 43, below, and 8:12). These events are described in the present parable of the Wicked Husbandmen, with which compare Isai. 5:1–7, to which passage it obviously alludes.—**B. Householder.** Under this image, as in 20:1, God is represented as the founder and owner of the vineyard (Isai. 5:2).—**C. Vineyard** (see 20:1, F.). Vineyards of great value were usually protected either by a thornhedge (Ps. 80:12), or a stone wall (Prov. 24:31). The act of entering and merely eating grapes was, however, permitted to any one who passed a vineyard (Deut. 23:24). The grapes, after being gathered, were placed in a broad and shallow excavation or *wine-press*, and trodden by men (Neh. 13:15; Isai. 63:3; Rev. 14:20). In such a place Gideon was once compelled to thresh wheat (Judges 6:11, Hebr. *"in the wine-press"*). The expressed juice flowed down through a closed grate or similar fixture into a receptacle called a *wine-vat*, from which it was ultimately removed in earthen vessels or in skins. The name *wine-press* sometimes includes the upper excavation and the lower vat, both of which were constructed on the side of a hill. A building resembling a turret or *tower* was erected in the vineyard and occupied by a watchman when the grapes were nearly ripe and until they were removed (comp. Job. 27:18; Isai. 1:8). It is not probable that each object mentioned in this verse has a special spiritual sense, as if, for instance, the laws of Moses were represented by the hedge, etc. Such a mode of interpretation cannot lead to satisfactory results; thus, the tower is an image, according to some, of the temple or the city; according to others, of the priesthood, etc. The Lord rather seems to mention all the precautions usually observed by owners of choice vineyards in order to indicate in general the many services which God had bestowed on His people for the purpose of glorifying His name by their devout spirit and conduct as the fruits. Such is obviously the sense of Isaiah's parable to which Christ here refers (Isai. 5:1–7).—**D. Let ... husbandmen** = after giving the Law as a guide, God "looked for righteousness" (Isai. 5:7) as the natural result. **Let it out** = rented, placed in charge of. The original word translated **husbandmen** strictly means a *tiller of the ground,* as in James 5:7. These husbandmen or vine-dressers may represent in a special sense the Pharisees and scribes (Matt. 23:2, 3), the religious teachers of the Jews, whose duty it was to strengthen and extend the kingdom of God.—**E. And went, etc.** = went abroad (comp. 25:14). God granted to man liberty of action, or the choice between good and evil, life and death (Deut. 30:15, 19; Josh. 24:15). The same responsibility now rests on all who live under the new covenant. The words do not imply that God is ever really absent, although sinful men may foolishly say: "The Lord seeth us not" (Ezek. 8:12); He is always invisibly present, and, moreover, always addresses men through the medium of His word.

³⁴ And when the season of the fruits drew near, he sent his servants to the husbandmen, to receive his fruits.

A. The time of the fruit = when the grapes had matured, and should furnish a suitable return to the owner; such a result of the divine action is indicated as might reasonably be expected in men's hearts and lives. *That* time for exhibiting the influence of faith on the heart and life *has already come* in the case of every individual.—**B. He sent, etc.** These servants were the prophets, who were divinely-appointed teachers of religious truth, sent to admonish and rebuke, to reveal the divine will, and to confirm the faith of the people. It was their general duty to urge men to bring forth the *fruits* of repentance and faith in their life and conduct.

³⁵, ³⁶ And the husbandmen took his servants, and beat one, and killed another, and stoned another. Again, he sent other servants more than the first: and they did unto them in like manner.

Matthew here gives only the substance of the Lord's words, which are more fully presented in Mark 12:2–5 and Luke 20:10–12. In all these passages the historic events are figuratively described which the sacred writer, after having reached the great catastrophe, the Babylonian Captivity, thus relates: "They mocked the messengers of God, and despised his words, and misused his prophets, until the wrath of the Lord arose against his people, till there was no remedy" (2 Chron. 36:16; see also Neh. 9:26; Acts 7:52; Hebr. 11:35–38). The lord of the vineyard, with wonderful long-suffering, affords new opportunities for repentance and amendment (comp. Jerem. 44:4). Such long-suffering is designed to lead to repentance (Rom. 2:4); its abuse by men is described in Eccl. 8:11. Thus they "treasure up unto themselves wrath against the day of wrath" (Rom. 2:5).

³⁷ But afterward he sent unto them his son, saying, They will reverence my son.

A. But ... all = when the period had arrived for granting the last revelation of the truth, or the period of the Christian dispensation, as set forth in the N. T.; after this period no new divine revelations until the end of the world are to be expected, according to Matt. 28:20; 2 Cor. 3:11; Hebr. 1:2; 7:15–25; 12:27, 28.—**B. His son** = Jesus Christ (John 3:16), His "one, well-beloved" Son (Mark 12:6), higher in rank and nature than men or angels (Hebr. 1:4, 5; 3:5, 6), being "with God," and Himself God (John 1:1); by Him preeminently "grace and truth came" (John 1:17). The Son, like the servants, claimed the "fruits" of the vineyard = repentance and its fruits (3:2; 4:17).—**C. Saying, etc.** These words are simply designed to express that which might, in the case of a mere human being, be reasonably expected (Isai. 63:8). As God cannot commit an error of judgment, they do not refer in any spiritual sense to Him, except for the general purpose of showing how "*slow* to anger" He is (Neh. 9:17).

³⁸ But the husbandmen, when they saw the son, said among themselves, This is the heir; come, let us kill him, and take his inheritance.

This verse describes the obstinately impenitent, whose extreme wickedness is equalled only by their blindness and infatuation. **They said among themselves** = the Pharisees and others deliberately formed a plan to destroy Christ (12:14; John 11:53). But could they with any reason believe that the crime which they meditated would be left unpunished? The husbandmen are the leaders of the Jewish people (see above, ver. 33, D.), who looked with jealousy and hatred on Christ, when they saw that while He resisted their pretensions, He was regarded by the people with even more reverence than they were (ver. 46); hence they desired to put Him to death (12:14). Their wickedness was great, but their folly in supposing that God would not punish such iniquity was also great. "Come, let us slay him," said Joseph's brethren" (Gen. 37:20). The **inheritance** is the vineyard, and represents the possession of authority and power to rule the chosen people of God. Possibly the Lord means here that many of the "rulers" as well as of the people knew that He was "the very Christ" = Messiah (John 7:26), but wickedly disowned Him. The two passages, Luke 22:34 and Acts 3:17, refer to an ignorance of the real extent of the crime, which indeed may leave room for repentance, but, as a voluntary ignorance, casts a heavy burden of guilt on the perpetrators. The parable is strikingly illustrated by the scene described in John 11:46–53. Christ is "appointed heir of all things" (Hebr. 1:2) in reference to His human nature; as God and Maker of all (John 1:3), He is already the Lord of all.

³⁹ And they took him, and cast him forth out of the vineyard, and killed him.

A. And ... him. In ver. 33–36 the parable referred to events of former ages; in verses 37, 38, it reached the time in which the Saviour Himself appeared; here, at ver. 39, as in 22:9, it assumes a prophetic character, corresponding to the words addressed to Nicodemus (John 3:14, 15).—**B. Cast him, etc.** For the execution of condemned persons, the Jews, in conformity to the spirit of the words in Numb. 15:35, always selected a spot on the outside of the city (1 Kings 21:13; Acts 7:58), and hence the Lord was conducted beyond the city gate to Golgotha (Matt. 27:32, 33; John 19:16, 17,

20). To this circumstance, and to a provision of the Law (Lev. 4:21; 9:11; Numb. 19:3), an allusion is made in Hebr. 13:11–13, and possibly here also by the Lord.

⁴⁰ **When therefore the lord of the vineyard shall come, what will he do unto those husbandmen?**

The Saviour unexpectedly demands a direct answer from His hearers. He still addresses such words to the impenitent sinner: What will God do to them who, after their hardness and impenitent heart, treasure up unto themselves wrath against the day of wrath? (Rom. 2:5.) The righteous blood which the Jews shed (23:35, as one specimen only of human guilt) would not fail to come upon the guilty (27:25). The execution of the sentence of divine justice will be acknowledged by the guilty themselves as richly deserved, however awful the retribution might be.

⁴¹ **They say unto him, He will miserably destroy those miserable men, and will let out the vineyard unto other husbandmen, which shall render him the fruits in their seasons.**

A. They = possibly certain of the Lord's hearers who did not perceive the spiritual application of the parable. There were some, too, who saw its true import, namely, the future ruin of the guilty nation, and who felt the power of the awful truth conveyed in the answer; these exclaimed in alarm: God forbid (Luke 20:16).—**B. He will ... men.** The words may be regarded alike as a description of the destruction of Jerusalem, and of the future punishment of the wicked (23:38; 24:2; Luke 19:41–44).—**C. And will let, etc.** According to Luke 20:15, 16, the Lord appears to confirm the truth of this answer by repeating it Himself. The transfer of the kingdom of God from the unbelieving Jews to believing

Gentiles, which is implied here and in ver. 43, below, is very frequently expressed in direct language (comp. Acts 13:46; 15:7; 18:6; 28:28; Rom. ch. 9—ch. 11; and comp. 8:11, 12). At the same time the position of Gentiles after their admission into the Church is specially explained by Paul, who declares that they shall enjoy God's "goodness" to them if they "continue in His goodness" (= believe in Christ and conscientiously follow Him, as fruits rendered in their season (Rom. 6:22; Eph. 5:9); otherwise, they also shall be cut off (Rom. 11:22).

⁴² Jesus saith unto them, Did ye never read in the scriptures, The stone which the builders rejected, the same was made the head of the corner: this was from the Lord, and it is marvellous in our eyes?

A. Jesus saith = after silently surveying His hearers with a searching look (Luke 20:17).—**B. Did ... Scriptures** = say not that the Lord deals unjustly with you. Had you not abundant opportunities to learn the value of the Gospel? Do you not, by your rejection of it, convict yourselves of folly and wickedness? Do you know the true meaning of certain expressions in that Psalm in which the people found words of welcome when I entered the city? See above (ver. 9, B. and C.).—**The scriptures** = the holy *writings* (Rom. 1:2), which constitute the O. T. Quotations from the latter are often introduced in the N.T. by the phrase: *It is written*, etc. (2:5; 4:4); the entire Hebrew Bible was first *printed* in a. d. 1488. Since these words were spoken, God has given the Scriptures of the N. T. also, and now the same term comprehends both collections of writings.—**C. The stone, etc.** The words occur in Ps. 118:22, 23 [in close connection with those which had supplied the Hosannaof the multitudes, ver. 9; Ps. 118:25]. The speaker refers to the deep distress and extraordinary dangers in which he had been involved, and then, with holy rapture, proclaims the complete victory which Jehovah had granted him. The inspired apostles teach us that these words specially refer to Christ (Acts 4:11; Eph. 2:20; 1 Pet. 2:7); the whole Psalm accordingly sets forth in prophetic language the humiliation and the exaltation of the Messiah, and corresponds to Phil. 2:5–11. A **corner-stone,** placed at the junction of two walls and serving as a support for them, in reality sustains the whole building see (the spiritual application of the name to Christ in Isai. 28:16, with which compare 1 Cor. 3:11). ["The allusion seems to have been drawn from one of the stones, quarried, hewn and marked, away from the site of the temple (1 Kings 5:7), which the builders, ignorant of the head architect's plans, had put on one side, as having no place in the building, but which was found afterwards to be that on which the completeness of the structure depended."—Plumptre.] The Psalm refers prophetically to the lowly appearance of the Saviour, which, in the eyes of the proud Jews, unfitted Him for the Messiah's great work (Isai. 53:2, 3). Nevertheless, precisely He who was even "hanged on a tree was exalted to be a Prince and a Saviour" (Acts 5:30, 31). The **builders** (= Jewish teachers of religion) declared that Christ was unfit to be the foundation of the kingdom of heaven; nevertheless, God made Him the head of the corner = the corner-stone. This result proceeds from divine wisdom and power ("from the Lord"), and is unexpected and wonderful; such divine acts "make foolish the wisdom of this world" (1 Cor. 1:20).

[43] Therefore say I unto you, The kingdom of God shall be taken away from you, and shall be given to a nation bringing

forth the fruits thereof.

A. Therefore = in the same way another divine act, equally as little anticipated by your worldly wisdom, will be performed, namely, the transfer of the name of *people of God* with all the positive blessings connected with it, from you to others.—**The kingdom of God** = the blessings flowing from the Messiah's kingdom, by which man is restored to communion with God.—**B. Taken ... given** (see above, ver. 41, C.).—**C. A nation.** This verse does not refer to any particular Gentile nation or race to the exclusion of others, but is used in the sense of the English word *people* when applied to a multitude, without regard to their respective countries; it so occurs, for instance, in 1 Peter 2:9, although the passage in Exod. 19:16, from which Peter quotes, refers to the Jewish nation. As the "scattered strangers" (1 Peter 1:1) of various races constituted, by the unity of the faith, *one* people or nation or Church (1 Cor. 12:12, 27; Eph. 2:14; 4:4, 5), so here too the new people of God or the **nation** consists of all true believers, irrespectively of their Jewish or Gentile birth and name.—**D. Bringing forth** (see ver. 41, C.).

[44] And he that falleth on this stone shall be broken to pieces: but on whomsoever it shall fall, it will scatter him as dust.

A. And whosoever ... broken. The Lord had announced in the foregoing verse in general terms the rejection of unbelieving Jews ("let out, etc.," ver. 41); here He proceeds to unfold more fully the actual results of their unbelief. He retains the image of a stone, by which He Himself is implied, but now, in allusion to Isai. 8:14, represents unbelief ("stumbling at the word, and disobedience," 1 Peter 2:8) as similar to the fatal stumbling of a thoughtless traveller, who is **broken** = dashed in pieces by the fall to which his recklessness conducted him.—**B. But on, etc.** The image of the stone is still preserved, but with a new application, in allusion to Dan. 2:34, 44. In that prediction the kingdom of Christ is compared to "a stone cut out without hands," which shall "consume" = *scatter, make chaff of,* that is, make an end of all its foes ("scatter him as dust;" comp. Isai. 60:12). The divine founder of the Church will overcome all His enemies (1 Cor. 15:25, 26). The eternal punishment and ruin of all the impenitent and unbelieving is still more explicitly taught below (24:51; ch. 25). With these solemn declarations the Lord concludes the present discourse.

⁴⁵ And when the chief priests and the Pharisees heard his parables, they perceived that he spake of them.

The individuals here mentioned are doubtless those who are introduced in ver. 15, and who had afterwards generally observed silence, without actually withdrawing from the Lord's presence ("at the same hour," Luke 20:19). To them as well as to other hearers (ver. 41, A.) the design of the foregoing parables was perfectly intelligible.

⁴⁶ And when they sought to lay hold on him, they feared the multitudes, because they took him for a prophet.

Such was the effect on these men of the Lord's preaching! It was to them the "savor of death unto death" (2 Cor. 2:16). The cause lies, according to (John 3:20; 5:40; and see above, 13:15, D.), in the wilful and determined purpose of their hearts to resist all the appeals of divine mercy, and all the influences of the Holy Ghost (Acts 7:51).—**They feared, etc.** (see above, ver. 23, B.).

7

Matthew 22

¹ And Jesus answered and spake again in parables unto them, saying,

A. Answered and spake = proceeded or continued to speak (see 11:25, C.). The close of the preceding discourse occurs in ver. 44 of the foregoing chapter. After an interval of unknown length, but probably on the same day and in the same place (21:23), the Lord again commenced to speak in parables **unto them** = the hearers to whom the previous words had been addressed.

² The kingdom of heaven is likened unto a certain king, which made a marriage feast for his son,

A. The kingdom of heaven (see 21:33, A., and Excursus I. vol. I). Here, the kingdom, as the kingdom of the Gospel, represents the Christian Church in its visible form; God's course of action is "like unto" that of this king. The Lord had delivered a parable on a former occasion and under entirely different circumstances (Luke 14:15–24), in which several incidents occur resembling those that are here introduced;

for an analogous case, see 25:14, A. He now sets forth in the present parable additional truths. Under the images of invitations, of murdered servants, and of the destruction of the criminals, He repeats the description of the unbelief, ingratitude and punishment of the Jewish nation which the foregoing parable contained (21:33, ff.), and discloses the divine purpose of calling the Gentiles; but He now proceeds (ver. 11–13, below) to teach the solemn lesson in addition, that if such divine judgments do not influence the members of the Christian Church, whose ancestors were Gentiles, to seek true righteousness, their doom will resemble that of the unbelieving Jews; they, too, will be cast away.—**B. A certain king**, lit. *a man, a king* = an image of God, the Sovereign of the universe, who dispenses both undeserved mercies and merited punishments.—**C. A marriage feast** = wedding banquet, as in Judg. 14:10; John 2:9; Matt. 25:10. The history of the institution of the passover (Exod. 12:3–14), and the circumstances related in Exod. 24:11, combined with the common oriental image of a banquet as an illustration of great enjoyment and honor (see above, 8:11, C.), furnish the sacred writers with various images descriptive of the bounty of God (Ps. 23:5; Prov. 9:2, ff.; Isai. 25:6; Zeph. 1:7). A marriage feast, in particular, exhibited the most perfect combination of joyful circumstances (Jer. 7:34). The latter, moreover, or marriage in general as an image of the relation between God and His people, is frequently introduced in the O. T. (see above, 12:39, A., and 9:15, A.). The marriage of the king's son may therefore be regarded as an image of the union which the Father desires to establish in His kingdom between His only-begotten Son and His believing people = the Church, His bride (Rev. 21:9); the honor and happiness which flow from that union are thus strikingly set forth. But the *bride* is not here introduced prominently as an image of the Church, since the latter is itself already presented under the image of groups of invited guests (comp. 25:1, F.); the Son or bridegroom also recedes from the view, in order that the guests, specially representing the visible Church, may be alone considered.

³ And sent forth his servants to call them that were bidden to the marriage feast: and they would not come.

A. Sent ... feast. An early invitation ("were bidden") was succeeded in the East, it is said (comp. Esth. 5:8 with 6:14, and see Luke 14:17), by another ("to call") immediately before the commencement of the feast, which sometimes continued several days (Judges 14:12; Gen. 29:27). The Saviour refers here to the numerous calls sent to His people through the prophet that they should walk in His ways and seek the heavenly inheritance (Hebr. 11:16); possibly, too, the special meaning may be involved, that the *chosen* people of Israel are now invited anew, and called to the Gospel feast.—**B. And they ... come** = "When I spake, ye did not hear" (Isai. 65:12; comp. Isai. 66:4; Jerem. 7:13; Zech. 7:11; Prov. 1:24). "Ye will not come to me, etc." (John 5:40). Such conduct shows how entirely alienated from God and rebellious the mind of fallen man naturally is (Col. 1:21). The eternal loss of the soul is the result of a deliberate rejection of the divine offers of mercy.

⁴ Again, he sent forth other servants, saying, Tell them that are bidden, Behold, I have made ready my dinner: my oxen and my fatlings are killed, and all things are ready: come to the marriage feast.

A. Again. The long-suffering God is described in the

Scriptures in very affecting and impressive language (Ps. 103:13; Jer. 31:35–37.—**B. Other servants** = new admonitions, repeated by other prophets (comp. 21:36). Possibly the Lord here shadows forth specially the mission of John the Baptist and of his apostles to the Jewish nation.—**C. Tell them, etc.** = divine love cannot yet abandon them (Isai. 49:16).—**Dinner.** The original Greek marks the first meal taken in the day; here, in a general sense = beginning of the feast.—**Fatlings** = young animals (for instance, the fatted calf, Luke 15:23), carefully fed with grain and intended for slaughter (comp. 2 Sam. 6:13). The **oxen, etc.,** are not respectively images of special divine mercies; the whole enumeration, as in 1 Kings 1:9; Prov. 9:2, is designed to set forth the *ample provision* made for the guests = the fulness of divine bounty, such as the "adoption, glory, covenants, law, service and promises" (Rom. 9:4) of the O. T.; all these involve assurances of the coming of Christ, who is "all, and in all" (Col. 3:11), and in whose all-sufficient (John 19:30), atoning work (1 John 1:7) we have emphatically "all things" (1 Cor. 3:21, 22).—The blessings of the Gospel are "prepared" for men by undeserved divine bounty, and never earned by them.

⁵ But they made light of it, and went their ways, one to his own farm, another to his merchandise:

Made light of it = cared not for it; the original word is rendered *neglect,* in 1 Tim. 4:14, *regarded not,* in Hebr. 8:9.—**His own farm,** an illustration of man's preference of his own will and temporal concerns to the divine will and service.—**Merchandise** = traffic, mercantile business. The worldly-minded in general are here represented, who permit their secular business (agricultural pursuits, trade, etc.) to exclude the subject of their religious duties from the mind and the heart. They think that they have no time to attend to God's business, and will not understand that this is really their own business. Their positive guilt consists in the dishonor and contempt with which they treat the heavenly "King," who cannot be "mocked" = treated in a scornful manner with impunity (Gal. 6:7: comp. 2 Chron. 30:10).

⁶ And the rest laid hold on his servants, and entreated them shamefully, and killed them.

The rest, as in Mark 16:13; Luke 8:10; Acts 2:37.—**Laid hold on,** as in 18:28, or 26:57.—**Entreated shamefully,** as in Acts 14:5 and 1 Thess. 2:2. The original describes insolent and injurious treatment. To **entreat** at present signifies to *solicit,* etc.; the translators used the word in the sense, now antiquated, of *treat* = behave towards, deal with.—**Killed,** as in 21:35, where a similar description is given of the persecutions which God's servants in former periods endured; possibly, scenes like the murder of John the Baptist may also be meant (Matt. 14:3, ff.) The class of persons here described differ from those mentioned in ver. 5, in so far that they exhibit a still more fully developed form of human depravity, or a deliberate, conscious and impious resistance to the divine will.

⁷ But the king was wroth; and he sent his armies, and destroyed those murderers, and burned their city.

A. Wroth = angry, as in 18:34, A. (comp. Acts 18:6; 1 Thess. 2:16).—**B. He sent, etc.** (comp. 21:41). At this point in the whole chain of historical events, the Lord, speaking prophetically, refers to the awful event of the destruction of the city of Jerusalem by the Roman soldiers, who, like the

Assyrians (Isai. 10:5), were unconsciously the executors of God's judgment. The circumstances connected with that catastrophe are more fully set forth in ch. 24, below (see Dan. 9:26).—**Murderers ... city** (see 23:37, B.; Acts 7:52).

⁸ Then saith he to his servants, The wedding is ready, but they that were bidden were not worthy.

A. The wedding is ready = the plan of salvation is precisely and fully adapted to the wants of fallen man (Hebr. 7:25); the blood of Christ *can* cleanse *all* men (1 Tim. 2:4) from *all sin* (1 John. 1:7).—**B. But they, etc.** = they, the Jews (Rom. 9:31), to whom the word of God came, did not correspond in heart and life to the divine purpose.—**Worthy** (see 10:11, B.); their "unbelief" (Rom. 11:20; Hebr. 3:19; 4:6, 11) unfitted them for the reception of the blessings of the Gospel (Acts 13:46).

⁹ Go ye therefore unto the partings of the highways, and as many as ye shall find, bid to the marriage feast.

A. Highways. The original, which gives a fuller phrase than the one occurring in Luke 14:23, and below, ver. 10, indicates by the term *partings* the square formed by the intersection or meeting of two or more streets, equivalent, probably, to *crossings of the* ways. In such places a promiscuous assembly could easily be found, and there, as we may gather from the analogous parable (Luke 14:21), the poor sat and begged. Grace makes no difference between the Jews and the Greeks (Rom. 10:12).—**B. And as many, etc.** = "whosoever will, let him take the water of life freely" (Rev. 22:17). The words in Matt. 21:43, and the language of Paul in Rom. 10:20, 21; 11:11, plainly show the meaning here to be: The Gospel which the Jews reject shall be preached to all the Gentile world (Mark 16:15; John 3:16; 11:52; Acts 22:21).

"All the ends of the earth shall see the salvation of our God" (Isai. 52:10; Luke 3:6). The parable, as in 21:39, becomes a prophecy.

¹⁰ And those servants went out into the highways, and gathered together all as many as they found, both bad and good: and the wedding was filled with guests.

A. Servants = the messengers of God, formerly prophets, now, the heralds of the cross.—**Highways** = roads, streets. Illustrations abound in the Acts of the Apostles, from the eighth chapter to the end, of the preaching of the Gospel to Gentiles.—**B. All ... found** = "preach the Gospel to *every creature*" (Mark 16:15; Col. 1:23).—**C. Both bad and good** = a proverbial phrase, here equivalent to *individuals of every kind,* as in 13:47. The language in another parable (the Tares, 13:38) indicates that mere membership in the Christian Church (the hearing of the Word and admission to the Holy Sacraments) is not an unerring index of the state of the heart (see illustrations in Acts 5:1, ff.; 8:13–23). The Gospel and the privileges of the Church have been offered to all men indiscriminately (Rom., ch. 11), but the unworthy will be ultimately rejected by the Lord. It is this point which the concluding portion of the parable is specially designed to illustrate.—**D. The wedding, etc.** = the banquet table was surrounded (lit. *filled*). The Christian Church, in its visible form, consists of an innumerable multitude of individuals.

¹¹ But when the king came in to behold the guests, he saw there a man which had not on a wedding garment:

A. And when ... guests. In this second part of the parable no special allusion to the Pharisees or the Jewish nation is made; it refers strictly to the Christian Church and its members, irrespectively of the mere circumstance of their birth or origin. It also directs attention prophetically, as in 25:31, ff., to the future judgment of men who in this world lived in a Gospel land. The king's course, as here described, is intended to teach three great truths: first, that each individual will hereafter be examined and judged, "came in to see;" secondly, that a certain preparation (= repentance and faith, Acts 20:21, and their fruits, the "wedding garment") is the indispensable condition on which invited guests will be permitted to enjoy eternal life as represented by the banquet; thirdly, that in the case of those who are not so prepared and cleansed, the sentence of punishment will be inevitable, sure and irresistible, "Bind, etc." (ver. 13).—**B. A man, etc.** This man, like the servant in Luke 19:20, is the representative of a large class of persons who outwardly confess Christ. It is well known that among oriental nations the gift of garments by kings and men of rank and wealth to their guests or others was a usual complimentary act (see Gen. 45:22; Judges 14:12, 19; 1 Sam. 18:4; 2 Kings 5:5, 22; Esther 8:15; Dan. 5:7; Luke 15:22). The rejection by a guest of such a gift, and his preference of his own unsuitable or "strange apparel" (see Zeph. 1:7, 8, to which passage the Lord here appears to allude), would naturally be regarded only as a deliberate insult, indicating a spirit in the guest which totally unfitted him for the enjoyment of the king's bounty. The gift was the more needed here, as these persons, taken from the highways, possessed no costly apparel of their own. The oriental customs of modern times furnish abundant illustrations of these statements; the modern *caftan* presented by the noble host is thrown over the ordinary clothing. The spiritual meaning of the wedding garment, which is the apparel corresponding to the king's rank and to all the circumstances, may be gathered from passages like Rom. 13:14; Gal. 3:27, which speak of "putting on" Christ, that is, being *clothed with* or *arrayed in* him, as the same Greek word is translated in Mark 1:6; Acts 12:21. This image is probably derived from words like those of the prophet, who, when he describes the Messiah, exclaims in rapture: "He hath clothed me with the garments of salvation, etc." (Isai. 61:10). The man may thus represent those who undervalue and despise the righteousness of Christ, which is "put on" = imputed to the believer. This interpretation is confirmed by the words in Rev. 19:8, where the fine linen in which the Lamb's wife is arrayed is explained to be "the righteousness of saints." The wedding garment is, accordingly, the symbol of the righteousness of the believer, which proceeds from faith in the crucified Redeemer: this faith purifies the heart (Acts 15:9), continually grows in depth and power by the grace of the Holy Spirit, and bears fruit in a holy life (see Rom. 9:30–32). This righteousness, says Paul (Phil. 3:9), is, not "mine own—it is through the faith of Christ—it is by faith" (see Rom. 3:22; Gal. 2:16). As the wedding garment is neither furnished by the guest nor earned by him, so our righteousness, by which we become fitted to enter heaven, is acquired, not by our works, but proceeds solely from the merits of Christ which are imputed to the believer (Rom. 4:5).

¹² And he saith unto him, Friend, how camest thou in hither not having a wedding garment? And he was speechless.

A. A friend (see 20:13, B.).—**B. How ... wedding garment?** = how couldst thou profess to know God and to be a Christian, and yet not bring forth the fruits of the Spirit? (Gal. 5:22–25). Didst thou not really deny thy Lord? Why hast thou preferred the "filthy rags" of thine own righteousness? (Isai. 64:6; Rom. 10:3). By thy unworthy walk and conduct (Tit. 1:16; Eph. 4:1; Phil. 1:27; Col. 1:10; 1 Thess. 2:12; 4:1) thou hast proved that thy faith was dead (James 2:17, 26), and that therefore thou hast not the true righteousness.—**C. He was speechless** = as he had without cause refused to receive the offered garment (comp. Jer. 23:24). If the heathen is "without excuse" (Rom. 1:20), how shall *he* answer God on the last day who lived and died in a Christian land without repentance and faith? (see Rom. 3:19). "If God spared not, etc." (Rom. 11:21).

¹³ Then the king said to the servants, Bind him hand and foot, and cast him out into the outer darkness; there shall be weeping and gnashing of teeth.

A. Bind ... foot = a mournful image of the hopeless and friendless condition of the lost sinner (comp. Ps. 76:7). The original here gives a word translated **servants,** which differs from the one so translated above (ver. 3, 4, 8, 10); it is sometimes translated *minister* (see 20:26, B.). Doubtless the angels, who *ministered* to the Lord, as related in 4:11, B., are here meant, as in 13:39, 41, 49; the *servants* named in ver. 2–10 then represent *men* who are messengers of the Lord.—**B. Take him away** = to everlasting punishment (25:46; comp. 2 Thess. 1:9); there, the bonds can never be loosed! (Luke 16:26).—**C. Cast him, etc.** (see 8:12, where the same words occur). He who is merely a nominal Christian, and does not live by faith (Gal. 2:20), but practically denies Christ, will perish as miserably as if no Saviour had existed.—**There** = in the outer darkness.

¹⁴ For many are called, but few chosen.

This language resembles that of a proverb, and may,

accordingly, be applied to a variety of cases. The call of the Gospel is addressed to large numbers, who are therefore described as "many"; hence the **called** (Matt. 9:13), as sinners by nature, are all who hear the Gospel, whether they reject the call, as in ver. 5, or become professing Christians, as in Rom. 1:6; 1 Cor. 1:24. Comparatively *few* accept the Gospel in faith and are thus qualified to enter the kingdom. The distinction, therefore, between the called and the chosen consists in the circumstance that the latter are those of the called who are obedient and therefore *approved*. As these accept the call, they are the *cherished,* the *beloved* of God, acceptable to Him. In this sense of *acceptable,* the word *chosen* or *elect* is applied to Christ (Luke 23:35) and to the angels (1 Tim. 5:21). It is then applied, like the corresponding term *saints,* that is, *holy* men (see 27:52, B.), to all true believers, whose faith or humble trust in Christ and His redeeming work renders them acceptable in the eyes of God. As the word in the sense of the *chosen ones,* the *selected,* the *choice ones,* implies the existence of others in whom the desired qualities are not found (comp. the verb in Luke 10:42; 14:7; Acts 6:5), it is here employed, as in 24:22, 24, 31 (where it is translated *elect*), to distinguish believers from unbelievers. It sometimes designates merely Christians by profession as distinct from the people of the world (Col. 3:12; Tit. 1:1). In 1 Peter 1:1, 2, the word "elect" is in the original prefixed to "strangers," whom the apostle does not personally know, but in the judgment of charity assumes to be sincere Christians. So Paul speaks charitably of all the Colossians (3:12), and Peter of Silvanus in 1 Pet. 5:12. The Greek word occurs more than twenty times in the N. T., and is always translated *elect* except here and in Matt. 22:14; Luke 23:35; Rom. 16:13;

1 Peter 2:4, 9; Rev. 17:14. These and other passages in which it is rendered *elect* (e. g. Acts 24:22; Rom. 8:33; 1 Peter 2:6; 2 John 1) prove the sense to be = truly acceptable to God. The chosen or elect are those among the *called* who make their "calling and election sure" (2 Peter 1:10). The corresponding Hebrew word (*bakhir*) originally signifies *to try* or prove, then, to *approve* or *choose,* and is thus applied to those who are acceptable in God's eyes, or the righteous (comp. Isai. 65:9, 15, 22; Ps. 105:43). "They are the *chosen,* who are not only called by the Gospel, but who also diligently hear it, believe in Christ, and manifest their faith in their life and conduct. If thy faith be still weak, pray to God for His Holy Spirit, and doubt not that Christ is thy Redeemer, and that if thou sincerely believe in Him, thou shalt be saved."—Luther.

¹⁵ Then went the Pharisees, and took counsel how they might ensnare him in *his* talk.

A. Then = when their last attempt had been unsuccessful (21:23–27).—**B. Took counsel** = consulted among themselves.—**C. Ensnare** = catch in a snare (Eccl. 9:12). **In his talk** = by an unguarded expression (Luke 20:20). They could not discover a single blemish in His life (John 8:46) which would justify them in seizing Him, but foolishly hoped that His prudence or wisdom might fail.

¹⁶ And they send to him their disciples, with the Herodians, saying, Master, we know that thou art true, and teachest the way of God in truth, and carest not for any one: for thou regardest not the person of men.

A. Their disciples = young men, not personally known to the Lord, and whose treacherous purpose, their teachers hoped, would not be suspected as their own might be. The secret "counsel" or snare which they devised (ver.

15), that is, a temporary coalition with another party, is now developed.—**Saying** = through their disciples, as in 11:3, A.—**B. The Herodians** = Jews who were the political partisans and adherents of Herod Antipas (14:1), who was now in the city (Luke 23:7). They were supporters of the alliance with the Romans and the political opponents of the Pharisees, who detested the Roman government. These hostile parties (as in the case of Herod and Pilate, Luke 23:12, between whom a personal enmity had existed) combine, as on a former occasion (see ann. to 12:14, B.), for the purpose of destroying Him whose holy doctrine condemned the vices of both.—**C. Master** (8:19, B.). The language is respectful, and even complimentary, but uttered by "spies which feigned themselves just men" (Luke 20:20), but were really wicked (ver. 18, below). They vainly hoped to gain the Lord's confidence by flattery. Nicodemus, on the other hand, spoke with sincerity, in John 3:2; comp. ann. to 27:57, C.—**D. Thou art true** = thou art sincere, always speaking thy real sentiments without prevarication or hesitation (comp. the same word **true** in 2 Cor 6:8).—**E. Teachest ... truth** = thou teachest conscientiously and without equivocation or mutilation ("in truth") the way or path of duty (Ps. 27:11), which God has prescribed in His word (see 21:32, B.).—**F. Neither carest, etc.** = thou dost neither show a weak partiality in the case of any favorite, nor manifest a timeserving spirit; thou dost court no man's favor, and fearest no man's frown—**Thou regardest, etc.** = thou esteemest man not according to his external rank and wealth ("person"), but according to the integrity of his character (comp. James 2:1, 3, 9). All the expressions in this verse are designed to reach the vanity and pride of which they ignorantly believed the Lord to be capable, and to instigate Him to utter rash and bold political opinions, which would endanger His life.

¹⁷ Tell us therefore, what thinkest thou? Is it lawful to give tribute unto Cæsar, or not?

A. Tell us = as thou art too conscientious and fearless to conceal the truth at any time.—**Tribute** = personal or poll-tax (see 17:25, C.).—**Cæsar.** This title, originally the name of a branch of the Julian family at Rome, was applied, after the death of Julius Caesar, to his successors, as the usual title of dignity (comp. the Russian title *Czar*). Here, and elsewhere in the N. T., it is equivalent to "the Roman emperor" (see 16:13, B.). The emperor who reigned at that time was Tiberius.—**B. Is it lawful** = consistent with the duty which a Jew owes to Jehovah, his only King, to give, etc. The snare concealed in the question was at once apparent to the Lord. The Jews had at former periods of national humiliation paid tribute to heathen rulers such as Persians and Babylonians. A party of Jewish zealots had, however, been formed before the public appearance of Christ, who, influenced doubtless in part by the numerous calls and extortion of the tax-gatherers, as well as by erroneous views of religious duty, maintained that it was sinful to acknowledge the authority of the heathen emperors of Rome by the payment of any tax or tribute; they appealed to passages like Deut. 17:15, which, however, really referred to times in which a choice between a heathen and a Jewish ruler was possible. The party was apparently crushed during the reign of the Emperor Augustus, when Judas of Galilee, mentioned by Gamaliel in Acts 5:37, was destroyed (Josephus, Antiq. 18, ch. 1). The great principle of this party was, however, secretly embraced by increasing numbers of the Jews and sustained by the Pharisees, until it ultimately led to the last Jewish war and the complete overthrow of the Jewish State by the Romans. If, then, the Lord had maintained the propriety of paying this unpopular tax, the Pharisees were prepared to stigmatize Him as a traitor to His nation and His God. If, on the other hand, He expressed His disapprobation of the tax, while that opinion would have been popular, it would have authorized the Herodians who were present (ver. 16, B.) in arresting Him on the spot as a rebel who threatened to overthrow the government (see Luke 20:20; 23:2). At the same time the Lord could not refuse to give a positive answer in any form without becoming suspected at once by all parties.

[18] But Jesus perceived their wickedness, and said, Why tempt ye me, ye hypocrites?

A. Their wickedness = hypocrisy (Mark), craftiness (Luke); as He knew what "was in man" (John 3:25), He saw that neither patriotism nor religion prompted the question, but solely a malevolent desire to endanger His life.—**B. Why tempt** = why do ye yield to the folly and malice of your hearts, by laying this snare for Me. For **tempt**, see 4:1, D.; the word here represents men as agents of the great Tempter.—**C. Ye hypocrites** = who pretend to be just and conscientious men (Luke 20:20); for **hypocrites**, see 6:2, D. The Lord is indeed "true," as these men said (ver. 16), when He exposed the wickedness of their purpose.

[19] Show me the tribute money. And they brought unto him a penny.

A. Show ... money = I will answer you at once; produce the tribute money = one of the Roman coins in which, as a legal tender, you always pay the tribute. The sense is: You have your answer marked on every coin which you handle in your secular business; let us examine one.—**B. Penny** = a denarius (see 17:24, B.). The obverse of this imperial Roman coin presented the portrait of the reigning emperor; the other side, the reverse, contained the inscription or name and title of the person whose image appeared on the obverse. If there were room on the former for the inscription, etc., it exhibited various symbols of cities, etc.

[20] And he saith unto them, Whose is this image and superscription?

The coin in the Lord's hand exhibited the head of the Roman emperor together with his name and title; the latter constituted the **superscription** or inscription.

[21] They say unto him, Cæsar's. Then saith he unto them, Render therefore unto Cæsar the things that are Cæsar's; and unto God the things that are God's.

A. Cæsar's = the portrait, name and title of the Emperor Tiberius.—**B. Then saith he, etc.** The Lord intends to furnish an answer which, without fulfilling the malicious design of those who question Him, may properly guide the conduct of the good citizen and the devout worshipper of God. The actual circulation of the Roman, that is, heathen money, among the Jews, of which the coin now produced was the indisputable evidence, indicated the true posture of Jewish affairs. The nation had been independent and free when it obeyed God; its subjection to the pagan Romans, as formerly to the Babylonians, was an evidence that they had sinned, and that God had punished them by the loss of their national independence (see 2 Chron. 12:8; Ezra 9:7; Neh. 9:27, 30). The common use of Roman coins was a daily admonition of their guilt; hence their question was equivalent to another: Is it lawful for us to endure the divine punishment of our sins, or not? Paul develops fully the duties of a citizen, when in Rom., ch. 13, he requires all Christians to respect the established government which Divine Providence (John 19:11) has sanctioned for the time (see also 1 Peter 2:13–17; 1 Tim. 2:1, 2). Questions referring to the civil law or to political difficulties the Saviour refrained from discussing (Luke 12:14), except in so far as they were connected with the paramount duties which men owe at all times to God. The sense of the words of the Lord then is: Render = pay (as the same word is translated in 5:26; 18:28) to the Roman emperor that which is his own; by your own confession and by the use of this coin, you acknowledge his authority over you; act towards him with a sense of justice, and observe the duties of honest men. But—adds the Lord—**render unto God the things that are God's.** The same Greek expression here translated, *things that are God's,* occurs in 16:23 and in Luke 2:49; in the latter it may be rendered: I must be in the things of My Father. The Lord does not here refer exclusively to the tribute money mentioned in 17:24, B., but doubtless conveys the following lesson: Your present relations to the Roman government, and, indeed, your duties as citizens, do not exempt you from the performance of your religious duties. Whether you be bond or free, you may be enabled, and you are solemnly bound, to fear, love and obey God (comp. 1 Cor. 7:20–22). Therefore, while you are controlled by the power of the Romans, in consequence of your sins, you are the more impressively urged to fulfil the duties of repentance and faith which are *God's things.* "*God's things* are the following: Love to God and man, faith in Christ, and devout obedience to the Gospel.... But what shall we do, if Cæsar command us to give God's things to him, that is, if the government oppresses the conscience? Then, it is our duty to endure persecution, but in all cases 'to obey God rather than men' (Acts 5:29)."—Luther.

²² And when they heard it, they marvelled, and left him, and went their way.

A. They marvelled = wondered (8:10, A.) at the divine wisdom which had furnished a direct answer that defeated all their own cunning and malice.—**B. Left him, etc.** = humiliated by their repeated defeats, and discouraged, but not filled with a salutary humility and a sense of their iniquity.

²³ On that day there came to him Sadducees, which say that there is no resurrection: and they asked him,

A. Sadducees. These persons, who belonged to a sect which was hostile to that of the Pharisees (rejecting all their traditions, etc.), evidently intended to perplex the Lord and expose Him to derision. On this remarkable day ("the same day") all the powers of darkness, represented by Herodians, Pharisees and Sadducees, make powerful efforts by an apparently organized combination to crush the Lord.—**B. Which say, etc.** As the Sadducees appear to have believed that the soul could not exist without the body (Josephus, Antiq. 18, 1, 4; War, 2, 8, 14), they denied the immortality of the soul, beside, the existence of spirits in general, and of angels also (Acts 23:8); this infidel opinion, which implied the extinction of the soul when separated from the body, necessarily led to the denial of the doctrine that the decayed bodies of the dead, who, according to their system, no longer existed in any form, would be raised from their graves.

²⁴ Saying, Master, Moses said, If a man die, having no children, his brother shall marry his wife, and raise up seed unto his brother.

The allusion is to Deut. 25:5, ff., where the Law of the Levirate (see 1:2, A.) is recorded. This law referred only to the case of a man who died "without issue" = without a son or daughter of his own (Numb. 27:8) to whom the inheritance could pass in regular order. It sanctioned a very ancient practice, of which an illustration occurs in Gen. 38:8. The first-born of a Jew and his brother's widow was enrolled in the family records as the seed or son of the deceased brother. The anxiety of the Jews to preserve every branch of a family from extinction, and to prevent the real estate originally belonging to a tribe from passing to another branch or tribe, led to the adoption of the principle of this law.

²⁵⁻²⁷ Now there were with us seven brethren: and the first married and deceased, and having no seed left his wife unto his brother;—In like manner the second also, and the third, unto the seventh.—And after them all the woman died.

A. Now there were, etc. The case which the Sadducees here describe, if not probable, was at least possible, although it is not now known as one that ever really occurred. Their purpose simply is to ridicule the more pointedly the whole doctrine of the resurrection (Acts 26:8), and the future existence of men, inasmuch as the case of a woman who had married only two brothers successively would have as effectually illustrated the point in question. The only means at their disposal for casting reproach on a scriptural doctrine consisted in appending to it unnatural and foolish opinions; these inferences, which the Lord distinctly exposes, were deduced from the Pharisaic doctrine that marriage ties would be renewed in the other world—a doctrine for which no evidence whatever existed.—**B. The woman died also** = without leaving a son or daughter, whose father might (as the Sadducees pretended to reason) claim her as his wife, in such a case, with a better right than the other six brothers, granting, as the Sadducees did, for the sake of argument, that all would rise from the dead.

28 In the resurrection therefore whose wife shall she be of the seven? for they all had her.

The Sadducees say: As no children were left by any one of the brothers, and as your doctrine of the resurrection must, further, imply that all the circumstances of this present material world (marriage, houses, private property, etc.) will be repeated in the future world,—will there not (they continue to ask) be a difficulty experienced in deciding with whom, if they all really live again, she shall live through all eternity? They really mean: Moses never could have believed in a resurrection of the dead, when he committed his laws to writing. Notwithstanding the profanity and impiety of these men, the Lord, for the sake of others who desire to learn, explains the subject fully, with His usual holy and calm dignity, and with divine and unerring wisdom.

29 But Jesus answered and said unto them, Ye do err, not knowing the scriptures, nor the power of God.

A. Ye do err, lit. *ye are led astray, deceived* (as in John 7:47; Tit. 3:3) by your presumptuous ignorance and by the spirit of infidelity. As the Scriptures themselves are unerring and true, the nearer we approach to Scripture doctrine, the more do we ourselves become free from error.—**B. Not ... Scriptures.** The Sadducees knew indeed the letter of the word of God, such as the historical events, laws, etc., which it set forth, but they did not "spiritually discern" (1 Cor. 2:14) its true sense and meaning. **To know,** often signifies in Scripture to *understand* (26:70; Mark 4:13; John 20:9; 1 Cor. 14:11, Jude, ver. 10). The **Scriptures** of the O. T., which the Lord here means, indicated the continued existence of the soul after the death of the body (for instance, Gen. 25:8; 2 Sam. 12:23; Isai. 14:9, 10), and also the resurrection of the body (for instance, Isai. 26:19; Ezek. ch. 37; Dan. 12:2.).—**C. Nor the power of God** = which can accomplish all things (Luke 1:37), as your father Abraham believed (Rom. 4:16, 17; Hebr. 11:19); *that* power can preserve the soul alive and restore the body even after it has turned to dust; it can establish human beings in a new condition of life and enjoyment, without repeating, according to your narrow and material views, all the modes, forms and peculiarities of this present material world.

[30] For in the resurrection they neither marry, nor are given in marriage, but are as angels in heaven.

All human beings that have ever lived and that now live are the descendants of the first human pair (Gen. 1:27, 28; 3:20; Acts 17:26; Rom. 5:12, ff.). The angels, on the other hand, were individually created in a fully developed form, and the relations of parents and children do not apply to them. Hence, even as other earthly transactions (buying, selling and getting gain, James 4:13, and losses by death) will not be repeated in the eternal world, which will materially differ from the present, so also "eating and drinking, marrying and giving in marriage" (24:38), births and deaths, are all peculiarities belonging only to man's life in this world. While the lost will be as "the devil and his angels" (25:41), the redeemed in heaven will be as God's angels who are immortal spirits (Ps. 104:4; Hebr. 1:7); their bodies, when raised from the grave, will be "spiritual bodies" (see 1 Cor. 15:42–44): new families will not be constituted, "neither can they die any more" (Luke 20:36). Even now already in Christ there is "neither male nor female" (Gal. 3:28). The whole tenor of the Scriptures, which the Sadducees did not "know," indicates that bodily peculiarities which are adapted specially or exclusively to this present world, will pass away with it. Divine wisdom has withheld a revelation of the precise condition of the risen bodies of the redeemed; "it doth not yet appear what we shall be" (1 John 3:2).

[31] But as touching the resurrection of the dead, have ye not read that which was spoken unto you by God, saying,

A. Touching = with respect to, concerning, as in 18:19, B. In these words the Lord furnishes to the Sadducees a special illustration of their ignorance of the true meaning of the Scriptures, and of the fact that former generations of men continue to exist.—**B. Spoken, etc.** The words quoted, although spoken to Moses at a very remote period, are, says the Saviour, "spoken unto you." All things in the Scriptures are "written for our admonition" (1 Cor. 10:11, and "are profitable for doctrine, etc." (2 Tim. 3:16).

[32] I am the God of Abraham, and the God of Isaac, and the God of Jacob? God is not *the God* of the dead, but of the living.

The words occur thrice in Exod. 3:6–16; there they constitute emphatically the Divine Name, in connection with the other name: "I am that I am" = Jehovah (Exod. 6:3). This sacred Name indicates the Eternity and Self-existence of God, and involves the sense of the words: "He who is, and who was, and who is to come" (Rev. 1:4). The Saviour here teaches that God, who means all that He says, speaks to Moses of Abraham, Isaac and Jacob, more than three centuries after Abraham's death, not as of ancestors who had ceased to live and were annihilated, but as of those whose existence was uninterruptedly maintained. He implies that they *live* to Him (Luke 20:38). Now if they were "dead" in the sense of the Sadducees, that is, if their souls were extinct, then God, who, in the days of Moses, called Himself their God, really called Himself the God of *nothing,* since, if they be not "living" = existing now, they have ceased to be, and are absolutely *nothing.* If God could not, or would not preserve them from annihilation, how could He still be their God? How could God's blessing be "forever" (1 Chron. 17:27), if death have power to destroy it? Could the infinitely holy and true God utter such unmeaning words? The sense of His words, as the Saviour reasons, must necessarily be the following:—I, the eternal God, created Abraham, Isaac and Jacob; their bodies have been long ago converted into dust, and the completeness of their nature, the union of the body and the soul (Gen. 2:7), is thus interrupted; but they shall be called from their graves; their souls, which now live, shall be reunited with their bodies, and they shall exist in their complete nature forever = I continue forever to be the God of their love and adoration. The Saviour does not refer to the passages in the prophets respecting the resurrection of the dead (mentioned above, ver. 29, B.), as the Sadducees, without openly rejecting the prophetic writings, were unwilling to believe doctrines which were not found in the writings of Moses; to the latter He accordingly here confines Himself, and by this procedure silenced them effectually (ver. 34). Even as the divinely inspired Epistle to the Hebrews explains many portions of the O. T. (for instance, ch. 7; ch. 9:8), so here, too, the true meaning of the divine address to Moses is unerringly revealed to man by the divine wisdom of Christ.

³³ And when the multitudes heard it, they were astonished at his teaching.

Astonished = at such unexpected disclosures of the deep meaning of the Scriptures. The speechlessness of the Sadducees convinced even those hearers who could not fully comprehend the subject, that the Lord's explanation was unanswerable and triumphant.

³⁴ But the Pharisees, when they heard that he had put the Sadducees to silence, gathered themselves together.

The Pharisees, on ascertaining that every effort to injure the Lord by extorting indiscreet words from Him had failed, had retired (ver. 22) and again consulted together for the purpose of devising new snares. The term here translated **together** (as also in Luke 17:35; Acts 3:1), and the circumstance that they are afterwards (ver. 41) found standing in a group near Christ, appear to indicate that, after leaving Him, the tidings that the Sadducees had also been silenced, so powerfully aroused their curiosity or their party feelings or their hope of obtaining new allies, that they at once returned to the spot.

³⁵ And one of them, a lawyer, asked him a question, tempting him.

A. One of them = of the Pharisees; **a lawyer** = a man versed in the Mosaic Law. This man, like the Pharisee Nicodemus (John 3:1; 19:39), appears from Mark 12:28, 34, to have regarded the Saviour without the usual malevolence of his sect. Another lawyer, mentioned in Luke 10:25, 29, exhibits far more of the self-righteousness of his class.—**B. Tempting him.** The original word (occurring above, ver. 18, in an unfavorable sense) is sometimes used, like a corresponding Hebrew term, as simply equivalent to *prove* (John 6:6), or *try* (Rev. 2:2), in cases in which, without hostile purposes, the knowledge, wisdom or skill of any one is to be ascertained by some test (comp. 1 Kings 10:1, and see 4:1, D.). Such appears, from the Lord's words in Mark 12:34, to have been the purpose of this man. He accordingly proposes, as a trial of the Saviour's knowledge of the Scriptures, a question which the Jewish teachers answered variously in their "strivings about the law" (Tit. 3:9), by respectively specifying the commandments concerning circumcision, or the sacrifices, or the Sabbath, etc.

36 Master, which is the great commandment in the law?

(See 5:19, A.).—**The great** = emphatically, the leading duty of man, as taught in the Law. The meaning of the question is: Among all the duties which God has commanded us to perform, which one is the most important = most worthy of our attention?

37 And he said unto him, Thou shalt love the Lord thy God with all thy heart, and with all thy soul, and with all thy mind.

The Lord here (ver. 37–40) assigns all our duties to the two classes which appear in the Decalogue: first, duties to God; secondly, duties to our fellow-men; a third class sometimes mentioned, that is, duties to ourselves, really contains those which are already embraced in the two former. The words quoted occur in Deut. 6:5, and comp. 2 Kings 23:25. The same passage is quoted also in Luke 10:27, where, as well as in Mark 12:30 and 33, slight verbal variations ("strength," "understanding") occur; the accumulation of the words ("heart," "soul," etc.), which indicates that they are to be taken as a whole rather than in their individual sense respectively, implies that love to God (see Exod. 20:6) must control the whole moral nature of man, so that his affections, understanding, conscience and will in their union shall regard Him as the Sovereign Good. The Lord's answer to the question is, in one word—Love!

³⁸ This is the great and first commandment.

The fulfilment of this great duty secures the fulfilment, from the purest motives and in the most acceptable manner, of every duty which man owes to God. It is this same principle which both explains the ascription of the title of *Father* to God, and which dictates the words of the Lord's Prayer: "Our Father, etc."

³⁹ And a second like *unto it* is this, Thou shalt love thy neighbour as thyself.

A. The second = if you next ask concerning your obligations towards your fellow-men, as you well may, since the test of a professed love to God is connected with them (1 John 4:20).—**B. Like unto it** = in spirit, authority and comprehensiveness.—**C. Thou shalt, etc.** The words, which occur in Lev. 19:18, were twice before mentioned by the Lord (see 5:43, C.; 19:18, 19, B., and comp. 25:35, 36).

⁴⁰ On these two commandments hangeth the whole law, and the prophets.

A. On these two = those who sincerely love God and man will be prompted by their love to fulfil every duty in every situation of life; such is the explanation of the "royal law" (James 2:8) given by Paul in Rom. 13:8–10; Gal. 5:14; "therefore love is the fulfiling of the law."—**B. Hangeth** = is *suspended, supported by,* as, for instance, a door by its hinges. Even as all the gracious purposes of God in granting a divine revelation are counteracted by the want of love, so, too, it is love alone that will fulfil the spirit as well as the letter of the law. True religion therefore consists not in the Pharisaic measuring, weighing and counting of outward duties (23:23), but in a course of life which is strictly guided by religious *principle*—the concurrent action of the understanding and the heart.—**C. The law and the prophets** = the inspired writings, the Word of God (see 5:17, C.). Love is the soul of all true religion. According to Mark 12:32–34, the lawyer now "answered discreetly" (= intelligently), confessed the truth and power of the Lord's words, and referred to confirmatory scriptural passages, such as 1 Sam. 15:22; Ps. 40:8; Micah 6:6–8.

[41] Now while the Pharisees were gathered together, Jesus asked them a question,

Although the Pharisees (see above, ann. to ver. 34) had manifested the utmost malice, the Lord makes an additional effort to humble their hearts and conduct them to penitence and to faith in His divine character and mission. He demonstrates here their utter ignorance of the true meaning of the Scriptures, which was betrayed by their indistinct views of the nature of the Messiah. The conversation occurs in one of the courts of the temple (Mark 12:35).

[42] Saying, What think ye of the Christ? whose son is he? They say unto him, *The son* of David.

What think, etc. = what is your doctrine respecting the promised Messiah? What is His true genealogy? **The Christ.** The Pharisees and scribes (Mark 12:35) give the usual reply (see above, 1:1, C.). The answer here given does not however convey the whole truth, as the Pharisees did not imply the divine nature of the Messiah. "Why does Christ propose this question here? He had just said: Thou shalt love, etc. But when the Law has given thee a knowledge of sin (Rom. 3:20), thou findest that thou canst not so love God, and thou sayest mournfully: I cannot love Thee, O God, as I should love Thee. Then Christ says: 'Come to Me; believe in Me.' Now when thou believest in Christ, He pours out abundantly His Holy Spirit on thee, and thou art made a new creature; *now* thou lovest Christ. Dost thou not see that thou canst not love God till thou *knowest* Christ? Therefore He proceeds here to show thee who He is."—Luther.

⁴³ He saith unto them, How then doth David in the spirit call him Lord, saying,

The point which the Lord's hearers, whom He here questions, could not explain may be thus set forth:—It is obvious that no man ever speaks of any one of his descendants who may appear in the world many centuries after his own death, as being his **Lord** = his superior, his sovereign. Now, proceeds the Lord, Psalm ex. was confessedly written by King David at a time when a divine revelation was made to him (—**in the Spirit** = by the direct inspiration of the Holy Ghost, 2 Sam. 23:2; Mark 12:36, and comp. Luke 2:27; Acts 1:16; 1 Cor. 12:3; 2 Peter 1:21; Rev. 1:10). Further, the Divine Spirit, in that Psalm, as ye Jews all know, refers to the Messiah's final and glorious victory (see Acts 2:34; 1 Cor. 15:25; Hebr. 10:13). But, continues Christ, David, His remote ancestor, and a mighty and independent monarch himself, who acknowledged no Lord but God, nevertheless in the first verse of Psalm 110 styles his descendant, the Messiah, his **Lord** = king, thereby confessing that his descendant is really his master and sovereign. But if the Messiah did not already exist, how do you explain this apparently unmeaning language, that a royal ancestor should acknowledge one of his distant descendants as his superior, nay, employ obviously the language of adoration? For David applied the term "Lord" to one who does not sit *at God's feet* as an inferior, but *at His side* as one co-equal in glory (Isai. 42:8). To David himself the true explanation was given (2 Sam. 7:12, 13; Ps. 89:3, 4; 132:11). The king was usually addressed in the age of David by the title "my lord" (1 Sam. 16:16; 22:12; 2 Sam. 2:5; 1 Kings 1:13, 17, 31).

[44] The Lord said unto my Lord, Sit thou on my right hand, till I put thine enemies underneath thy feet.

A. The ... Lord, lit. according to the Hebrew: (This is) the declaration of Jehovah to my Lord (= my king), namely, Sit, etc.—**B. Sit ... hand.** It was esteemed a high privilege when the subject of an oriental king was permitted to *stand* (or be stationed) at his right hand (Ps. 45:9); no higher honor could be bestowed than that which consisted in the privilege of *sitting* at his right hand (1 Kings 2:19; see above, 20:20, B.), inasmuch as it also communicated vast power to the favored individual, and, in the case of the king's son, imparted royal power (Exod. 11:5; 1 Kings 1:13, 17). The whole constitutes an image (feeble, indeed, as all human things are only feeble images and "patterns" (Hebr. 9:23, of heavenly things) of the power and glory of the Son of God (comp. 26:64, C.). Christ's seat at the Father's right hand, which is so often mentioned in the Scriptures (Mark 14:62; Rom. 8:34; Eph. 1:20; Col. 3:1), is an image of His participation in the divine power and omnipresence, and, generally, of His possession of all the attributes of God (see 19:28, D.).—**C. Till I, etc.** The act which is illustrated in a special case in Josh. 10:24, and to which these words seem to allude, represented the complete subjugation of a dangerous enemy; the sense therefore here is, that all the enemies of the Messiah and His kingdom shall ultimately be completely overcome (1 Cor. 15:25)—**Till** = till Thy mediatorial glory is universally acknowledged by all, after their defeat (see Rev. 11:15, and 1 Cor. 15:24, 25).

⁴⁵ If David then calleth him Lord, how is he his son?

The difficult point mentioned above (ann. to ver. 43), is here distinctly presented = in what sense could David, the independent monarch, humbly acknowledge the superiority of one of his own descendants, and represent that descendant as participating in the divine glory of Jehovah Himself? The same mysterious divine conversation which is shadowed forth, for instance, in Gen. 1:26; 3:22; 11:7), ("let us"), is here resumed. Who *is* David's **Lord** to whom Jehovah speaks? No answer is here given by the Pharisees, but it lay already in Ps. 2:7, and was given audibly at the Redeemer's Baptism (see 3:17). Christ is David's son "according to the flesh" (Rom. 1:3, 4) = in His human nature (1:1), but the Son of God in His divine nature (John 1:1, 14; see above, 8:29, C.).

⁴⁶ And no one was able to answer him a word, neither durst any *man* from that day forth ask him any more *questions*.

The repeated failures of the Lord's enemies "to ensnare him in his talk" (ver. 15) prevented any further exhibition of their hostility in this form—**any more questions** = proceeding from unholy motives.

8

Matthew 23

¹ Then spake Jesus to the multitudes, and to his disciples.

Then = turning to the people after His enemies had ceased to address captious questions to Him. The discourse in this chapter is the last of the Lord's public addresses; those that follow were addressed to the disciples alone. Various lessons and warnings which the Lord had delivered on former occasions (Luke, ch. 11 and ch. 13) are here repeated with additional remarks. The Lord, whose parting words are now addressed to the people, unveils for the last time all the vices of the Pharisees and scribes. The severity with which He speaks is occasioned by the fact that while undisguised vice often repels, vice disguised in the garb of religion is on that account the more plausible and the more dangerous to the unwary; consequently, it deserves even a more pointed rebuke. At the same time, the Lord does not indicate individuals, but is describing the general spirit and tendency of the Pharisaic sect.

² Saying, The scribes and the Pharisees sit on Moses' seat:

A. **Sit** = have seated themselves. They had acquired an official rank and authority in the course of time as public teachers of religion. Such an office was essentially necessary for obvious reasons, and had originally been assigned by Moses to the priests, the sons of Levi through Aaron (Lev. 10:11; Deut. 17:9; 31:9; 33:10; 2 Chron. 19:8; Neh. 8:4, 9; Mal. 2:7) After the Babylonian Captivity, when teachers of the law who belonged to other tribes rose to eminence, and synagogues were established, the priests appear to have receded, and the scribes, who were originally transcribers of the law or interpreters (Neh. 8:8), gradually formed a recognized class, and became the official teachers of religion. Their authority had become firmly established during the century which preceded the birth of Christ. The claims of the office itself are here fully recognized by the Lord, independently of the personal character of those who were invested with it.—B. **Moses' seat.** "Moses sat to judge the people" (Exod. 18:13), and through him the law was given. When these persons officially read and interpreted the laws of Moses, the Lord figuratively describes them as occupying the "seat of Moses." "But when they began to teach doctrines at variance with the spirit of the law, whatever their pretensions might be, they no longer sat in *Moses seat*. So, too, when the Pope tells me to earn my salvation by my works, and when he makes no account of the merits of Christ, he certainly does not sit in St. Peter's chair."—Luther.

³ All things therefore whatsoever they bid you, these do and observe: but do not ye after their works; for they say, and do not.

A. **All things therefore ... do.** The word *therefore* can refer to no other circumstance than the high authority possessed by the law, as coming from Moses, the inspired teacher. The sense is: Do all that Moses commands: give heed to his own words as these are publicly read to you. The word **all** evidently means *all things consistent with God's word,* as in Col. 3:22, and does not include commands or religious observances which flow from an exclusively Pharisaic and corrupt source, and which make the law "of none effect" (15:6); against such lessons the warning is here emphatically directed. The Bereans, who applied the Scriptures as a sure test of the truth, are mentioned in Acts 17:11 as a model for Christians.—**B. But do ... works** = do not act in accordance with their special precepts; do not make it a matter of conscience to observe the religious duties which are devised and required by them as meritorious "works." The **works** which the traditions of the Pharisees required were not enjoined by the law, and, in reality, constituted a mere mechanical religion—a religion of cold and heartless formality, such as the cases mentioned in 15:1–6, and the extra fasts, public distribution of alms, conspicuousness in the act of praying, and similar points which are specified below, for instance, in ver. 23. The "works" accordingly, here mentioned, do not mean the *conduct* of the men, which to the public eye appeared to be eminently correct and pure, but in general their *motives* and their doctrines, for which see 16:12, B.—**C. For ... not** = for, while they pretend that the higher sanctity derived from such practices is necessary to all, they themselves in reality forbear to follow after true holiness: they do not keep even the laws which Moses has set forth, but totally neglect them (ver. 23, below; comp. Rom. 2:17–24).

4 Yea, they bind heavy burdens and grievous to be borne,

and lay them on men's shoulders; but they themselves will not move them with their finger.

A. For ... shoulders (see 11:28, B.). The Lord, who proceeds to furnish the grounds of the foregoing prohibition, compares the many minute specifications of men's religious duties, as enumerated by Pharisaic hypocrisy, to a very heavy weight, using a word which describes a bundle composed of pieces of wood and intended for fuel, under which the carrier staggers, or the cargo of a vessel (Acts 27:10).—**Grievous to be borne** = difficult to carry, oppressive; the sense is, that they perplex the consciences of men by wickedly imposing duties which God never prescribed. Thus they convert the service of God, which should be a source of joy to a grateful heart, into a laborious and unsatisfactory mechanical employment. On the other hand, "*His* commandments are not grievous (lit. *heavy*)" (1 John 5:3), since a living faith in the heart produces a love to God so strong and so deep, that the keeping of His commandments (John 14:15) is gratefully acknowledged to be an honor, a privilege and a blessing (comp. Matt. 11:30, and see Ps. 119).—**B. But they, etc.** = they, on the contrary, knowing the emptiness and folly of their pretended religious acts, are never disturbed by any reproaches of conscience for not observing their own precepts in their private and domestic life; further, they scorn the "weightier matters of the law" (ver. 23), the true duties of religion, and thus they really emancipate themselves from every religious obligation (ver. 5, A., below), like the sluggard to whom the act even of bending one of his fingers is a labor which he shuns.—**Not move ... finger** = a proverbial phrase indicating the entire absence of interest and effort (comp. Rom. 2:17–23).

⁵ But all their works they do for to be seen of men: for they make broad their phylacteries, and enlarge the borders *of their garments.*

A. But ... men (see 6:1, 2, 5, 16, which passages amply illustrate the present words). The Lord evidently means that the religion of the Pharisees was altogether hollow and delusive, and that they sought, not the divine approbation, but exclusively human applause and admiration; the inference seems authorized that they did not pray, give alms, or perform any "good work" from religious principle, or when admiring spectators were not present. "Closet prayer" had no attractions for them.—**B. Phylacteries** = guards, memorials, means of observing the law. These were prayer-fillets or strips of parchment enclosed in leather, on which certain portions of the law were written, as, Exod. 13:3–10; ver. 11–16; Deut. 6:4–9; 11:13–21. In consequence of a literal interpretation of Exod. 13:9, 16; Deut. 6:8; 11:18 (where, as in Prov. 3:3; 6:21; 7:3, a constant and earnest attention to the divine will is figuratively described), one of these articles was attached to the forehead, and another to the left arm next to the heart on the inside, between the elbow and shoulder; both were worn during the act of prayer. The practice, which is still observed by the Jews, probably originated after the Babylonian Captivity; it encouraged the hypocritical spirit of the Pharisees, and was, besides, connected, in the course of time, with many superstitious opinions, according to which these articles were regarded as amulets or charms, protecting against external injuries, evil spirits, etc.—**C. Enlarge the borders, etc.** (see 9:20, C.). In both of the cases here mentioned, the increased size was intended to attract public attention, and to express emphatically the piety of the wearers. The Pharisees measured religion by inches! Can we wonder that the Lord solemnly exclaims in this chapter: "Woe unto you, Pharisees!"?

⁶ And love the chief place at feasts, and the chief seats in the synagogues.

A. Chief ... feasts, lit. *the first place of reclining* (at the table), or post of honor (comp. Luke 14:7, ff., and see ann. to 8:11, D.).—**B. Chief seats,** lit. *first seats* (Luke 11:43; 20:46), elevated and conspicuous, and considered more honorable than the others (comp. James 2:3). The ambition which covets such a petty distinction is no mark of a true Christian, and ought not to be entertained by him.

⁷ And the salutations in the market-places, and to be called of men, Rabbi.

A. Market-places (11:16, B.); the large numbers there assembled furnished the vain Pharisees with spectators of the honorable **salutations** which they received.—**B. Rabbi.** The Hebrew word Rab = *much, great,* was specially employed as a title of office, and is translated *captain* (2 Kings 25:8), *officer* (Esth. 1:8), *master* (Dan. 1:3; see also Matt. 2:1, E.). It was afterwards applied to the Jewish teachers of the law as a term of respect, in the sense of *master, teacher.* When such a teacher was addressed with special reverence, as in the case of Christ (Matt. 26:25; John 1:38), he was styled *Rabbi = my* master. The latter form is retained by the modern Jews, *Rabbi, Rabbins.* During the age preceding the appearance of Christ, and particularly at the time when He commenced to teach, every Jew who professed to be a teacher of the law eagerly sought after such titles of honor as *rab, rabbi,* and the repetition of the latter was deemed an additional mark of honor. The nearly equivalent terms Rabban and Rabboni (the latter in John 20:16, as a Galilean form) were regarded as still more emphatically honorable terms of address. This puerile desire for unsubstantial honors on the part of the Jewish teachers really seemed to indicate their own consciousness that they deserved none which were real.

⁸⁻¹⁰ But be not ye called Rabbi: for one is your teacher, and all ye are brethren. And call no man your father on the earth: for one is your Father, which is in heaven. Neither be ye called master: for one is your Master, *even* the Christ.

As in ver. 6, the Lord by no means forbids any one to occupy prominent places, but only rebukes the vanity or pride which covets the honor, so, too, a distinction is here made between the mere acceptance of titles and a puerile and corrupt desire for them. The Lord's meaning in uttering these prohibitions may be gathered from the following considerations: Official titles, descriptive of the duties of an office, and appellations which respect and affection are prompted to bestow (8:19, B.) are abundantly sanctioned, within proper limits, by the N. T. Thus, the term *teacher* ("Master" in John 1:38) is the equivalent of *Rabbi*, and corresponds to the original word translated in ver. 8 and 10 **master** (lit. leader, guide); so the title *teacher* is adopted in Acts 13:1; 1 Cor. 12:28; Eph. 4:11. The Lord Himself recognizes the title in John 3:10 as belonging to Nicodemus (in the original emphatically: *the* master). The term **father,** as a respectful appellation, occurs already in the O. T. (2 Kings 2:12; 6:21; 13:14). Paul regards himself as the spiritual *father* of those whom he was the means of conducting to Christ (1 Cor. 4:15; Gal. 4:19; 1 Tim. 1:2; Philem. ver. 10), and repeatedly claims the highest titles known in the Church (1 Tim. 2:7; 2 Tim. 1:11). John addresses certain believers as "fathers" (1 John 2:13, 14). The present words are evidently directed against that unholy spirit of party which elevates human teachers to an equality with Christ, of which a striking illustration is given in 1 Cor. 1:12. The sense is the following:—Yield implicit faith, resign your judgment and conscience completely to no human teacher, as if he were perfect and infallible; such homage belongs to *One* alone, who is unerring (Col. 2:3); He alone is your **master** (lit. leader, guide). Obey the commands of no human being ("on earth") with the feeling that his power, or wisdom, or love can never fail; such are the divine attributes of your Father in heaven alone. (See John 6:45; 1 Thess. 4:9.)—**All ye are brethren** = ye are all equals, the children of one Father; hence, let no one of you assume "dominion over the faith" of others (2 Cor. 1:24); there shall be no privileged class in the Christian Church. Do not, then, imitate the Pharisees, nor covet empty titles of honor, when such a course has the effect of substituting your authority and opinions in the place of the divine authority and wisdom. Mere titles applied by respect and affection are not only harmless but appropriate, when the divine honor is neither intentionally nor virtually impaired. Hence Luke addresses Theophilus by the title "most excellent" (Luke 1:3), and Paul applies the same to Festus (Acts 26:25, "most noble"). The more modern title of *Doctor* (which is merely the Latin word for *teacher*) of Medicine, Divinity or Laws simply indicates one who has studied a particular science so diligently that he has become qualified to be a *teacher* of it, either by his example in the regular practice of his profession, or by direct instructions as a professor.

[11] But he that is greatest among you shall be your servant.

The Lord's purpose to extinguish vanity and pride in His disciples leads Him to remind them of similar lessons which He had already inculcated (see above, 20:26, B., and 18:4, B.).

¹² And whosoever shall exalt himself shall be humbled; and whosoever shall humble himself shall be exalted.

Luke describes two additional cases (14:11; 18:14), in which the Lord uttered the same impressive words, and which appear to allude to Ezek. 21:26; in the former case (14:7–11), the parable or illustration employed by the Lord explains the sense at once; even as the foolish love of distinction is there described as succeeded by shame and mortification, so, in a spiritual sense, God will disappoint and abase the proud, while He "giveth grace unto the humble" (James 4:6; 1 Pet. 5:5, and comp. Isai. 57:15; 66:2; Job 22:29; Luke 1:51, 52).

¹³ But woe unto you, scribes and Pharisees, hypocrites! because ye shut the kingdom of heaven against men: for ye enter not in yourselves, neither suffer ye them that are entering in to enter.

A. Woe (see 11:21, A.). The frequent repetition of this word in the present direct address to the scribes and Pharisees indicates the awful doom which their persistent iniquity was bringing upon them (comp. 2 Peter 2:3, ff., and see below, 24:51).—**Hypocrites,** 6:2, D.—**B. Because ye, etc.** The Lord compares the kingdom of grace which He came to establish to a palace or temple; the "key" (Luke 11:52) is a saving knowledge of His Person and work (John 17:3; Luke 1:77). The twofold impiety of the Pharisees, which conducts them to perdition ("woe"), consists in their own unbelief and rejection of the Saviour, and in their unceasing efforts to deter others who are inclined to receive Christ ("are entering") from believing in Him and following Him, as in John 9:24; 1 Thess. 2:16.—**Against men,** lit. *before* men = when it is at hand, and already in their presence.

¹⁵ Woe unto you, scribes and Pharisees, hypocrites! for ye compass sea and land to make one proselyte; and when he is become so, ye make him twofold more the son of hell than yourselves.

A. Compass = *travel about,* go up and down, as in 4:23; Acts 13:11.—**B. Sea and land** = every spot where you hope to find one—a proverbial expression.—**C. Proselyte.** The word (signifying any one that has *come up to, approached*) occurs also Acts 2:10; 6:5; 13:43, and designated originally a convert from paganism to Judaism. A proselyte is sometimes called "one that fears God, devout" (Acts 13:16, 50); the name, as in the case of Cornelius (Acts 10:2), describes heathen who had learned to believe that Jehovah alone was God. Those who renounced idolatry and acknowledged the God of Abraham, without submitting to circumcision, were termed "proselytes of the gate" = did not fully enter the Jewish communion. He who embraced the Jewish religion in its full extent, according to Exod. 12:48, was termed a "proselyte of righteousness." It was agreeable to the divine will to reclaim blind heathen and conduct them to the only true God. The Pharisees, however, were not influenced by a holy missionary spirit, but solely labored to make *Pharisees,* that is, sectarian Jews, in order to strengthen their own party, and were not anxious to increase the number of true worshippers of God. Hence their converts, who were not governed by the fear and love of God, but were influenced by mere temporal considerations in making a profession of the Jewish faith, often retained all their heathen vices and added to these all the hypocrisy and impiety of the Pharisees, exhibiting a frightful degree of wickedness and disgracing the name of religion even more than the original Pharisees. They were, in this sense, **twofold** worse than their guides, by bringing even greater reproach than the latter on revealed religion.—**D. Son** (see 8:12, A.) = *fitted for*, as in Deut. 25:2, where the Hebrew words translated "worthy to be beaten" are equivalent to: *a son of stripes*. So in 1 Sam. 26:16, David calls Saul's attendants "sons of death" in the Hebrew = pre-eminently worthy of the punishment of death (comp. 1 Sam. 20:31, margin). So Judas is a "son of perdition" (John 17:12) = fitted by his voluntary acts for no other lot (see 26:24, D.).—**Hell** = *geenna* (see 5:22, G.). The ungodly Pharisee himself, and his ungodly heathen convert, both receive their sentence here, which consigns them to eternal punishment; both are "sons of hell" = correspond in their ungodly feelings and conduct to that abode of darkness and pain, where the love and fear of God have no home.

16-17 Woe unto you, ye blind guides, which say, Whosoever shall swear by the temple, it is nothing; but whosoever shall swear by the gold of the temple, he is a debtor. Ye fools and blind: for whether is greater, the gold, or the temple that hath sanctified the gold?

A. Blind guides (see 15:14, B.). The Lord had, in the Sermon on the Mount (5:33–37), exposed the levity and profanity of the Pharisees as exhibited in their doctrine concerning oaths. He resumes the subject here, and exhibits in detail their unfitness to be religious teachers; they are *blind guides,* whose lessons only lead into danger. According to their impious system (see above, 5:34, A.), an oath in which neither the name of God nor a direct reference to Him occurred, while it *seemed* to impose an obligation, was, in reality, *no* oath—it apparently made the declaration of the Pharisee worthy of reliance, but in fact left him, as he supposed, at liberty to utter any falsehood. The Lord, on the contrary, denounces him in such a case as a perjured man.—**B. It is nothing** = an oath in the form: "By this temple I swear that, etc.," is nothing in itself—said the Pharisees; it does not require the truth to be spoken.—**C. The gold** = either the treasury (13 chests in the court of the women, Mark 12:41), or, more probably the sacred utensils mentioned in Exod. 25:17, 29, 31, 38. If the phrase, "the gold of the temple," be substituted in the oath for that of "the temple" (*naos*, 4:5, E.), then, as the Pharisees said, he who thus swears is a **debtor** = is bound to keep the oath (ver. 18, B.).—**D. Fools** (see 5:22, F.). The Lord, who is the sovereign Judge of men, here already pronounces a sentence according to His absolute authority and unerring knowledge and wisdom. They were **fools** (= devoid of all understanding) in supposing that an inanimate thing, as gold, can be a witness to an oath independently of the living God.—**E. Whether** = which (of the two), as in 9:5; 21:31.—**F. Is greater, etc.** = why do you declare that an oath "by the gold" is one that must be kept, but not one "by the temple," when the former oath can have no meaning nor solemnity, unless there be in it a reference to the temple, the "house" of God (21:13, B.), the sacred character of which alone, as the **greater** (= more important of the two), gives a sacred character to, or **sanctifieth,** the gold of the treasury belonging to it (ver. 21).

^{18, 19} And, Whosoever shall swear by the altar, it is nothing; but whosoever shall swear by the gift that is upon it, he is a debtor. Ye blind; for whether is greater, the gift, or the altar that sanctifieth the gift?

A. Altar. Two altars were employed in the service of the tabernacle and temple, the altar of burnt offerings (Exod. 27:1–8), and the altar of incense (Luke 1:11); for the latter, see Exod. 30:1–10; 37:25; 40:26; 1 Kings 6:22; 7:48; Rev. 8:3. The former, which is mentioned in ver. 35, below, and is also meant here and in 5:23, stood in the court of the priests in the open air (Exod. 27:1, ff.; 29:12; 38:1, ff.; 1 Kings 8:22; 9:25; 2 Chron. 4:1; 7:7);—**it is nothing** (see ver. 16);—**swear** (see 5:34, A.).—**B. Gift upon it** = any offering (see Lev., ch. 1–4); the gift itself was not accepted by the Lord unless it was brought to the holy place which He had appointed (Deut. 12:13, 14) and "touched the altar" (Exod. 29:37). Hence, as the altar alone gave a religious character to the gift, the former obviously possessed a higher character itself. By a device as impious in design as it was puerile in form, the Pharisees transferred the character of the altar to the gift, and alleged that an oath by the latter alone bound the person.—**Debtor,** bound to keep his oath.

20 He therefore that sweareth by the altar, sweareth by it, and by all things thereon.

The sense is: If you profess a willingness to bind yourselves by an oath, but intend to evade the obligation, you utterly fail; both an oath "by the altar" and one "by the gift" are alike either binding, or are alike mere mockery; such an oath can have no meaning, unless it be a direct appeal to Him to whom both the altar and the gift are alike consecrated.

21 And he that sweareth by the temple, sweareth by it, and by him that dwelleth therein.

Your oath "by the temple" (ver. 16)—the Lord proceeds—if it be not meant as a mockery of the Most High, is one that binds you; for why is the temple at all mentioned as a holy place, if the appeal be not made directly to Him whose presence alone converts it into a holy place? (Matt. 12:4; 1 Kings 8:13).

²² And he that sweareth by the heaven, sweareth by the throne of God, and by him that sitteth thereon.

(See above 5:34, C.) On the distinction between lawful and unlawful oaths, see above, 5:34, B. Such awful irreverence and deliberate violations of every law of God lead the Lord here, in His holy displeasure, to term such religious teachers, hypocrites, fools and blind leaders.

²³ Woe unto you, scribes and Pharisees, hypocrites! for ye tithe mint and anise and cummin, and have left undone the weightier matters of the law, judgment and mercy, and faith: but these ye ought to have done, and not to have left the other undone.

A. Tithe. The word means *a tenth part*. Besides the first-fruits, the law required of the Jews the tenth part of all the produce of the earth, chiefly, however, of fruit-bearing trees and fields, namely, corn (grain), wine and oil; the tithes of articles of comparatively insignificant value, as the produce of a garden, were not specially exacted; the proceeds were designed for the temple service, the support of the priests and Levites, etc. (see Lev. 27:30; Numb. 18:21, 24, 26; Deut. 12:6, 17; 14:22, 23, 28, 29). The Pharisees, however, for the sake of maintaining their reputation for piety, added new points to the requisitions of the law, and offered tithes of "all manner of herbs" (Luke 11:42) = garden plants.—**B. Mint** = garden or spear mint, with which the Jews strewed the floors of their houses;—**anise**, properly, *dill,* as the margin also renders the word,—an aromatic plant;—**cummin,** or **cumin,** a plant bearing seeds of a pungent and disagreeable taste, and, like the two former, of little value.—**C. Weightier,** lit. *heavier = more* momentous, important, impressive or solemn, as in 2 Cor. 10:10;—**the law** = the divine law given through the agency of Moses. The Lord doubtless refers here to Micah 6:8. An illustration of the Pharisaic observance of forms and violation of divine commandments is found below (26:59, C.).—**D. Judgment ... faith.** These are mentioned as representatives of the "weightier matters" or things of the law, for the neglect of which they could not atone by trivial offerings like tithes of common garden vegetables. Luke mentions in 11:42 "judgment and the love of God."—**Judgment.** The use of the corresponding Hebrew term, also translated *judgment* (Gen. 18:19; Ps. 33:5; 101:1; Isai. 1:17; Hos. 12:6) indicates that the Lord here means equity or integrity in general, and specially, impartiality and disinterestedness in judicial decisions, as the result alike of the true fear and love of God, and of an enlightened love to man (see 12:18, E.). The word **mercy,** in the sense of pity or compassion, may be designed to represent specially those duties to man which are repeatedly mentioned below (ch. 25:35–45), and the neglect of which betrays a want of love to God.—**Faith** may here indicate that reliance on God's truth, and that implicit confidence in His promises of redemption, which, when firmly established in the mind and heart, give a new character to the life and conduct, and of which bright examples are found in the sacred records, such as those mentioned in Hebr., ch. 11.—**E.**—**These** = the fear and love of God, and love to man, are the great duties prescribed by the law (see ch. 22:36–40).—**F. And not to, etc.** While the tithes of mint, etc., were of no great value, and were not absolutely required, nevertheless the Lord often teaches that in matters apparently trivial ("one jot or one tittle" of the law, 5:18) a holy spirit may be manifested (see ann. to 10:42). Hence, the offering of such tithes ought not in a contemptuous spirit to be left **undone** = neither the performance nor the omission of an act is so insignificant in God's eyes, that He does not discern in the one case and in the other either reverence and love to Him, or selfish and sinful sentiments.

²⁴ Ye blind guides, which strain out the gnat, and swallow the camel.

A. Blind guides (see ver. 16).—**B. Which strain out.** The ordinary process of reaching or drawing off wine from the lees is not here meant, but rather a religious practice. "It was the custom of the more accurate and stricter Jews to strain their wine, vinegar and other potables through linen or gauze, lest, unawares, they should drink down some little unclean insect therein, and thus transgress (Lev. 11:20, 23, 41, 42),—just as the Buddhists do now in Ceylon and Hindostan—and to this custom of theirs the Lord refers."—Trench.—**Gnat,** here = any small insect.—The **camel** (for which see above, 3:4, A.; 19:24, B.) was an unclean animal, as it "divideth not the hoof" (Lev. 11:4), and hence its flesh was not allowed to be eaten. The proverb which the Lord here quotes, resembling that of the mote and the beam in 7:3, represents one who is painfully scrupulous or conscientious in insignificant matters, and whose narrowness of mind, ignorance or hypocrisy nevertheless allows him to be guilty of the grossest, vilest and most culpable acts. The conscience of the Pharisees would not allow them to swallow an unclean insect, but it allowed them to "devour widows' houses" (Luke 20:47; see another illustration below, 27:6).

²⁵, ²⁶ Woe unto you, scribes and Pharisees, hypocrites! for ye cleanse the outside of the cup and of the platter, but within they are full from extortion and excess. Thou blind Pharisee, cleanse first the inside of the cup and of the platter, that the outside thereof may become clean also.

A. Ye cleanse. The Lord had uttered the same rebuke on an earlier occasion (Luke 11:39). The laws of Moses taught that the touch of a defiled object communicated a legal uncleanness to the person (see above, 15:2, B.). It was at all times possible, when a Jew went abroad, that he might touch an unclean person and become unclean himself by the contact, and that dishes and articles of furniture might have been similarly defiled. Hence the Pharisees found here new opportunities for displaying the spirit which they termed the spirit of religion, or piety. They accordingly added many rules to the laws of Moses, to which Mark refers (7:3, 4); they cared only for the letter of the law and of their traditions, but were totally destitute of faith and love. To them Paul's words were applicable: "Even their mind and conscience is defiled" (Tit. 1:15).—**B. Platter** = a plate or dish.—**C. They** = the cup and platter.—**D. Are full of extortion** (= rapacity) **and excess** (= dissoluteness, intemperance, incontinence). The sense is: While you pretend to observe your self-imposed religious duties, and scrupulously cleanse your dishes, you allow yourselves to acquire the food placed in them by the most ungodly means.—**E. Cleanse first, etc.** = observe honesty and justice towards others; revere the divine law in your efforts to provide for your wants; such pretended piety, which cleanses the exterior of the dish, but fills it ("that which is written") with the proceeds of fraud, can never avail before God. If your heart be right in His eyes, the ordinary rules of cleanliness and the divine laws respecting moral purity will need no religious additions derived from human wisdom. At the same time, the Lord doubtless means that the inconsistent procedure of the Pharisees, as here described, was an image of their moral conduct; they exhibited a studied conformity in their outward deportment to the requisitions of the law, but, by retaining in their hearts all manner of impurity, they deprived their outward acts of all value in the eyes of God.

27 Woe unto you, scribes and Pharisees, hypocrites! for ye are like unto whited sepulchres, which outwardly appear beautiful, but inwardly are full of dead men's bones, and of all uncleanness.

A. Whited sepulchres. According to the law (Numb. 5:2; 6:6; 19:16), he who touched a corpse or bone or grave was unclean seven days. The Jews, influenced by this consideration and by their interpretation of Ezek. 39:15, carefully designated the spot in which any one had been interred, in order to secure passengers from involuntary defilement (Luke 11:44). In the course of time they ostentatiously adorned their family sepulchres, and annually, early in the spring, whitewashed and decorated them anew ("beautiful").—**B. Within** = the monument, however tasteful and rich, was merely the veil which concealed, not a corresponding object, but only a foul and putrid mass.

28 Even so ye also outwardly appear righteous unto men, but inwardly ye are full of hypocrisy and iniquity.

The sense is: Ye Pharisees appear outwardly as righteous (= devout and godly) men; but your outward piety is merely the veil that hides the unmixed evil ("full of") of your hearts, that is, hypocrisy and ungodliness, by which ye yourselves become foul and loathsome in the eyes of God.—**Iniquity**, according to the original *word = lawlessness,* and translated "lawlessness" in 1 John 3:4, where it occurs as a description of *sin*. The thought may also here be conveyed: Ye Pharisees carry with you, whithersoever ye go, all the pollution of the grave.

²⁹ Woe unto you, scribes and Pharisees, hypocrites! for ye build the sepulchres of the prophets, and garnish the tombs of the righteous.

Ye build, etc. = erect costly monuments to their memory.—**Prophets**—**Righteous** (see 10:41, B.).—**Garnish** = adorn, decorate with columns, garlands, etc., as in 12:44. The same structure may often be termed indifferently a tomb or sepulchre. There is in this verse an illustration of the parallelism of Hebrew poetry, as in 15:8, C., thus: build—garnish; tombs—sepulchres; prophets—righteous.

³⁰ And say, If we had been in the days of our fathers, we should not have been partakers with them in the blood of the prophets.

A. And say = ye seem by the act to allege as your motive.—**B. If we, etc.** = your ostentatious reverence for the murdered prophets is intended to imply: We are far more devout and holy than our fathers were. They were guilty of murder, and, finally, of rebellion against God; we, on the contrary, reverently and piously listen to the messages which God sends, and devoutly honor the memory of the victims of the ungodly spirit of our fathers.

³¹ Wherefore ye witness to yourselves, that ye are sons of them that slew the prophets.

Wherefore = *so that,* as the original word is frequently translated, as in 8:28; 13:2. The sense is: You admit that you are the descendants of these murderers of the prophets; your efforts to destroy Me also furnish to your own consciences the evidence that, although you pretend to censure the sanguinary spirit of your ancestors, you have, nevertheless, inherited their ungodly temper, *so that* ye are undeniably their *sons* indeed, both by descent, and also by similarity of character. The Lord further implies the following: The proof that you have acquired a better spirit than that of your ancestors would, on the other hand, be furnished, not by showy monuments which you build, but by a devout attention to the divine messages sent to you.

³² Fill ye up then the measure of your fathers.

Predictions of evils that God permits, but does not desire, are often expressed in the language of command; this circumstance simply indicates that such results of human depravity will not be prevented (see 1 Kings 22:22; Isai. 6:9, 10; 8:9; 13:6; 29:9; Jer. 1:10; John 13:27; and comp., 13:14, B., above). Thus the language, as in the word "run" in 2 Sam. 18:23, or "send" in 2 Kings 2:17, is used in a permissive sense only. Sometimes, as below (ver 38, and in John 5:40), such an event is merely stated as a fact that is about to occur, or that has occurred. The present words, which are closely connected with the preceding verse and are to be interpreted in the sense of the parable in ch. 21:33–40, imply: Your fathers killed the prophets, who were mere men; *ye* intend (12:14) to kill the Prince of life (Acts 3:15; 7:52; 1 Thess. 2:15); if the wickedness of your fathers did not proceed to the utmost possible degree (figuratively = did not make the vessel or measure full), you desire to reach that ultimate point of iniquity ("fill, etc."), beyond which divine justice cannot allow you to proceed. Hence you exceed in guilt your fathers whose murderous acts you profess to condemn.

33 Ye serpents, ye offspring of vipers, how shall ye escape the judgment of hell?

Ye serpents, etc. (see 3:7, B.) = your ancestors breathed the spirit of the serpent which "beguiled Eve" (2 Cor. 11:3) by means of impious and blasphemous language (Gen. 3:4, 5), and ye are their genuine offspring. Such wickedness as you exhibit will necessarily lead you to perdition (see ver. 15, D., and 5; 22, G.). The Lord, in His unerring wisdom, truth and justice, assigns to these men their appropriate titles, and reveals their ultimate, awful doom.—**How shall.** The sense of the Lord's question is, not that God had made their escape impossible; He rather asks this question: How shall or will you escape, if you persist in such unbelief and impiety? With all your pretended sanctity, you will perish because of the unchanged wickedness of your hearts.

34 Therefore, behold, I send unto you prophets, and wise men, and scribes: some of them shall ye kill and crucify; and some of them shall ye scourge in your synagogues, and persecute from city to city:

A. Therefore = ye have inherited the murderous spirit of your ancestors and will imitate their acts; **therefore**—Christ continues—the words of the Scriptures which refer to the part (as in 2 Chron. 24:19; 36:15, 16; Jerem. 7:25, 26; 25:4) are also a prophetic description of your present and future history.—**B. I send.** In Luke 11:49, where the Lord also alludes to the substance of these passages in the prophets, He represents the writers as inspired men, "the wisdom of God said." As He was Himself God from all eternity (John 1:1; 8:58; 17:5), and as His Spirit was in the prophets (1 Peter 1:11), He refers to the words spoken by His prophets as being His own words (see ver. 37, C.), and quotes the substance; He accordingly says: *I send* = I do and will send;—**prophets,** the apostles included (Luke 11:49; Eph. 4:11; see 13:52, B.);—**kill** (Acts 12:1–3);—**scourge** (10:17, C.); **crucify;** possibly this expression refers to the crucifixion of the aged Simeon of Jerusalem in the year 107, during the reign of Trajan (Euseb. Eccl. Hist. iii. 32). Still, as the Lord here appears, according to the succeeding verses, to refer to events occurring during the interval between His death and the destruction of Jerusalem, and as He alludes, not to His own crucifixion, but to that of certain *others* whom He *sends,* it may be inferred that the Jews did crucify some apostles or teachers, the circumstances of whose death history has not recorded. ["The meagreness of the history of the Apostolic Age must be taken into the account."—Meyer. "That in their *synagogues* (note this particular) they should answer the undeniably God-given wisdom with *scourging;* that they should persecute from city to city even *scribes,* in order to thoroughly suppress their quiet testimony—in this the guilt of their resistance to the truth rises to a higher pitch. They leave unpersecuted not even the least one who merely dares, by way of testimony, to interpret the Scripture against them."—Stier.]

³⁵ That upon you may come all the righteous blood shed on the earth, from the blood of Abel the righteous unto the blood of Zachariah son of Barachiah, whom ye slew between the sanctuary and the altar.

A. The divine judgment which the sins of the people deserved, and which was manifested in the destruction of Jerusalem—a type or image of the future judgment of sinners—is now revealed. **That ... may come.** The words *that may,* as in 5:45; Mark 5:23, and elsewhere, indicate a certain consequence or result = *insomuch that,* or, *so that.* The sense is, not that the Jews deliberately intended and desired to bring the "righteous blood, etc." (= punishment and ruin), upon themselves, but that their conduct would have such consequences (comp. Acts 13:46), where the conduct that is rebuked resembled that of persons pronouncing a sentence against themselves.—**B. Upon you may come.** Similar phrases in Deut. 21:8; 28:2, 15; Jonah 1:14; Matt. 27:25; Acts 5:28; Eph. 5:6, compared with the language "be required of" in Luke 11:51, indicate the sense to be: The punishment due to such sins will ultimately fall upon you;—**upon you** = "this generation" (ver. 36, and comp. 24:34), persons then living (see 11:16, 17, A.). The siege of the city of Jerusalem was commenced by Titus 38 years after these words were spoken; the city was taken about 5 months afterwards (24:22, A.).—**C. The righteous blood** = the punishment (1 Kings 2:32) of the murder of righteous men, believers (Rev. 6:10); **from the blood** = from the time of the act of shedding the blood, taking away life (Deut. 12:23; Joel 3:19; comp. 2 Kings 21:16; Jer. 26:15; see also 27:4, A.).—**D. Abel ... Barachiah.** Abel (Gen. 4:8; 1 John 3:12; Hebr. 12:24) was the first human being whose blood was shed after the "foundation of the world" (Luke 11:50), in the contest which began between good and evil; thus he became the representative of all martyrs viewed as an aggregate. Stephen (Acts 7:59, 60; 22:20) was the first *Christian* martyr who died for the truth, as a faithful *witness* (which is the meaning of the word *martyr*). The death of Zachariah is described in 2 Chron. 24:20–22. His father is there named Jehoiada, and also in 2 Kings, ch. 11, 12; 2 Chron., ch. 23, 24. The names of eminent persons were often changed among the Hebrews, of which practice numerous cases are mentioned in the O. T., e. g. Gen. 17:5, 15; 32:28; 35:18; 2 Sam. 12:24, 25; 2 Kings 23:34; 24:17. Thus the son of Joash is called in the same chapter (Judges 8:29, 32; comp. with 6:32, and 7:1) both Jerubbaal and Gideon. The cases in the N. T. of several apostles, such as Simon, who is also called Peter, of Saul, "who also is called Paul" (Acts 13:9), and others (Acts 1:23; 4:36; 12:12, 25; Col. 4:11) are familiar (see also 26:36). It is possible that the distinguished services of the high-priest Jehoiada, described in the chapter mentioned above, and consistently and energetically continued to the advanced age of 130 years (2 Chron. 24:15), may have secured to him at a comparatively late period in the grateful recollections of the people the honorable name of *Barachiah,* which is accordingly given to him in the passage before us; it signifies: *Blessed of Jehovah,* or, *Whom Jehovah has blessed;* it is more emphatic than the analogous name *Jehoiada,* which signifies: *Whom Jehovah knows.* So Nathan gave the name of Jedediah (signifying: *Beloved of Jehovah,* 2 Sam. 12:24, 25) to Solomon, which name signifies simply *Peaceable* (1 Chron. 22:9). Various traditional names, facts, etc., not recorded in the O. T., are incidentally mentioned in the N. T., as familiarly known to the people, for instance, the names in 2 Tim. 3:8, and the facts stated in Acts 7:22, which, like the name of Barachiah here given to Jehoiada, belong to the countless details not furnished by the O. T., but preserved in other records of the Jews to a late period. More than 200 years after the murder of Zachariah occurred that of the prophet Urijah (Jerem. 26:23). According to the arrangement of the several books of the O. T. adopted by the Jews in the time of the Saviour, and still retained in our printed Hebrew Bibles, the Chronicles occupied the last place; the Lord therefore selects the case of Abel from the first book, Genesis, and that of Zachariah from the last, 2 Chronicles, in order to indicate *all* similar cases in the whole extent of the Scriptures; in both cases also (Gen. 4:10 and 2 Chron. 24:22) a solemn appeal is addressed to the justice of Him to whom "vengeance belongeth" (Hebr. 10:30). The name of the father of the prophet Zachariah (ch. 1:1), who is not here meant (he lived three centuries later than the other Zachariah), was also Barachiah, and a nearly similar case of an earlier date is incidentally mentioned in Isai. 8:2. The name *Zachariah* (meaning: *Whom Jehovah remembers*) was a favorite one among the Jews, and is applied to a number of persons in the Old Testament.—**E. Slew between, etc.** = in the court of the priest (2 Chron. 24:21) where the altar of burnt offerings stood, opposite to the entrance of the sacred edifice (see above, ver. 18, B.).—**Ye slew** = ye, the Jewish people.—**Temple,** the *naos,* as above ver. 16, C.

36 Verily I say unto you, All these things shall come upon this generation.

A. Verily (see 5:18, A.).—**B. All these things** = the punishment of the long series of rebellious and sinful deeds to which ver. 35 alludes; the final destruction of the Jewish state is meant, with no hope of a future restoration such as that which succeeded the Babylonish Captivity.—**C. Came upon, etc.** = (see ver. 35, B.).

37 O Jerusalem, Jerusalem, which killeth the prophets, and stoneth them that are sent unto her! how often would I have gathered thy children together, even as a hen gathereth her chickens under her wings, and ye would not.

A. O Jerusalem, Jerusalem. The Lord's revelations

respecting the destruction of the city and the unparalleled horrors which accompanied it (24:21), although all was inflicted as the deserved penalty of obstinate unbelief and rebellion against God, powerfully moved the compassionate Redeemer. "He beheld the city, and wept over it, saying, etc." (Luke 19:41, ff.). Hence He mournfully and even reproachfully mentions the name of the city twice, appealing to it in the language of deep emotion (see 11:23, A.). For other instances in which cities, etc., are thus addressed, see 2:6, A.—**B. Which ... her** = the murderers' city (22:7, and see Nehem. 9:26; Lament. 4:13; Hebr. 11:36, ff.). "It cannot be that a prophet perish out of Jerusalem" (Luke 13:33) = if any act of rebellion against God has ever been committed, it was only an imitation of the acts of that city, and will be found in the catalogue of its sins;—**stoneth** (21:35; Acts 7:58).—**C. How often ... wings.** The original furnishes the general name of *bird*, equivalent here to *fowl*, or understood specially of the hen. The bird's protecting wings afford many beautiful images in Scripture of the tender care of God (Deut. 32:11, 12; Ruth 2:12; Ps. 17:8; 61:4; Isai. 31:5). Even so the Lord Jesus often would have gathered, on the highway, in the temple, in dwellings, the children (= inhabitants) of Jerusalem, etc.; a chief city frequently received the name of mother among oriental nations (2 Sam. 20:19). The Lord had sent His prophets to them repeatedly (1 Peter, 1:10, 11, and ver. 34, B. above), and then spoken to them Himself (21:37; Hebr. 1:1). The whole object of all such appeals was the preservation of the people both from the temporal calamities which their obstinate unbelief was now bringing upon them, and from eternal ruin.—**D. And ye would not!** "Ye will not come to me, that ye might have life" (John 5:40).

"Men loved darkness, etc." (John 3:19; see Isai. 28:12; 30:15; 65:12). The loss of the sinner's soul is occasioned by his own unconstrained, voluntary and deliberate rejection of the means of salvation which the Lord has freely offered to him, but which He compels none of those to accept who choose death rather than life (Deut. 30:15–20; Josh. 24:15; Ezek. 18:31; Rev. 22:17).

38 Behold, your house is left unto you desolate.

Your house. This term probably refers not specially to the temple (see below, 24:15), but involves an allusion to Ps. 69:25 (quoted in Acts 1:20), and indicates here the desolation and ruin to which divine justice would soon abandon the homes (viewed in the aggregate as the abode) of the unbelieving people.—**Behold** (see 1:20, B.)

39 For I say unto you, Ye shall not see me henceforth, till ye shall say, Blessed *is* he that cometh in the name of the Lord.

A. The words quoted by the Lord: "Blessed, etc.," had already occurred above, 21:9, C., which see.—**For** = the coming calamity is now inevitable.—**Ye ... henceforth.** Here the Lord closes all the public appeals and warnings which He purposed to address personally to the Pharisees; the succeeding discourses are confined to the circle of His disciples (24:3, ff.; 26:1, ff.). The Lord never appeared personally to these unbelievers after His resurrection (Acts 10:40, 41). The sense is: I have first sought you, and ye now find Me ready to pardon and to save; henceforth I leave you. Never again shall ye receive from Me the offer of mercy, until ye yourselves seek Me in your town, and, seeing Me with the eye of faith, in deep contrition and penitence, confess My truth and power.—**B. Till.** There is no reason to assume that this word refers to any precise point of time, such as the resurrection, the outpouring of the Holy Ghost, the destruction of Jerusalem, etc. It rather refers to any future period after His death, in which His pity leads Him to expect a change in His hearers (comp. Jerem. 3:12–14). It is accordingly related in Acts, that various Jews who had previously rejected Christ afterwards repented and believed—the people, in 2:23, 37, 43; 4:4; 5:14; priests, in 6:7, and Pharisees, in 15:5. When such persons were awakened and received Christ as the true Messiah, they gladly **blessed** His name and confessed that He came from God. To these original enemies of Christ who "hereafter believed" Paul was a "pattern" = a glorious illustration of the "long-suffering" of Jesus Christ (1 Tim. 1:16).

9

Matthew 24

PRELIMINARY OBSERVATIONS

Obs. A.—The interpretation of this chapter is attended with peculiar difficulties. The Lord evidently refers in it to two distinct events, one of which, the destruction of Jerusalem, occurred eighteen centuries ago; the other, the end of the world, is still a future, and, possibly, a very distant event. To the former, for instance, He undeniably alludes in ver. 6–9, to the latter in ver. 14, for it occurs *after* the Gospel shall have been "preached in all the world;" to the former, again, in ver. 15, ff., to the latter, evidently, in ver. 30, 31; to the former, very plainly, in ver. 34, to the latter, almost as plainly, in ver. 36, 37. These transitions in His discourse, from the one to the other of two events which are so widely separated in time and character, are so frequent, that, without the adoption of some key, which may open up the cause of such changes from one to the other, it is often very difficult to account for them, and, in several verses of the chapter, to determine to which of the two His words specially refer. It is not to be supposed for one moment that the Lord spoke in a confused or incoherent manner, or passed from one event to the other without a sufficient reason. A great diversity of interpretations has been occasioned by the apparently desultory manner of speaking which some have here ascribed to the Lord; of the various modes of explaining the whole which have been attempted no one has yet been generally adopted.—The key which we here propose is described below, Prel. Obs. F.

Obs. B.—As our Lord often employs illustrative similitudes in His discourses (like those in 6:29; 11:16; 23:27), besides fully developed parables (as in ch. 13), in order to give distinctness and vividness to His lessons, so, too, as many interpreters believe, He adopts the same method in this chapter. The fearful events which preceded and attended the destruction of Jerusalem are, as they maintain, regarded by Him as appropriate images of the solemn scenes which will occur at the end of the world. If, therefore, the same prophetic words in any verse do not directly refer to both events, they may still, even when they describe the fall of Jerusalem, only be intended to furnish an image of another and more awful event—the end of the world. This mode of interpretation, however, without accounting for the apparent confusion of thought in the discourse, obscures the meaning of various verses, and has always failed to remove the reader's perplexity.

Obs. C.—The laws of perspective have been here presented by other interpreters as an illustration of the language of prophecy, and then applied to this discourse. To a spectator standing on a lofty eminence, two remote objects may appear to be in close proximity; when he subsequently proceeds to the locality, he finds that they are really far asunder. In the sketch of the artist, buildings, bridges, etc., that are near him, are distinctly defined; those that are very remote seem crowded together, and the intermediate distance is scarcely perceptible. So prophecy often refers to events belonging to the future which are really separated by wide intervals of time, by years, and even by centuries; yet they are described rapidly, without any intimation of the fact that they will actually occur at periods of time very far remote from each other. Compare 2 Sam. 7:12–16, where the history of Solomon and the establishment of the Messiah's throne are both revealed, without any specification of the times. Thus, too, no intimation is given in Isai. 9:6, 7, that the full development of the Messiah's kingdom will occur long after His birth (comp. also Isai. 11:1–6; ch. 53; 60:1–3; Jer. 23:5; 31:31–34; Ezek. 34:23–28; 36:24–38; Dan. 2:36–45). This mode of interpretation does not remove the apparent obscurity of the present chapter, and is not successful in explaining it; the fatal objection to its application in the case before us is furnished by the fact that the Lord, unlike the ancient prophets, *does* here intentionally discriminate between the times of the two events.

Obs. D.—While God has been pleased to reveal future *events*, He has always absolutely withheld all precise statements respecting the *times* of their occurrence; of this circumstance even two of the last of the prophets furnish illustrations (Hag. 2:6–9; Mal. 3:1). The O. T. abounds in predictions respecting the Messiah, and describes His whole history from His birth in Bethlehem to the completion of His atoning work and the permanent establishment of His Church. But even the most definite expression of the *times* which it affords, namely (Dan. 9:24–27), "seventy weeks," is obviously and purposely given in obscure terms. It seems that it would have been unwise in itself and of an evil influence, if the times of predicted events had been revealed to man; his watchfulness, his spirit of prayer, his faith in God—all his Christian graces owe their brightness to his continual preparations for his death (see 24:42, C.). When Daniel asked a question like that of the disciples in ver. 3, the significant answer was: "Go thy way, Daniel, for the words are *closed up and sealed* till the time of the end" (Dan. 12:8, 9). Hence the risen Saviour absolutely and in the most positive terms refused such revelations even at the last moment when He was parting from His disciples (Acts 1:7). They lived and they died without that knowledge (1 Thess. 5:1, 2; 2 Peter 3:10), and only knew that the end of all things might be long deferred (2 Thess. 2:2). So strictly has the Almighty withheld such knowledge from all His creatures that "of that day and hour knoweth no man, no, not the *angels* of heaven" (Matt. 24:36); indeed, so unsuited to human nature is a knowledge of this deep mystery, that Christ remarks that even *He*, in His State of Humiliation, refrained for the time from the use of His knowledge of "that day and that hour" (Mark 13:32). Under such circumstances, we may naturally expect that all the revelations given in the present chapter will be so presented to our feeble eyes as if a veil partially shrouded the heavenly light; if all were fully revealed it would dazzle and overpower our nature.

Obs. E.—While thus the mere curiosity of man is by no means gratified, the Lord amply provides in the present chapter for our spiritual and real wants in the following manner:—It cannot be essential to our true welfare to know the *precise time* of the end of the world—an event which will occur long after our death. But it *is* of unspeakable importance to us to be properly prepared for the judgment which will be held at that time. Now, our future and eternal condition in the other world will be decided altogether by our acceptance of Christ in true faith, or our rejection of Him in this present life; no means of grace, nor any opportunity to repent and reform, will be furnished after death (Obs. F. § 5). Hence, the day of our own death as individuals will virtually be the same to us as if it were the "day of the coming of the Lord to judgment." Those who had died previously to this event, including ourselves, and those who shall then be living on earth, when it does occur, will be treated by the Judge precisely in the same manner, according to 1 Thess. 4:15. To all these, without distinction, the words in 2 Cor. 5:10 apply. Hence, as, on the one hand, no apostle could indicate the time of the end of the world, and as, on the other, the death of the individual placed him, as far as his own sentence was concerned, precisely in the situation of those who shall be alive when the end of all things does come, the sacred writers regard both of the times—the day of the individual's death and the day of the Lord's coming—as equivalent, or virtually coinciding, the one with the other (see, for instance, Phil. 4:5; 1 Peter 4:7; James 5:8, 9; 2 Peter 3:10–14; 1 John 2:28).—Thus the Lord teaches us by His personal instructions, and by those which He imparts through His apostles, to live daily in the expectation of His coming, that is, to live daily with eternity in view.

OBS. F.—The interpreter of the following chapter will

possibly not be perplexed by any apparent confusion in it, arising from a supposed unaccountable transition from the one event to the other, if the following circumstances be considered:—

§ 1. No one of the four evangelists attempts to record *all* the sayings and deeds of the Lord (John 21:25). The one omits circumstances which another maybe induced by the general object for which he writes, and under the guidance of the Divine Spirit, to introduce fully. Even in the present discourse, while Matthew furnishes much matter which Mark and Luke omit (for example, 24:27–41; ver. 45–51, and the whole of ch. 25, except the reference in Mark 13:24), he omits certain portions which they record (Mark 13:35–37; Luke 21:24, 34, 36). Hence we learn that, as on other occasions (comp. Matt. 19:2 with Mark 10:1), *all* the words of the Lord have not been preserved; much less can we expect that all *the questions or remarks of the disciples* should be written in full.

§ 2. *Matthew sometimes omits portions of conversations* between Christ and His disciples or the people; thus He occasionally presents answers of the Saviour only, without introducing the questions or remarks of His hearers which occasioned these answers. This important fact, which constitutes the key that is applied in the following explanations, is verified by the following references:—The command given in Matt. 4:19 and the immediate obedience of the two fishers are made perfectly plain only by a reference to Luke 5:3–10. The cause of the cry described in 8:29 is explained in Mark 5:8 and Luke 8:29. The reason of the charge given in 12:16 is found in Mark 3:11, 12. In 14:8 the substance only of the conversation is furnished which appears in Mark 6:24, 25.

In 14:16, 17, the substance again is given of a conversation recorded in Mark 9:33–35. The words in 19:9 seem to be a continuation of an address to the Pharisees, but, as ver. 10 also indicates, they really constitute an answer to a question privately addressed to the Lord by the disciples, according to Mark 10:10. The words in 26:31 were doubtless called forth by language like that occurring in John 13:37. So, too, many details are omitted in 9:20, ff.; 17:14, ff., which are found respectively in Mark 5:25, ff.; Luke 8:43, and in Mark 9:14, ff.; Luke 9:38, ff. See also Matt. 26:31, B. Luke furnishes illustrations not found in Matthew of occasional interruptions of the Lord's discourses by short questions of the disciples, in 12:41; 17:37.

§ 3. The whole of the present discourse is exhibited by Matthew in an unbroken form, beginning at 24:4 and extending to the end of ch. 25. However, he furnishes himself the key to the whole in 24:3, where the disciples are introduced as addressing certain questions to Him (see below, at the verse). Since their occasional questions convey no definite information, *he repeats none* that are afterwards directed to the Lord, but records continuously the *Lord's own words only*. We may here assume, therefore, without precisely fixing the forms of the several questions, that *this long discourse embodies extended answers* of the Lord *to a succession of questions* from the perturbed disciples. The latter are greatly perplexed; they are not yet aware that many centuries will intervene between the fall of the city and the end of all things; they ask many questions, the substance of which alone is given in 24:3.

§ 4. The whole discourse as here presented furnishes, accordingly, the substance of a prolonged *conversation* held "privately" (24:3) between the Lord and "Peter, James, John and Andrew" (Mark 13:3), of whom the three former were admitted to various solemn scenes which no other disciple witnessed (see above, 17:1, B.). Luther remarks incidentally in one of his sermons: "Matthew here records not a formal discourse, but a *free and unconstrained conversation*," and Stier (without, however, further applying the principle in his explanation of the chapter): "It is probable that our Lord did not speak continuously and without certain pauses, or precisely in the form in which the discourse is here presented." A similar arrangement of extended answers to questions occurs in ch. 18 (see ver. 1 and 21), after which Matthew remarks in 19:1 that "Jesus finished these sayings" = these discourses. The same expression, occurring below in 26:1, indicates that here also the Lord's several answers to various questions implied by the word "all" are combined as one discourse. Thus one of the pauses in the conversation, at the end of ver. 31, not marked by Matthew is very distinctly visible in the parallel passage (Luke 21:29); the remark there made that the Lord now introduced a parable shows that He did not speak continuously or without occasional pauses, or questions from the disciples. At another parallel place (Luke 21:10) there is also an indication of a pause in the discourse. And in the abrupt transition in Matt. 25:14, there appears a trace of another interruption indicating that various connecting words have been omitted; a comparison with Mark 13:34, where the whole parable is compressed in one verse, will exhibit even more extensive omissions in the latter.

§ 5. We may then explain the contents of ch. 24 and ch. 25 according to the following principle:—This whole discourse really consists of several distinct series of "sayings" (26:1) or remarks which are pronounced partly in answer to occasional questions of the four disciples not recorded by Matthew, but indicated by Mark and Luke to a certain extent, and partly prompted by the Lord's knowledge of their wishes or spiritual wants. An exact specification of the time or times of future events He refuses to give; but the signs of coming events He reveals, on the one hand, while, on the other, He desires to impress on them and those whom they should afterwards instruct, the truth that to each individual his own death is equivalent to the end of all things. The following divisions of ch. 24 and ch. 25 seem to offer themselves to our view:—(*a*) ch. 24:4–13. Here, in answer to the question in ver. 3 respecting the sign (= indication) that "these things" mentioned in 23:36 are at hand, the Lord presents a rapid view of the trials of believers which will precede the fall of Jerusalem, (*b*) 24:14. To that point in the question which assumed that these events will coincide in time with His last coming at the end of the world, the Lord carefully distinguishes between the two answers in the negative (see below, ver. 14). (*c*) 24:15–26. Here the disciples possibly express their deep interest in the former events, that is, in their future trials, the dispersion of their nation, etc. The Lord, resuming the subject by saying, "therefore" (see below, ver. 15, A.), now gives additional warnings and instructions intended to guide their conduct, (*d*) 24:27–31. This passage, introduced by the word "For" (see below, ver. 27, B.), is doubtless the answer to a question expressed or indicated, and is intended to show that the scenes which will precede His final coming to judgment will differ materially from those that shall precede the fall of the city, (*e*) 24:32–35. Here the Lord makes a pause in the discourse, distinctly marked in Luke 21:29, but not mentioned by Matthew. He recurs to the point which most of all interested His disciples, who exhibit deep emotion and possibly renew their questions; He reminds them that He has now revealed with sufficient fulness the character of the events which shall precede the fall of the city. (*f*) 24:36–41. The Lord, who hitherto had spoken not for the purpose of gratifying an idle curiosity, but rather of reaching the heart, desires now to impress *this* truth in the minds of His disciples, that His last coming and the end of the world are events of far greater importance than the fall of the Jewish State. This whole passage, as an independent portion, is omitted by Luke, ch. 21, between ver. 33 and ver. 34. (*g*) 24:42–25:30. At this point the disciples are apparently so deeply moved that they cannot interpose new questions; the Lord proceeds to discuss the new point already introduced in in 24:36, ff., namely, that the death of each individual is really "the end" in his own case, and illustrates man's responsibility by parables (see below, 24:44, C.). (*h*) 24:31–46. He completes the solemn revelations by a description of the Last Judgment, which will extend to all the individuals of the human race.

Obs. G.—Various remarks which occur in this conversation had been previously made by the Lord in His public discourses (comp., besides the parallel passages in Luke, ch. 21, also Luke 12:36–40 and 17:24–36). These remarks, which were not then fully understood by the disciples (see below, ver. 36, A.), are now repeated in a connection which renders their meaning more distinct.

[1] And Jesus went out from the temple, and was going on his way: and his disciples came to him to shew him the buildings

of the temple.

A. Departed ... temple. The Lord never returned to it—before the week closed, He was crucified.—**B. Disciples ... shew.** They did not exhibit these buildings to Him as to a stranger; the Greek word implies that they *pointed out, called His attention* to them, as it is also used in Luke 17:14; 24:40; Acts 9:39. They indicated that *these* were the special objects of their interest at the moment, thus inquiring indirectly whether the awful words just pronounced: "Your house, etc." (23:38), could possibly refer to these sacred buildings.—**C. Buildings.** The term comprehends all the magnificent structures (cloisters, pillars, walls, etc.) which were connected with the temple (4:5, E.), and which Herod during his long reign, and the Jewish authorities after his day, had erected or completed (John 2:20; see Josephus, Antiq. 15, ch. 11; 20, 9, 7; War, 5, ch. 5). The latter remarks that Herod "chose out 10,000 of the most skilful workmen," whose number was subsequently increased to 18,000, and that the "goodly stones" (Luke 21:5) of the sacred edifice, or rather of its foundation, were "white and strong; their length was 25 cubits, their height was 8, and their breadth about 12" (Antiq. 15, 11, 2 and 3). He elsewhere (War, 5, 5, 6) describes some of the stones of the walls as having been "45 cubits in length, 5 in height, and 6 in breadth" (for *cubit* see 6:27, B.). Josephus, a Jewish historian of undoubted veracity (born a. d. 37), has left a full account of the Jewish War, which, without any such intention on his part, affords many remarkable illustrations of the words spoken by the Lord in this chapter (see K. von Raumer's "Credibility of Josephus," in *Palæstina*, p. 466).

² But he answered and said unto them, See ye not all these

things? verily I say unto you, There shall not be left here one stone upon another, that shall not be thrown down.

The sense is: These various objects to which you point I *do* mean; all these massive walls will inevitably be broken down, and devastation and ruin will overwhelm the whole. The Romans literally fulfilled this prediction, according to Josephus (War, 7, 1, 1), inasmuch as, after the capture of the city, when "the army [of the Romans] had no more people to slay or plunder," then "they demolished the entire city and temple," except some portions which were spared as trophies of their victory; the very foundation was dug up, and all traces of an inhabited city were destroyed, as he informs us. (Compare the description in Ps. 79:1–4 of the Babylonian Conquest.)

³ And as he sat on the mount of Olives, the disciples came unto him privately, saying, Tell us, when shall these things be? and what *shall be* the sign of thy coming, and of the end of the world?

A. As he sat ... Olives. The original implies that after He had reached this spot on leaving the temple, and seated Himself, the disciples came to Him. The temple and the city, the approaching ruin of which filled their minds with gloom, were in full view. For the **mount of Olives,** see ann. to 21:1.—**B. The disciples ... privately.** Only *four* of the whole number are here meant (Mark 13:3, and see Prel. Obs. F. § 4). The term **privately** (= *apart*, 17:19; *when they were alone*, Mark 4:34) doubtless refers to the absence of the other disciples, as on somewhat similar occasions of deep import.—**C. Tell us ... world.** According to the view presented above (Prel. Obs. F. § 3), Matthew places these questions here in order to indicate that the prolonged discourse which follows was occasioned by certain interrogatories to which the Lord furnishes replies. The first of the *two* questions refers to *the precise time* of the occurrence of "these things" which the Lord had mentioned in 23:36, and now repeats in ver. 2. The second question is to be viewed in connection with the following facts:—There were certain lessons which, previously to the day of Pentecost, when the Holy Ghost was poured out (Acts, ch. 2), the disciples were not prepared to learn (John 16:12, 13). Even after His resurrection their impatience to know the future, and their incorrect views, are gently rebuked by the Lord (Acts 1:6, 7). Here the same ignorance or confusion of thought is manifested by them. They are not distinctly conscious that the end of the world will be widely separated in time from the overthrow of the Jewish State, and imagine that the "coming" of the Lord, when Jerusalem shall fall, on the one hand, and the end of the world, on the other, will coincide in the time. The questions as here stated by Matthew probably contain the substance of several others referring chiefly to the signs of those momentous events, by which the disciples may know that they are at hand. They, moreover, appear to imagine that the "end of the world" is so near, that they may still live when it occurs. They remember indeed the remarkable words spoken in 16:27, 28, and 19:28; but of the *times* of the events there revealed and of the events themselves, they had yet no clear conception.—**D. Thy coming.** On this subject, see above, 10:23, B.—**E. The end of the world.** For the term here translated **world**, see 12:32, C. Precisely the same Greek phrase occurs in 13:39, 40, 49, and 28:20; neither there nor in the present verse can it possibly mean simply the end of the Jewish State, but can only refer to the end of all things = the passing away of this earth (2 Peter 3:10).

⁴ And Jesus answered and said unto them, Take heed that no man lead you astray.

That is:—Be on your guard; and believe no one whose doctrines differ from Mine; you will be exposed to many trials of your faith before these massive buildings shall be cast down. Such watchfulness will be of more value to you than a knowledge of the time ("when"). The warning is repeated by Paul (Eph. 5:6; Col. 2:8; 2 Thess. 2:3). As in a similar case (Luke 13:23, 24), so the Lord here, while refusing to give a direct answer, replies by uttering a solemn admonition: "He began to say, etc." (Mark 13:5), that is, He introduced in succession several topics of deep interest.

⁵ For many shall come in my name, saying, I am the Christ; and shall lead many astray.

Each will falsely assume My name and character, saying, I am the promised Messiah; each of these impostors will succeed in persuading "many" that he is the promised Deliverer. Many impostors and deceivers arose among the Jews, according to the testimony of Josephus (Antiq. 20, 8, 6; War, 2, 13, 5), before the city was destroyed. Thus, he mentions "that Egyptian" whom the chief captain, in the first alarm, supposed Paul to be (Acts 21:38); this man, like others, pretended that he could exhibit signs and wonders, and, as it was estimated, about 30,000 individuals were "deceived" by him. Others, who pretended respectively to be "some great one," or "the great power of God," like Simon the sorcerer, Theudas and Judas of Galilee, are already mentioned incidentally in Acts 5:36, 37; 8:9, 10. Our historical records have not preserved the name of any impostor who ventured, before the fall of the city, to announce himself *publicly* and without any reserve as the "very Christ" (John 7:26; Acts 9:22) or Messiah Himself; such pretensions were no doubt confined to the small circles of the initiated while the Jewish authorities retained their power. Hence Dositheus the Samaritan, the founder of a numerous sect during and after the age of the apostles, publicly claimed to be only the prophet announced in Deut. 18:18, but in private may have described himself as "the Christ." But after the fall of the city, when detection was less prompt and easy, many "false Christs" appeared, of whom the one best known, Barchochebas or Bar-Cochba (= *Son of a star*, the ambitious title which he assumed in allusion to Numb. 24:17), perished in the year 135. Such a "false Christ" could possibly claim that he was the Lord Jesus himself, and that His promised "coming" now occurred. Hence the Lord discriminates carefully in the subsequent discourse between the era of the fall of Jerusalem, which alone concerned the disciples personally, and the distant period when the General Judgment will occur.—**Deceive many** (see ver. 11).

⁶ And ye shall hear of wars and rumors of wars: see that ye be not troubled: for *these things* must needs come to pass, but the end is not yet.

A. Wars ... wars = while a bloody war prevails in one part of the Roman Empire, ye will be alarmed by tidings that other wars are on the point of commencing elsewhere. The Romans repeatedly threatened war against the Jews before the reign of Vespasian. The Lord possibly alludes to the wars of the Romans with the Parthians, to the enormous numbers of Jews slain in the Syrian and other cities (Jos. War., 2, ch. 18; Antiq. 20, ch. 3 and 4), to the wars of rival emperors, Otho,

Vitellius, etc. Large portions of the Roman Empire were convulsed by war during the whole period preceding the fall of the city.—**B. Be not troubled** = do not vainly believe that these convulsions, which will occur long before the Gospel shall have reached all nations, indicate the actual end of the world. It is worthy of observation that when Paul imparts precisely the same lesson to the Thessalonians, he employs the same word, rendered **troubled** = *disturbed, alarmed* (2 Thess. 2:2).—**C. For all, etc.** = for "the end" of the world, concerning which ye inquired (ver. 3), is not indicated by these events. Hence, vast and bloody wars, and even the fall of empires, by no means constitute sure signs of the near approach of the end of the world.—**All these things** = now mentioned in reference to the fall of the city (see ver. 34).—**Must** = certainly will (see 16:21, C.).

7 For nation shall rise against nation, and kingdom against kingdom: and there shall be famines and earthquakes in divers places.

The Lord here refers to the language of the prophets (for instance, Isai. 19:2; Jerem. 51:46), as well as 2 Chron. 15:6 with which the disciples were familiar, and which described in general terms great political convulsions, national calamities, and wars; the terms employed refer here to facts and are to be literally understood.—**Famines.** One of great severity which occurred a. d. 49 is incidentally mentioned in Acts 11:28, whereas in Acts 7:11, the same Greek word is rendered *dearth;* it is sometimes rendered *hunger*, as in Luke 15:17; 2 Cor. 11:27, but *famine* in Rom. 8:35 (see Jos. Antiq. 20, 2, 5).—**Pestilences.** Here a general name is employed, indicating calamities like the oriental Plague or any malignant diseases that are contagious or infectious as well as epidemic and mortal. One pestilence alone, in a. d. 65, in a single autumn carried off 30,000 persons in Rome. The appalling scourge of the pestilence is often mentioned in the O. T. (Lev. 26:25; 1 Kings 8:37; Ps. 91:3, 6; Ezek. 7:15)—**Earthquakes.** These are also frequently mentioned in the O. T. (e. g. Isai. 24:20; 29:6), and have occurred in the Holy Land as well as in other countries. In addition to several others that took place between a. d. 46 and a. d. 60 in "divers (= sundry, various) places" in the Roman Empire and are mentioned by historians, there was a violent earthquake in the year 63, that is, about seven years before the fall of the city, in the neighborhood of Mount Vesuvius, which partially destroyed Pompeii (Tac. Ann. 15:22); the earthquake which completely ruined it as well as Herculaneum occurred about 16 years afterwards, a. d. 79. Previously, during the reign of Tiberius, thirteen cities of Asia Minor were destroyed in one night by an earthquake. The imperfect historical records referring to that period which are extant do not furnish full details of the events which the Lord here predicts.

⁸ But all these things are the beginning of travail.

That is: Such events, as a mere "beginning," will be succeeded by greater horrors which will ultimately overwhelm the city and the whole nation. The Greek word for **sorrows,** occurring also in Acts 2:24, indicates originally pangs which are intense, but also of comparatively short duration = (throes, 1 Thess. 5:3; John 16:21).

⁹ Then shall they deliver you up unto tribulation, and shall kill you: and ye shall be hated of all the nations for my name's sake.

A. Then shall ... you. The word **shall** is here simply the sign of the future tense = will. Similar predictions had already been made in 10:17; 23:34. They possibly refer to cases like that of Stephen (Acts 7:59), James (Acts 12:2), and the persecution of the Christians under the Emperor Nero, during whose reign the apostles Peter and Paul are said to have suffered martyrdom.—**B. Ye shall be, etc.** = the Jews will regard you as enemies of their religion, and consequently as enemies of God; and all nations (= Gentiles) will hate you (see above 10:22, A., and comp. John 16:2 with Acts 6:14; 26:9; 28:22; 1 Cor. 4:13; 1 Peter 2:12; 3:16; 4:14).—**For my name's sake** = as Christians (Peter 4:16), adherents of Christ whom the Jews with impious unbelief denied and slew, and to whose disciples they transferred their original hatred of the Lord Jesus (Acts 4:2; see 10:22, B.). An ancient writer states that the very name—a *Christian*—when it was heard by the heathen, provoked a war against itself, as if it implied a crime.

[10] And then shall many stumble, and shall deliver up one another, and shall hate one another.

A. Offended = will stumble and fall, will allow such trials to shake their faith, to destroy their confidence in God, and will renounce the Christian religion (13:21). For the word **offend**, see 5:29, C., and for illustrations, 2 Tim. 1:15; 4:10, 16; 1 John 2:19, and comp. Hebr. 12:3, ff.—**B. Betray one another** = through fear of persecution or through bribes, some professing believers will denounce their brethren to their persecutors. Such scenes occurred during the reign of Nero, a few years before the fall of the city (Tac. Ann. 15, 44).—**C. Shall hate, etc.** = these treacherous and apostate Christians will act as enemies that hate. The Lord here repeats, according to Mark 13:12, words that He had uttered once before (see above, 10:21).

¹¹ And many false prophets shall arise, and shall lead many astray.

(See 7:15, B., and above, ann. to ver. 5.) These cautions are repeated by Paul (Acts 20:29, 30; Rom. 16:18; 2 Cor. 11:13; Gal. 1:7; 2:4; 1 Tim. 4:1; 2 Tim. 3:1), by Peter (2 Peter 2:1), and by John (1 John 2:18; 4:1; see below, ver. 23).

¹² And because iniquity shall be multiplied, the love of the many shall wax cold.

The **iniquity that abounds** (= multiplies, increases; comp. the same word in Acts 12:24; 1 Peter 1:2) is the iniquity or unbelief of the persecutors, aggravated or rendered more trying by the unfaithfulness and apostasy of professing Christians (comp. 2 Tim. 3:1–5).—**Wax** (see 13:15, A.). Love, the great Christian principle (22:37–40), the most holy emotion which the human heart is, by grace, made capable of entertaining, is compared to the sacred fire which burned perpetually on the altar (Lev. 6:9–13).—**Many,** forbearing to watch and pray and to hold fast to the divine promises, will allow the grateful love with which they had professed the name of Christ, and the fraternal love with which they had regarded their brethren, to be extinguished by fear or other unholy emotions, and will renounce a cause which involves them in severe earthly trials (2 Thess. 2:3; 2 Tim. 1:15; Hebr. 10:25).

¹³ But he that endureth to the end, the same shall be saved.

For the future encouragement of believers when the trials here predicted shall occur, the Lord graciously promises eternal salvation (= perfect and eternal deliverance from all evil, 2 Peter 2:9; 2 Tim. 4:18) to those who in faith **endure** (= bear, sustain) their trials unto the end of their course on earth (comp. 2 Tim. 2:12 and James 1:12; 5:11).—**Unto** (the)

end = of life (Rev. 2:10), as in John 13:1; Hebr. 3:14; Rev. 2:26. The definite article *the*, which in ver. 6 and ver. 14 gives prominence to the *great* end = the end of all things, is here omitted, and the adverbial form of the Greek phrase simply indicates the idea of *finally, perseveringly*.

¹⁴ And this gospel of the kingdom shall be preached in the whole world for a testimony unto all the nations; and then shall the end come.

A. The rapid transition in this verse from the fall of the city to the "end" of the world may be thus explained. The disciples had heard the Lord speak previously (ver. 6) of a certain *remote* "end"; here, at the close of ver. 13, in which He had employed the same word "end" (meaning the close of the individual's life on earth), they inquire whether He declared that immediately after the events just mentioned as signs of the approaching fall of Jerusalem, the "end of the world" itself (ver. 3) would occur. The phrase, **this gospel,** which indicates that some reference had just been made to the *Gospel*, and also the absence of the words found in Luke 21:18, 19, show that Matthew has here omitted a portion of the conversation and proceeds with his report only when the Lord Himself resumes the regular discourse. *After* the fall of the city and *before* the "end" of the world, the tidings of the Gospel shall be carried to all nations, thus showing that the interval would be of comparatively great length.—**B. And.** The word so translated, and its corresponding Hebrew connective, admit of various modes of application. The latter even begins several books (Exod. 1:1; 1 Kings 1:1; Ezra 1:1) and letters (2 Kings 5:6; 10:2), and is translated *now,* referring generally to preceding words or facts, or it indicates that a general subject is resumed or a new one introduced. In the N. T. it is sometimes equivalent to *then, after that,* as in Matt. 3:16; 4:3, or is translated *but* (Mark 12:12; Acts 10:28); *therefore* (1 Cor. 5:13) and *for* in Acts 23:3; 1 John 1:2; 3:4. It is sometimes equivalent to *namely,* as in John 1:16 (= namely, grace, etc.; 1 Cor. 3:5, "even"). Here it implies that the disciples had here interposed a question, and that the Lord said in reply: *That* end of the world itself shall not come then, *for* this gospel, etc.—**C. This gospel of the kingdom.** The word **this** may allude to the joyful intelligence of salvation involved in the words: "shall be saved" (ver. 13; comp. 26:13, A.); but it more probably refers to the Gospel which the disciples and their successors were to preach, and which possibly had been just mentioned in the intermediate conversation; for the whole phrase, see 4:23, C.—**D. World.** The original word (*oikoumene*), differing from that which is similarly translated in ver. 3, and signifying *the inhabited* (*earth*), although used sometimes in a restricted sense (Luke 2:1; Acts 11:28; 19:27 = Palestine, or = the Roman Empire), is evidently intended, as the words "all nations" and the statement in Rom. 11:25 show, to designate the habitable globe, the whole world, as in Acts 17:31; Rom. 10:18; Hebr. 1:6. In the analogous passage (Matt. 26:13), another word (*kosmos*), translated "world," is the one occurring in 4:8; 13:38; 16:26. The ancient prophecies had repeatedly declared: "The earth shall be full of the knowledge of the Lord, etc." (Isai. 11:9; Hab. 2:14). America and other portions of the globe, the homes of millions of men, were not then known even by name. Nevertheless, the Gospel was to be sent to those parts of the world, too, before the "end" should come.—**E. For a witness ... nations** = bearing witness, according to the great purpose of the Gospel (John 1:17; Tit. 2:11), to all men concerning the love of God revealed in Christ (1 Cor. 1:6; 2:1; see ch. 8:4, D.).—**F. And then, etc.** The day of judgment will not arrive until the Gospel shall have been previously proclaimed to all nations = "the whole world" (Matt. 26:13).—**Then** = *thereupon, after that*. The word is decisive as to the order of the events, without indicating the length of the interval between them.

¹⁵ When therefore ye see the abomination of desolation which was spoken of by Daniel the prophet, standing in the holy place, (let him that readeth understand).

A. Therefore. At this point the painful interest which the disciples felt in the coming events that so nearly concerned them and their nation, manifests itself by exclamations or questions, and the Lord pauses. The evidence of this fact is found in the variations occurring in the reports in Mark 13:14 and Luke 21:20; both of these evangelists prefix other words to this verse, showing that the conversation had been resumed and had interrupted the Lord's discourse. At the point where He again proceeds with His discourse, the three evangelists coincide substantially. Christ now furnishes additional and detailed instructions in ver. 15–26 respecting the conduct of the disciples and of their Christian associates when the times of trial should be at hand. The introductory word **therefore** indicates that He resumes the subject which He had discussed to the end of ver. 13, but temporarily dropped while uttering the words in ver. 14. Such resumptions after short interruptions or parentheses, by means of the word *therefore,* are frequent (see 7:24; 10:32, and comp. John 6:24 with ver. 22 of that chapter, or Hebr. 4:11 with ver. 6).—**B. Abomination ... place.** The prophet Daniel, who lived six hundred years before the Christian era, was permitted to see many future events in his visions. Among these are the remarkable revelations which he received concerning the Messiah. Josephus says: "Daniel also wrote concerning the Roman government, and that our country should be made desolate by them" (Ant. 10, 11, 7). The words in the Book of Daniel to which the Lord here refers are found in ch. 9:26, 27; 12:11.—**The holy place** (in the original simply "a *holy place*") is supposed by some to be the temple, although Matthew, in 13:14, instead of this phrase, says: "where it ought not." That the temple cannot be meant is obvious; for when the Romans actually did offer sacrifices to their ensigns on the site of the temple, the sacred buildings had been already burned (Jos. War, 6, 6, 1), while here our Lord evidently refers to a time preceding the destruction of the temple, when the escape of fugitives was still possible (ver. 16). Probably Judæa, or the region around the city, called "the holy land" (Zech. 2:12), is implied; like the city (4:5, C.), the whole land belonged to the Lord and was regarded as *holy* (see Lev. 25:23; Jer. 2:7; Hos. 9:3). Christ here indicates that His disciples should withdraw from the city before the temple should be taken and destroyed; moreover, Luke, who omits these words, supplies the following: "When ye shall see Jerusalem compassed with armies" (21:22), which evidently alludes to the approach of the Roman armies with their standards exhibiting the well-known Roman eagles. (These were figures of gold or silver about the size of a pigeon, and were borne on the tops of spears with their wings displayed; when the army marched, the eagle was always visible to the legions.) These representatives of living creatures were abhorred by the Jews on account of the idolatrous rites represented by them (Jos. Ant. 17, 6, 2). The word **stand** (lit.*standing*) indicates a prolonged presence of the **abomination of desolation** = the desolating abomination. The original word for **abomination** which Daniel employs designated any vile and odious thing, particularly when connected with the pollutions of idolatry (Zech. 9:7; Nahum 3:6; 2 Kings 23:24). Possibly the ensigns and the images of the Roman emperor are included, such as Pilate in vain attempted at an earlier period to introduce into Jerusalem (Jos. War, 2, 9, 2). So, too, when Vitellius intended to conduct an army through Judæa, the Jews remonstrated effectually against the passage of the troops through their country, on account of the images in their ensigns (Jos. Ant. 18, 5, 3). The sense of the whole may then be:—When the armies and standards of the pagan Romans establish themselves on the soil of the holy land, with the evident intent to spread desolation over it, then, etc. But if "the holy place" be understood in its technical sense, the reference in "the abomination of desolation" may be to the scenes of violence, murder, consecrations of usurping priests, etc. (see Jos. War, iv. 686–8).—C. **(Whoso ... understand.)** Some suppose that Matthew himself introduces this parenthesis; but as it occurs also in Mark 13:14, it is evidently a part of the Lord's discourse. He Himself, whose own words Matthew is here very careful not to interrupt at all, calls the attention of His disciples specially to the angel's language occurring in the ancient prophecy (Dan. 9:23; 12:10), as a guide for their own future meditations. Such brief parenthetical remarks are not uncommon (see 13:9, 43; John 7:22; Rev. 2:9).—**Whoso readeth** = for the instruction of himself and of others.

¹⁶ Then let them that are in in Judæa flee unto the mountains:

That is: If ye had hitherto still lingered, do ye and all who receive my words, at once abandon the whole land, for the siege of the city and the ruin of the country are at hand.—**Flee ... mountains** = seek places of refuge (Gen. 19:17; Judg. 6:2; 1 Sam. 13:6).—It is said (Euseb. Eccl. Hist. iii. 5) that shortly before the fall of the city, the Christians, in obedience to this command, withdrew in a body and went beyond the Jordan to Pella, a city situated in the northern part of Peræa (Jos. War, 3, 3, 3), in the mountainous region on the north-eastern confines of the Holy Land. (Comp. Jos. War, 2, ch. 19, 6, and ch. 20, 1, respecting the flight of many inhabitants of Jerusalem.)

¹⁷ Let him that is on the housetop not go down to take out the things that are in his house:

The roofs of the houses were flat, affording conveniences for walking, and were sometimes chosen, as in Peter's case (Acts 10:9), by those who sought retirement. The housetop was reached both from the interior of the house, and also by a staircase on the outside (9:2, D.). The image is that of a man to whom the suddenness of the danger leaves no time to collect provisions and clothing for his flight: if the Christians linger too long in the city when the Jewish war is beginning, they will find all means of escape cut off (comp. Luke 17:31, and see above, Prel. Obs. G.).

¹⁸ And let him that is in the field not return back to take his cloak.

This additional image enforces the precept of the former verse, that no time should be wasted in escaping from the doomed city. The Lord designs to extinguish the last hope of His disciples that the city will be spared.—**Clothes.** The mantle or cloak (5:40, B.; 26:65, A.) was not worn during the labors of the field or when other work was performed (comp. John 13:4; Acts 7:58).

[19] But woe unto them that are with child, and to them that give suck in those days!

Woe = alas for, etc. (11:21, A.). The Lord refers to the unspeakable miseries of the times, the dispersion of families and the painful trials which the helpless fugitives will endure, particularly referring to mothers; the allusion is to that holy principle of love which will not allow a mother to consider her own safety unless she first provide for that of her offspring, whence she is liable to perish with the latter.

[20] And pray ye that your flight be not in the winter, neither on a sabbath:

That is: Let prayer and uninterrupted communion with God sustain you. The Lord here evidently refers to believers whose faith would prompt them to prefer a painful flight to a continuance in the city. They are permitted to pray for two alleviations: first, that the privations and sufferings which necessarily attend such a flight may not be aggravated by the severity of the season of the year; and, secondly, that their flight may not be attended by circumstances or apparently necessary acts that might either offend the Jews as violations of the letter of the law, or disturb their own peace of conscience. This point is illustrated by a reference to the manner in which a conscientious Jew regarded the observance of the Sabbath (Exod. 16:29; Jer. 17:22). Two sources of trial are specified: first, natural causes; secondly, social or religious institutions. Josephus remarks (Ant. 13, 8, 4) that it was not lawful for a Jew to journey on a Sabbath or a festival day; for the distance called a "Sabbath day's," see 21:1.

²¹ For there shall be great tribulation, such as hath not been from the beginning of the world until now, no, nor ever shall be.

The sense is: The miseries which are approaching will justify you in encountering the greatest perils in effecting your escape. These unexpected disclosures of the future trials of Jews and Christians, as connected with the fall of the city, doubtless produced a marked movement among the disciples. They are deeply distressed, but have reached a period when, in the Lord's view, it is essential that they should be prepared by Him for personally encountering danger in any form without timidity or hopelessness. Hence He here reasserts in proverbial terms which refer to extraordinary calamities (see Exod. 10:14; 11:6; Joel 2:2), that all these things will come to pass, and even exceed in severity all other known calamities, referring with emphasis to the words in Dan. 12:1. The allusion doubtless is to the appalling events which preceded and followed the capture of Jerusalem; this city was crowded at the time by Jews from a distance who had assembled to keep the passover (Jos. War, 6, 9, 3 and 4). The "great distress" mentioned in Luke 21:23, 24; the murders (large fires quenched by the flowing streams of blood, Jos. War, 6, 8, 5); the famine and the enormous crimes which it engendered (a mother, named Mary, for instance, killing her babe, roasting and eating one half of the body, Jos. War, 6, 3, 4); the crucifixion of so many hundreds of Jewish prisoners "that room was wanting for the crosses, and crosses wanting for the bodies" (Jos. War, 5, 11, 1); the slaughter of more than a million of Jews ("eleven hundred thousand perished during the whole siege," besides ninety-seven thousand who were led into captivity (Jos. War, 6, 9, 3),—these were indeed events to which no former age, and none that succeeded, can afford a parallel; the Lord's prophetic view of them moved Him to tears (Luke 19:41); additional remarks on the same event are found in Luke 21:24.

22 And except those days had been shortened, no flesh would have been saved; but for the elect's sake those days shall be shortened.

A. Except (lit. *if—not*) **... saved** = if the Lord (Mark 13:20) had not in His infinite compassion determined to arrest the course of these calamities, and restrain the passions of cruel and wicked men, **no flesh** (= *no mortal,* as in Jer. 12:12; Rom. 3:20; 1 Cor. 1:29) could **be saved** (= *escape bodily death,* as in 8:25; 14:30)—death, in the form of pestilence or famine, in addition to the sword, would rage till all had perished (comp. Gen. 6:13).—**Shortened** = diminished in number. The siege and capture of Jerusalem occupied a much shorter time than Titus had expected. The former commenced early in the spring of a. d. 70; the latter occurred five months afterwards, early in the autumn of the same year.—**B. But ... elect's sake, etc.** For **elect,** see 20:16, B. The sense is: God will not permit these calamities to prevail so long that they shall overwhelm and destroy His own believing people, the Christians. "He knoweth them that trust in him" (Nahum 1:7; 2 Tim. 2:19). These 16 words, which refer to the overruling providence of God, are designed to soothe and encourage the disciples and all afflicted believers; the latter, by their presence, their faith, and their prayers, prove to be a protection even to the unrighteous (comp. Gen. 18:26; Acts 27:24, 34, 44).

23, 24 Then if any man shall say unto you, Lo, here is the

Christ, or, Here; believe *it* not. For there shall arise false Christs, and false prophets, and shall shew great signs and wonders; so as to lead astray, if possible, even the elect.

A. Then = duringthe period described in the foregoing words. The writings of the apostles and the history of primitive Christianity show that few dangers were more insidious and formidable than those with which false teachers and religious pretenders of all kinds threatened the Church. The Lord had uttered similar warnings at the commencement of His ministry (7:15); He repeats them above (ver. 4, 5, 11); here He specially refers to those impostors who shall assume the name of **Christ** = Messiah; **Christ**, lit. *the* Christ, as in ver. 5.—**B. Great signs and wonders.** Josephus remarks that before the fall of the city there was "a body of wicked men—not so impure in their actions, but more wicked in their intentions—who deceived and deluded the people under pretence of divine inspiration, etc." (War, 2, 13, 4). "They pretended that they would exhibit manifest wonders and signs" (Ant. 20, 8, 6). This prophecy of the Saviour and the later history of the Jewish writer precisely agree. The signs and wonders which these false Christs and prophets promised or pretended to perform were "lying wonders" such as Paul mentions (2 Thess. 2:9), and, like every ungodly thing, were "after the working of Satan."—**C. If it were possible.** The original phrase is simply: *if possible*, and does not deny the possibility of the fall of the elect (mentioned in ver. 22, above), as the English version seems to do by the unnecessary insertion of the italicized words *it were*. So, too, in 26:39, the Lord evidently does not pray for an acknowledged impossibility. Precisely the same two Greek words again occur in Acts 20:16; Rom. 12:18; Gal.

4:15; in the first two of these passages a possibility may exist; in the last one it is, for the sake of argument, assumed to exist. While the word **if** frequently introduces a doubt, it also frequently indicates that a particular circumstance may easily occur or really does exist, as in 5:29; 6:30; 7:11; 12:28. Accordingly, the Lord here by no means teaches that the **elect,** or indeed any human beings, are infallible, or incapable of being deceived or of falling, and that hence they no longer needed the prayer: Lead us not into temptation (Ezek. 18:24; Matt. 26:41; 1 Cor. 10:12; Phil. 3:12). The sense of the words is very clearly given by one of the four disciples to whom they were spoken (Prel. Obs. F. § 4, above). He addresses those who had obtained "like precious faith" with him, that is, the "elect" (1 Peter 1:1, 2, comp. with 2 Peter 1:1), in the following manner: "Beware lest ye also, being led away with the error of the wicked, fall from your own steadfastness" (2 Peter 3:17). The Lord's words: "What I say unto you, I say unto all, Watch" (Mark 13:37), are repeated continually to each individual until his race on earth is fully run.

²⁵ Behold, I have told you beforehand.

Behold ... before = so that, when all shall come to pass, your faith may not waver, but rather be confirmed by such evidence of My divine foreknowledge (John 13:19; 14:29).

²⁶ If therefore they shall say unto you, Behold, he is in the wilderness; go not forth: behold, he is in the inner chambers; believe *it* not.

A. Wherefore = as the lesson to be deduced from these warnings, if they, etc.—**B. If they** = indefinitely, any agents or blind adherents of these impostors.—**C. Behold he** (= *Christ,* as in ver. 23) **is, etc.** Some of the impostors and false Christs would secure a retreat in the desert, and thither call their deluded followers; others, who still abode in the city, before its fall, would either affect a mysterious air, or conceal their pretensions from the public view, and secretly gather disciples (= **secret chambers,** a term indicating privacy, mystery; for the word, see 6:6, B.).—**Chambers** = some one of several (21:5, F.). Whatever character the impostor might assume, he was not *the Christ* whom the disciples had known, and must be instantly and unhesitatingly disowned.

²⁷ For as the lightning cometh forth from the east, and is seen even unto the west: so shall be the coming of the Son of man.

A. After the Lord had reached this point, and described the signs that would indicate the near approach of the destruction of the city, He again refers to the questions in ver. 3, which seemed to imply that His last coming at the end of the world would occur at the same time. Mark omits here a portion of the Lord's words; the conversation is probably resumed, and Matthew, in ver. 27–31, gives the substance of the reply addressed to the disciples. Christ *now* shows that the end of the world would be introduced by signs and attended by circumstances of a character entirely different from those which He had just described in ver. 15–26. As these events still belong to the future, and we have no other precise and definite revelations of them, they, like in all unfulfilled prophecies, are so veiled that no interpreter can furnish a full and particular explanation (ver. 29, A.).—**For.** This word generally introduces a reason which is given for words previously uttered. We may suppose either that words like those in ver. 6, "the end (of the world) is not yet," had been repeated, or that the Lord had said that new and peculiar signs would announce His coming, which He now proceeds to describe, "for," continued He, "as the lightning, etc."—**B. As the lightning, etc.** Two features of the lightning are here indicated: first, its celerity, suddenness or unexpectedness (whence it is frequently used as an image of unlooked-for events); and, secondly, its conspicuousness, distinctness, or the widely extended space in which it is seen ("east ... west," as in Job 37:3), on which account it is at once distinguished by all from any other luminous appearance.—**So shall, etc.** = so, too, when I, the Son of man (8:20, B.), shall come the second time (10:23, B.), in order to judge the world, that event will be both unexpected ("as a thief in the night," 2 Peter 3:10 and ver. 43, below), and also will be marked by such divine glory (2 Thess. 1:7, 8), that all the world ("east ... west") shall be able to distinguish it unerringly from the appearance of any pretender or false Christ (Rev. 1:7; comp. Luke 17:24, and see Prel. Obs. G.).

[28] Wheresoever the carcass is, there will the eagles be gathered together.

That is: The well-known proverb which implies that certain operating causes inevitably produce certain results (the carcass inevitably attracting the birds of prey that are still unseen) is here applicable: the confusion in the world, the sins of men, the interpositions of divine grace, and the whole course of events from the fall of Adam to the preaching of the Gospel for a witness unto all nations (ver. 14), necessarily call for an ultimate divine adjustment, a retribution, a divinely arranged new order of things (comp. Rom. 2:5–10; 2 Thess. 1:6–10; Rev. 21:1, 5). The proverb here quoted (which was not unknown to other ancient nations) was current among the Jews, and is found in substance in Job 39:30: "Where the slain are, there is she (the eagle)" (see 7:6, A.);

the same image is introduced in Deut. 28:49. The original name, however, and particularly the corresponding *Hebrew* word, embraces also, in a broader acceptation than the modern word, a species of vulture (*vultur perenopterus*) in some respects resembling the eagle; it has part of the head denuded of feathers, to which feature there is an evident allusion in Micah 1:16, where the name is translated *eagle*, as well as in Job 9:26; Hos. 8:1; Hab. 1:8; in all these cases the allusion doubtless is to a vulture. The latter prefers carrion ("carcass," Prov. 30:17), while the eagle, as it is well known, prefers to seize its prey alive; besides, while vultures were numerous in Palestine, the eagle was less frequently seen. The text cannot therefore refer, as it is supposed by some, to the Roman eagles (described above, ver. 15, B.), implying that Jerusalem or Judæa is the carcass; still less, as others believe, can the eagles be images of destroying angels (the carcass representing the spiritually dead); least of all can they, as others, again, have assumed, represent the assembly of believers surrounding the crucified and risen Redeemer as the carcass. Oriental travellers have observed that a carcass lies undisturbed for a season, and, nevertheless, in a very brief space of time, vultures which have perceived it at an immense distance dart in large numbers suddenly from the air upon it. The sense then is: As a carcass will inevitably attract vultures, although none may yet be visible, so the mixture of good and evil in the world will surely lead to a divine interposition ultimately, even though men in their false security may entertain no apprehensions (2 Peter 3:3, 4). The Son of man will come and judge the whole race, whose habitation, the earth, will then pass away. The same words occur in Luke 17:37.

²⁹ But immediately, after the tribulation of those days the sun shall be darkened, and the moon shall not give her light, and the stars shall fall from heaven, and the powers of the heavens shall be shaken:

A. Immediately ... days. The remark made above (ver. 27, A.), that no interpretation of these prophecies can possibly furnish reliable details beyond the words of the text, applies here with peculiar force. **Those days** embrace the period preceding the Lord's coming to judgment. During this time intervening between the first indications of the Lord's coming and the actual advent, **tribulation** (for which word see above, 13:20, 21) will be endured, but this transition period will not be of long continuance ("immediately after"); with this interpretation the words "in those days" in Mark 13:24 fully concur. The pause which is usually made here by interpreters does not appear to be sustained by any solid arguments. The Greek words for "immediately after," which cannot possibly admit of any essentially different translation, necessarily imply a very brief interval, and cannot comprehend the many centuries intervening between the fall of the city and the end of the world; hence, the events of this verse are very closely connected with the foregoing in ver. 27, 28. In the present verse the *last* coming of the Lord is meant; that event must also be meant in ver. 27.—**B. The sun ... from heaven.** Similar language occurs frequently in the O. T., as in Isai. 13:10; 34:4; Ezek. 32:7; Joel 2:30; Hagg. 2:6, referring to great and striking events, some of which are intimately connected with Gospel times. Here, however, there is a distinct reference to great and visible changes in the appearance of the heavenly bodies, which may possibly be the beginning of that dissolution of all things revealed in 2 Peter 3:10, 11. As in ver. 7, so the words here employed are not mere figures of speech, but are to be literally understood.—**The stars shall fall.** It is not said that they shall *fall on the earth;* they shall *fail, pass away,* as the original word found here is rendered in Luke 16:17; in this sense, too, it is applied to Babylon in Rev. 14:8; 18:2, "is fallen."—**C. And the powers, etc.** As these **powers** are here *distinguished from* the sun, moon and stars (sometimes called the *host of heaven* (Ps. 33:6; Isai. 34:4), they possibly refer to the intelligent heavenly "hosts" or the angels (1 Kings 22:19; Ps. 103:21; 148:2), who also appear to be the "powers" mentioned in Rom. 8:38; 1 Peter 3:22; Col. 1:16, comp. with Eph. 1:21, and are called "angels of power" in 2 Thess. 1:7 in the original. They are **shaken** = *roused, deeply interested* in the solemn scenes, without the accompanying "trouble" of the Thessalonians (2 Thess. 2:2); the word originally describes the oscillating movements of a vessel occasioned by the action of the waves. The angels had previously been interested in the divine plan of salvation (1 Peter 1:12), and rejoice both at the Saviour's birth (Luke 2:13, 14), and also when they perceive that His saving grace influences the sinner (Luke 15:10); they will themselves be actively employed in these solemn scenes (ver. 31).

[30] And then shall appear the sign of the Son of man in heaven: and then shall all the tribes of the earth mourn, and they shall see the Son of man coming on the clouds of heaven with power and great glory.

A. And then. The length of the several divisions of time here respectively indicated is not revealed (ver. 14, F.).—**B. The sign of the Son of man.** The nature of this sign (different from the one mentioned in 12:39, C.), the Lord has not described; it is sufficient for us to know that when it shall appear, it will be so distinct and intelligible, that, like the signs of the manger (Luke 2:12) and the star (Matt. 2:2, 7, 9), on previous occasions, none can mistake its meaning. It may consist in the whole character of these events, their suddenness, grandeur or visible and direct heavenly origin, as Luke (21:25) seems to imply; it may be a celestial light like that which "suddenly shined round about" Paul on the road to Damascus (Acts 9:3),—a sign that would be the more distinct in consequence of the darkness which, according to ver. 29, precedes it. Or, in reference to Dan. 7:13, and the repeated introduction of the remarkable name *Son of man* (see above, ver. 27, B.), the sign may consist in the new appearance of the God-Man Jesus Christ in His human nature, yet invested with all divine glory, such as was temporarily revealed at His Transfiguration (see ann. to 17:2).—**C. And then ... mourn** (comp. Zech. 12:10–12; Rev. 1:7). At that time men will be found in all parts of the world who will either mourn as penitent sinners, or mourn that they did not "obey the Gospel," and now are to be "punished, etc." (2 Thess. 1:8, 9);—**mourn** = *bewail*. The same word occurs in 11:17.—**D. And they shall see, etc.** = all shall have abundant evidence of the presence and power of the Judge (Dan. 7:13). The **clouds**, doubtless, like the "bright cloud" mentioned in 17:5, are to be understood as brilliant masses of celestial light (comp. Acts 1:11; Exod. 16:10). The **power and great glory** of the Son of man will be demonstrated, first, by the attendance and adoration of "his mighty angels" (2 Thess. 1:7), who, while they "excel in strength" (Ps. 103:20, 21), declare by their prompt obedience the greatness of Him to do whose pleasure is the great purpose of their existence;

and, secondly, by His wonderful works, the raising of the dead, etc. (John 5:25; see 26:64, D.).

31 And he shall send forth his angels with a great sound of a trumpet, and they shall gather together his elect from the four winds, from one end of heaven to the other.

A. And ... angels (see 13:39, C.). When the Lord afterwards (25:31), at the conclusion of the discourse, resumes the subject of the General Judgment, the presence of the angels is again mentioned.—**B. With ... trumpet.** When God came down upon Mount Sinai, one of the wonders that announced His presence consisted in sounds like "the voice of the trumpet exceeding loud" (Exod. 19:16). Similar voices, loud as trumpets (**sound,** lit. *voice*), will not only proclaim the presence of the Judge, but also announce the actual resurrection of the dead, according to revelations given, after these words of Christ had been spoken, in 1 Cor. 15:52; 1 Thess. 4:16.—**C. Gather the elect.** For the **elect,** see above, 20:16, B. "The dead in Christ"—they that are Christ's—"shall rise first" (1 Cor. 15:23; 1 Thess. 4:16), and then also "they that have done evil" (John 5:29).—**D. From the four, etc.** (see Mark 13:27, and comp. Deut. 4:32; 13:7; 1 Chron. 9:24; Rev. 7:1). All the terms in these passages are equivalent to the phrase: "all parts of the earth," or, "from every direction," "from every point of the compass." The language„ as in Deut. 30:4; 2 Sam. 22:8, is suggested by the appearance in nature, according to which the sky (**heaven**) seems at a vast distance from the spectator, or at the horizon or boundary of vision, to rest on the earth at points where the **ends** of both appear to meet.

32 Now from the fig tree learn her parable; When her branch is now become tender, and putteth forth its leaves,

ye know that the summer is nigh:

A. Now learn. The word translated *Now* is simply the connective often rendered *and* or *but*, as in ver. 19, 36, or altogether omitted, as in ver. 29 at the beginning. The Lord here makes a pause in His discourse; this pause is distinctly marked in Luke 21:29, where a new division of the discourse is announced by the words: "And he spake to them a parable." The Lord had probably been interrupted by an exclamation or question of the disciples; He answers by reminding them that they have now had sufficiently full revelations of the two events which so deeply interested them, and that He expects them to meditate, and, by watching the course of Providence, to **know** (= to discern "of their own selves," Luke 21:30) the respective "signs of the times" (Matt. 16:3).—**B. A parable.** The sense is: The illustration of these things is furnished by the fig tree; even as it affords indications of the changes of the seasons, so the events already mentioned (ver. 4–13; 15–26) will be sufficiently clear indications of the downfall of the city.—**C. Branch ... tender** = when the sap has risen, and the branch, after being dry and rigid in the winter, becomes moist and soft. For **fig tree**, see 21:19, A.—**D. Summer.** This season, extending in that region from April to October, was characterized by the absence of rain; the appearance of the latter during that period is described as miraculous in 1 Sam. 12:17, 18. During this season the wheat harvest occurred, for which important event preparations were made when the leaves of the fig tree began to appear (comp. Prov. 6:8), when *summer* and *harvest* are viewed as nearly coincident.

[33] Even so ye also, when ye see all these things, know ye that he is nigh, even at the doors.

A. All these things = the signs of the approaching fall of the city, as mentioned in ver. 32, B.—**B. It is near.** *What* is near? As no nominative or subject of the verb is occurs in the original, the translators suggest in the margin *he* for *it* (see Introd. § 6), but the parallel passage, Luke 21:31, contains the direct answer: *"the kingdom of God"* is near. This phrase (comp. Excursus I. vol. I. p. 379) indicates fundamentally communion with God, a more or less perfect recognition of His glory by His creatures, and their own consequent happiness. Now the destruction of Jerusalem and its temple exercised an incalculably great influence not only on the spirit and character of the Christian Church, but also on its external growth or expansion. All the bonds that had hitherto connected believing Jews with the ancient religion (visits to the temple, observance of Jewish ceremonies, etc., Acts, ch. 15; 18:18; 21:21–26) were dissolved when the temple service with its sacrifices, etc., ceased, and when this awful evidence of the divine rejection of those who had slain the Lord Jesus had been given. The Church of Christ, viewed as a more fully revealed form of the kingdom of God, emerged from the ruin of the nation as an independent and new organization, with a life, a power and a spirit of its own, and with a worship and a law totally distinct from those of the old religion. Then, as never before, the prophetic words of the Saviour addressed to the Samaritan woman (John 4:21–24) began to be fulfilled, and a more widely-extended development or manifestation of the spirit of the Christian Church as distinct from Judaism, together with more freedom in its movements, commenced. In such a sense the fall of Jerusalem was an impressive token or sign that the manifestation of "the kingdom of God" in its proper Christian form was **near, even at the doors.** The latter phrase indicates the very closest proximity (James 5:9). Hence, as the fig leaves (ver. 32, D.) announced the gathering of the grain, so the fall of the city announced a gathering of people, a harvest for the Church among Jews and Gentiles immeasurably greater than any accessions which it had previously received. Of the history of the Church during the period in question, extending from a. d. 70 (when Jerusalem fell) to a. d. 100, the notices or records that are extant are very scanty; one well-known fact, however, sheds a flood of light upon it. Pliny, the governor of Bithynia and Pontus in Asia Minor (Acts 16:7; 1 Peter 1:1), wrote a letter to the Emperor Trajan in a. d. 107, about 37 years after the fall of the city, which presents the following facts:—In that remote region, on the south of the Black Sea, nearly the whole population had been converted to Christianity; the heathen temples had been almost forsaken, the pagan religious rites had generally ceased, etc. The facts show that a powerful impulse was given to the Church by the great catastrophe to which the Lord here refers.

[34] Verily I say unto you, This generation shall not pass away, till all these things be accomplished.

This generation, etc. (see above, 23:35, B.). The word here, like the corresponding Hebrew term in Numb. 32:13, evidently refers to persons then living, contemporaries, as above, 11:16, A.; 12:39; 16:4; 17:17, and in Acts 2:40; 13:36; Hebr. 3:10; contemporaneous existence is meant in such cases. A **generation** was reckoned, after the era of Moses, at 30 or 40 years (see Deut. 1:35; 2:14). The destruction of Jerusalem occurred about 40 years after these words were spoken.—**All these things,** as in ver. 6, above = that are mentioned as signs of the approaching ruin of the city.—**Pass** = *pass away,* as the same word is rendered in the next verse, and in James 1:10 (see 5:18, C.).

³⁵ Heaven and earth shall pass away, but my words shall not pass away.

To this event—the passing away of the present visible creation—mentioned in Ps. 102:25, 26; Isai. 51:6; 2 Peter 3:10, 12, the Lord had already prophetically referred in 5:18. The sense here is: You cannot rely on the stability of any visible object, for all that you behold above, around or beneath you is transitory; but My words shall not come to nought; they are reliable = on their fulfilment you can confidently rely. This is language which no creature could presume to employ ("my words"); it is here uttered by God the Son.

³⁶ But of that day and hour knoweth no one, not even the angels of heaven, neither the Son, but the Father only.

A. When the conversation of the four disciples and their Master had reached this point, the former appear to have refrained from further interruptions of the Lord's discourse. As in Mark 9:32; Luke 9:45, the disciples, although perplexed and distressed by certain mysterious words of Christ which they long could not understand (Luke 18:34), nevertheless "feared to ask" for more precise explanations; so here, too, they appear to be troubled in spirit, but do not venture to interpose new questions. This new division in the discourse is distinctly seen both in Mark (ch. 13:32), who here, after adding a short summary, discontinues his report, and also in Luke (ch. 21:33), who adopts the same course; both leave to Matthew the task of reporting in full the discourse *from this point.* The Lord proceeds to speak uninterruptedly, as it seems, to the close of the next chapter, on a new subject, namely, the personal application of the great truths which He had so far revealed. He designs to give a practical character to His predictions by introducing the following solemn lesson:—While the events already foretold are in themselves of vast importance, yet in the case of each individual, whether he dies in one century or in another, the hour of his death, after which he can no longer work out his salvation (John 9:4; Phil. 2:12), is really equivalent to the coming of the Son of man to judgment, inasmuch as his own future and eternal lot is at that moment virtually decided. This impressive doctrine is unfolded in ver. 36–41, and then affectingly illustrated and applied in the remaining portion of the discourse.—**B. But ... hour** (see above, Prel. Obs. D.). The Lord, well understanding the anxious looks of His disciples, nevertheless absolutely withholds from them the knowledge of the precise time (**day and hour**) of the actual end of the world. His words, which may be translate: "*Concerning* that day, etc.," and which point back to ver. 30, clearly show that we have here a transition to another subject, entirely distinct from "these things" which that generation will live to see (ver. 34). **That day,** as in 7:22, C., and 2 Tim. 1:12, 18; 4:8, is the "day of the Lord" or "end" mentioned in ver. 14, and in 2 Peter 3:10; 1 Thess. 5:2. So, frequently, the words *that, those,* used, as here, in opposition to *this, these,* refer to a more remote subject previously mentioned; in Luke 18:14, *that one* (translated "the other") is the Pharisee mentioned in a former verse. In Mark 16:20, *those* (translated "they") are the disciples mentioned in a foregoing verse.—**C. Knoweth no man, etc.** = it is not a subject which a creature ought to know or can endure to know (comp. Acts 1:7);—**Not the**

angels. Mark adds (13:32): "neither the Son" (see PREL. Obs. D.).—**But ... only** = "such knowledge is too wonderful" for man (Ps. 139:6), it can be grasped by the Divine Mind alone.

37 And as *were* the days of Noah, so shall be the coming of the Son of man.

But as, etc. = as men in the days of Noah (when he proclaimed the approaching judgment, 2 Peter 2:5) despised the divine warnings, and paid no attention to the revelation of the precise time when the deluge would occur (in 120 years, Gen. 6:3), and perished in their sins, so, even if the Lord would reveal the precise time of the end of the world ("the coming, etc.," ver. 27), such a revelation would again be utterly slighted by the thoughtless and profane. Indeed, if it were revealed that the time of that event would be more remote than the probable death of the individual, the revelation would only harden his heart the more and confirm his security in sin. The Lord here prepares the way for developing in ver. 42 and the remainder of the discourse the lesson already mentioned (see ann. to ver. 36, A.).

38 For as in those days which were before the flood they were eating and drinking, marrying and giving in marriage, until the day that Noah entered into the ark,

See Gen. 6:1–6, "the wickedness of man was great."—**Flood** = of water (Gen. 6:17; 7:6), the deluge, as in 2 Peter 2:5;—**eating, etc.** = men continued to be absorbed in the affairs of this life;—**giving in marriage,** as in 1 Cor. 7:38), is the act of parents who arrange the marriage of their children;—**until the day** = showing not the least regard to the divine revelations of the time of the deluge. The Lord, as in His description of the rich man (Luke 16:19) specifies no gross crimes, as murder, etc.; but His description represents the antediluvians as totally alienated from the life of God (Eph. 4:18), as neither glorifying nor thanking God (Rom. 1:21), and as ultimately abandoned by divine grace in consequence of their inexcusable ignorance and wickedness (Rom. 1:20, 24, 26, 28). Hence, their worldly life, not being influenced by divine grace, exhibited nothing but vice and iniquity (comp. Rom. 1:29, ff.; 2:10–18; 14:23). The description applies to every godless and wicked generation, living in thoughtless security.

^{39} And they knew not until the flood came, and took them all away; so shall be the coming of the Son of man.

And knew not = *did not reflect, care for,* as in Gen. 39:6; Isai. 1:3, the corresponding Hebrew word signifies, like the same Greek word in John 10:14.—**B. Took ... away** = carried them off, caused their death; the Greek word, as an exclamation, "away," occurs in Luke 23:18; Acts 21:36; 22:22.—**C. So shall** (will), **etc.** = so, too, at the end of the world, many will be totally unprepared to meet their Judge.

$^{40,\ 41}$ Then shall two men be in the field; one is taken, and one is left.—Two *women shall be* grinding at the mill; one is taken, and one is left.

In these two verses the Lord declares that when the time of His coming is at hand, impenitent sinners will be found absorbed in temporal concerns and totally regardless of their eternal interests; but other persons, again, in similar stations of life, without neglecting their earthly calling, will be found to have lived a life of faith. He selects illustrations which comprehend both sexes and various conditions. Two *men* may be engaged in agricultural labors; one of them may be a believer; he will be **taken** = received into the care of the angels (ver. 31; compare **take** in 2:20; Acts 21:24).

Two women (as the original indicates) may be intimately associated in the same household duties (for **grinding,** etc., see 18:6, C.); one of them may be **taken** = be acknowledged as a true believer; the other, a worldly-minded woman, be unfit, through want of a new heart, to be admitted into the joy of the Lord (comp. Luke 17:28, 32, 35).

⁴² Watch therefore: for ye know not on what day your Lord cometh.

A. The subject which the Lord now introduces, that is, the duty of each individual to prepare for his approaching death, as if the day of that event actually coincided with the day of the Lord's coming, He proceeds to unfold in the following words, to ch. 25:30. He primarily applies the lesson to His own disciples, as the first heralds of the cross and teachers of the Church. That a new division of the discourse here commences is shown by the manner in which Luke in ch. 21:36 (with which comp. Mark 13:33–37) here closes his report, indicating that the special subject hitherto discussed is now dismissed and a new one introduced. (Compare for this verse and those which follow, Luke 12:37–40, and Prel. Obs. G.)—**B. Watch therefore** = in view of the uncertainty of the hour in which death may call you away, be always prepared for the coming of your Judge. "And what I say unto you, I say unto all, Watch" (Mark 13:37). "Watch and pray" (Matt. 26:41; comp. 1 Cor. 16:13; 1 Thess. 5:6; 1 Peter 5:8); in the latter passage the same word is translated: "be vigilant."—**C. For ye, etc.** = precisely your ignorance of the exact time of your end is to have the effect of keeping your faith alive, of maintaining the spirit of prayer, of animating you to live near to God (see above, Prel. Obs. D.). Such daily communion with God (1 Cor. 15:31; Gal. 2:20) alone can preserve you from Satan's snares and qualify you for the enjoyment of the presence of God in heaven.

⁴³ But know this, that if the master of the house had known in what watch the thief was coming, he would have watched, and would not have suffered his house to be broken through

A. Goodman ... house = householder (see 20:11, B.).—**B. In what, etc.—watch** = night-watch (14:25, A.), here equivalent to: *at what hour of the night*. *The thief's arrival* was a proverbial expression of the Jews, indicating any event the time of the occurrence of which was very uncertain (see above, 7:6, A.; 18:3, C.). The sense here is:—A wise man, who receives an intimation that danger is approaching, will prepare for it and be found ready when it arrives.—**Broken up** = broken into, entered into, through an opening in the wall (6:19, B.).

⁴⁴ Therefore be also ready: for in an hour that ye think not the Son of man cometh.

A. Therefore, lit. *On this account* = as your case is the same (being forewarned of approaching danger), imitate that man's example; while the arrival of death, on the one hand, is certain, the precise time, on the other, is uncertain.—**B. Be ... ready.** The original word for *ready* is equivalent *to prepared* (22:4, 8; 2 Cor. 9:5), and, as in 25:10 and Tit. 3:1; 1 Peter 3:15, describes persons who have made all proper arrangements for an approaching event, the precise time of the occurrence of which is unknown.—**C. For in such, etc.** While it is obvious that the disciples died before the second or last coming of Christ, it is equally obvious, in view of the sense and application of the parables which immediately follow, that the "coming" which is here announced is a decisive and final event (comp. 25:10); it is the day of "reckoning" for all men (25:19; comp. with 24:46, 51). This *coming* can therefore not be the destruction of Jerusalem, with which the death of the several disciples did not coincide, nor can it refer to any other striking public event in the current history of the world; it can indicate only the death of the disciples respectively, and of other individuals (see 10:23, B.). In one sense of the proverb (founded on Eccl. 11:3): "As the tree fall, so it lies," the future and eternal state of each individual will depend on the life and spirit which characterized him at the time when he died (see ver. 36, A.). The Lord therefore here says:—In place of inquiring with unnecessary anxiety concerning future events in which you are not personally interested, rather prepare for the hour of your own death; that hour may come suddenly, in some tumult raised by persecutors or otherwise; therefore, regard each day as your last, as if the end of the world were very nigh.

45 Who then is the faithful and wise servant, whom his lord hath set over his household, to give them their food in due season?

A. Who ... servant. In this passage, ver. 45–51, the Lord appears to allude primarily to the apostolic duties of His disciples as His agents in founding the Church and communicating the Gospel to the world. In their capacity as the original heralds of the cross ("pillars," Gal. 2:9; "the salt of the earth," "the light of the world," Matt. 5:13, 14; "sitting upon twelve thrones," 19; 28), they assumed a heavy responsibility, and would, after their death, be subjected to a strict examination of the degree of fidelity which they had exhibited to their sublime mission. At the same time, the particulars mentioned in Mark 13:34 and 37, but omitted here ("to every man his work, etc."), show that every individual, in whatever position he may be placed, is regarded by the Lord as a responsible agent, who is solemnly bound to labor faithfully in the service of God. Matthew appears to regard the apostles particularly, but without confining the application of the word to them alone.—**Wise** = here, descriptive of a man of forethought and prudence; the same term occurs in 25:2.—**Household** = the aggregate of the "fellow-servants" in ver. 49 (comp. Luke 12:42).—**B. To give, etc.** The servant here described as a model for the apostles is a *steward* (Luke 12:42), a servant also, but invested by his master with authority over others, like Eliezer (Gen. 15:2; 24:2, and see above 20:8, B.). Paul regards himself and his fellow-laborers as "stewards of the mysteries of God" (1 Cor 4:1), and Peter assumes that "every man that hath received the gift (lit. *a gift*) "is" a steward of the manifold grace of God" (1 Peter 4:10).—**Meat** = food (3:4, C.).—**In due season** = at the proper time; in the spiritual sense, a wise and judicious, as well as conscientious and zealous fulfilment of religious duties is here implied.

⁴⁶ Blessed is that servant, whom his lord when he cometh shall find so doing.

The blessings described in the Sermon on the Mount (5:3–12) are here promised anew in all their fulness and eternal glory; they will be granted on the last day (25:34), for then the Lord "cometh" (25:31). Such precious promises, received in faith, cheered the disciples in all their subsequent trials (see 2 Cor. 4:17, 18; Phil. 1:21–23; 2 Tim. 4:6–8; James 1:12; 2:5; 1 Peter 5:4, 10; 1 John 3:2; Jude, ver. 21).—**So doing** = always, without abatement, working, watching and praying.

⁴⁷ Verily I say unto you, that he will set him over all that

he hath.

A. As these remarkable words refer to acts of the Lord and to conditions of the redeemed, all of which belong to the future, and the scene of which is heaven, the precise meaning of the former cannot at present be known to mortals. St. Paul refers to the same subject in Rom. 8:17, 18, and calls the redeemed "joint heirs with Christ"; he there also speaks of "the glory which shall be revealed in us," and elsewhere (2 Tim. 2:11, 12) declares that the faithful shall "live" and "reign" with Christ. As these visions of heavenly glory, if unveiled, would dazzle and overcome feeble mortals while they are in the flesh, St. John says: "It doth not yet appear, etc." (1 John 3:2).—**B. Make him, etc.** The sense of the image (taken from scenes like those in Gen. 39:4–6; 41:40) is:—Even as such a lord advances the faithful servant to a position of the highest honor and enjoyment, so God will raise the redeemed to the full and unlimited enjoyment of heavenly glory (comp. 25:21).

[48] But if that evil servant shall say in his heart, My lord tarrieth;

A. But and if. The word **and** is here superfluous; it does not occur in the original Greek phrase, which elsewhere, as in 5:13; 6:23, is translated simply: *but if = if, however,* or, *should, however.*—**B. That evil servant** = if that highly trusted servant should be found to have been evil, faithless, dishonest.—**C. Say in his heart** = *secretly think,* as in Ps. 10:6, 11, 13.—**D. My lord, etc.** = the time of my death is still distant. "Though it tarry, wait (look) for it; because it will surely come, etc." (Hab. 2:3).

[49] And shall begin to beat his fellow-servants, and shall eat and drink with the drunken;

And shall, etc. = and shall walk after the flesh (Rom. 8:1; 2 Peter 2:10), indulging the corrupt inclinations of his heart, and scorning all religious duties. The selfish, oppressive, carnally minded (Rom. 8:6) servant is here the image of the nominal Christian, of the unconverted, worldly-minded sinner (James 4:17), and also of the hypocrite (ver. 51).

⁵⁰ The lord of that servant shall come in a day when he expecteth not, and in an hour when he knoweth not.

That servant will harden his heart more and more, inasmuch as obstinate impenitence brings with it the curse of increased insensibility to the warnings of truth; thus the "day" and "hour" of death will come when he is least prepared to meet his God and Judge.

⁵¹ And shall cut him asunder, and appoint his portion with the hypocrites: there shall be the weeping and gnashing of teeth.

A. And shall ... asunder. This horrible mode of inflicting capital punishment, called *dichotomy,* was practised by the ancient Babylonians (Dan. 2:5; 3:29), Egyptians and Persians; it differed from another barbarous mode of execution called *serratura,* or *sawing asunder,* to which there is an allusion in Hebr. 11:37, where the prophet Isaiah, according to later traditions, is meant. Neither mode was tolerated by the laws of Moses. The acts described in 2 Sam. 4:12, and probably 12:31, were mutilations of the bodies of criminals after their death, the purpose of which was to attach ignominy to the punishment of death. Under this image the Lord describes the eternal and awful doom of the impenitent.—**Portion** = fruit, reward, result, as in Eccl. 2:10; Rev. 21:8, "part."—**Hypocrites** (see 6:2, D.). Here the Lord reveals that their eternal condition in the other world will be one of unmitigated punishment and misery; they are in reality "unbelievers" (Luke 12:46).—**B. There shall, etc.** (see 8:12, D. "The wages of sin is death," Rom. 6:23).

10

Matthew 25

PRELIMINARY OBSERVATIONS

Obs. A.—After the Lord had given answers to the questions in ch. 24:3, He introduced the momentous truth that the hour of the death of each individual is "the end" of all things, virtually, in his own case; it is, as He teaches, the duty of man not so much to inquire after the precise time of the fall of Jerusalem or of the end of the world, as, rather, to make diligent preparations for his own death, which may occur when it is least expected (see above, 24:36, A., and ver. 44, C.).

Obs. B.—This important lesson is now more fully taught and illustrated by two parables. These will lose much of their meaning and force, unless they be studied in connection with the foregoing chapter. The images in both (a festival, as in 8:11, in the one, and a final reckoning in the other) plainly indicate the "end" of all things. The former—the parable of the Ten Virgins—principally illustrates the uncertainty of the hour of death, and the importance of being at all times prepared for it. That such is the scope of the parable is revealed in ver. 13, which assigns the purpose for which the parable was delivered. The second parable—of the Talents—is designed to explain the reasons which render such a preparation for death necessary. These are derived from the circumstance that as each individual had been intrusted with objects of great intrinsic value (life, religious privileges, etc.), he will be required to give an account of his character and conduct to the Supreme Judge on the Day of Judgment.

Hence, the second parable gives special prominence to man's responsibility for his mode of applying the gifts which divine grace has bestowed. While the near relations of the virgins to the bride, and of the servants to their Lord, seem to indicate that the responsibility of the disciples is chiefly designed to be illustrated, there is no reason for supposing that the solemn lessons and warnings here given are applicable to them alone—surely, "every man" (ver. 15), without any exception, is solemnly bound to be a faithful servant of his Lord in heaven.

¹ Then shall the kingdom of heaven be likened unto ten virgins, which took their lamps, and went forth to meet the bridegroom.

A. Then = at the "end" of all things, when the Lord's final coming to judgment occurs; the latter virtually coincides, in the case of every individual, with the day of his death (24:36, A.).—**B. Kingdom ... likened unto** = the Messiah's kingdom in its transition, when its earthly forms, which exhibited a mixture of good and evil (tares and wheat, ch.

13), pass away, and when it is to be revealed in its pure and heavenly character (see Excursus I. § 10).—**Likened unto** (see 18:23, B.).—**C. Ten.** Among the Jews various cardinal numbers (such as 3, 7, 10, 12, 40, 70) were peculiarly significant, chiefly in consequence of the association of the latter with prominent points in the law, historical events, etc. (see 10:1, A.; 18:21, A.). The number **ten** reminded the Jew of the "words of the covenant, the ten commandments" (Exod. 34:28; Deut. 4:13); it reappeared in the laws respecting *tithes* (see 23:23, A.), and elsewhere frequently. It indicated completeness or sufficiency, and was used at times to represent a large number (Gen. 31:7, 41; 1 Sam. 1:8; Job 19:3; Eccl. 7:19). It also expressed, according to Jewish usage, the limit or lowest number of which a company could consist that ate the paschal lamb in conformity to the law in Exod. 12:4, "so that a company not less than ten belong to every sacrifice" (Jos. War, 6, 9, 3). Hence, the nobleman in Luke 19:13, who had a full and complete household, had "ten servants." In the present case the phrase, *ten virgins,* is equivalent to the *customary* or appropriate number of female friends and attendants of a Jewish bride.—**D. Virgins.** On the occasion of a marriage, the bridegroom, attended by his "companions" (Judg. 14:11, and see Matt. 9:15, A.), advanced, after the setting of the sun (hence the "lamps"), to meet the bride, who was attended by a corresponding number of "virgins, her companions" (Ps. 45:14). These were sometimes more than ten in number, in the case of families of wealth and rank. The judgment is represented as a joyful event, since it transfers the faithful (as all ought to be) to scenes of joy and glory. It is possibly on this account that the Lord, as in Luke 12:36, chooses the image of a marriage festival. The persons in this and the next parable are simply representatives of general classes of men, and no special spiritual meaning appears to be connected with the literal meaning of the terms *virgins* and *servants*.—E. **Lamps,** or *torches,* as the word is rendered in John 18:3. Such a torch consisted of a staff or rod, to one end of which a small vessel or pan containing a wick saturated with oil was attached (see 12:20, A.); the latter, while burning, was regularly supplied with oil from another vessel with which it was connected (ver. 4 and 7, and see Numb. 4:9, "lamps, oil-vessels").—**Went forth** = from their own respective homes to the house of the bride (comp. ver. 6, C.).—F. **The bridegroom.** The Lord Jesus is supposed by many to be indicated by the bridegroom; the bride would then represent the Church. The coming of the Lord as the Judge of men, at a future but uncertain time, is doubtless implied by the expected arrival of the bridegroom. The bride herself is not introduced, while her attendants are the prominent personages (see 22:2, C.). Now, the true members of the Church, as it is designed to exist (Eph. 5:27), will also be required to give an account as well as others; hence the interpretation of this portion of the parable is simplified if we assume that its main object is to set forth, on the one hand, the uncertainty of the hour of death (viewed as virtually equivalent to the day of judgment), and, on the other, the necessity of being prepared for death at all times. The details here given (the number *five,* ver. 2; the sleeping of all, ver. 5, etc.) do not, respectively, represent spiritual things: this view is sustained by the words occurring in ver. 13, which explain the intention of the parable. So, too, the "oil and wine" of the good Samaritan (Luke 10:34) do not respectively represent special spiritual things, but, with other details, set forth the thoughtfulness, tenderness and fulness of love.

² And five of them were foolish, and five *were* wise.

Five—five. The Lord does not intend to teach that the number of enlightened Christians is precisely equal to that of impenitent sinners; He merely takes the lowest number (ver. 1, C.) which the case suggested, and presents accordingly *two* groups (comp. 21:28; Luke 15:11). Even as in Luke 13:23, 24, He withheld a direct answer to a question respecting the actual number of those "that be saved," so here He refrains from indicating even remotely the relative proportions of the two classes; He introduces a general division, which, while it gives the strongest force to the contrast between the two classes, is equivalent to: "some—some."—**Foolish** = *dull, inconsiderate,* as in 7:26; 23:17; Tit. 3:—see above 5:22, F. Comp. Prov. 14:8; Ps. 111:10; 2 Pet. 1:5–9).—**Wise.** The original word here, as in 7:24, is equivalent to *prudent, thoughtful, intelligent,* and occurs in such a sense in Matt. 24:45; Luke 12:42; 16:8; 1 Cor. 10:15; it is different from the word which strictly corresponds to the English word *wise,* and which occurs in Matt. 11:25; 23:34; Rom. 1:14; 1 Cor. 1:19.

³,⁴ For the foolish when they took their lamps, took no oil with them: But the wise took oil in their vessels with their lamps.

Lamps—oil—vessels (see above, ver. 1, E.).—**With them** = with themselves. The *wise* virgins, aware that the emptiness of the oil-vessels would defeat the whole design for which the lamps were carried, furnished themselves with oil, and were consequently ready at any moment. The others, occupied with the present moment alone, made no provision for the future. Their moral conduct was, as far as the world could judge, correct ("lamps"), but was not sanctified by Christian or holy principles ("oil"). This fact constitutes the essential difference between nominal Christians and hypocrites, on the one hand, and those who have an experimental knowledge of Christ (Phil. 3:8, 10), on the other. "Good works without faith are like lamps without oil, which are soon extinguished."—Luther. The Lord exhibits by means of such images the wisdom of those who daily and hourly prepare to meet their God, and the folly of those who live in impenitence and sin. The lamps may thus be regarded as symbols of a moral life regulated by the principles of worldly decorum, and the oil as a symbol of that living faith without which even an outwardly moral life exhibits no works that, in the eyes of God, are truly good and acceptable. Such special explanations, however, while they may involve important truths, are not necessarily a part of the immediate purpose of the parable. Hence the explanations or applications may vary; some may take the lamps as images of the sacred writings, and the oil as an image of the light of the Holy Spirit, who gives the true interpretation of the Scriptures.

⁵ Now while the bridegroom tarried, they all slumbered and slept.

A. Tarried = *deferred, delayed his coming,* as in 24:48.—**B. They all, etc.** As *all* the *wise* virgins also slept, while no censure falls upon them for yielding to a tendency of the bodily nature established by the Creator Himself, and as no evil results follow, the sleep here mentioned, as in 13:25, cannot be interpreted as an image of spiritual sloth. It is probably only one of the details which impart a natural character to the historical frame-work of the parable. Or, possibly, this interval which all spent in sleep may represent that portion of time given to lawful secular pursuits, such as trade, agriculture, etc., which belong only to this life; to these the believer gives a proper share of attention while "waiting for the coming of our Lord Jesus Christ" (1 Cor. 1:7; 1 Thess. 1:10).

⁶ But at midnight there is a cry, Behold, the bridegroom! Come ye forth to meet him.

A. At midnight = when, under ordinary circumstances, no visitor was expected (Luke 11:5–7); the Lord probably illustrates the words just pronounced, in 24:44, where a solemn warning against all false security respecting the time of our death is given (see also 2 Pet. 3:3, ff.).—**B. A cry ... bridegroom** = the shouts, the voice of mirth etc., characteristic of a marriage procession in ancient Jerusalem (Jerem. 7:34; 16:9; 25:10; Ps. 45:15).—**C. Come ye, etc.** The virgins are represented as waiting in the dwelling of the bride, where they had previously assembled (see ver. 1, C.) until the approach of the bridegroom with his companions should be announced.

⁷ Then all those virgins arose, and trimmed their lamps.

Trimmed. The Greek word may include the act of applying the sharp-pointed wire usually attached to the lamp or torch; it designates in general the process of *putting in order,* preparing, or furnishing, for instance, a table with food (Ezek. 23:41, in the Sept. or Greek translation), a house with utensils (Luke 11:25), a grave with garlands (Matt. 23:29), a bride with ornaments (Rev. 21:2), and here, possibly, a torch or wick with oil (ver. 1, C.). The time of replenishing the lamp in order to obtain the brightest light represents the moment when all are called to present themselves before the

Judge.

⁸ And the foolish said unto the wise, Give us of your oil; for our lamps are going out.

Are going out = are nearly extinguished or *quenched,* as the word is elsewhere rendered (Matt. 12:20; Mark 9:44; Hebr. 11:34). The soul which devotes its whole time and attention to the affairs of this life (see ver. 5, B.), and neglects to seek a living faith in Christ, is not fitted to enter heaven. The obstinately impenitent sinner discovers too late the gross self-delusion to which he had yielded in this life. The wise virgins represent those who, while they "use this world" (1 Cor. 7:31), have their "conversation (= citizenship) in heaven" (Phil. 3:20), and their "affections set on things above" (Col. 3:2), where their "treasures" are (Matt. 6:20). At the close of this discourse (ver. 41–46), the Lord more fully describes the condition of those whose lamps have no "oil" = who appear before the Judge without the righteousness of Christ which is imputed to those who receive Him with a living faith (Phil. 3:9).

⁹ But the wise answered, saying, Peradventure there be not enough for us and you: go ye rather to them that sell, and buy for yourselves.

A. But the wise ... so. The refusal is not here expressed as fully and emphatically as in 13:29, but rather implies some apprehension which occasions the non-compliance; for instance, *it is to be feared that* there be not enough; in Rom. 11:21 the words "take heed" are accordingly inserted (comp. Acts 5:39, "lest haply"). The speakers, who have enough oil for themselves only, direct the others to resort to the same source which had supplied them. The spiritual sense is: Every individual will be judged according to his own character and conduct; the righteousness of one mortal will not save another. It is the blood of "the Lamb of God which taketh away the sin of the world" (John 1:29), that alone "cleanseth us from all sin" (1 John 1:7). No application to saints or angels can avail, and no righteousness of our own can atone for our guilt. There are no works of supererogation (= good works done over and above the actual duty of the individual) which can be put to the account of another, as the Papists vainly imagine (Luke 17:10). "The just shall live by faith" (Hab. 2:4; Gal. 3:11), that is, by his own personal faith. "No man cometh unto the Father but by me" (John 14:6). See the gracious invitations in Isai. 55:1; Matt. 11:28.—**B. Go ye, etc.** This advice seems to indicate a feeble hope of success before the actual arrival of the bridegroom; it may represent the charitable judgment or hope entertained respecting the result of a deathbed repentance of a friend or acquaintance. In such cases God will decide with mercy, but also with strict justice. Can they that have oil to sell—the Saviour—be so easily found, if sought for only at the last moment, when death, already convulsing the body with pain and clouding the thoughts of the departing spirit, has commenced his work? Is *that* a favorable time for leaving and walking in the way of salvation? Even as Moses and the prophets, when too long slighted, did not aid the rich man (Luke 16:29), so Christ and the apostles cease to be saving guides when death has carried his prey away.

¹⁰ And while they went away to buy, the bridegroom came; and they that were ready went in with him to the marriage feast: and the door was shut.

A. And while ... came = when death makes its appearance, the day of grace, the season of probation, is closed. "While it is said, To-day, etc." (Hebr. 3:15).—**B. They that ... marriage.** The Lord recurs to this circumstance below (ver. 34).—**Marriage** = marriage-feast, as in 22:2, 4, **B.—And the door, etc.** (comp. Luke 13:25), where the spiritual meaning, which occurs here also, is obvious from the connection; the eternal exclusion of all "workers of iniquity "from heaven is plainly taught. After this life, the door of heaven will never be reopened! The "great gulf" between heaven and hell is impassable (Luke 16:26). (The Greek word for *gulf* (chasm) often describes a wide and extended space, and is applied to the ocean and the sky.)

11 Afterward come also the other virgins, saying, Lord, Lord, open to us.

A. Afterward = when life on earth, the season of probation, had been misapplied and had passed away forever.—**B. Lord, Lord, etc.** "Many will seek to enter in, and shall not be able" (Luke 13:34). The time when these scenes will occur is the Day of Judgment (see 7:21–23). The wicked, discovering their folly too late, will in vain implore the Judge to pardon them; they had wantonly despised His warnings while it was called To-day (Hebr. 3:13).

12 But he answered and said, Verily I say unto you, I know you not.

(See the explanation in ann. to 7:23, B.) Here the language is appropriately used by the bridegroom, who already found in his presence all that had appeared in the procession and were entitled to enter. To many on the last day the sense will be: I never saw you in the closet (6:6), at my Table (1 Cor. 11:20), etc.

13 Watch therefore; for ye know not the day nor the hour.

(See above, 24:42, for the explanation.) We have in these

words the Lord's own declaration respecting the general purpose of this parable; it teaches the solemn lesson implied in Eccl. 9:10.

¹⁴ For it *is* as *when* a man going into another country, called his own servants, and delivered unto them his goods.

A. For ... a man. The parable—of the Talents—somewhat resembles that of the Ten Pounds in Luke 19:12–27; the latter was delivered at an earlier period and in another place, and differs materially from the former both in its general design, as stated in Luke 19:11, and in the details. The image in both cases of a lord and his dependants was a natural and familiar one, and, as in a similar instance (see above, 22:2, A.), could easily occur in different parables, as well as that of a man who "had sons" in Matt. 21:28 and Luke 15:11.—**B. Going ... country.** The Lord grants freedom to men during their life on earth, the period of their probation (see 21:33, E.); the Saviour, since His ascension to the Father, is not personally visible to men (John 16:10; 20:17).—**C. His own servants** = over whom he possessed undisputed authority (see the force of the word **own** in John 10:12).—**D. His goods** = his *property,* as in 19:21, B. The Saviour here represents all that men possess (life, bodily and mental endowments, etc.) as objects only intrusted to them by God, who retains His claim to all. "What hast thou that thou didst not receive?" (1 Cor. 4:7, and see James 1:17; 1 Peter 4:10).

¹⁵ And unto one he gave five talents, to another two, to another one; to each according to his several ability; and he went on his journey.

A. Unto one ... ability. Talent = a Greek denomination of a certain fixed weight, and then of a certain amount of money, for which see 18:24, B. The word, probably through the influence of this parable, is now often applied to any distinguished mental endowment;—**ability** = *capacity, fitness,* which his lord had already fully ascertained; a faithful employment of the gifts of God's grace is followed by an increased measure of grace—"grace for grace" (John 1:16). Similar "diversities of gifts," granted by the Spirit "as he will," are mentioned in 1 Cor. 12:4–11. The divine distribution of temporal and spiritual gifts is not the result of any divine procedure resembling the caprice or whim of a man, but is governed by the highest wisdom, justice and love, although the divine purposes in special cases may not be known to us. Such gifts are always adapted to the **several** = personal or particular fitness of the individual, or the task which God assigns to him.—**B. Took his journey.** God, whom we cannot perceive with our senses, does not at once arrest the unfaithful and impenitent, but is long suffering and patient, reserving to Himself the determination of the time of the judgment. The interval between this lord's departure and his return, during which the incidents in ver. 16–18 occur, represents the period intervening between Christ's ascension and His second coming, in the history of the Church, as well as in that of the individual, the period which closes at the death of the latter.

[16] Straightway he that had received the five talents went and traded with them, and made other five talents.

This servant applied the money actively and judiciously to the purpose of trade, in accordance with his master's intention; during the absence of the latter he doubled the amount originally received. The spiritual sense is: Our life and strength belong to God's service; the gifts of His grace, offered in Christ, are to be diligently applied by every one in the fulfilment of the duty of dying to sin, of acquiring the spirit and mind of Christ (Phil. 2:5), and of following His steps (1 Peter 2:21); then, if Christ is "our life" (Col. 3:4), our death is "gain" (Phil. 1:21). Our growth in grace, moreover, in knowledge, faith and love, is proportioned to our earnestness and zeal. The conscientious employment of God's temporal gifts is here obviously also a part of our duty.

¹⁷ In like manner, he also that *received* the two, gained other two.

All are not apostles, etc. (1 Cor. 12:29); all have not the same abilities and opportunities for producing important results in the kingdom of grace. Nevertheless, he who receives only two talents = inferior gifts, opportunities, etc., can display as much diligence, forethought and conscientiousness in seeking his salvation as he who receives five. Hence the lord who is here introduced subsequently speaks not of the *success* or actual results, but solely of the *faithfulness* of his servants. He who believes that he has received *one* talent only is, nevertheless, as fully held accountable for his conduct and its influence or results as others who appear to be originally more highly favored.

¹⁸ But he that received the one went and digged in the earth, and hid his lord's money.

The Lord had already in 24:48, 49, described a faithless and wasteful servant = the vicious, profane and hardened sinner. Here He presents an illustration of the class of moral but unconverted and unsanctified persons (see ver. 25, A.). These do not absolutely oppose the cause of religion; they may even profess to be its friends; this feature of their conduct is represented by the act of hiding the talent and preserving it from harm. But they neither acquire spiritual gains for themselves by following Christ, nor promote the spiritual welfare of others by an example of Christian fidelity and zeal. The offer of pardon and salvation is practically spurned when they neglect the means of grace and fail to fulfil the duties of repentance and faith; as "wicked and slothful" servants, they will be "cast into outer darkness" (ver. 26, 30). Every impenitent sinner who rejects the offer of divine mercy is the servant who "hides his lord's money."

¹⁹ Now after a long time the lord of those servants cometh, and maketh a reckoning with them.

Cometh = when the General Judgment is held (see ch. 24, Prel. Obs. E.);—**reckoneth** = *taketh account,* as in 18:23, C. (see 12:36, C., and comp. 2 Cor. 5:10).

²⁰ And so he that received five talents came and brought other five talents, saying, Lord, thou deliveredst unto me five talents: lo, I have gained other five talents.

A. Other five talents = five that had been gained in addition to the five originally received. The time, ability, opportunity and spiritual grace offered to each individual enable him both to secure the growth of grace in his own heart, and also to promote the extension of the Redeemer's kingdom on earth; he labors for these objects by precept, example and continued, fervent prayer.—**B. I have gained, etc.** Here are to be supplied in the interpretation (according to John 15:5, "without me, etc.") the words: "Yet not I, but the grace of God which was with me" (1 Cor. 15:10). The five additional talents were gained only through the five that had been originally given (comp. John 3:27).

²¹ His lord said unto him, Well done, good and faithful servant: thou hast been faithful over a few things, I will set thee over many things: enter thou into the joy of thy lord.

A. Well done. This expression (comp. 2 Sam. 3:13; Ruth 3:13, "well") is here a commendatory exclamation not confined to oriental nations = Very good! Excellent! (Comp. 1 Cor. 4:5), "have praise.")—**B. Few things.** The gifts of God in this life, however undeserved and precious, are inconsiderable when compared with the exceeding and eternal weight of glory (2 Cor. 4:17; Rom. 8:18) which will be the portion of the **good and faithful** = those who have been renewed and sanctified by grace on earth.—**C. I will ... things.** For the sense, see above, 24:47, A. and B.—**D. The joy, etc.** A somewhat similar expression in Esther 9:17, 18, 19, 22, and the image employed by the Lord in Matt. 8:11, E., both indicate that the **joy** here mentioned is an allusion to a banquet employed as a familiar illustration of the highest degree of enjoyment which can fall to the lot of a human being (see ver. 30, below).

22, 23 And he also that *received* the two talents came and said, Lord, thou deliveredst unto me two talents; lo, I have gained other two talents.—His Lord said unto him. Well done, good and faithful servant; thou hast been faithful over a few things, I will set thee over many things: enter thou into the joy of thy lord.

Two very important lessons are here taught: first, the advantages, opportunities, etc., granted by the Lord to different individuals, vary in amount or extent; the actual results of the labors of many may seem to be insignificant (comp. 10:42, B., D.). As God, however, does not, like an earthly lord or king, really need the aid of any man, the spirit of faith and love in which the widow gave her last mite (Mark 12:41, ff.) was as acceptable in His eyes as that of any wealthy and liberal contributors could be. The outward form of the probation in this life is immaterial, provided that the result, demonstrating holy purposes, is favorable. Secondly, the language of the Judge on the last day, and the reward which He bestows, will depend (ver. 23) on the fidelity and zeal of the individual exclusively, and not on the actual amount of his labors on earth. While Peter's labors, and especially those of Paul, are described in the Acts as exceedingly rich in results, several of the apostles, who doubtless labored as faithfully, disappear from the historical pages of the N. T. at a very early period. Nevertheless, in all such cases the eternal reward may be equally great and glorious.

24 And he also that had received the one talent came and said, Lord, I knew thee that thou art a hard man, reaping where thou didst not sow, and gathering where thou didst not scatter.

A. Then he ... talent = not one individual will be able to escape on the great day of reckoning.—**B. I knew thee, etc.**—**Hard** = *harsh, stern*. *Scattered* is here applied either to the act of *scattering* the chaff by winnowing (3:12), or, more probably, to a particular mode of distributing seed = sowing (comp. *cast abroad, scatter, cast in,* in Isai. 28:25; in either case it represents the master as both grasping and also unjust or dishonest. So, too, many thoughtless men seem to regard the duties of religion as tasks to be performed for God's benefit, while in reality the whole benefit is assigned to the diligent and obedient. Since Christ describes the master as a judicious, generous and just man, how did the servant **know** him to be a *hard* master? That servant's sloth and other evil traits of character had previously taught him to experience the justice of his master rather than his bounty. So the unconverted and wicked, whose own consciences rebuke them, regard God rather as a master who condemns and punishes than as a gracious lord rewarding the faithful. As servants of sin, they know only the justice of God; His tender love they never sought, whereas the obedient "have boldness in the day of judgment—perfect love casteth out fear" (1 John 4:17, 18).

25 And I was afraid, and went away and hid thy talent in the earth: lo, thou hast thine own.

A. Afraid = of losing the talent, and of being punished. This servant is not an avowed enemy, but one who owns that he is in his master's power. He represents, not the unblushing infidel or grossly immoral scorner of religion, but rather a class of indolent and worldly-minded people (see ver. 18). They indulge the flesh, disregard the claims of religion, and lay up no treasure in heaven; when conscience rebukes them, they attempt to tranquillize it by the impious thought that God exacts more than the position and circumstances of His creatures sanction. It is not love to God and moral purity, but a mere servile fear of punishment ("afraid"), that withholds them from excesses or vicious outward acts. The conduct of those who hesitate to assume personally and decidedly the duties of religion by an open confession of Christ and a public union with His Church, is also illustrated by this man who was "afraid" *to do his duty.*—**B. Hid.** He did not appropriately apply it. The time and the opportunities for glorifying God, and for growing in grace, granted to each individual, are slighted and misapplied by those whom this servant represents. We must hereafter answer not only for the evil which we have done, but also for the good which we have left undone.—**C. Lo, thou, etc.** Such persons seem by their conduct to address God thus: We have not desired Thee;

we have not been idolaters, murderers, thieves; we have, on the contrary, been moral and honest; we have been good neighbors; we have read our Bible, visited the sanctuary, etc. But is this *all* that God requires? Is this all that Paul means, when he says: "To me to live is Christ"? (Phil. 1:21); **that is,** *thine own* = all that thou oughtest to expect, as in 20:14. But the Lord justly claimed more than this sum of money; the time and strength of the servant also belonged to the Master; of the fruits which these should have produced, the servant had defrauded him.

²⁶ But his lord answered and said unto him, *Thou* wicked and slothful servant, thou knewest that I reap where I sowed not, and gather where I did not scatter.

A. His lord ... him. Although no positive dishonesty is related, he is charged as "wicked and slothful." The term **wicked** (applied to another servant, 18:32) plainly shows here that the omission of duty is not simply a negative evil, but a positive transgression of the divine will, and actual *wickedness*.—**B. Thou knewest, etc.** The words form an indirect question = Didst thou know—or, Didst thou think that, etc.? The whole language of the servant was as insulting as it was untrue. His master replies in the following terms, resembling those occurring in another but similar parable (Luke 19:22, and see above, ver. 14, A.). By thy own confession "much shall be required" by me (Luke 12:48), and such a belief on thy part should have roused thee and prompted thee to make zealous efforts. No excuse will be admitted on the last day by the Judge for any transgressions proceeding from false religious views. Inasmuch as we are abundantly enabled to become "sound in the faith" (Tit. 1:13; 2 Tim. 1:13), religious errors and delusions increase the guilt of the offender.

²⁷ Thou oughtest therefore to have put my money to the bankers, and at my coming I should have received back mine own with interest.

The *bankers* here mentioned were persons who received money on deposit at interest, in order to loan it to others at a still higher rate. The extortions which moneylenders practised gave an odious sense, in the course of time, to the word *usury* = illegal interest. The spiritual sense is: Thou hast not only not sought after eminent attainments in knowledge, faith and love, but thou hast not even attempted to fulfil with an honest heart the lowest and most ordinary duties of religion. If we Christians cannot all personally preach the Gospel to heathen nations, visit the sick, provide for all the poor, etc., we can at least avail ourselves of Bible, mission and other benevolent societies and Church institutions, by making them our "exchangers" = agents, almoners, etc. It is the intention of the heart, the honest desire to live and labor for God's honor, to which the Judge will look.

²⁸ Take ye away therefore the talent from him, and give it unto him that hath the ten talents.

Possibly angels are here addressed, whose ministry is described in 13:41, 49. The sense is: The mere outward morality of man, which proceeds not from an internal living principle of faith (Rom. 14:23), but from other influences (decorum, the civil law, the usages of society, etc.), will be utterly discarded by the Supreme Judge ("take from him"). While such morality is doubtless, in its outward form, preferable to open vice, any merit which it may seem to possess is really due to the invisible but resistless influence of religion in the world and to the acknowledged excellence of its precepts = "give it, etc."

²⁹ For unto every one that hath shall be given, and he shall have abundance: but from him that hath not even that which he hath shall be taken away.

For the explanation of these words, see ann. to 13:12, A.

³⁰ And cast ye out the unprofitable servant into the outer darkness: there shall be the weeping and gnashing of teeth.

See ann. to 8:12 for the explanation.—**Unprofitable.** The connection in which the same word in the original occurs in Luke 17:10 shows that its ordinary meaning of *useless, without value,* is to be retained here also. Impenitence, spiritual sloth, and the neglect to seek Christ are all traits of conduct that bring down God's punishment (see 8:12, B.).

³¹ But when the Son of man shall come in his glory, and all the angels with him, then shall he sit upon the throne of his glory.

A. At this point the last division of the discourse commences; the Lord had already referred (24:27–31) to His second coming (which will be followed by the resurrection of all the dead and the General Judgment), but had temporarily suspended His remarks on that subject (see above, ch. 24, Prel. Obs. F. § 5, (*e*). He now completes His remarks. That the judgment of *all* the individuals of the human species is here meant is a truth proved by the words "all nations" (ver. 32; see Rom. 3:6; John 5:28, 29); at that time, according to Matt. 24:14, and many passages in the prophets, like Hab. 2:14, no heathen nations will have remained to which the Gospel had not at least been "preached" (comp. John 10:16; Rom. 11:25). Even those heathen nations which had appeared on earth and passed away long before the birth of Christ will also be judged; their case is considered in Rom.

1:18, ff.—**B.** The following passage is, on the one hand, not a mere parable intended only to illustrate some general truth, but rather a prediction of certain future *events;* yet, on the other hand, figurative expressions ("sheep—goats"), as well as illustrations furnished by the oriental mode of administering justice, are introduced, even as in 8:11, 12; 9:36, the figurative terms convey additional information, without converting the facts themselves into mere figures of speech.—**C.** As the circumstances here described belong to the future, they are, as in all prophetic descriptions, purposely veiled.—**D. When the Son, etc.** (see 16:27; 24:30, 31).—**Throne of his glory** = be revealed in His divine glory as the Saviour and Lord of all; **throne** (comp. 19:28, D.). The time when the General Judgment which is here described will be held is concealed from men; such a conviction of the absolute uncertainty of "the times or the seasons" (Acts 1:7) is regarded by Paul as a part of the Christian's creed (1 Thess. 5:1, seq.). That the judgment will occur at the end of the world had already been taught in 13:40, 49, and in ch. 24.

[32] And before him shall be gathered all the nations: and he shall separate them one from another, as a shepherd separateth the sheep from the goats.

A. All nations. This language is so comprehensive and emphatic, and it so carefully excludes all limitations as to generations or countries, that the words **all nations** are clearly to be understood literally = all human beings that ever lived on earth, irrespective of their Jewish or Gentile origin.—**B. He shall ... another.** These terms also, which describe a promiscuous assembly, the individuals of which are not yet arranged according to classes, distinctly teach that the Judge will call before him *all* men, the good and the evil. The act of separating is here introduced as equivalent to the whole process of the Judgment, namely, the trial of each individual and the decision of the Judge in each case. Additional revelations concerning the Judgment are found in Rom. 2:5–9; 2 Thess. 1:6–10.—**C. As a shepherd, etc.** All men (including heathen, Rom. 1:20) have been sufficiently endowed in order to constitute them responsible agents. Sheep and goats—the images here employed—were alike regarded by the law as suitable for being offered as sacrifices to God (Lev. 1:10; 5:6; 22:19); flocks of both kinds usually fed together (Gen. 30:33; 32:14). The latter, however, were deemed to be less valuable than the former (Luke 15:29), and their temper, which was less tractable than that of the sheep, fitted them, as in this case, to be images of men who are disobedient to God. The good shepherd (John 10:1–18) who gave His life "for all" (2 Cor. 5:14; Rom. 5:18) "is the Saviour of all men, specially of those that believe" (1 Tim. 4:10).

33 And he shall set the sheep on his right hand, but the goats on the left.

This arrangement indicates the distinct and complete separation [Augustine dwells here on the thought that there is no third place: "He who will not be found on the right must be found on the left"] of the two classes of human beings on the Day of Judgment. There is also possibly an allusion to the higher honor assigned *in some cases* to the right hand, when it is specially contrasted with the left (see Gen. 48:13–19; Eccl. 10:2, but comp. also 20:20, B.; 22:44, B.; 26:64, C.).

34 Then shall the king say unto them on his right hand, Come, ye blessed of my Father, inherit the kingdom prepared for you from the foundation of the world.

A, The king. Christ assigns this name to Himself, because

His divine glory shall be so fully revealed that all, whether willingly or unwillingly, must bow the knee before Him (Phil. 2:10), and confess the truth that He has all power in heaven and in earth (28:18).—**B. Ye blessed of my Father** = whom My Father blessed on earth (Eph. 1:3), and blesses now; a construction similar to that of the original occurs in John 6:45, "taught of (by) God," and in 1 Cor. 2:13, which, literally translated, is: "words taught by human wisdom—taught by the Holy Ghost."—**C. Inherit.** This word, primarily alluding to property received from a father or ancestor, represents the believers as *children* of God; St. Paul now adds: "if children, then heirs; heirs of God, etc." (Rom. 8:17; see also above, 5:5, B.).—**D. Kingdom** = the blessedness enjoyed in heaven by those who dwell eternally in God's presence (see Excursus I. vol. I.).—**E. Prepared, etc.** The allusion is to the gracious purpose of God in devising a plan of salvation for fallen men, even before sin and death entered the world, as set forth in Eph. 1:3–5; 2 Thess. 2:13, 14; James 2:5; 1 Peter 1:2.—**Prepared** (see 20:23, B.).—**Foundation—world** (see 13:35, E.).

$^{35,\,36}$ For was an hungered, and ye gave me meat: I was thirsty, and ye gave me drink: I was a stranger, and ye took me in:—Naked, and ye clothed me: I was sick, and ye visited me: I was in prison, and ye came unto me.

Here the reasons for which the redeemed are regarded as "righteous" (ver. 37) and received into heaven are stated. The doctrine implied is the following: "A man is justified by faith without the deeds of the law" (Rom. 3:28; Gal. 2:16; Eph. 2:8, 9). This justifying faith, however, is a living or active faith; a nominal faith which has not power to produce fruit = works, is of no value; faith is made perfect (demonstrated) by works

(James 2:22) in the sense that a true faith cannot possibly exist without producing as its evidence the holy life described in Rom. 12:1, 2, for "every good tree bringeth forth good fruit" (7:17); the failure of the latter proves that the former was not "good." Hence Paul says that the law is not made void but established through faith (Rom. 3:31). Now, justifying faith influences man's whole nature, and so effectually purifies the heart (Acts 15:9), that, according to Gal. 5:6, it cannot be said to exist in reality, when it fails to produce, among other fruits, a genuine love to man (1 Cor. 13:2). Indeed, love, the offspring of faith, existing only when faith appears in full power, is regarded as indubitable evidence of the existence of faith. If, then, the Saviour represents genuine love as the characteristic feature of His disciples in John 13:35, He does so because its presence demonstrates the presence of that faith which He declares in Mark 16:16 to be essential to salvation. When Paul, again, describes the operation of love, and remarks that "he that loveth another hath fulfilled the law" (Rom. 13:8–10), he describes a course of conduct which is really the result of a living faith (comp. Rom. 8:4). In the same manner, the doctrine that men shall be judged hereafter according to their works or deeds (Matt. 7:21; 16:27; Rom. 2:6; 2 Cor. 5:10) is founded on the principle that these works, as indications of the spiritual state, derive their good or evil character solely from the presence or absence of a living faith in the soul. The same truth, that God regards not merely the outward form of works, but considers the internal principle from which they proceed, and requires love to man as an evidence of a devout heart, is repeatedly proclaimed by the prophets (Isai. 58:6, 7; Micah 6:6–8). The Lord therefore mentions works of love in the present case as evidences of the justifying or saving faith of those whom He addresses.—**An hungered** (see 4:2, C.).—**Stranger ... took me in** = into your houses, sheltered Me when I was a homeless wanderer.—**Naked,** here = insufficiently clad, as in James 2:15; Job 22:6. The word sometimes, as in John 21:7; Acts 19:16; 1 Sam. 19:24, means *half-naked* = without the upper garment, sometimes *entirely nude,* as, possibly, Mark 14:51.—**Visited,** as in James 1:27 = visited for the purpose of affording substantial aid and comfort.—**In prison** = ye did not, through want of delicate and tender love, or through fear, desert Me when I was afflicted and persecuted. The earthly trials and sorrows of God's people are evidences of His love (Hebr. 12:6).

37-39 Then shall the righteous answer him, saying, Lord, when saw we thee an hungered, and fed *thee?* or athirst, and gave *thee* drink?—And when saw we thee a stranger, and took thee in? or naked, and clothed thee?—*And* when saw we thee sick, or in prison, and came unto thee?

A. Righteous = those who are justified by faith (see 1:19, B., and above, ann. to ver. 35, 36).—**B. Shall** (will)—**answer.** This conversation, like the one between Abraham and the rich man, in the parable (Luke 16:24, ff.), is introduced in a figurative manner, for the purpose of setting forth the thoughts or sentiments entertained by those who are found in the circumstances here described.—**C. When saw we, etc.?** Two important truths here especially claim attention: first, this language, which is plainly represented as proceeding from unaffected surprise and not from a pretended humility, indicates, on the one hand, the amazement of the speakers at the glory and honor bestowed upon them, which will far exceed the hopes which they had entertained on earth; it alludes, on the other hand, to the many unexpected discoveries which believers themselves will make on the Day of Judgment; they, too, labored on earth under the influence of many defective views and even errors of judgment, and descended into the grave while they were still ignorant of many important facts respecting themselves. The language, secondly, illustrates the Lord's command in 6:3, and implies that the true disciple of Christ is conscious only of his defects and sins, while he has through grace become free from all spiritual pride arising from the performance of "good works."

⁴⁰ And the King shall answer and say unto them, Verily I say unto you, Inasmuch as ye did *it* unto one of these my brethren, even these least, ye did it unto me.

It was a high honor conferred on the human race when the eternal Son of God assumed human nature (Hebr. 2:14), and, in this respect, became our equal = our brother. But it was, further, a direct and unspeakable blessing when, through His atoning work and the gift of His Spirit, He renewed and sanctified His people, so that they might become "partakers of the divine nature" (2 Peter 1:4), and be converted into *children of God* (Rom. 8:15; Gal. 4:6). Thus He who was eternally the Father of our Lord Jesus, the only-begotten Son (John 3:16), became in another, but also in an emphatic sense, *our* Father (John 20:17), "for which cause he is not ashamed to call them brethren" (Hebr. 2:11). Hence the present phrase, **my brethren,** is not, as in 28:10, applied by the Saviour to the company of the disciples only, but, as in Hebr. 2:17, to all true believers also. The exalted degree of glory of the redeemed, and the manner in which they will be "like" Christ, is not yet fully revealed (1 John 3:2). The present language, in which the Lord seems even to identify Himself with His followers, is expressive of the highest degree of infinite love. So absorbing is the Saviour's love to His people, that any service rendered to one of them on earth pleases Him as if *He* had been in want and distress, and had been personally relieved.—**Even these least.** The Lord had, while He dwelt on earth, repeatedly termed His followers "little ones" (10:42, A.; 18:6, B.). With overflowing love, He here alludes to that name, and implies that even he who may have seemed to men to occupy the very lowest or most obscure position, or had even undeservedly (1 Peter 3:17), like the apostles, been "made the filth of the world" (1 Cor. 4:13), had become, by his faith, very precious to his Lord.—**These** = this whole number, on the right hand. The doctrine that the two natures of Christ are united inseparably and eternally is illustrated and confirmed by His use of the word "brethren," as well as in Acts 7:55; 9:4.

⁴¹ Then shall he say also unto them on the left hand, Depart from me, ye cursed, into the eternal fire, which is prepared for the devil and his angels:

A. Ye cursed. To be *cursed,* in the emphatic and awful sense of the term, is to be consigned irremediably to punishment and ruin (comp. Mark 11:21). All the world is guilty before God (Rom. 3:19); we are by nature the children of wrath (Eph. 2:3); Christ came to deliver us from the wrath to come (1 Thess. 1:10; see 3:7, C.). Now, impenitent and unbelieving sinners not only remain in their original condition, but also by their personal transgressions treasure up unto themselves wrath against the day of wrath (Rom. 2:5; Col. 3:6), and, accordingly, "the wrath of God *abidetlh* on them (John 3:36)—they are the "cursed" ones (see 2 Thess. 1:7–10).—**B. Eternal fire.** For this expression, see 5:25, 26,

C., and comp. 18:8, 9, C., and ver. 34, C., where additional passages are quoted which teach the absolute eternity of the future punishments of the wicked. The words at the close of this address (ver. 46) convincingly set forth the same awful truth; for if the "life" = the blessedness of the redeemed, is "eternal" = never ends, then (as the same Greek word occurs in both members of the verse) the "punishment" of the wicked never ends.—**Fire** (comp. 2 Thess. 1:8, and see above, 5:22, G.).—**C. Prepared for, etc.** Very little is revealed respecting the history of the fallen angels and the nature of their punishment. From the passages mentioned in ann. to 8:29, E., we learn that while their present state is one of great misery, their sentence will be still more explicitly pronounced on the last day. No human beings were originally subjected to any degree of reprobation; the Scriptures speak of a "Book of Life" (Phil. 4:3; Rev. 3:5; Ps. 69:28), but never of a *book of death;* hence this punishment had been prepared for the devil and his angels, whose fall occurred before Adam and Eve were placed in paradise. But when the latter also disobeyed God, and sin had entered the world, and when impenitent men consented to be the servants of Satan, they, like his angels, made themselves partakers of his everlasting punishment (John 12:31; 14:30; 16:11; 2 Cor. 4:4; Eph. 6:12).

43, 44 For I was an hungered, and ye gave me no meat: I was thirsty, and ye gave me no drink: I was a stranger, and ye took me not in: naked, and ye clothed me not: sick, and in prison, and ye visited me not.

Even as in ver. 35, 36, the works of love performed by the righteous are declared to be evidences of their saving faith, so here the absence of Christian love is regarded as the evidence of a want of that faith without which it is impossible to please God (Hebr. 11:6). The sense evidently is: Your entire want of love demonstrates that you were not the children of God—you did not resemble Him (comp. 5:44, 45). A striking illustration of the pernicious character of those sins to which the world often gives the palliating name of "mere sins of omission."

44 Then shall they also answer him, saying, Lord, when saw we thee an hungered, or athirst, or a stranger, or naked, or sick, or in prison, and did not minister unto thee?

The impenitent often tranquillize their conscience in this life by frivolous arguments derived from their external morality, good resolutions, etc.; but they overlook the fact that God recognizes only two classes of men, His friends and His enemies (Rom. 6:16; James 4:4; see 12:30, B.; 13:43, A.). Many descend with their self-delusion into the grave, who will only after their death, as here described, learn with wonder and despair that they had totally mistaken the true nature of religion. As the righteous were not fully conscious of the high value which the Judge assigned to works of love as evidences of faith, so the impenitent and wicked are not aware of the extent of their guilt. They imply: Lord, we would certainly have relieved Thee under such circumstances, if we had found the opportunity. But does any one lack the opportunity to know and love God and keep His commandments?—**Minister** (see 4:11, B.).

45 Then shall he answer them, saying, Verily I say unto you, Inasmuch as ye did it not unto one of these least, ye did it not to me.

The Judge unfolds to the wicked the true nature of their evil course, their neglect to seek a new heart, etc.; they should have learned these solemn truths during their life on earth; *now,* on the day of judgment, the recognition of their errors and sins is *too late!*—**The least of these.** The Judge points to those at His right hand.

⁴⁶ And these shall go away into eternal punishment: but the righteous into eternal life.

(Comp. John 5:29.) In the original the same word occurs in both members of the verse, but was translated in the Authorized English N. T., in the one case "everlasting" and in the other "eternal" (see above, ver. 41, B.). [A variation in the English for purely stylistic purposes that has been often diligently used to confuse the minds of the people, who do not know that one and the same word was used by the Lord. Hence the important change in the R. V.] The eternal condition of men in the world to come, as determined on the Day of Judgment's here revealed. After that solemn day no change will ever occur; the righteous will "ever be with the Lord" in heaven (1 Thess. 4:17), the wicked abide in "shame and everlasting contempt" (Dan. 12:2), "and the smoke of their torment ascendeth up forever and ever" (Rev. 14:11). Their **punishment** will be unutterably great (18:34, B.). With these solemn words the Lord closes His discourse.

11

Matthew 26

¹ And it came to pass, when Jesus had finished all these words, he said unto his disciples,

These words = the several distinct addresses, answers and explanations which are recorded in ch. 24 and 25. At this point Matthew commences the recital of the "passion" (= suffering, Acts 1:3) of our Lord; the term includes His last sufferings and death (Luke 22:15).

² Ye know that after two days the passover cometh, and the Son of man is delivered up to be crucified.

A. After two days. For the sake of convenience the modern names which represent the first, second, etc., days of the week will be employed in the following explanations; the Jews designated these days by numbers (Acts 20:7; 1 Cor. 16:2), our Sunday being *the first* day, and the Sabbath of the Jews being the *seventh* or last day. As our Lord was crucified on a Friday (B. § 5, below), which began on the previous evening at sunset (B. § 2), these words may be understood, according to the usual mode of expressing time among the

Jews (see 12:40, A.), as having been uttered on the previous Tuesday.—**B. The feast of the passover,** literally, *after two days is the passover.*

§ 1. *Two distinct festivals,* so intimately connected in their historical origin, religious purpose and time of celebration, as to constitute in practice *one* great festival of *eight* days, are to be here understood by the word *passover.*

§ 2. The feast of the Passover, which was instituted on the occasion of the departure of the Israelites from Egypt, consisted, strictly speaking, of only *one day* of twenty-fours; *"this day* shall be unto you for a memorial; and ye shall keep *it* a feast to the Lord, etc." (Exod. 12:14). It referred to the Lord's mercy in *passing over* or passing by (= the transition of) those houses of the Israelites, the door-posts of which had been marked with the blood of the slain lamb, and sparing the first-born or eldest son of each of such families (Exod. 12:13); hence originated the Hebrew name, which, with a slight change occurring in the Greek mode of representing it, assumes the form of *pascha;* the English translators happily employed an English name, *passover,* somewhat resembling the Hebrew in sound as well as in sense. The Hebrew means *to leap over, pass by, spare* (see Exod. 12:13, 23, 27, and comp. Josephus, Antiq. 2, 14, 6). The law commanded that it should be regularly kept on the *fourteenth* day of the first month of the year (corresponding to the close of our March or the beginning of April, Lev. 23:5; Exod. 12:6; Numb. 9:2, 3); it commenced at sunset and continued till the next sunset. The Jewish day of twenty-four hours began, not as with us at midnight, but on the previous evening, in reference to Gen. 1:5, 8, 13, 14 (comp. Lev. 23:32.) The old name of the passover-month was *Abib* (Exod. 13:4; Deut. 16:1), for which the name *Nisan* was afterwards substituted (Esth. 3:7; Neh. 2:1). The Jewish month invariably began with the first appearance of the new moon, and the first day of the month was a festival (Numb. 10:10; 28:11; 1 Sam. 20:5; Isai. 66:23), so that the passover, fourteen days afterwards, occurred precisely at the time of full moon (27:45, B.). The paschal lamb was a type or sign of Christ (John 1:29, 36; Rev. 5:6; Isai. 53:7), who is called in 1 Cor. 5:7 "our passover = paschal lamb (comp. Deut. 16:5, 6). For the time of killing the lamb, see below, ver. 17, C.

§ 3. As the departure of the Israelites from Egypt, when they were to take possession of the "land of promise" (Hebr. 11:9; Gen. 15:18), was an event of the highest importance not only in reference to their own future political history, but also to the introduction of Christianity (Luke 24:46, 47; John 4:22; Rom. 9:4, 5), God commanded that, like the passing-over of the firstborn, it should be annually commemorated immediately after the passover or memorial-day by a special festival called "the feast of unleavened bread; "to this feast *seven* days were assigned (Exod. 12:14, 15). Thus the double festival (Numb. 28:16, 17) extended, according to Exod. 12:18, from "the fourteenth day of the month at even ... until the one-and-twentieth day of the month at even," both included = *eight* days. The second feast, when distinguished from the passover-day (see below, § 4), commenced on the fifteenth of Nisan, according to Lev. 23:6; Numb. 28:17, at even, or at the time when the fourteenth (the passover) ended, namely, when the evening of the natural day or the beginning of the fifteenth arrived, and it included the twenty-first day of the month. While, then, the passover specially commemorated that sparing of the Jewish first-born, the feast of unleavened bread rather commemorated the whole or general event of the deliverance of the Israelites from Egyptian bondage (Exod. 12:17; 13:3; 23:15). It derived its name—*feast of unleavened* (= sweet, unfermented) *bread* (Exod. 23:15, 17)—from the circumstance that God most earnestly commanded that leaven (yeast) in all its forms should be removed from every house during the festival (Exod. 12:15, 19; Deut. 16:2–4. For *leaven,* see 13:33, B.). As this substance, which is mixed with the dough before the latter is baked, requires a period of several hours in order to produce the desired fermentation, its entire absence was intended, as God declared through Moses (Deut. 16:3, 4), to remind the Jews, on the one hand, of the. "bread of affliction" (= daily affliction and sorrow, Exod. 3:7), of their life in Egypt, and, on the other, of the "haste" with which they left Egypt, when they "baked unleavened cakes of the dough ... because they were thrust out of Egypt, and could not tarry" (Exod. 12:11, 33, 39); for the same reason the flesh of the lamb was directed to be eaten or burnt before the next morning (Exod. 12:10; 34:25). Thus when Abraham or Lot prepared a *hasty* meal for unexpected guests, they furnished *unleavened* bread (Gen. 18:6; 19:3).

§ 4. That a distinction exists between these two festivals, however closely they are allied in time and purpose, is proved by the language in Lev., ch. 23, where, in ver. 5 and 6, the time of each respectively is stated; the same discrimination is made in Numb. 28:16, 17; 2 Chron. 30:15, 21; Ezra 6:19, 22. Hence Josephus says: "The feast of unleavened bread *succeeds* that of the passover, and falls on the fifteenth day of the month, and continues seven days" (Antiq. 3, 10, 5). Nevertheless, as the general purpose of both festivals—the commemoration of God's special mercies (Exod. 13:9)—was the same, and as no interval of time occurred between them, the two were frequently regarded and described as only *one* great festival consisting of *eight* days, one for the passover, and seven for the other feast. Hence, either name, *the passover*, or the *feast of unleavened bread*, was given interchangeably to this entire sacred season or festival of eight days; for instance, Exod. 13:3; Numb. 9:2, ff.; Deut. 16:1, ff. Accordingly, Josephus uses this popular mode of expression when he says: "This happened at the season when the feast of unleavened bread was celebrated, which we call the passover" (Antiq. 14, 2, 1, and ib. 17, 9, 3). "The feast of unleavened bread is called the passover by the Jews" (War, 2, 1, 3). "The feast of unleavened bread was now come, it being the fourteenth day of the month" (War, 5, 3, 1). Josephus also, in Antiq. 11, 4, 8, speaks of the two festivals as if they were virtually only one. The N. T. employs a similar phraseology. In Acts 12:3, 4, the period of eight days is called "days of unleavened bread," and immediately afterwards "passover" (which word, however, the English translators here render "Easter," while in the other twenty-eight passages in which it occurs they render it "passover"). So, in Luke 22:1, both names occur, indicating the one period of eight days. In Luke 2:41, the "passover" is not the one day strictly constituting that festival, but includes the additional seven "days" (ver. 43) of the connected festival. In Mark 14:1, both names are with great precision fully given, in order to designate the whole period of eight days. Indeed, so plainly does either name indicate the whole sacred season, that even in Exod. 23:15; 34:18; Deut. 16:16; 2 Chron. 8:13, one name alone is employed, without excluding the other festival, which was also to be perpetually kept (Exod. 12:14).

§ 5. This Jewish usage of giving either name indifferently to the whole period of eight days, of which the language of Josephus just quoted, and the passages in the N. T., furnish striking illustrations, will explain several passages in the Gospel of John which seem to conflict with the other three Gospels. As the period which embraced both festivals, from the 14th to the 21st of Nisan, consisted of eight days, it is here interesting and important to notice the fact that when Josephus combines the two as one actual festive season, he says: "We keep a feast for *eight* days, which is called the feast of unleavened bread" (Antiq. 2, 15, 1). That our Lord ate the paschal supper at the usual time, the evening of the 14th of Nisan, when all the Jews kept the festival, is apparent from Matt. 26:2, 17; Mark 14:12; Luke 22:7. (That the evening of the 14th refers to the *first* hours, or the *beginning* of that term of 24 hours, is also apparent from Jos. Antiq. 2, 14, 6.) Christ could not have adopted the extraordinary course of anticipating the day and observing the passover 24 hours before the regular time, according to these passages; indeed, the precise terms in Exod. 12:3, 6, plainly require that the whole nation should *simultaneously* keep the festival. When the *fourteenth* of the appointed month was not punctually observed, the law prescribed that the *fourteenth* of the succeeding month might be substituted (Numb. 9:10, 11; 2 Chron. 30:2, 15), but the *thirteenth* day was not recognized. It appears from Numb. 33:3 and Exod. 12:22, compared with Exod. 12:31, that during the daytime, or latter part of the 14th (when the paschal lamb had already been eaten the previous evening and the first-born of the Egyptians had been slain), all the Israelites gathered together, and then left Rameses, the general place of meeting, on the

15th, possibly in the evening (Deut. 16:6), or before the night succeeding the one in which the first-born in Egypt were slain. "From the time when Pharaoh dismissed Moses and Aaron in the night of the 14th day of the month (according to the Jewish reckoning) until the morning of the 15th day, when the people set off (Numb. 33:3), there was an interval of some 30 hours, during which these leaders could easily reach Rameses from the court of Pharaoh, whether this were at Memphis, or, as is more probable, at Zoan or Tanis. (The Psalmist places the scene of the miracles of Moses in the region of Zoan, Ps. 78:12, 43.)"—Robinson: Bibl. Res. I. 55. (See above, 2:13, C.)

The third day after the crucifixion, the one on which our Lord rose from the grave, was also the day after the Sabbath, or the first day of the week (Sunday, Mark 16:1, 9), our Lord having been crucified on the preceding Friday, the day before the Sabbath (Mark 15:42; see below, ver. 17, A.). He had, according to the first three Gospels, like all the Jews, eaten the paschal supper on the previous Thursday evening, a few hours before He was betrayed and seized. Now it had been commanded that on each of the seven days of the feast of unleavened bread special sacrifices should be offered (Numb. 28:17–24); the Jews, on such occasions, also brought "free-will offerings," portions of which they ate, and they "rejoiced before the Lord" (Lev. 23:38; Deut. 27:7; comp. Solomon's sacrifices and religious feast, 1 Kings 8:62–66). To these successive days of "feasting" or "eating before the Lord" the name *passover* was also applied, in a general or familiar sense. The evangelist John, who wrote his Gospel long after the first three had been given to the Church, consequently omits large masses of matter which they record, and supplies chiefly events and discourses which they omit; for instance, he describes the Lord's act of washing the feet of the disciples (ch. 13) without repeating their narrative of the institution of the Holy Supper, which, at the time when he wrote, was familiarly known to all Christians. In no case can it be supposed that one inspired writer contradicts another. Hence the words in John 13:1, "before the feast of the passover," which refer to the last evening of the Lord, or the evening (= commencement) of the passover-day, are equivalent to the words: before the actual commencement of the feast of seven days (Luke 22:1) of unleavened bread, during which the special daily offerings were brought. In John 18:28, the Jews, who had unquestionably all eaten the paschal lamb on the previous evening, declined to enter the judgment-hall of a heathen ruler, which act would have defiled them, and unfitted them legally for "eating the passover." This latter phrase refers to the festive or sacrificial offerings and banquets, of which, as in the days of Hezekiah and at other times, they partook ("seven days, offering peace offerings, etc.," 2 Chron. 30:22). So, too, many thousands of animals were given by Josiah and others as "passover-offerings" (2 Chron. 35:7, ff.). The original Hebrew in 2 Chron. 30:22 contains a phrase corresponding to John's language, for the words, literally translated, are: "they did eat the feast" = the festive offerings. So, too, in Ps. 118:27, and in Exod. 23:18, the Hebrew word translated *sacrifice* is *feast* (= festival sacrifices), as the margin also states in the latter passage; and in Deut. 16:2 all the animals slain during the whole festival, whether of the flock or of the herd, are called collectively, as here in John, "the passover." In John 19:14 the phrase, "the preparation of the passover," which here designates Friday, the day of the crucifixion, and the day succeeding the general eating of the paschal lamb, is readily explained from ver. 31, 42, of the same chapter. The name of the sixth day of the week (Friday), on which food, etc., was prepared for the Sabbath-day (Exod. 16:22; 35:2, 3), was currently called "preparation-day." Thus, in an imperial decree quoted by Josephus, the Jewish phrases of which were evidently furnished by Jews, the latter are exempted from the duty of "going before any judge on the Sabbath-day, or on *the* [day of the] *preparation* to it" (Antiq. 16, 6, 2). The word occurs in the same sense (= Friday) in Matt. 27:62; Luke 23:54, and is so explained in Mark 15:42, so that there can be no doubt respecting the meaning of the word in John 19:14. The Sabbath which occurred during the holy passover festival of eight days was specially sacred, and the sixth week-day preceding it was called "the preparation-day of the passover." Hence the Sabbath-day itself, in view of the additional solemnity imparted to it by the festival, is called in ver. 31 "a high day." Finally, the "feast" mentioned in John 13:29 also refers to the sacrificial offerings and banquets of the seven days, of which the disciples still supposed that they and their Master would continue to partake. When the 13th of Nisan, which ended on Thursday at sunset, is called in Matt. 26:17 (see ann.) and Mark 14:12 "the first day," this appellation is given to it either in the sense of *the introductory day* = the day preceding (as the same word here translated "first" is translated "before" in John 1:15, 30), or rather, in the sense that as the paschal lamb was then prepared and leaven already removed from the house, the day virtually constituted the *first* of the whole festival season. For a strict observance of the words in Exod. 12:18 would exclude the use of leavened bread during the natural day on the evening of which the 14th commenced (see below, ver. 17, A.).

§ 6. It may be added that a *third* circumstance gave new interest and solemnity to this festival; it was a Jewish spring festival. On the day succeeding the first Sabbath which occurred during the eight days, the sheaf of the first-fruits of the harvest (barley) was offered (see Exod. 23:16; Lev. 23:9–14; and comp Jos. Antiq. 3, 10, 5).

C. The Son of man, etc. The Saviour again (16:21; 17:22; 20:19) foretells His crucifixion; the treachery of Judas is an act of the performance of which He is so certain that He speaks of it as if it had already occurred = *is* betrayed.—**To be crucified.** The Lord represents His death as coinciding in time with the observance of the passover festival, which ended with the evening of the natural day on which His death occurred.

³ Then were gathered together the chief priests, and the elders of the people, unto the court of the high priest, who was called Caiaphas.

A. Then = possibly, on the day when the Lord made the remark in ver. 2. The persons here indicated constitute the council (ver. 59), or sanhedrim; the present is, however, not a public or regular meeting, but one of a private and informal character.—**B. Caiaphas.** Josephus informs us that this priest was known by the name of Joseph as well as that of Caiaphas (Antiq. 18, ch. 2, § 2, and ch. 4, § 3). He was subsequently deposed from his high office, which he had dishonored by his Saducean doctrine and his unholy conduct generally.

⁴, ⁵ And they took counsel together that they might take Jesus by subtilty, and kill *him*,—But they said, Not during the

feast, lest a tumult arise among the people.

A. Took counsel. They had long before "sought to lay hands on" the Lord (21:46), but the impious plan of actually slaying Him seems to have been first distinctly proposed by Caiaphas (John 11:50); his wicked project, however, was so controlled by divine power that the result corresponded to the "determinate counsel and foreknowledge of God" (Acts 2:23). Hence, like Balaam (Numb., ch. 22–24), he became, in opposition to his original purpose, a prophet of "good things to come" (Hebr. 10:1).—**B. By subtilty** = in a crafty manner (Mark 14:1), or in such a way that their own personal safety and influence would not be affected.—**C. Not** = let this seizure not occur *during the feast*, that is, before the entire festivals of passover and of unleavened bread have terminated. The subsequent proposal of Judas induced these men, however, to vary from this purpose.—**D. Lest, etc.** We learn from Josephus (Ant. 17, 9, 3; 20, 5, 3), that as the great festivals brought vast numbers of Jews to the city (see for an illustration Acts 2:9–11), there was in that age a tendency manifested by seditious persons to create *tumults*. The enemies of the Lord, knowing that many believed on Him, apprehended that the public arrest of His person would create a tumult which might prove disastrous to themselves (comp. 21:46 and Luke 22:2).

⁶ Now when Jesus was in Bethany, in the house of Simon the leper.

A. In Bethany (see 21:17). In Luke 7:36, ff., a somewhat similar act of anointing the Lord is related; it occurred at a different time (before the close of the public ministry of Christ, Luke 8:1) and place (in the city, Luke 7:37); the persons, also (there, "a woman which was a sinner," Luke 7:37;

here, the devout Mary, John 12:3), and the circumstances (a Pharisee, the Lord's rebuke of him, etc.), all differ from those described in the present case. John has related the same occurrence (12:1, ff.), and remarks that it had occurred "six days before the passover," probably the Friday of the preceding week. It is here introduced by Matthew (as in 14:3 he goes back to an earlier date) in order to explain the original source of the enmity which Judas manifested towards his Master, and which appears to have been roused or fully developed by the Lord's words in ver. 10, ff., below.—**B. Simon the leper.** Authentic history has preserved no account of his life and character. Martha's presence as one that "served" (see 8:15, B.) where her brother was a guest (John 12:2) indicates that Simon was an intimate friend, possibly a relative of Lazarus and his sisters. He retained the name of **leper** after having doubtless been healed by the Lord, whom he now gratefully receives as an honored guest. So in 11:5 the *lame* and *deaf* are those who *had been* lame and deaf, as in John 9:17 "the blind man" is no longer blind, but still retains that name.

⁷ There came unto him a woman having an alabaster cruse of exceeding precious ointment, and she poured it upon his head, as he sat *at meat*.

A. A woman = Mary (John 12:3). She came as He reclined at the table; the guest, in that position, turned the feet away from the table, and hence these (as in Luke 7:38) as well as the head could be reached by any one who approached the table (8:11, D.).—**B. Alabaster ... ointment.** Vases of alabaster (a white, semi-transparent mineral) were believed in ancient times to be better adapted for preserving perfumes and ointments than vessels made of other materials. At a later period the name, in the sense of *ointment-vessel*, was given generally to vases with long narrow necks that were made of glass or metals. In the present case the ointment used was "spikenard" (Mark 14:3; John 12:3). The oil which gave value to it was derived from an oriental plant, the fragrance of which was very highly prized (Song of Sol. 1:12).—**Very precious** = of great price, expensive. ["Such preparations, like genuine attar of roses in the modern East, consisting, as they did, mainly of the essential oils of carefully cultivated flowers, often fetched an almost fabulous price."—Plumptre.]—**C. Poured, etc.** The practice of anointing the head, and the body generally, which was widely extended among the oriental nations, is still retained by them from considerations connected with their personal comfort and health (Deut. 28:40; Ps. 104:15; see 6:17). Guests to whom the host intended to render distinguished honor at a banquet were anointed profusely (Ps. 23:5; Amos 6:6; Luke 7:46). The ointment was, as a mark of special honor and reverence, applied even to the feet of the guest; the latter act was here also performed by Mary (John 12:3), who thus anointed the Lord's "body" (Matt. 26:12; John 12:7). Mary's active faith, fervent love and deep gratitude for the restoration of her brother to life (John 11:2), and for her own spiritual life, which the Lord had imparted to her (Luke 10:42), combined to draw from her this decided expression of her holy sentiments.

⁸ But when the disciples saw it they had indignation, saying, To what purpose is this waste?

Matthew does not intend to relate the details, but to state simply the general fact which led the Saviour to utter the words that follow. From John 12:4–6 we learn, first, that

Judas was the treasurer of the company of the disciples, that is, took charge of the gifts of those who "ministered unto Christ of their substance" (Luke 8:3) = contributed to His support, and provided Him with money for distribution among the poor; and, secondly, that he was a "thief." Hence his dissatisfaction when Mary's gift was presented in such a form as to prevent him from pilfering. Some others of the disciples (Mark 14:4) thoughtlessly concurred with Judas, not being aware of his private and selfish motive.—**Waste,** here = *total loss,* an expenditure which produces no abiding benefit for any one. The connection sometimes requires the original word to be translated *destruction,* as in 7:13; 2 Peter 2:1.

⁹ For this *ointment* might have been sold for much, and given to the poor.

For much = money. According to the parallel passages in Mark and John, the ointment, in view of its quality and the large quantity ("a pound," John 12:3), was valued at 300 pence = at least $42.00 (see 17:24, B.). [Ch. 20:2 shows that it represented a laborer's wages for a whole year.] Mary's act was certainly, when all the circumstances are considered, one of the most munificent on record.—**Given to the poor,** that is, the *money* for which the ointment could have been sold (see 19:21, C.).

¹⁰ But Jesus perceiving it, said unto them, Why trouble ye the woman? for she hath wrought a good work upon me.

A. But Jesus perceiving it = what was thought and said.—**B. Why trouble ye** = give, or, occasion trouble, vexation, etc., as in Luke 11:7; 18:5; Gal. 6:17; He alludes to the embarrassment and discouragement of Mary, occasioned by the remarks of Judas.—**Wrought** = performed, done, as in 3 John 5, "doest to."—**C. A good work**—proceeding from an enlightened and living faith and a holy love (see 5:16). The intrinsic excellence of the work or act did not depend on the pecuniary or commercial value of the gift; the farthing of the poor widow (Mark 12:42) was even less than the ten-thousandth part of Mary's gift (see 5:25, B.), in a business point of view (see above, ver. 9), but acquired inestimable value from the widow's holy motives and desires.—**For** = inasmuch as.—**Upon me** = towards Me; the deed, irrespectively of the actual value of the gift, was sanctified by the enlightened motive, and by the divine character of Him to whom it referred = **me**.

¹¹ For ye have the poor always with you; but me ye have not always.

A. For. The intermediate thought here omitted, but indicated by **for,** is: Ye cannot complain that ye have by this expenditure lost an opportunity to aid the poor, for—adds the Lord, alluding to Deut. 15:11—ye always have these near you. The frequent mention in the N. T. of alms-giving, as a regular practice (Matt. 6:1, ff.; Acts 10:2), the apparently common sight of beggars (Luke 16:20), and the very prominent attention paid by the first Christians to the poor as to a numerous class, of which illustrations abound in the Acts (for instance, ch. 6:1) and the apostolic epistles (e. g. Gal. 2:10), are evidences that vast numbers of the people at this period were reduced by the troubles of the times to the most abject poverty (comp. 19:21, C.).—**B. But me, etc.** = My visible presence will soon be withdrawn from you; after My ascension (Acts 1:9) such testimonials of love cannot be given to Me personally, but indirectly only, through My afflicted brethren (25:40).

¹² For in that she poured this ointment upon my body, she did it to prepare me for burial.

For. The connection is: She hath wrought a good work, **for** while the motive is holy, the act, in view of My approaching death and burial, is eminently appropriate and commendable. The ancient practice of embalming the dead (Gen. 50:2) was, to a certain extent, retained in some cases among the later Jews (John 19:40); the body was wrapped in a clean linen cloth (Matt. 27:59; John 11:44), between the folds of which large quantities of aromatics or spices and ointments were placed (Luke 23:56). Nicodemus brought "about a hundred pounds' weight" for that purpose (John 19:39). Even if Mary were not distinctly aware that the Lord's burial was so near at hand, He declares that the approaching event fully justifies the act. Still, Mary's thoughtful character, as illustrated in Luke 10:38, ff., and in John, ch. 11, and her profound attention to her Master's words (such as those in 26:2, which some of the disciples may have communicated to her, or which the Lord Himself addressed to her, Luke 24:6, 7), seem to indicate on her part a painful apprehension that death would soon remove Him from her. To such secret thoughts of Mary the Lord appears to allude.

¹³ Verily I say unto you, Wheresoever this gospel shall be preached in the whole world, that also which this woman hath done, shall be spoken of for a memorial of her.

A. This gospel. For the word, see 4:23, C. He probably refers to the "good tidings" of His death, to which He alludes in the word "burial," and which is our life (Rom. 14:8, 9; Matt. 20:28; 2 Cor. 5:15; 1 Thess. 5:10; comp. the same expression in 24:14, C.).—**B. For a memorial** = in memory of her. The word, as in Acts 10:4, describes any object, act or practice which preserves the memory of a person, event, etc. Here, as in 24:14, He not only regards the Gospel as designed for, but also predicts that it actually will be preached to, the whole world, carrying with it this glorious illustration of the power of divine grace, namely, the work in Mary's soul. The monument which the humble Mary unconsciously erected to her own memory by this act of devotion, having now been incorporated into the Gospel record, will ultimately be seen and admired throughout the world. The meaning undoubtedly is, that her conduct, springing from a living faith, should constitute an example for all.

14 Then one of the twelve, who was called Judas Iscariot, went unto the chief priests.

Judas, whose sordid love of money had already, through the neglect of watchfulness and self-examination, acquired such control over him as to lead to the commission of petty crimes (ver. 8, above), was thus led "concerning faith to make shipwreck" (1 Tim. 1:19). The Lord's disclosures concerning His own crucifixion also may have tended to discourage Judas, whose expectations, possibly like those of the scribe mentioned in 8:19, 20, were of a worldly character. The gentle rebuke of his hypocritical language (ver. 10, ff.) imbittered his feelings; If—he may have said to himself—if this Jesus of Nazareth, my Master, be the Son of God, He can extricate Himself again as He has done heretofore (Luke 4:30; John 10:39); if, on the other hand, His apprehensions of a violent death should be realized, I can derive no advantage by adhering to Him; but, in either case, I can gain money by betraying Him. If Judas used the word "safely" (Mark 14:44) ironically, like "hold him fast" (ver. 48, below), he possibly believed that his Master would be able to extricate

Himself (comp. Matt. 27:3, A.). [A speculation, then, on his Lord's omnipotence, intended to defraud the Jews!] He privately made the proposition to the "chief priests" = the highest Jewish authorities. Matthew adds here and ver. 47, reproachfully: **one of the twelve** (= not a stranger, not a heathen, but a "familiar friend," Ps. 41:9), in order to give prominence to the atrociousness of the crime.

15 And said, What are ye willing to give me, and I will deliver him unto you? And they weighed unto him thirty pieces of silver.

A. What ... give me. The language seems to indicate that the leading motive of Judas, after his reverence for the Lord had been suppressed by Satan's influences, was the desire to gratify his love of money.—**B. I will deliver ... you.** The original Greek word is translated, sometimes, *deliver*, sometimes, *betray* (see 17:22). The *treachery* of Judas consisted in the following circumstance: The Lord's enemies eagerly desired to seize Him at the earliest possible moment; at the same time they wished, according to ver. 5, to accomplish their design at such a favorable place and hour that no public tumult would be occasioned. The proposition of Judas accordingly contained in substance the offer to give them notice when they could find the Lord alone, and when they would have no cause to apprehend a rescue on the part of His adherents.—**C. They weighed him.** The words in 27:3, and their unquestionable eagerness to secure Judas as an accomplice, indicate that they at once paid him the stipulated sum, after having at the commencement of the interview (Mark 14:11) promptly agreed to pay money for such a service. Now it was customary, before the precious metals were coined, to make payment by weight = to place silver or gold in a balance (Jerem. 32:10). The original word translated in A. V. **covenanted** is employed in the Greek version of the O. T., for a Hebrew word translated *to weigh* in Ezra 8:25, 26, 33; Isai. 46:6, and precisely in the prophecy Zech. 11:12 mentioned below, 27:9.—**D. Thirty, etc.** = $16.80 (see 17:24, B.; the amount was only a little more than one-third of the value of Mary's ointment, ver. 9). This sum was fixed in Exod. 21:32 as the compensation due to the owner of a slave that had been killed by an ox. The chief priests doubtless designed by specifying this amount to show their contempt for Christ (see below, 27:9).

¹⁶ And from that time he sought opportunity to deliver him *unto them*.

Opportunity = a fit time. Judas watched for an hour when the Lord would be found in some solitary spot where His arrest could be quietly made. His crime was deliberately committed.

¹⁷ Now on the first *day of* unleavened bread, the disciples came to Jesus, saying, Where wilt thou that we make ready for thee to eat the passover?

A. Now (on) **the first day** = Thursday (see the ann. above to ver. 2). The 14th day of Nisan began in that year on Thursday evening at sunset (see above, ver. 2, B., § 5, and for the beginning of the month, see § 2). During the 13th day = Wednesday up to sunset, all leaven or yeast was removed from the houses of the Jews; hence this portion of the 13th of Nisan, which immediately preceded the passover-day (the natural day, at the close of which the 14th commenced), was popularly termed the **first day**, since in reality all leavened bread was removed, and, according to a rigid construction of Exod. 12:18; Lev. 23:5; Numb. 9:3; Deut. 16:6, its use was avoided, although the festival, strictly speaking, did not begin until sunset (see ver. 2, B., § 5, near the end).—**B. Where wilt thou** = special accommodations for such purposes were always furnished by the inhabitants to Jews who visited the city on such occasions.—**C. To eat the passover** = the paschal supper. The lamb had been selected on the previous "tenth day of the month" (Exod. 12:3); it was slain on the afternoon of the 13th day "in the evening" (Exod. 12:6), literally, "between the two evenings," that is, before sunset (see 14:15, A.), and eaten after sunset, when the 14th commenced.

¹⁸ And he said, Go into the city to such a man, and say unto him, The Master saith, My time is at hand; I keep the passover at thy house with my disciples.

A. Go ... city = Jerusalem. They are probably still in or near Bethany, ver. 6.—**B. To such a man.** This peculiar expression indicates a person whose name, for special reasons, the speaker or writer does not wish to mention (comp. Ruth 4:1; 1 Sam. 21:2). According to the Lord's statement, derived from His foreknowledge, the disciples would meet a particular individual on their entrance into the city, "bearing a pitcher of water (Mark 14:13; Luke 22:10). They are directed to notice the house which he enters, and then accost the occupant of that house. The Lord evidently desires to conceal both the name of the man and the situation of the house; indeed, the commission appears to have been privately given to Peter and John (Luke 22:8). All these circumstances imply that the Lord, who was aware of the secret plan of Judas (ver. 14), and did not desire to be disturbed at the supper, purposely withheld from the latter all knowledge of the locality. The occupant of the house, who evidently knew *who* "The Master" (= teacher, 8:19, B.) was, no doubt was one of the many adherents of Christ who are not mentioned by name in the four Gospels (see above, 21:3, A.). Like the seventy disciples, Lazarus and other believers, he observed the festival with his own family, and not in the Lord's company. According to Jewish usage (founded on Exod. 12:4, which required each "household" as a general rule to observe the festival separately), the company at the paschal meal could not consist of less than ten individuals (see Jos. War, 6, 9, 3), nor of more than twenty (see 25:1, C.).—**C. My time is at hand,** lit.*is near*, as the same word is translated in Mark 13:28. This language *may* imply: The time for My celebration of the passover is come. But, on the one hand, such a message conveyed no new information, since the precise time of the celebration was known to all (ver. 2, B., § 5), and, on the other, the original term for **time** often refers to special, momentous or decisive periods, as in 8:29; 21:34; Luke 21:8; John 7:6, 8, with which compare the word "hour" occurring as an equivalent in Mark 14:41; John 2:4; 7:30; 8:20. Hence it is clear that the Lord designs to inform the occupant of the house that the **time** of His atoning death was at hand.—**Is** = *will* very shortly *be;* so in John 17:4, 13, He describes the time of the completion of His work as having already arrived.—**D. I will keep, etc.** The words plainly imply that, while the occupant of the house was friendly to the Lord, no previous arrangement had been made with him, and that, as in the case of Zaccheus (Luke 19:5), the Lord's visit to his house was an unexpected honor.

¹⁹ And the disciples did as Jesus appointed them; and they made ready the passover.

The disciples were Peter and John (Luke 22:8).—**Appointed**

= directed. As the Lord had predicted, the occupant of the house (not the man who carried the pitcher, Luke 22:10, 11) at once conducted them to "a large upper room furnished and prepared" (Mark 14:15) = with tables, cushions or couches (see 8:11, D.); hither the disciples brought the lamb, "roast with fire," the "bitter herbs" (Exod. 12:8), unleavened bread, wine, and all that was needed for the paschal meal, thus "preparing," or "making ready" (the same Greek word being used in ver. 17 and 19). The *upper room* (Mark 14:15; Luke 22:11) was in the second story, immediately below the roof (see 9:2, D.), and, from its retired situation, was well adapted for the present purpose. It is obvious that the blessing connected with the celebration of the Lord's Supper may be received by devout communicants, whether they partake of it in an upper room, as at this time, or elsewhere, with burning lamps, as here, or without them, standing, sitting or kneeling, etc. The Lord Himself did not precisely observe all the forms prescribed for the first passover in Exod. 12:11.

[20] Now when even was come, he was sitting at meat with the twelve.

A. The even = Thursday evening, after sunset, at the commencement of the 14th day of the month (see ver. 2, B., §5).—**B. The twelve.** Hence Judas, who had accompanied the other disciples, is now also present; he probably remained until the conclusion of the meal. Did he then also partake of the Holy Supper? The words in John 13:30 seem to imply that he left the house before the Supper was instituted. His absence can, however, have been only of brief duration, for, according to Luke 22:19–21, he is represented as present at the time of the institution and immediately after it, and the whole motive in the present chapter (for instance, ver. 25, 26) indicates that Matthew regards him as present at the time. Moreover, the word "all" seems to indicate emphatically that all the twelve received both the bread and the wine. This view is confirmed by the circumstance that if he had withdrawn before the institution of the Lord's Supper, and had not ascertained the place to which the Lord afterwards proceeded (ver. 36), he could not have conducted the officers and armed men (Luke 22:47; Matt. 26:57; John 18:3) with such precision to the spot. Accordingly he must have remained until the Lord left the house with the disciples (ver. 30), and *at that moment*, in the darkness of the night, have silently withdrawn (see below, ver. 31, B.).

21 And as they were eating, he said, Verily I say unto you, that one of you shall betray me.

A. They did eat = the paschal meal. According to the Jewish usage, the head of the family commenced with a prayer, or gave thanks, and then the first of *four* cups of red wine, mixed with water, was tasted by all the company. The 113th and 114th Psalms were sung (see below, ver. 30, A.), and the meal proceeded. It was probably during the earlier part of the meal that the occurrences related in Luke 22:24–30 and John 13:1–20 took place.—**B. Verily, etc.** The Lord was "troubled in spirit" (John 13:21), or grieved by the wicked course to which Judas abandoned himself, and now alludes to his proposed acts: "Ye are not all clean," said he (John 13:11) = even your limited number does not consist entirely of faithful adherents.—**Betray** (see ver. 16).

22 And they were exceeding sorrowful, and began to say every one, Is it I, Lord?

A. And they ... him. Each one of the eleven, conscious of his own deep devotion to the Lord, and ignorant of the plans of Judas, was distressed by the doubt which the Lord appeared to express respecting their fidelity.—**B. Is it I?** = thou surely canst not doubt *my* devotion and love to Thee (see John 13:23, ff.).

²³ And he answered and said, He that dipped his hand with me in the dish, the same shall betray me.

A. He answered. The Lord's words were, according to John 13:25, 26, addressed by Him privately to John, who lay on "Jesus' breast" = next to Him at the table; indeed, the words could not have been addressed to all aloud, as the question of Judas, in ver. 25, below, shows that he had not heard them.—**B. Dipped ... dish.** According to the well-known usage of the times (15:2, B.), the head of the family dipped pieces of the bread into the dish or bowl of thick broth (containing also dates, figs, etc., besides the "bitter herbs," Exod. 2:8), and gave them to the guests in rotation; the others continued to eat, dipping pieces in the common dish themselves. This answer, combined with John 13:26, informs us that at the moment when Judas reached forth his hand for that purpose, the Lord presented to him the "sop" (John 13:26), that is, a morsel or piece of bread moistened in the broth. By this sign John, "the beloved disciple" (John 13:23), was privately made acquainted with the name of the only traitor in the company. The Lord (John 13:18) affectingly alludes to the prophecy in Ps. 41:9.—**C. Betray** = deliver up into the hands of enemies (see ver. 15, B.).

²⁴ The Son of man goeth even as it is written of him: but woe unto that man by whom the Son of man is betrayed! good were it for that man if he had not been born.

A. The Son of man goeth = goeth hence to His death (Ps. 39:13).—**B. As it is written of him** (see Gen. 3:15, the first

Gospel promise; Numb. 21:8, 9, comp. with John 3:14, 15, and 12:32, 33; Ps. 22; 41:9; Isai., ch. 53; Dan. 9:26; Zech. 13:7). He died in accordance with the "determinate counsel and foreknowledge of God" (Acts 2:23; Luke 22:22; 24:26, 27). Since Christ was "foreordained before the foundation of the world" (1 Peter 1:20) as our Redeemer, the prophets were in due time commissioned to reveal the gracious plan of salvation. The foreknowledge of God respecting the crime of Judas did not compel him to commit it, even as that divine knowledge did not compel Saul and the men of Keilah (1 Sam. 23:7–13) to carry out their designs against David.—**C. But woe.** This exclamation, which often indicates deep sorrow or pity (11:21, A.), here expresses the Saviour's grief that Judas would be "lost" (John 17:12).—**Good were it, etc.** When the oriental nations, whose language of passion was characterized by very bold figures, designed to say that they endured the highest degree of misery and suffering, they often uttered in the wildest terms their regret that they had ever been born (see Job 3:3, ff.; Jerem. 15:10; 20:14). In conformity to this usage, the sense of the present proverbial language simply is: Since that man, Judas, has acted in direct opposition to the wise and benevolent design for which God created him, and has voluntarily rejected Me, he will, in consequence of his own folly and wickedness, suffer unutterable and everlasting pain (comp. 18:7, C.); he is "the son of perdition" (John 17:12; see 8:12, A., and 23:15, D.), because he did not, like the eleven disciples, keep God's Word (John 17:6).

25 And Judas, which betrayed him, answered and said, Is it I, Rabbi? He saith unto him, Thou hast said.

A. Then = after the private conversation between the Lord and John (ver. 23, A.).—**B. Judas ... I?** The Lord's last warning word in ver. 21 should have alarmed the conscience of Judas; but his persistent hypocrisy in speaking as a friend while he cherished hostility in his heart reacted on him and hardened him the more, according to the process described in 2 Cor. 4:4. Hence, as, according to Luke 22:3, he had previously listened to a suggestion of Satan in place of saying: Get thee hence, Satan (Matt. 4:10), now, "after the sop, Satan entered into him" (John 13:27) = took full possession of him as an unresisting prey. Hence proceeds the effrontery with which he here asks the question.—**C. Thou hast said** = *Yes,* or, *It is as thou sayest.* Such was the ancient mode of uttering an affirmative answer (comp. ver. 64, below). This narrative, like that of the evangelist John, indicates that the question of Judas, and the answer to it, were both uttered in low tones, and were not distinctly heard by the other disciples. The succeeding words, recorded in John 13:27, were spoken aloud. Afterwards Judas withdrew temporarily (ver. 20, C.), but returned during the progress of the paschal meal (ver. 31, B.).

26 And as they were eating, Jesus took bread, and blessed, and brake it; and he gave to the disciples, and said, Take, eat; this is my body.

A. And ... eating = had eaten the paschal lamb, but not yet concluded the whole meal. At this point the history of the institution of the sacrament of the Lord's Supper commences. A *sacrament* is a religious ceremony, instituted by Christ Himself, in which certain outward signs or symbols are used, and which imparts to those who exercise faith the divine gifts themselves, which are indicated by the symbols. Only two sacraments were given to the Church by its Head, namely,

Baptism and the Lord's Supper.—**B. Jesus took bread** = a loaf of the bread already prepared for the paschal meal. This bread consisted of a thin, broad, flat "cake of bread" (2 Sam. 6:19; Gen. 18:6), shaped like a plate or wafer (comp. Exod. 29:23; 1 Kings 19:6; Hos. 7:8). It was of moderate size, one inch or less in thickness, and scarcely more than eight or ten inches in diameter, the dimensions being determined by convenience. The size may be estimated from passages like 1 Sam. 25:18; 2 Sam. 16:1; Luke 11:5; John 6:9. As these loaves were light and small, they often bear in the N. T. the plural name *breads*, translated simply *loaves*, as in 14:17; 15:34; 16:9, 10.—**C. And blessed** = the bread; so, too, the cup was blessed (1 Cor. 10:16). Here the following words occur in the margin of the English Bible: "Many Greek copies have *gave thanks*," that is, in place of *culogesas = blessed*. Many ancient manuscripts have a different Greek word, *eucharistesas*, signifying *gave thanks;* the latter occurs immediately below (ver. 27). For the two Greek words, which nearly coincide in sense, and one of which has furnished the name *Eucharist* for the Lord's Supper, see above, 14:19, B. The Saviour's act here is one of consecration (comp. Luke 9:16; 1 Sam. 9:13).—**D. And brake it.—Brake** = *broke*. Owing to the peculiar form of the bread (see B., above), the loaf was not cut but always broken (comp. 14:19; 15:36; Acts 27:35; Lam. Jerem. 4:4). In the parallel passage (1 Cor. 11:24), the same word *broken* is applied to the Lord's body. This particular word is not applied in the Gospels to the body of Christ in the narrative of the institution of the Holy Supper, and, in 1 Cor. 11:24, is simply equivalent to "given," which is the word employed in Luke 22:19. Inasmuch as the Scripture had declared: "A bone of him shall not be broken" (John 19:36; Exod. 12:46; Numb. 9:12; Ps. 34:20), the act of *breaking* the bread used in the Communion, which act by no means represents the *piercing* of the Lord's Body with nails and a spear, can have no significance, and does not necessarily belong to the holy rite. Paul introduces the word in 1 Cor. 10:16 because the first Christians used similar bread = so baked that it did not admit of being cut, but was broken, and this circumstance afterwards suggested the word *broken* in 1 Cor. 11:24 (see below, 27:56, C.).—**E. And gave it to the disciples** = that they might actually partake of the gift. The emphatic words, **Take, eat,** indicate that the ordinance is not simply a ceremony performed by a few individuals, and intended to commemorate a past event by the exhibition or display of bread and wine, but that its benefits can be received solely by those who actually *eat*.—**F. This is my body.** In the original Greek the pronoun **this** by its form and termination, which cannot be precisely represented in English, indicates that it does not directly refer to the word *bread*. The sense is: This, which I give you, is, etc. It is obvious that the disciples ate bread and not the mere semblance of bread, for, according to 1 Cor. 10:16, bread remains unchanged even after the consecration. The doctrine of the Papists, according to which the bread is converted into the Lord's flesh, while it retains only the color and taste of simple bread, is, therefore, altogether unscriptural. While, however, the bread continues to be bread, the remarkable language of St. Paul in 1 Cor. 10:16; 11:27, and in Eph. 5:30, shows that he believed that the true body of Christ, His "glorious body" (Phil. 3:21 = His glorified body), was connected with the bread, so that the communicant received alike bread *and* the Lord's body, and wine *and* the Lord's blood. This sacramental union of the body of Christ with the bread is as incomprehensible as the passage of His body through "shut doors" (John 20:19, 26). Indeed, if the Lord's Supper constituted simply a commemorative rite, it would not possess a higher character or value than a "shadow" of the law (Col. 2:17), and the Lord would have merely reintroduced the types and figures of the law, while a very different view is presented in Eph. 5:30–32; Hebr. 9:9; 10:1. That presence of Christ is real and true, although incomprehensible, even as the holy influences of the Divine Spirit on the soul are real and true, although human reason cannot fully explain their nature. "Thou canst not tell, etc.," said the Lord to Nicodemus (John 3:8).

²⁷ And he took a cup, and gave thanks, and gave to them, saying, Drink ye all of it;

A. And ... cup = "after the same manner" (Luke 22:20; 1 Cor. 11:25), that is, after blessing it, as He blessed the bread. Both bread and wine had been previously on the table, as they were essential to the observance of the passover. The cup of wine, mingled with water, was circulated in connection with solemn prayers and thanksgiving, as a part of the entire ceremony. The **cup** here mentioned was probably the fourth, which was usually given after the lamb had been eaten.—**B. Gave thanks** = to God, as in the case of the bread (ver. 26, C.).—**C. Drink, etc.** The Papists, in direct opposition to both the spirit and the letter of these words—**ye all**—withhold the cup from all communicants, conceding it to the officiating priest alone. For the presence of Judas, see ver. 20, C.

²⁸ For this is my blood of the covenant, which is shed for many unto remission of sins.

A. For. This word introduces the reason on account of

which the Lord directs His disciples actually to drink as well as to behold the wine = *all* need the blessing which it conveys, and are equally bound thus to confess His name (ver. 26, E.).—**B. This ... covenant.** The original Greek word translated in A. V. **testament** occurs thirty-three times in the N. T.; it is rendered *covenant* twenty times, but *testament* in the other thirteen places. In all of the latter, as it is generally admitted, the word *covenant* would be more appropriate than *testament*, except in Hebr. 9:15–17, where the meaning apparently is *testament* = a will, or a legal declaration of a person's will respecting the disposition of his property after his death. But even in that passage, the word *covenant* would have been rightly chosen; the assertion that any one is the mediator of a last *will* is unintelligible, while the phrase, "mediator of a covenant," that is, a person who negotiates between the parties, is plain. The first covenant is not called elsewhere a *testament* in the sense of a *last will;* neither did a testament or a will of a dying or deceased man require, as ver. 18 says, a dedication with blood, which language applies only to covenants. The words translated: "there must ... be the death of the testator" (ver. 16), rather means: "there must be a death [namely, of a covenant-making victim] brought in [as the margin reads], or, furnished by the covenant-maker." The phrase in ver. 17: "after men are dead," seems rather to refer to the death of the animals (= of force because, or, in consequence of, slain, dead, victims), for the word *men* is not in the original. In the conclusion of ver. 17, the sense, finally, is:—There is no strength (validity) while the covenant-making victim lives = the covenant-maker's act never has force (legal authority) while the animals still live or have not yet been slain, in order to bind the contracting parties. The first or old covenant (see Hebr., ch. 8—ch. 10) was made in Horeb (Deut. 5:2); God graciously engaged on His part to be the benefactor of the Israelites, and they were pledged to serve Him alone (Exod. 19:5–8; Deut. 4:23). The new or better covenant, of which Christ is the Mediator, and which is promised in Jerem. 31:31, ff.; Ezek. 37:26, is described in Gal., ch. 3 and ch. 4, as one of grace and truth (John 1:17). According to its terms, God will grant everlasting life to all who truly believe in the Crucified Redeemer (see 2 Cor. 3:6, ff., and the Epistle to the Hebrews). In very ancient times, when solemn covenants were made, the contracting parties ratified their engagements by shedding the blood of animals (comp. Gen 15:8–18). According to Hebr. 9:18, ff.; Exod. 24:6–8, Moses, as the mediator of the first covenant, resorted to the "shedding of blood," and said: Behold the blood of the covenant, etc. It is in allusion to this blood of animals, which, according to Hebr. 9:13, 14; 10:4, could not really cleanse from sin, that the Saviour here says, while He presents the cup: This is *My* blood = more efficacious than the blood of the first covenant (Exod. 24:8), since it "cleanseth from all sin" (1 John 1:7), thus establishing a *better* covenant. As true blood was employed by Moses, the **blood** given in the Holy Supper must be the true blood of Christ (as in the case of His body and the bread), in conjunction with the wine; nevertheless, as gross flesh and blood were obviously not presented by Him, the body and blood which He gave were communicated in a manner incomprehensible to man. So, too, the union of the invisible soul with the human body is a fact believed by all, but capable of being distinctly understood and explained by none. The phraseology in Luke 22:20 and 1 Cor. 11:25: "This cup, etc.," indicates verbal variations which may be readily explained, when we reflect that the Lord doubtless, during the distribution, repeated substantially the same truths with various slight changes in the mere words.—**C. Which is shed for many** = shed for you (Luke 22:20). The Lord possibly said "for you," and then, in reference to the whole human family for which He died, viewed as **many** when compared with the *twelve*, He added: "and for many;" that the word is here equivalent to "all" is shown in ann. to 20:28, F. The "many" who are dead are "all" in Rom. 5:12, 15.—**Shed for** = in your place. That the sufferings and death of Christ, viewed as an atoning sacrifice, were *vicarious*, that is, endured in our place, is taught not only in Isai., ch. 53, but also in various portions of the N. T. (see the passages, 20:28, E.).—**D. Unto remission of sins.** When sin entered the world, it separated man from God and introduced death (Rom. 5:12; James 1:15). The work of Christ, in its whole extent, comprehends the entire deliverance of man from sin, that is, both the removal of our guilt (derived from original sin and personal sinful acts), and also the sanctification of our nature. Hence, the **remission** (= pardon) **of sins** is equivalent to our full restoration to divine favor and to happiness (comp. Rom. 5:6–21). The circumstance that neither Matthew nor Mark records the words in Luke 22:19; 1 Cor. 11:24, 25, "in remembrance of me," shows that the Lord's Supper is not chiefly, much less exclusively, intended to be a memorial of Christ's death, but rather a means of grace; the agreement of all in recording the words: "This is my body—blood," shows, on the other hand, that the communication of the Lord's body and blood in the sacrament is pre-eminently characteristic of the ordinance. The word employed by Paul in 1 Cor. 11:26: "ye do *shew* the Lord's death" (translated usually *preach*, Acts 4:2; 13:38, and also *declare*, Acts 17:23; 1 Cor. 2:1; *speak* of, Rom. 1:8), teaches that he viewed the Lord's Supper also as a public confession of faith.

²⁹ But I say unto you, I will not drink henceforth of this fruit of the vine, until that day when I drink it new with you in my Father's kingdom.

A remarkable accumulation of figurative terms occurs in this verse; even *wine* ("the blood of the grape," Deut. 32:14; Gen. 49:11) is here called the **fruit** (= *produce, result;* comp. *fruits* in 2 Cor. 9:10) **of the vine.** The Lord frequently employs the image of a banquet when He designs to describe very great happiness and enjoyment (comp. 22:2, C.). In ch. 8:11, E., it represents the blessedness of the redeemed in heaven. Now, at this paschal supper, He had used the language found in this verse both in reference to the bread and to the wine, according to Luke 22:16, 18, before He actually instituted the Holy Supper itself, as it there appears from ver. 19. Then, as Luke relates (ver. 30), He introduced the same expressions for the third time, saying: "That ye may eat and drink at my table in my kingdom." And, finally, in Rev. 19:9, the "marriage supper of the Lamb" is described; but this banquet (like the "fine linen" which there, in the foregoing verse, is explained to be an image of "the righteousness of the saints") is clearly an image only of the glory and bliss of the redeemed in heaven, and cannot be understood literally of the act of eating or drinking. Further, the word **new,** as here applied to the wine, cannot be literally understood, for, according to the well-known fact, "the old (wine) is better (than the new)" (Luke 5:39), while here the "new" wine is obviously so named in the sense of *better*, as that word frequently is used, for example, in Ps. 33:3; 2 Cor. 5:17; Gal. 6:15; Eph. 4:24; Hebr. 8:8, 13; 2 Peter 3:13; Rev. 2:17; 3:12; 5:9; 21:1, 5. The **kingdom** here, as in Matt. 13:43; 2 Tim. 4:18, is the kingdom of glory in heaven, after the judgment has been held and the world has passed away. Luke's record of the words (22:30) resembles the language in Matt. 19:28, E., and refers to a future period when the Gospel preached by the apostles shall generally diffuse its blessings in the world. But in the present passage (Matt. 26:29) the term **that day,** which designates the time of the end of the world and of the judgment (see 7:22; 24:36, shows that the period here specified is that in which the blessedness of the redeemed shall begin, when they are admitted into heaven on the Gospel terms which had been proclaimed by the inspired apostles, "the judges of the twelve tribes of Israel" (see 19:28, E.). It may yet be added that Paul describes the termination of the practice of celebrating the Lord's death in the Holy Supper as coincident with His coming to judgment (1 Cor. 11:26). The sense of the present verse then is: This is the last passover which I shall celebrate with you. When we next meet in order to abide together, seeing face to face (1 Cor. 13:12; Gen. 32:30; Exod. 33:11), it will be under circumstances far more blessed than the present are, and our union will then be eternal. (The words of Peter in Acts 10:41 refer, not to ordinary meals in which the Lord joined the disciples after His resurrection, but to the incidents described in Luke 24:42; John 21:13, which were simply designed to furnish evidence of the reality of the Saviour's presence (comp. Acts 1:3). Hence the words: "did eat and drink," as in Luke 13:26, are equivalent to: We held intimate communion with Him in reality, and not in dreams or visions.)

³⁰ And when they had sung a hymn, they went out unto the mount of Olives.

A. Sung a hymn = had hymned, sung praises. It was customary, at the conclusion of the meal, to sing the words of Ps. 115–118; these four Psalms, and the two which preceded them (ver. 21, A.), constituted the so-called *Great Hallel* = Praise. The Hebrew word *Hallelujah* (Rev. 19:1, 3, 4, 6) signifies: Praise ye Jehovah (see Ps. 106:1, margin).—**B. They went, etc.** = towards Gethsemane (ver. 36; John 18:1). For **mount of Olives,** see 21:1. The words recorded in John (ch. 14—ch. 17) had been previously spoken.

³¹ Then saith Jesus unto them, All ye shall be offended in me this night: for it is written, I will smite the shepherd, and the sheep of the flock shall be scattered abroad.

A. Then = after having left the house.—**B. All ... night.** This language enables us to determine the moment when Judas finally withdrew. He could not retire at an earlier moment, unless temporarily (ver. 20, C., and 25, C.), without attracting attention, which circumstance his plan required him to avoid. When, however, all had left the house at a very late hour of the evening, and he now knew the place of destination, the darkness enabled him to depart without observation, as he hoped, and to inform the Pharisees that a favorable opportunity for seizing his Master in comparative solitude had arrived. Nevertheless, the all-seeing eye of the Saviour followed Judas, and a remark in reference to his absence, or, probably, a distinct revelation of the apostasy of Judas, was made. Possibly the disciples then referred, by way of contrast, to their own fidelity; in order to unveil to them their own weakness, Christ now replied: **All ye,** who still remain, shall (= will) be, etc.—**C. Offended** (see 5:29, C.). The sense is: Ye, too, alarmed and discouraged, will betray weakness of faith, and even desert Me, before this night has passed away. The literal fulfilment of this prediction is mentioned below (ver. 56).—**D. For it is written.** The language does not mean that this prediction itself caused the dispersion of the disciples, or rendered it necessary. So, in Acts 27:9, the "fast" did not render the sailing dangerous, but the late season of the year, with which the feast coincided, was the cause (comp. 1:22, A.). Here the sense is: Your flight was foreseen by the omniscient God and foretold; being a foreseen event, it will occur, as the prophet accordingly wrote. An essential difference exists, on the one hand, between the temporary unfaithfulness of the disciples, when they were seized by a panic, and hastily fled without any deliberate purpose to abandon their Lord, and, on the other, the conduct of Judas, who deliberately and calmly devised and arranged his treacherous plan. Hence the Lord utters the following words (ver. 31, 32), which embrace, first, a prophetic passage, and, secondly, a gracious promise that includes a renewed prediction of His resurrection. The disciples now learn that their conduct would not take their Master by surprise.—**E. I will smite, etc.** The words are found in Zech. 13:7. In that remarkable chapter, which opens with a glorious revelation of the atoning work of Christ, the prophet refers to the period of four centuries, extending from Malachi to the advent of the Saviour, during which the voice of prophecy was silent; he implies, in highly figurative language, first, that when the great Prophet announced by Moses (Deut. 18:15) shall finally appear, He shall be denied, persecuted and slain; and, secondly, that His adherents ("sheep—flock") shall be dispersed. The feelings of the distressed disciples during the short (Mark 16:14) period of their dispersion are illustrated in Luke 24:21, ff.

[32] But after I am raised up, I will go before you into Galilee.

Risen again (see 16:21; 20:19).—**Go before, etc.** The Lord, according to 28:16, named ("appointed") the mountain where the meeting should occur, but the locality is now unknown. The whole spirit of the words—serenity and confidence—indicating that the Lord would victoriously live again, and renew His intercourse with His people, is animating in the highest degree.

[33] But Peter answered and said unto him, If all shall be offended in thee, I will never be offended.

A. Peter answered. The impetuousness which originally predominated in the character of Peter (comp. 14:28; 16:16, 22; 26:51; John 13:8, 9; 20:6; 21:7), and which prompted him to speak and act while others deliberated, was subsequently so controlled and elevated by grace as to assume the form of heroic and enduring courage (comp. Acts 2:14).—**B. If all, etc.** The general character and conduct of Peter furnish satisfactory evidence that these words *only seem* to reflect unkindly on the fidelity of his fellow-disciples. That Peter referred to the disciples is indicated in John 21:15, ff. He simply expresses his own conviction that *he* could never be guilty of deliberate apostasy; the words **If all** indicate that a case is supposed which, in the speaker's view, will not probably occur. He does not desire to lower others in his Master's esteem, and is unquestionably sincere; but he relies too presumptuously on his own strength.—**Offended.** Peter repeats the word employed by his Master (ver. 31).

[34] Jesus said unto him, Verily I say unto thee, That this

night, before the cock crow, thou shalt deny me thrice.

A. Jesus said. The Lord designed to elevate Peter to an important post; but humility and reliance on divine grace exclusively were indispensable qualifications. The Lord reveals to Peter the approaching fall of the latter, so that the lesson of self-abasement which it taught might, by the distinctness given to it in this conversation, make an indelible impression.—**B. Before ... crow** = before the morning comes. The third watch of the night, extending from midnight to three o'clock in the morning, was called by a Greek name signifying *cock-crowing* (Matt. 13:35). The first cock-crowing was assumed to occur at midnight, the close of the second watch, and the second about three o'clock A. M., at which time the fourth watch began. In Mark 14:30 the word "twice" is added; this expression defines with precision that the three denials of Peter would occur at or after midnight and before the rising of the sun (comp. ver. 69, ff., with 27:1).—**C. Deny.** The word here (see 16:24, B.; comp. with Luke 12:9) is equivalent to *disown*, disclaim all relationship or connection with any one (see ver. 74). The sense is: Thou wilt, in place of boldly and consistently adhering to Me, three times distinctly disavow Me and My cause.

³⁵ Peter saith unto him, Even if I must die with thee, *yet* will I not deny thee. Likewise also said all the disciples.

A. Even if ... deny thee. Peter now uses still more emphatic language.—**B. Likewise, etc.** The disciples, too, sincerely loved their Master; when Peter expressed his devotion to the Lord in such unequivocal terms, he merely expressed common feeling, which had been once before acknowledged by Thomas, in John 11:16.

³⁶ Then cometh Jesus with them unto a place called Geth-

semane, and saith unto his disciples, Sit ye here, while I go yonder and pray.

A. Then. The foregoing conversation appears to have been held on the way.—**B. A place called Gethsemane** = a plantation or "garden" (John 18:1) extending along the brook Cedron, at the foot of the Mount of Olives (Luke 22:39). The name, which signifies *oil-press*, indicates the business of the proprietor. It was a favorite place of resort of the Saviour (John 18:2). Tradition points to its site on the east of the city. In the enclosure Robinson found, in 1838, "eight very old olive trees" (Bibl. Res. I. 234).—**C. Sit ye, etc.** The disciples to whom these words are addressed are the eight that remained after Judas withdrew, and after Peter, and James and John, the two sons of Zebedee (4:21), accompanied the Lord somewhat further (ver. 37, 38). The eight were on several other occasions excluded from scenes to which the three just mentioned were admitted (see 17:1, B.).—**D. While I, etc.** (see 14:23, A.). On this solemn occasion the Lord's threefold act of prayer (ver. 44; comp. 2 Cor. 12:8) was marked by a continued increase of intensity of feeling (Luke 22:44).

37 And he took with him Peter and the two sons of Zebedee, and began to be sorrowful and sore troubled.

A. Peter ... Zebedee (see ver. 36, C.).—**B. Began.** The Lord had always been calm or composed in His demeanor, sometimes happy and cheerful, often very grave, but never gloomy. The present unusual disquietude is indicated by the word **began.—To be sorrowful** = to be painfully affected. The word employed in Mark 14:33, "sore (= greatly, 17:6) amazed," is translated in Mark 16:5, 6, "affrighted," and indicates an overwhelming sense of distress.—**Sore**

troubled. The original term, occurring also in Phil. 2:26, here indicates *anguish*, a painful feeling of desolation, or those sensations which sometimes cause a *shuddering*. ["The confused, restless, half-distracted state, which is produced by physical derangement or by mental disorders."—LightFoot.]—**C.** The Lord's "agony" (Luke 22:44), or "travail (= anguish) of soul" (Isai. 53:11), in Gethsemane, which even the three favored disciples were not permitted to witness fully, is, particularly in view of His own remarkable expressions (ver. 39), a very mysterious subject.

§ 1. He twice refers to it by way of anticipation: first, in Luke 12:50 ("straitened" = distressed; comp. the allied word "distress," Luke 21:25; "anguish" 2 Cor. 2:4); and, secondly, in John 12:27 ("troubled," which word is found in Matt. 14:26, B.). Now, we read in Hebr. 5:7 that in "the days of his flesh" (= after the eternal Son of God had assumed human nature, John 1:14, and before He died on the cross), "He offered up prayers and supplications with strong crying and tears ... and was heard in that He feared;" the latter clause, as many explain it, signifies: His prayer was answered, and He was delivered from His distress. In Luke 22:53, after the agony had passed away, but while the pains of the cross still impended, the Lord says to His enemies: This is your hour and [is] the power of darkness (comp. the latter clause with passages like 2 Cor. 6:14, 15; Eph. 6:12). The words doubtless refer to renewed manifestations of the malice of Satan, who departed from Him only "for a season," after the temptation (see above, 4:11, A.), but perpetually renewed his assaults (16:23, B.). He was now permitted once more to exercise all his powers of temptation. The result was, that the Saviour, according to Hebr. 2:10, 17, 18; 4:15, was not only "in all points tempted like as we are," but by His prayers and faith, which secured the victory, was made "perfect through suffering," and thus could give assurance to every sorrowing soul that He was "touched with the feeling of our infirmities" = a sympathizing Mediator. The Lord's agony had no connection with the natural dread of suffering a painful death; for that dread many martyrs of both sexes, when put to the rack or cast into the fire, and even many prisoners of war, have overcome. Neither did it proceed from any consciousness of bearing the Father's wrath as if He were personally guilty, for, on the contrary, He was always conscious of His Father's love (John 10:17). God "made him to be sin for us, who knew no sin" (2 Cor. 5:21) = "laid on him the iniquity of us all" (Isai. 53:6), that is, allowed Him to sustain the anguish and the penalty to which our sins lead. "Christ endured my sorrow, in order to bestow His joy on me."—Ambrose.

§ 2. Such scriptural declarations teach that the Saviour endured a struggle in Gethsemane of unusual intensity and anguish, which no mortal can understand. He was on the point of completing that great atoning work on which all heaven gazed with deep interest (1 Peter 1:12). In the awful moments which preceded His cruel death He was overwhelmed with grief; the whole enormity of the guilt of the human race oppressed Him, for He alone could see it in its whole fearful extent. Even as death, with all its eternal results, is a far more solemn event in the eye of an enlightened Christian than in that of an ignorant and stupid heathen, so the spiritual evils of men were more distinctly revealed to the Saviour's eye in all their horror than to our own. The burden was too weighty for His mere human nature: "His sweat was as it were great drops of blood" (Luke

22:44). Who can measure or conceive of the anguish of His soul, while this inward conflict prevailed? Or who can approach that mysterious presence and unveil or explain that agony which the eye of the Father alone beheld? As after the first temptation (Mark 1:13), so here His human nature was bowed down under the awful burden laid upon it; it would have been prostrated if "an angel had not appeared unto him from heaven, strengthening him" (Luke 22:43).

§ 3. At the same time, another glance which the Scriptures permit us to cast on the Saviour's agony reveals the fact that He did not entertain any sense of personal guilt, and that hence the Father's presence and love were not for one moment withdrawn, as we learn from John 8:29; 10:17 and 16:32. The awful struggle of the Saviour must have therefore consisted in part in some powerful temptation (indicated perhaps by the word "agony" in Luke 22:44 = *conflict*), the nature of which is not revealed, or else in an agonizing feeling of the accumulated weight of "the sin of the world," which His vicarious sufferings and death were intended to expiate (John 1:29).

§ 4. The intense sufferings of the Lord, which far exceeded those of any martyr, are thus explained by Luther in a sermon on the sufferings of Christ in the Garden: "We, who are ordinary mortals, and who are conceived and born in sin (Ps. 51:5), have a nature (flesh) which is unclean and destitute of delicacy of feeling. Yet even we find that we are less obtuse and insensible to bodily pain in proportion to the degree in which the blood is pure, the health vigorous, the mind clear, and the whole bodily organization in a natural state. Now, as Christ was altogether holy and free from sin, His sensations both of pain and of pleasure must have been far more exquisite than our own, so that He must have suffered much more intensely from the pains of death than we, with our corrupt bodies, can do. He was therefore the greatest martyr that ever lived, and the 'terrors of death' overwhelmed Him with more horror (Ps. 55:4, 5) than ordinary mortals in their depraved state experience."

§ 5. The expression "this cup," in Matt. 26:39, does not refer exclusively to the actual death of Christ, which from the beginning He was willing to suffer (Hebr. 10:5–10), but to those intense sorrows of soul which He experienced in that awful hour (20:22, B.); it is so explained in Mark 14:35: "He prayed that ... the hour might pass from him." *That* cup did pass away (see above, § 1), when He prevailed, and was strengthened by an angel (§ 2, above). Afterwards, in John 18:11, the same term, indicative of suffering, is extended in sense (corresponding to the comprehensive term "passion," see ann. to ver. 1), and applied alike to the pain which the treachery of Judas occasioned, to the personal indignities offered to the Lord, and to the whole of the subsequent sufferings.

³⁸ Then saith he unto them, My soul is exceeding sorrowful, even unto death: abide ye here, and watch with me.

A. My soul ... sorrowful (see ann. to ver. 37).—**B. Even unto death.** A proverbial expression = I am ready to die under the crushing weight of My distress. "The sorrows of death compassed me" (Ps. 18:4).—**C. Abide** = remain here while I go "forward a little" (Mark 14:34, 35). The soul often shrinks from exposing its deepest emotions to the gaze of mortals. No eye but that of God could witness the whole intensity of the Saviour's conflict.—**D. And watch with me.** The word for **watch,** translated *wake* in 1 Thess.

5:10, often refers to the full consciousness of a living person, as opposed to a state of unconsciousness = death; here it similarly implies, in a warning tone, that the disciples should remain wakeful and be on their guard (see below, ver. 41).—**With me** = *along*, or *together with* Me, that is, as well as I watch. The Lord does not ask them to pray with (in company with) Him; that communion of His soul with God none could aid; "the heart knoweth his (its) own bitterness" (Prov. 14:10).

³⁹ And he went forward a little, and fell on his face, and prayed, saying, O my Father, if it be possible, let this cup pass from me: nevertheless, not as I will, but as thou wilt.

A. Fell on his face. Prayer, when performed in this attitude, indicated the deepest degree of self-abasement (Numb. 16:22; Neh. 8:6; and see Matt. 6:5, B.). Such a posture was, likewise, the expression of overpowering emotion (comp. Matt. 17:6). Here it is an affecting illustration of the Lord's "travail of soul" (ver. 37, C.).—**B. If it be possible** = "if thou be willing" (Luke 22:42; see 24:24, C.). The Lord does not ask to be exempted from death itself, but to be delivered from the inexpressible agony of soul which at that moment He endured. The sense is: If it be consistent with Thy will to deliver Me, etc.—**This cup** = this agony (see above, ann. to ver. 37, C., § 5, and ch. 20:22, B.).—**C. Nevertheless, etc.** (comp. John 5:30; 6:38). These sublime words express the sentiments which every intelligent creature of God should entertain. When the eternal Son of God "in the days of his flesh" (ver. 37, C., § 1) endured a trial transcending the strength of ordinary mortals, He nevertheless unreservedly and fully yielded to the Father's will. Hence He could say: "I do always those things that please him" (John 8:29).

⁴⁰ And he cometh unto the disciples, and findeth them sleeping, and saith unto Peter, What, could ye not watch with me one hour?

A. Findeth them sleeping, and saith. The language of the Lord gently rebukes the disciples for yielding to their inclination to sleep. Still, this language may be misunderstood unless we notice the remarkable words of "Luke, the beloved physician" (Col. 4:14), who, in ch. 22, ver. 45, represents them as "sleeping for sorrow," and also the statement in Luke 9:32, that on the occasion of the transfiguration the same disciples were "heavy with (= weighed down by) sleep" = in a torpor. In both cases the feelings of these disciples had been excited in an unusual degree; in the latter especially they understood that a fearful crisis had arrived, and their alarm and anxiety, of which we can scarcely conceive, completely exhausted all their bodily strength. It has been remarked by medical writers that in situations which create unusual uneasiness, profound grief and anxiety or any other excessive tension of the soul, nature seeks relief in the unconsciousness of heavy sleep or stupor. This circumstance fully explains the continued drowsiness of the disciples, which arose, not from the feeble but rather the powerful interest with which they beheld their Master's danger.—**B. Saith unto Peter** = who had rashly professed, ver. 25, that he could overcome even the terrors of death.—**C. What, could, etc.,** lit. Are ye *so* (= in this manner, or, to such a degree) unable to watch, etc. The same Greek phrase ("Is it so, that") occurs in 1 Cor. 6:5. The rebuke, which recognizes the unusual oppression of the disciples, implies that it should have called forth unusual efforts to prevail over their grief. [Can you not even *watch* with Me, while I agonize for you?] It mournfully alludes to the Lord's lonely state in the hour of His deepest grief (comp. Ps. 69:20).

⁴¹ Watch and pray, that ye enter not into temptation: the spirit indeed is willing, but the flesh is weak.

A. Watch. This word had occurred in ver. 38, D.; here it is evidently employed in the more usual spiritual sense (comp. 24:42, B.; Acts 20:31; 1 Cor. 16:13). The following is implied: The tempter is near; you may at any moment be led away from the path of duty; therefore be on your guard. (See, for such a twofold sense, the word "dead" in 8:22, and the word "sleep" in 1 Thess. 5:6, 7, comp. with ver. 10).—**B. Pray** = seek direct communion with God, and ask for His divine aid—for the "shield of faith, wherewith, etc." (Eph. 6:16; comp. 17:20; Mark 9:23).—**C. That ye ... temptation** = that the temptation to which ye will be exposed may not prevail through your own neglect, nor occasion your fall, by your act of consenting to it.—**Enter into** (see 6:13, A., and comp. 1 Tim. 6:9). Peter doubtless recalled to mind the present scene with deep feeling, when he afterwards wrote the words in 1 Peter 4:7; 5:8.—**D. The spirit, etc.** The Lord in His infinitely tender love designs to say that He by no means ascribes to these disciples the unholy purposes of Judas, and that he well knows that they desire to be faithful. Still, no man, since the fall of Adam, possesses any strength of his own, or can believe in God, love Him and keep His commandments, without divine aid. Even the upright believer can, at best, only repeat Paul's words in Rom. 7:18.—**Willing** = *prompt, ready*, as in Mark 14:38; Rom. 1:15. The terms **spirit** and **flesh** in this passage, which refers to those who are already believers, maybe explained from Rom. 7:18, 22, 25, and ch. 8;

Eph. 3:16. The former designates here the "inward man" or "mind" = the moral nature, the soul, enlightened and renewed by grace; the latter here specially indicates not so much our bodily or human nature, as rather our human nature in its present disordered or corrupt state, as in John 3:6; Gal. 5:16, 19; Eph. 2:3. The Christian daily struggles with the evil tendencies of his nature, until at death he is freed from the last traces of original sin.

⁴²⁻⁴⁴ Again, a second time, he went away, and prayed, saying, O my Father, if this cannot pass away, except I drink it, thy will be done.—And he came again, and found them sleeping: for their eyes were heavy.—And he left them again and went away, and prayed a third time, saying again the same words.

The Saviour went away thrice and prayed, first kneeling (Luke 22:41), then falling on His face (ver. 39, above).—**Their eyes were heavy** = with sleep, as in Luke 9:32 (see ver. 40, A.).—**Saying the same words,** but with emotions increasing in power, which gave new meaning to the words in the eyes of God (ver. 36, D.). Thus "the same words" of the Lord's Prayer, or of appropriate forms of prayer regularly read at public worship, may be repeated continually with new fervor and devotion, even as the *same hymns* are often sung by a congregation. It is not the *repetition itself* of the same prayer, and even of the very words, which is censured in 6:7, A., but the absence of devout feeling or of faith and love.—["Lower forms of sorrow may, as it were, play with grief and vary the forms of its expression, but the deepest and sharpest agony is content to fall back upon the iteration of the self-same words."—Plumptre.]—"How forcibly this exhibition of the Saviour's course teaches us to persevere in prayer in seasons of temptation."—Luther.

⁴⁵ Then cometh he to the disciples, and saith unto them, Sleep on now, and take your rest: behold, the hour is at hand, and the Son of man is betrayed into the hands of sinners.

A. Sleep on now. As the disciples are informed that "the hour is at hand," and are commanded, in the next verse, to "rise," some interpreters have proposed to read these words interrogatively = do ye sleep? But the original phrase translated **now,** as in Hebr. 10:13, rather means *henceforward,* or, more literally, *"the rest,"* namely, *of the time,* and could not be introduced into such a question in a natural manner. The sense doubtless is: My struggle is over; now am I ready; until the betrayer comes, **take your rest** = seek repose, until they come! Here a pause of some length occurs, such as, in a similar case, must evidently be assumed at the end of John, ch. 14, before the words in 15:1 are uttered. The disciples accordingly slumber, and the Saviour remains at their side in silence, recovering from the exhaustion which followed His agony, and seeking in silent prayer the strength which He would need in the new conflict that was at hand. The English text would indicate this interpretation if printed thus: "and take your rest.—Behold, the hour, etc."—**B. Behold, etc.** These words, introduced by the exclamation, "It is enough" (Mark 14:41), and indicating haste, are uttered after the interval of rest just described above in **A.,** and are intended to arouse the slumbering disciples.—**The hour is at hand,** lit. *has drawn near* = the time of My death and victory (comp. John 12:23; 13:1).—**Is betrayed** (or, *delivered,* 17:22, 23) = the deed is done! Judas has consummated his crime!—**Sinners** = Judas, the Jews and the Roman soldiers (Acts 2:23).

⁴⁶ Arise, let us be going: behold, he is at hand that betrayeth

me.

Let us be going = to meet the approaching enemies. The Lord exhibits divine fortitude, although He knew "all things that should come upon him" (John 18:4).—**He is at hand, etc.** The Lord calls the attention of His disciples to the approaching light of the torches gleaming through the trees of Gethsemane, and to the sounds of the clashing weapons mentioned in John 18:3. As the Jewish month always began with the new moon, the passover, which was on the 14th day, necessarily occurred at the time of full moon (see above, ver. 2, B., § 2). Hence, these torches were designed to enable the men to explore the dark recesses of the garden.

⁴⁷ And while he yet spake, lo, Judas, one of the twelve, came, and with him a great multitude with swords and staves, from the chief priests and elders of the people.

A. Judas ... twelve (see ver. 14).—**B. A great ... staves** (John 18:3; Luke 22:52). There was a temple-guard, consisting of Levites, regularly maintained in the city, which was, with the officers, subject to the orders of the high priest; Judas had previously seen the captains (Luke 22:4). The mention of **swords**, in addition to **staves** (here = rods, clubs, see 10:10, D.), and the occurrence of the Greek military terms "band" (a cohort, or, possibly, *manipulus*) and "captain" (answering here nearly to the modern *colonel*) in John 18:3, 12 (comp. Matt. 27:27; Acts 10:1; 27:1), seem to indicate that a troop of soldiers, sent forth by Pilate at the request of the Jews, constituted a part of this **multitude.** Some resistance may have been apprehended by the Jews on the part of the disciples, who, as Judas knew, possessed two swords (Matt. 26:51; Luke 22:38). For the *temple-guard*, see 1 Chron. 9:17, 27; 24:5; Acts 4:1; 5:26; Jos. War, 2, 12, 1; 6, 5,

3.—C. From the chief priests, etc. = according to whose official directions the band of armed men here acted.

[48] Now he that betrayed him gave them a sign, saying, Whomsoever I shall kiss, that is he; take him.

A. A sign = a private signal, intended to identify the individual whom the band should seize. Judas probably **gave them a sign** = notified them, while they were marching, and immediately before He came forward, as the word "forthwith" in ver. 49 shows.—B. Kiss. The oriental custom, according to which a kiss indicated both friendship and love between persons of the same sex (2 Sam. 15:5; Ruth 1:14) when they met or when they parted (Gen. 33:4; Exod. 4:27; 1 Sam. 10:1; Luke 7:45; Acts 20:37), and also reverence and devotion (Ps. 2:12; 1 Kings 19:18; Hos. 13:2), is often mentioned in the Scriptures. The kiss was imprinted on the lips (Gen. 33:4; 1 Sam. 20:41), or the beard (2 Sam. 20:9—a custom which the Arabs still retain), the hand, the knees, or even the feet or ground occupied by the feet of princes, as an act of homage (Isai. 49:23; Micah 7:17; Ps. 72:9; Luke 7:38). In accordance with this oriental custom of indicating love or reverence, persons of the same sex, among the primitive Christians, gave "the holy kiss" to each other (Rom. 16:16; 1 Cor. 16:20; 2 Cor. 13:12; 1 Thess. 5:26; 1 Peter 5:14). Jacob's kiss (2 Sam. 20:9) was, like that of Judas, the "deceitful kiss of an enemy" (Prov. 27:6).

[49] And straightway he came to Jesus, and said, Hail, Rabbi; and kissed him.

A. Came to Jesus. It appears from Luke 22:47 that Judas "went before" the multitude, partly for the purpose of giving the appointed signal, and partly, no doubt, with the hope of concealing the fact from his former associates, that he acted in concert with the band.—**B. Hail, Rabbi.** Judas employs the friendly term of salutation (see 28:9, A.), which was usual both in personal addresses and in letters; it was also in some cases a recognition of the high character and the rank of the person saluted (27:29), and hence applied even to emperors. The Greek word here employed is, in its different forms, translated *greeting, farewell, God-speed* (see Luke 1:28; Acts 15:23; 23:26; 2 Cor. 13:11; James 1:1; 2 John 10, 11). The English word **Hail** originated in an old Anglo-Saxon term equivalent to *wholeness, health, prosperity*. On this occasion Judas also applied the title of honor: *Rabbi* (for which see 23:7, B., and John 1:38; 6:25).—**C. And kissed him** (ver. 48, B.). The bold manner in which Judas executed his plan is evidence that "Satan had entered into him" (Luke 22:3). His history is completed below (27:3–5).

⁵⁰ And Jesus said unto him, Friend, do that for which thou art come. Then they came, and laid hands on Jesus, and took him.

A. Friend = Thou, mine own familiar associate! (Ps. 41:9; 55:13; see 20:13).—**B. Do that ... come.** ["The language is somewhat abrupt; *Friend, mind what you are here for! attend to that*. With these words He spurns the kisses with which the traitor was overwhelming Him. Instead of hypocritical kissing, Jesus would prefer that Judas should at once proceed with his dark deed."—Meyer.]—**C. Then came they, etc.** = after recovering from the terror which had suddenly overpowered them on first seeing the Lord, as described in John 18:4–9.

⁵¹ And, behold, one of them that were with Jesus stretched out his hand, and drew his sword, and smote the servant of the high priest, and struck off his ear.

A. One of them = Peter (John 18:10).—**B. Stretched out, etc.** (see John 18:10). Peter ["to regain what he had lost, by neglecting to watch and pray"—Besser] again yields to the impulse of his feelings, without first ascertaining his Lord's will. His Master at once "healed" the wounded man (Luke 22:51), and then addressed Peter. The company of the disciples had previously furnished themselves with two swords (Luke 22:38); when the Galileans travelled to Jerusalem, they often carried weapons with them, as at that period the roads were rendered insecure by robbers.

52 Then saith Jesus unto him, Put up again thy sword into its place: for all they that take the sword shall perish with the sword.

A. Put up (= return ...) **sword** = into the sheath, scabbard (John 18:11). The sense is: My kingdom is not of this world (John 18:36), and does not need the aid of "carnal weapons" (2 Cor. 10:4).—**B. For all they, etc.** There is here doubtless an allusion to Gen. 9:6, where all private revenge, especially in the form of the taking of another's life, is forbidden (comp. Rom. 12:19). Peter had forgotten, in his excitement, the obvious circumstance that the enemies in his presence could easily return the blow, or cause it to be legally punished by death (Rom. 13:4; see Matt. 10:34, E.). The Lord's words are designed to rebuke Peter's excessive self-reliance, in as far as it came in conflict with faith, or trust in divine protection, and with submissiveness to the will of Providence. ["He imagined if he did not defend his Master, He must remain undefended, that all depended upon *him*. But surely God can have no need of any man's help."—Rieger.]

53 Thinkest thou that I cannot beseech my Father, and he shall even now give me more than twelve legions of angels?

A. Thinkest thou = is thy faith beginning to waver?—**B. That I cannot now** = even in this crisis, when I seem to be unable to prevail over My enemies.—**C. Pray, etc.** = canst thou really believe that at this moment My enemies have greater power than I? (comp. John 10:18; 11:42; 19:11). The **legion** was a division of the Roman troops possessing a distinctive character as a separate or independent army, and consisted of both cavalry and infantry. The number of men in a legion varied at different periods, but seldom exceeded 6,000. The term, in allusion to the completeness of the organization of this military body, was sometimes used figuratively to indicate a large number, as here and in Mark, 5:9. The Lord, possibly alluding also to 2 Kings 6:16, 17, says **twelve,** contrasting with the twelve feeble disciples who had hitherto attended Him twelve vast divisions of the innumerable host of the angels (Luke 2:13; Hebr. 12:22; Rev. 5:11; Dan. 7:10). Illustrations of the irresistible power with which God can endow a single angel are found in 2 Sam. 24:16; 2 Kings 19:35. The sense is: How canst thou think that My safety depends on thy feeble arm and sword, as if I could not invoke and freely exercise the almighty power of God, whose hosts of "mighty angels" (2 Thess. 1:7) do His pleasure? (Ps. 103:21).

[54] How then should the scriptures be fulfilled, that thus it must be?

A. How then ... fulfilled = if I should resort to such means of defence and not voluntarily lay down My life (John 10:18), and suffer death for sinners as their ransom (see 20:28, E.), how then, agreeably to the divine plan of salvation (1 Peter 1:20; Eph. 1:4; Rev. 13:8), is the gracious promise of pardon to be fulfilled, which is founded exclusively on My atoning death (Acts 4:12; Rom. 3:25; 1 Cor. 3:11; 1 Tim. 2:5, 6), as the Scriptures have already declared? (ver. 24, C., above).—**B. That thus,** lit. *for* (because) *thus,* in accordance with the divine plan and promise, it must all occur = it is proper and right (see 16:21, C.; comp. Acts 2:23).

⁵⁵ In that hour said Jesus to the multitudes, Are ye come out as against a robber with swords and staves to seize me? I sat daily in the temple teaching and ye took me not.

A. To the multitudes = and their leaders (Luke 22:52).—**B. Are ye ... seize me?** He reproaches them for the indignity offered Him in the mode of the arrest, which implied that He was capable of resorting to the desperate acts of a common highwayman. When—He asks—had His conduct indicated a disposition to employ violence against His enemies? (comp. Luke 4:29, 30; John 7:30, 44; 8:20). So, too, Paul was unwilling that a blemish should unnecessarily adhere to the cause which he advocated, or to his own good name (Acts 16:37).—**C. I sat, etc.** The Lord first vindicates His own character and conduct by referring to His upright, pacific, and yet fearless course of action (**sat daily** = when in Jerusalem), which evinced a good conscience; He, secondly, rebukes severely with these words their unholy feelings of malice and hatred, which compelled them to resort to secret and cowardly means of arresting Him. The words in Luke 22:53, like those addressed to Pilate (John 19:11), imply that His enemies could accomplish nothing, if divine wisdom should decide to check them.—**In the temple** = in one of the courts, possibly in Solomon's porch (John 10:23; Acts 3:11), which was connected with the court of the Gentiles (4:5, E., and see 21:12, A.).

⁵⁶ But all this is come to pass, that the scriptures of the

prophets might be fulfilled. Then all the disciples left him, and fled.

A. But all ... fulfilled. With these words, which give the substance of an additional remark of the Lord found in Mark 14:49, Matthew resumes the narrative, and, as in 1:22; 21:4, refers to the fidelity of God in keeping His ancient promises of accomplishing a redeeming work (comp. ver. 54).—**B. Then** = at the moment when Jesus expressed His willingness to yield without resistance and was actually seized.—**Forsook ... fled** (see ver. 31). After the disciples had recovered from their terror, which carried them temporarily away from the presence of the band, they, or at least Peter and John, returned (ver. 58; John 18:15). Their subsequent fidelity and heroic faith demonstrate that they had involuntarily yielded to a temporary alarm. At this point, probably, the incident occurred which is related in Mark 14:51, 52, and which possibly refers to Mark himself; he may have resided at that time in the city with his mother Mary (Acts 12:12).

⁵⁷ And they that had taken Jesus led *him* away to the house of Caiaphas the high priest, where the scribes and the elders were gathered together.

A. The events that followed the seizure of the Lord are not all related by each of the four evangelists; the one supplies incidents which another omits. A comparison of their respective accounts furnishes the following results:—The Lord was subjected first of all to an examination before Annas, who then sent Him to Caiaphas (John 18:13, 24); after the latter had also examined Him, and the Sanhedrim had in the mean time held a secret meeting, very early on Friday morning, He was placed before their tribunal.

After these persons had professedly investigated the case, He was conducted to the Roman governor, Pilate; the latter sent Him to Herod, and subsequently examined Him a second time (Luke 23:6–15). It was during these repeated public examinations, which consumed the whole night (Luke 22:59, 66), that the various indignities described in the four Gospels were offered Him.—**B.** The high priest's palace, like all large oriental houses, had a quadrangular interior court, which was paved; the arched passage which conducted to it from the street was protected by a heavy folding gate, in which a wicket was inserted. In this *court* (translated "hall" in Luke 22:55), which was open to the sky, the "fire of coals" mentioned in John 18:18 was made by the guards—**C. Caiaphas** (see ver. 3, B.). The members of the Sanhedrim were already coming together for consultation; they doubtless considered the question whether they should adhere to their original plan (ver. 5), or at once proceed to inflict death on Christ.

⁵⁸ But Peter followed him afar off unto the court of the high priest, and entered in, and sat with the officers, to see the end.

A. Peter ... off = not yet fully recovered from his alarm (ver. 56).—**B. Went in** = from the street into the interior court of the palace (ver. 57, B., and ver. 69).—**C. To see the end** = still hoping for his beloved Master's escape from danger.

⁵⁹ Now the chief priests, and the whole council, sought false witness against Jesus, that they might put him to death;

A. The time here indicated in Luke 22:66 is the early dawn: the consultations mentioned (ver. 57) had terminated.—**B. The whole council,** in formal session. Annas, the former high priest, a man possessed of great weight of character, was probably the president (Acts 4:6), and Caiaphas, although the high priest at the time, only one of the members (John 11:49, "one of them"). The Herodian family and the Romans had already introduced the policy of diminishing the power of the high priests, in consequence of which that office no longer entitled the incumbent to act as the presiding officer of the council.—**C. Sought false witness** = inasmuch as they well knew that no witness that was true could be unfavorable to Christ (John 8:46). Although the sentence "to put him to death" had already been framed, their own reputation demanded that at least the forms of a trial should be granted to the accused; the circumstance that they were guilty of a direct violation of the letter and spirit of the divine law in Exod. 26:16 was of no consequence in their eyes (see 23:23, C.).

⁶⁰ And they found it not, though many false witnesses came. But afterward came two,

A. Found it not = not even the many false witnesses could invent slander in such a form that their "witness agreed together" (Mark 14:56). The sense is: Even these bitter foes were ashamed to proceed on such contradictory charges, none of which could be substantiated. As the enemies of the Lord had seized Him before their plans were fully matured (ver. 4, C.), the subornation of witnesses had not yet been effected.—**B. Afterward, etc.** The letter of the law, and its repeated declarations (Numb. 35:30; Deut. 17:6; 19:15), which the Sanhedrim pretended to reserve, compelled them to furnish at least *two* witnesses.

⁶¹ And said, This man said, I am able to destroy the temple of God, and to build it in three days.

A. Said. These two false witnesses (Ps. 27:12) refer to certain words once employed by the Saviour, and recorded in John 2:19–21; He had applied the term *temple* to His own body (comp. Col. 2:9), and alluded to His death and resurrection. He had said: Destroy ye = if ye should destroy, etc. Here, by a malicious perversion, one of these witnesses (Mark 14:58) declared that the Lord had expressed His intention to destroy the sanctuary (the *naos,* 4:5, E.; 21:12, A., and not the whole area, often called collectively the *temple*). Now, such language, as the words in Acts 6:13 show, were understood to be an impious declaration of hostility to Him who dwelt in the sanctuary, and the charge here made, after the words of Christ had been distorted by His enemies, was, consequently, one of a very serious nature. It was, however, also obvious, that even if these witnesses spoke the truth, the offender could not have been an enemy of God, for He proposed to rebuild the temple; the accusation refuted itself. "But neither so did their witness agree together" (Mark 14:58, 59), since one of them, in his eagerness to secure the bribe, added words of his own invention: "I will destroy, etc.," which seemed to contradict the statement of the other, whose words Matthew here reports.

⁶² And the high priest stood up, and said unto him, Answerest thou nothing? what is it which these witness against thee?

A. The high priest arose = either through great excitement, or, possibly, in order to intimidate the Lord.—**B. Answerest thou, etc.** = hast thou no reply to make to such grave charges? The Lord had not attempted to refute the testimony of the false witnesses: first, because its falsity was known to all (John 18:19–21), and, secondly, because no reply would have altered the decision already made in private against Him (Luke 22:67, 68). "He opened not his mouth" (Isai. 53:7). It is also apparent that a full reply, including a reference to the Lord's resurrection on the third day, would have been inappropriate at that moment and before that audience. His expressive silence seems to imply: Why should I speak? Your fierce passions will allow you to hear neither "the voice of the prophets" (Acts 13:27) nor My own.

⁶³ But Jesus held his peace. And the high priest said unto him, I adjure thee by the living God, that thou tell us whether thou be the Christ, the Son of God.

A. Held his peace (see 20:31, A.).—**B. Answered** = resumed, in answer to the significant silence of the Lord (see 11:25, C.).—**C. I adjure thee.** This language of a judge was equivalent to the modern legal act of "administering an oath" = "to make any one swear," as the corresponding Hebrew term is translated in Gen. 24:3; 2 Chron. 36:13. The person so addressed, after "hearing the voice of swearing" (Luke 5:1) = listening to the form of the oath (comp. 1 Sam. 14:28), and assenting to it, was assumed to be bound by the oath. As our Lord replied, not to the slanderous charges, but to the oath which was here administered, He sanctioned this mode of eliciting the truth, when properly observed (see above, 5:33, A.; 34, B.).—**D. By the living God** (see 16:16, D.). In adjurations the term **living** refers to God both as a witness who knows the truth, and as an avenger who punishes perjury (comp. Hebr. 10:31).—**E. The Christ** = the promised Messiah, as in 16:16 (see 1:1, B.).—**F. The Son of God.** That the Jews understood this name to imply that Christ was divine = God (8:29, C.), appears from John 10:32, 33; 19:7; and comp. 16:16. The chief priest, who had hitherto failed to prove any of his charges, and was well aware of the earlier declarations of Christ that He was the Son of God, was satisfied that the accused would not hesitate to reassert His claims. He therefore reverts to the present method in order to justify the execution of Christ on the ground that He had "blasphemed" = ascribed to Himself a divine nature (see ver. 65).

⁶⁴ Jesus saith unto him, Thou hast said: nevertheless I say unto you, Henceforth ye shall see the Son of man sitting on the right hand of power, and coming on the clouds of heaven.

A. Thou hast said = *Yes* (see ver. 25, C.). The same sense attaches to "I am" (= that which thou hast said) in Mark 14:62. We have here an unequivocal recognition by the Lord of the established Church doctrine respecting His Deity.—**B. Nevertheless** = *but further*. The original word is sometimes used in such a sense, as here and in 11:22; "but" in Luke 19:27, when the speaker indicates that he now proceeds to a new subject.—**C. Henceforth ... power** = ye who now hear Me shall personally witness My divine glory, as foretold by Daniel (ch. 7:13), and then be convinced of My truth.—**The right hand of power** = of the power of God (Luke 22:69). The divine attribute of power or omnipotence here represents the nature and being of God generally (comp. Hebr. 1:3; 8:1). For **the right hand** (= place of honor), see 25:33, and comp. 1 Kings 2:19. The Lord alludes to Ps. 110:1 (see above, ann. to 22:43 and 44), where a prediction of Christ's exaltation and of His kingdom and glory occurs. The language indicates Christ's equality in honor and power with the Father, according to Acts 2:33; 5:31; 7:55, 56; Rom. 8:34; Hebr. 1:3; 1 Peter 3:22. This language, which in the Scriptures invariably refers to the Lord after His ascension, indicates the exaltation of His *human* nature (Phil. 2:9, ff.), which is now inseparably or forever connected with His divine nature; that divine nature always had been invested with the Father's glory (John 17:5; see 28:18, B.).—**D. Coming.** Different events connected with the Lord's deeds of power are described by terms analogous to this word "coming" (see the ann. to 10:23, B.). The present prediction appears to refer to future revelations of the Lord's glory which all His friends and enemies will witness, and to designate, as the similar expressions imply, the same events which are mentioned in 24:30, D. The sense of the whole verse is: Of My right to such a title ye shall receive ocular demonstration not only when I shall be revealed and acknowledged in eternity as the possessor of all power in heaven and in earth (28:18), but also previously, or, at a preceding period when I shall come to judge the living and the dead.

[65] Then the high priest rent his garments, saying, He hath spoken blasphemy; what further need have we of witnesses? behold, now ye have heard his blasphemy.

A. Rent his garments. A single article of clothing is occasionally, as in this instance, designated by the general term *garments*. The garment torn was the cloak or mantle (see 5:40, B.), or, when several articles of clothing were worn, one of the intermediate garments, usually where it extended over the breast. The act here described, which was common in the East, indicated some powerful emotion, usually grief (Josh. 7:6; 2 Sam. 3:31), or holy indignation and horror (Acts 14:14). By such emotions the hypocritical high priest, in imitation of the men mentioned in 2 Kings 18:37; 19:1, pretends to be governed. In common cases, such as the loss of relatives by death, the high priest was not permitted to perform the act (Lev. 10:6; 21:10).—**B. Spoken blasphemy** = irreverently claimed to be divine, that is, the Son of God (see ver. 63, F., and for **blasphemy,** 9:3, C.).—**C. What further, etc.** Caiaphas betrays in these words his embarrassment occasioned by the absolute impossibility to substantiate a single charge against the holy doctrine, conduct and character of Christ; he eagerly catches the words of the Lord as a pretext for condemning Him, and imperiously assumes that none can contradict him.

⁶⁶ What think ye? They answered and said, He is worthy of death.

A. What think ye? = pronounce your judgment in the case. The present investigation is preliminary in its character. According to Jewish usages (Jerem. 21:12), and also the Roman law, no sentence of death pronounced by a tribunal at night was legal and valid, neither was such a sentence usually pronounced by the Jewish authorities on the same day on which the accused person had received his trial. The former right, to which every one that was accused was entitled, was evaded by holding a formal session of the Sanhedrim very soon afterwards, according to 27:1, at which the sentence of death was pronounced anew ("when the *morning* was come"). The latter was evaded by the shallow pretext that the trial had been held before daylight in the presence of Caiaphas and individual members of the council, and consequently before the natural day on which the sentence mentioned in 27:1 was pronounced (Luke 22:66). These gross violations of law and justice, and the contradictions in which the Lord's enemies involved themselves, could not escape the notice of the spectators. But passion and might were permitted to prevail.—**B. They answered, etc.** = they voted apparently with entire unanimity, and doubtless in the absence of Nicodemus (John 7:50) and Joseph of Arimathea (Luke 23:50, 51; John 19:38), that Jesus should be sentenced to death. Blasphemy and similar offences were unquestionably punished with death according to the law (Lev. 24:16; Deut. 13:1–5; 18:20), but in this case the crime was not explained and proved.

67 Then did they spit in his face, and buffeted him; and some smote him with the palms of their hands.

A. They = "some" (Mark 14:65), possibly both members of the council (Matt. 27:41) and the attendants (Luke 22:63).—**B. Buffeted,** lit. inflicted blows with the fist on Him; similar outrages occur again (27:30). The indignities heaped on the holy person of the Saviour, and of which numerous instances are recorded by the several evangelists, could not be exceeded in atrocity; all that barbarity and malice could suggest, hypocrisy sanction, and cowardice perform, is combined in the blasphemous language (Luke 22:65) and personal violence to which the Lord was subjected.—**Spit—face** = the highest insult which could be offered among oriental nations (Numb. 12:14; Isai. 50:6). The Saviour's deep humiliation had already been predicted (see Isai. 50:6; 53:3–7; Micah 5:1), and was previously known to Him (John 18:4); but such was His love to man that He whom all the angels of God worshipped (Hebr. 1:6) "despised (here = disregarded, 6:24, C.) the shame" even of the cross (Hebr. 12:2; Phil. 2:7, 8), in view of the glory and joy which awaited Him after giving Himself for the redemption of a lost world.—**C. Smote, etc.** = "struck him on the face" (Luke 22:64). That such is the sense here appears from Matt. 5:39, where the same word is rendered simply "smite."

⁶⁸ Saying, Prophesy unto us, thou Christ, who is he that struck thee?

Prophesy. This word, which conveys the general sense of uttering truths unknown to man, by means of a divine communication (see 7:22, D.), is here intended to deride the Lord's claim to knowledge which mortals cannot acquire by their own efforts; the men had, namely, first covered the Lord's face or blindfolded Him (Mark 14:65; Luke 22:64). The sense then is: Thou who claimest to be Christ (= the Messiah), and to be endowed with divine knowledge and power, prove now Thy truth by naming the man who smote Thee, without having seen him. The vile character of persons who could be capable of such conduct is obvious.

⁶⁹ Now Peter was sitting without in the court: and a maid came unto him, saying, Thou also wast with Jesus the Galilean.

A. Was sitting without = on the outside of the chamber in which the Lord stood (**without,** as in 12:46), but in the interior court in which the fire had been kindled (Mark 14:67), and in this sense he sat **in the palace** = within its enclosure (see above, ver. 57, B., and 58). The spot which the Lord occupied in the interior of the building, where, however, all that took place in the court could be observed, was reached by steps (Mark 14:66) "beneath." The three denials are here grouped together (ver. 72, A.).—**B. A maid,** lit. *one maid,* that is, the first one as distinct from the second mentioned in ver. 71; the first one was the appointed door-keeper, according to John 18:17. The word translated **maid** sometimes designates in the N. T. a female servant (Luke 12:45) or bond-woman, bond-maid, as in Acts 16:16, 19, and is so translated in Gal.

4:22, 23, 30, 31. Among the Jews such persons frequently had charge of the door (comp. Acts 12:13).—**C. Came unto him, etc.** = immediately after his entrance (John 18:16, 17).—**Thou also** = as well as John. This female either asked in a spirit of levity, or, possibly, in a servile manner desired to show her zeal by assailing all to whom her master, the high priest, was known to be unfriendly.—**Jesus of Galilee**, lit. Jesus the Galilean. The Lord's protracted abode in Galilee led many to regard Him as a native of that region, and the term *Galilean* was subsequently applied to Him by way of contempt (21:11; John 7:52).—**Thou wast with** = thou belongest to His party (see 12:30, A.).

⁷⁰ But he denied before *them* all, saying, I know not what thou sayest.

A. Denied = disowned Christ (ver. 34, C.), refused to acknowledge that he had any connection with Him.—**Before them all** = the high priest's servants, the officers, etc.—**B. I know not, etc.** Peter assumes to be so entirely a stranger to the accused Jesus, as not even to "understand" (Mark 14:68) the meaning of the maid's words. "How grievous a sin may be committed in uttering only a few words! (comp. ch. 12:24; Acts 5:8)."—Bengel.—**C.** The sudden terror which had seized Peter and the other disciples (ver. 56), and which had subsided, now takes possession of him again. It was the "hour" of Christ's enemies and "the power of darkness" (Luke 22:53) = the time in which iniquity was allowed to prevail. According to the Lord's words (Luke 22:31), Satan, who had once exercised all his power to conduct Job to a fall (Job, ch. 1 and 2), now "desired to have Simon Peter that he might sift him as wheat" (= agitate, prove in the most severe manner). Hence the temptation was in this case unusually powerful.

As he had in his language in ver. 33, 35, forgotten that he could do nothing without his Master's divine grace (John 15:5), he is here taught by bitter experience to see himself as he really is, and, like Job, to "abhor himself and repent in dust and ashes" (Job 42:6).

⁷¹ And when he was gone out into the porch, another *maid* saw him, and said unto them that were there, This man was also with Jesus the Nazarene.

A. The porch = the gateway, portal or arched passage (see above, ver. 57, B.) to which Peter retreated. Mark (ch. 14:68) gives it another but equivalent name, also translated "porch," and more precisely designating the spot *before* the interior court = *entrance*.—**B. Another maid** = together with a man (Luke 22:58), and indeed various persons ("them that were there") of the group (John 18:25).—**C. Said to them.** The *man* who spoke directly addressed Peter (Luke 22:58).—**D. This fellow** (see 12:24, B.).—**E. Was also, etc.** = is an adherent of Him who is now on trial (ver. 69, C.).—**Jesus the Nazarene.** This appellation was not necessarily contemptuous (see John 1:45; Acts 10:38); the Lord was supposed by many to be a native of Nazareth, as "he had been brought up" there (Luke 4:16; see Matt. 2:23, A.; 21:11).

⁷² And again he denied with an oath, I know not the man.

A. Again = the second denial. The three denials did not occur in very rapid succession (ver. 73, and Luke 22:59), but rather during the whole period of the protracted examination of the Lord; they are simply placed together by Matthew for the sake of exhibiting Peter's case as an independent part of the general narrative, as well as of avoiding any interruption of the preceding narrative.—**B.**

With an oath = one of the usual oaths of the Jews mentioned in 5:34, ff.; 23:16, ff.—**C. I know not, etc.** = I have not the most remote connection with Him.

⁷³ And after a little while they that stood by came and said to Peter, Of a truth, thou also art *one* of them; for thy speech bewrayeth thee.

A. Came ... stood by = including a relative of Malchus whom Peter had wounded, and who now refers to that act (John 18:10, 26); the terror which this new circumstance produced now completely paralyzes Peter.—**B. Surely** = undeniably. The term refers to the previous oath of Peter, the reliability of which this word positively denies.—**C. For** = in addition to other circumstances.—**D. Thy speech bewrayeth** (betrayeth) **thee** = exposes thee, makes thee known as a Galilean (Mark 14:70).—**Speech** = dialect. The inhabitants of Galilee did not distinguish accurately between certain letters of the alphabet termed *gutturals,* for which we have no precise equivalents in the English alphabet, and which, as in a somewhat analogous case in Judg. 12:6, they could not "frame to pronounce right;" their dialect generally was harsher than that of the inhabitants of Judæa.

⁷⁴ Then began he to curse and to swear, I know not the man. And straightway the cock crew.

A. To curse and to swear. The increased violence of Peter arose from the circumstance just mentioned in ver. 73, A.; in his excitement, after losing all self-control, he uttered imprecations in addition to his oath (possibly using the form occurring in 1 Sam. 3:17; 14:44; 20:13) in order to substantiate the truth of his declaration that no connection existed between him and Jesus.—**B. And ... crew** = the second time (Mark 14:68, 72), according to the Lord's words

(Mark 14:30). At this moment the Lord, who stood in full view, "turned and looked upon" him (Luke 22:61). That glance of the Saviour, so expressive in its silence, so mournful, and yet so full of divine pity, arrests and saves Peter in the extremity of his danger, when, as once before, "he was beginning to sink" (14:30), and was nigh unto destruction.

75 And Peter remembered the word which Jesus had said, Before the cock crow, thou shalt deny me thrice. And he went out, and wept bitterly.

A. Peter remembered = see ver. 34.—**B. He went out** = by the outer gate into the street (see ver. 57, B.).—**C. And wept bitterly** (comp. Isai. 22:4; 33:7). The crisis has passed, the unnatural excitement of Peter is suddenly arrested, and, by the infinite grace of his Lord, "he comes to himself" (Luke 15:17). Compare the case of Paul (Acts 9:9, 11). Both experienced anguish of soul, but both *prayed* in humble trust and faith.

12

Matthew 27

¹ Now when morning was come, all the chief priests and the elders of the people took counsel against Jesus to put him to death.

A. Morning = of Friday, the eventful day of the Lord's crucifixion.—**B. Took counsel, etc.** = deliberated on the best plan for securing the immediate execution of the sentence of death (already pronounced in 26:66, and now formally repeated), before a rescue should be attempted by His friends. As they could not proceed without the official consent of Pilate (ver. 2), it was important to exhibit the Lord to him in the character of a political offender. Hence they adopted the expedient which appears in ver. 11, below, namely, they determined to represent Him as a seditious person and a pretender to the throne (see also John 18:29 and 19:12).

² And they had bound him, and led him away, and delivered him up to Pontius Pilate the governor.

A. Bound him = again, after having loosened his bonds (John 18:12, 24) during his examination before Caiaphas.—**Delivered** (see 17:22).—**B. To Pontius, etc.**

= "to the Gentiles" (Luke 18:32). After the deposition of Archelaus (2:22, A.), which occurred a few years subsequently to the birth of Christ, Judæa and Samaria were attached by the Roman government to the province of Syria, and the whole territory was governed by a Roman officer who was styled a *proconsul*. From this time also the Jewish authorities no longer possessed the right to inflict capital punishments without the official consent of the Roman governor. This circumstance explains the present appeal to Pilate (see John 18:31). An officer of inferior rank, styled a *procurator*, was entrusted at times specially with the government of Judæa; the powers granted to these rulers frequently varied in extent. The governor of Judæa appears to have usually resided in Cæsarea, on the Mediterranean Sea (16:13, B.). Pilate, who was at this time the procurator of Judæa, occupied Jerusalem with a large military force, since at the celebration of the great festivals serious disturbances frequently arose (see ann. to 26:4, D.). His administration was harsh and oppressive, and his conduct was so emphatically resented by the Jews and the Samaritans, whose accusations were very serious, that he was ultimately removed from office and sent to Rome, in order to sustain a trial. The Emperor Tiberius died before Pilate reached the city. Eusebius (Eccl. Hist. II. 7) relates that the calamities which overwhelmed him drove him to the commission of suicide. He was fully aware of the Saviour's innocence (ver. 18, 23, 24, below), and he long hesitated to issue the order for the execution, not being able to resist entirely, with all his heathenish contempt of revealed religion, the force of the Saviour's words; but the threat of the Jews, who implied that they would accuse Him before the jealous Emperor Tiberius of favoring a rebel

(Luke 23:2), and even a competitor for the throne (John 19:12, 15), alarmed his selfish fears, and extorted the order for the Lord's crucifixion. His character appears in the whole transaction in a most unfavorable light, and no redeeming trait distinguishes him from the multitude of corrupt pagan rulers of his age.

³ Then Judas, which betrayed him, when he saw that he was condemned, repented himself, and brought back the thirty pieces of silver to the chief priests and elders,

A. Then Judas ... condemned. This language may possibly imply that Judas had not expected that the Lord, whose vast power over the elements and unclean spirits as well as over men He had often observed, would be actually placed under constraint and slain by His enemies (26:14). But it, more probably, indicates that this man's eagerness to gain money had prevented him from considering the whole enormity of his crime, until it had been committed, and its consequences had become visible.—**B. Repented himself.** The original word, sometimes descriptive of a change of views and feelings that is equivalent to genuine repentance (see 21:29), here indicates *remorse* = the pain of guilt, the reproaches of conscience occasioned by a view of the criminality and danger which he had incurred, but not accompanied by faith in divine grace and by hope; in the language of Paul he was not "made sorry after a godly manner" (2 Cor. 7:9, 10). That repentance which the Word of God demands is always connected with a humble hope of finding pardon through Jesus Christ. The original Greek word occurs only in four other places (Matt. 21:29 and 32; 2 Cor. 7:8; Hebr. 7:21); wherever the words *repent, repentance,* occur elsewhere, a different Greek word is used (see above,

3:2, A.).—**C. Brought again, etc.** But could that act undo the crime which he had perpetrated? Could it rescue his Master?

⁴ Saying, I have sinned in that I betrayed innocent blood. But they said, What is that to us? See thou *to* it.

A. Saying ... blood. Judas had already been taught by his Master's words (for example, Luke 15:21) to understand the awful nature of *sin;* he is now fully aware of the extent of his guilt.—**Betrayed ... blood** = exposed *Him* to death who is free from all guilt (comp. 23:35, C.); indeed, Judas had never accused the Lord of any offence (ver. 23). The word **the** before **innocent** is not in the original.—**B. They said, etc.** They imply: Thy innocence or guilt, and the innocence or guilt of Jesus, can have no influence on our present proceedings, since we have secured Him (comp. John 21:22).—**See thou, etc.** = the responsibility rests on thee alone (ver. 24, C.); if thou hast involved thyself in guilt and danger, provide for thyself as thou best mayest; thou hast served our purposes, and we now discard thee (comp. Acts 18:15). Such is the sympathy of the ungodly with the ungodly.

⁵ And he cast down the pieces of silver in the temple, and departed, and he went and hanged himself.

A. Cast ... temple. The Greek word here translated **temple** is the specific name of the sacred edifice itself, *naos,* as distinguished from the courts and their appurtenances (see 4:5, E.; 21:12, A.). As a meeting like the present could not have been permitted in the interior of the former, but must have been held in the court of the Israelites, it is possible that Judas, in his desperate state of mind, either rushed into the forbidden enclosure, or, at least, turned towards it, at the same time hurling from him the money which was burning his very soul, and which fell in the interior of the sacred edifice.—**Departed.** The Greek word here used occurs at times in the Septuagint or the Greek Bible (for which see ann. to 17:10), as the version of two Hebrew words, both of which describe the act of those who "flee away" (Judg. 4:17; 1 Sam. 19:10; Jerem. 4:29; Hos. 12:12).—**B. hanged** (= strangled) **himself,** like the perfidious Ahithophel (2 Sam. 17:23). The horrible event naturally created a deep sensation in the city (Acts 1:18, 19). It is possible that the wretched man committed the awful crime of suicide in the gloomy valley of Hinnom (5:22, G.), near one of its many precipices, and that there the hideous circumstances occurred which were connected with the fall of the suspended body, after the cord or the branch of the tree broke, and which are described in Acts 1:18; they are recorded for the purpose of inspiring all men with a salutary awe.

⁶ And the chief priests took the pieces of silver, and said, It is not lawful to put them into the treasury, since it is the price of blood.

The sacred **treasury,** consisting of the gifts of the Jews (15:5, 6, A.; Luke 21:1), was designed chiefly for the expenses of the temple service.—**It is the price of blood** = we paid that money for the opportunity of putting Jesus to death. These Jews, precisely as the Lord had characterized them ("strain at a gnat, etc.," 23:23, 24), were too scrupulous to perform an act which might seem to be a violation of Deut. 23:18, to which the words: "It is not lawful, etc.," refer, but they deliberately shed the innocent blood of Jesus.

⁷ And they took counsel, and bought with them the potter's field, to bury strangers in.

A. Bought ... field = a field, the clay of which had been used by a potter for the manufacture of earthenware; hence the field, no longer suited for tillage, was purchased at such a low price (see 26:15, D.).—**Took counsel** = held a consultation. The peculiar circumstances in the present case gave unusual notoriety to *the* potter's field thus purchased, and furnished the name *Aceldama,* a Syro-Chaldaic term signifying: *Field of blood* (Acts 1:19) = bought with blood-money. Judas was thus indirectly the author of the purchase (Acts 1:18, "this man purchased"), even as the Jews, whom Peter addresses in Acts 2:23, had not personally, or with their own hands, but indirectly, or through others, crucified the Lord.—**B. To bury, etc.** The **strangers** are probably foreign Jews and proselytes who had attended the festivals, like those mentioned in Acts 2:9, ff., and possessed no near relations among the inhabitants of Jerusalem, where death overtook them. The dislike with which the Jews regarded heathen would scarcely have allowed the chief priests in the present instance to provide for friendless Gentile strangers who had no religious claims on their charity. Special burial-places had long before been assigned for the humble and the poor of their own population (Jerem. 26:23).

[8] Wherefore that field was called, The field of blood, unto this day.

(See ver. 7, A.)—**Unto this day** = the time when Matthew wrote this Gospel, many years after these events occurred (28:15, D.).

[9, 10] Then was fulfilled that which was spoken by Jeremiah the prophet, saying, And they took the thirty pieces of silver, the price of him that was priced, whom they of the children of Israel did price;—And they gave them for the potter's field, as the Lord appointed me.

A. Spoken by Jeremiah the prophet. When the writers

of the N. T. quote the prophets, they occasionally omit the names, assuming that their readers are familiar with the words of the O. T. (e. g. 2:5, and ver. 35, below). Sometimes they combine two passages without specifying the names of the prophets (see an instance above, 21:5, A., and comp. 2:23, B.). So Paul in Rom. 9:33 combines Isai. 8:14 and 28:16, and Mark in 1:2, 3, connects Mal. 3:1 and Isai. 40:3. Further, it is well known that the later prophets occasionally refer to the words of their predecessors; Zechariah, in particular, often quotes words, thoughts, etc., of Jeremiah, who lived somewhat less than a century before him (comp., for instance, Zech. 1:4 with Jerem. 18:11 and 35:15; 3:8 and 6:12 with Jerem. 23:5 and 33:15; 11:3–5 with Jerem. 50:6, 7, 44; 11:9 with Jerem. 15:2; 14:10, 11, with Jerem. 31:38–40). Now in three places (18:1, ff.; 19:1, ff.; and 32:7, 9), Jeremiah describes circumstances which involved a deep prophetical meaning, and which the Divine Spirit interpreted and unfolded more fully in Zech. 11:12, 13. The low estimate placed on the Redeemer by the Jews, His humiliating *sale* for the price of a slave (see 26:15, D.), and the apparently accidental purchase of a potter's field, with the attending circumstances, are foreshadowed in the ancient history of the people, even as the history of Jonah (Matt. 12:39), and of the serpent of brass (John 3:14; Numb. 21:9), furnished types of Christ. Now Matthew had already alluded in 26:15, indirectly, to Zech. 11:12, 13, but reserved the direct use of the passage until he should in his narrative reach the present events. Even as in 2:23 he made a combination of various prophetic passages, so here he combines with the passage in Zechariah those that occur in Jeremiah and which are mentioned above; he simply names Jeremiah as the original source; the familiar words in Zechariah, which he quotes more fully, suggest at once to the reader the name of the latter, and hence, according to Matthew's custom, he does not mention it specially.—**B. They took the ... silver.** This fact (see 26:15, C. and D.) is a striking illustration of Isai. 53:3; the words occur in Zech. 11:12.—**C. The price ... priced.** The Lord's enemies in their blindness regarded their own act of shedding blood as a mere business transaction like Jeremiah's lawful purchase of Hanameel's field (32:7–9); their estimate of the Lord's value fell infinitely below His real value. There is indeed something awful and most shocking in this mode of dealing with the blessed Saviour, to which Matthew calls our attention in the words: "the price ... did value," while he also alludes to Zech. 11:13.—**D. And gave ... field.** Matthew refers to their act mentioned in ver. 7. The prophet typically performed the act (Zech. 11:13).—**E. As the Lord appointed me.** The words in Zech. 11:13 contain the Lord's appointment = commission; on the other hand, the transaction described in Jerem. 18:1–6 was intended to illustrate by the potter's movements the absolute power of God over His people; the prophet then makes mention of a potter, of the valley of the son of Hinnom, and of the awful doom of Jerusalem, as well as of the symbolic act of breaking the earthen bottle (Jerem. 19:1–12). All these impressive scenes which Jeremiah exhibits, the later prophet Zechariah is guided by the Spirit in applying in the peculiar language of prophecy to the Messiah. The veil still resting on these ancient transactions and words is now removed, and in Matthew we receive a revelation of the typical meaning of the whole. The mention here of the **children of Israel** (ver. 9) may possibly allude to the unnatural act of Joseph's own brethren (Gen. 37:28), as an additional illustration of the turpitude of the conduct of Judas and the priests.

¹¹ Now Jesus stood before the governor: and the governor asked him, saying, Art thou the King of the Jews? And Jesus said unto him, Thou sayest.

A. Stood before, etc. (ver. 2).—**B. Asked ... Jews?** Pilate had naturally made inquiry respecting the nature of the offence with which Jesus was charged (John 18:29–31); the Jews also knew that Pilate, as Gallio, another heathen, afterwards did (Acts 18:14, 15; comp. also Acts 25:18–20), would have refused to entertain a charge referring merely to Jewish religious controversies; hence they found it expedient to give a political character to their accusation (see Luke 23:2, 3). This latter circumstance led to the present question: **Art thou, etc.?** = do you really claim to be the King of the Jews?—**C. Thou sayest** = I am (26:25, C.). The Lord's additional words, explaining the spiritual nature of His kingdom, are found in John 18:36. Paul refers to the whole in 1 Tim. 6:13.

¹² And when he was accused by the chief priests and elders, he answered nothing.

Accused by. The first meeting of Christ and Pilate in the hall of judgment appears to have been without the presence of witnesses (John 18:28, 29). The Jews apprehended that by entering the house of a pagan they would become legally unclean (Numb. 19:22, and comp. Acts 10:28; 11:3). He went out to the Jews and expressed his conviction that Jesus was guilty of no political "fault" (John 18:38). Then they "accused" the Lord anew, as related in Luke 23:2, 5. The Lord, having been led forth to the spot where the Jews stood, was assailed by reproaches on all sides, to which He submitted in humility and silence.

¹³ Then saith Pilate unto him, Hearest thou not how many things they witness against thee?

Hearest thou not, etc. = Thou hast a right to reply to these numerous charges; what self-defence dost Thou make?—**Witness against** = here, *accuse Thee of;* in the whole disorderly trial the accusers are not distinguished from the witnesses. Pilate wished for a denial on the part of the accused, which would have compelled the accusers to furnish positive evidence of the guilt of Jesus. But Pilate the heathen was not competent to decide on the real character of the Messiah, and hence the Lord was silent.

¹⁴ And he gave him no answer, not even to one word, insomuch that the governor marvelled greatly.

Even Pilate, as the absence of all displeasure on his part shows, did not expect the Lord to reply in detail to charges so obviously proceeding from malice alone (ver. 18); but he wondered at the calmness, holy dignity and meekness of one so bitterly assailed, and yet so self-possessed and pacific.

¹⁵ Now at the feast the governor was wont to release unto the multitude one prisoner, whom they would.

The practice of releasing prisoners on occasions of public rejoicings (the accession of a king to the throne, a victory, etc.) was observed in many countries and in different ages. The Roman government, which frequently granted indulgences to subject nations, permitted the Jews, in honor of their great festival, the passover (John 18:39), to select any condemned prisoner of their nation, "whom they would," as the recipient of the boon of liberty. The custom was opposed to the spirit of the Jewish law (Exod. 21:12; Hebr. 10:28), and its origin is not known.

¹⁶ And they had then a notable prisoner, called Barabbas.

A notable = *noted, notorious* insurgent and murderer (Mark 15:7; Luke 23:19; Acts 3:14), whom **they** = the officers of justice, had seized and held in confinement. No details respecting Barabbas have been preserved in history.

¹⁷ When, therefore, they were gathered together, Pilate said unto them, Whom will ye that I release unto you? Barabbas, or Jesus which is called Christ?

A. When they = the mass of the Jews.—**B. Whom will, etc.** Pilate was desirous of releasing the innocent Jesus, whose deportment had deeply impressed him, and hence he allowed a choice only between Him and a man of infamous character then in the hands of justice; he supposed that the multitude would scarcely prefer the latter to one who, as he here intimates, had received the honorable Jewish appellation of **Christ** = Messiah (John 9:22; Matt. 1:1, B.).

¹⁸ For he knew that for envy they had delivered him up.

For envy = through, on account of, envy. Pilate was satisfied in his own mind that Jesus had committed no illegal act; he also ascertained that Jesus had acquired a degree of influence among the people by His benevolent and pure course of conduct that threatened to impair the religious and political power which the heads of the Jewish nation had acquired by their hypocritical conduct. This probable result, for which he wished (in addition to the deep impression which he had received from the Lord's conduct and word), increased his desire to spare Jesus. Hence, during the trial, having hastily concluded that our Lord was a Galilean, he sent Him to Herod, whom the festival had brought to the city (see 2:1, D.; 2:22, C., and 14:1, B.; 2, B.), with the hope that the latter would assume the responsibility and release

Jesus (see Luke 23:6–15).

¹⁹ And while he was sitting on the judgment seat, his wife sent unto him, saying, Have thou nothing to do with that righteous man: for I have suffered many things this day in a dream because of him.

A. **While he was sitting** = in order to conduct the trial to a regular issue, after his first efforts to release Christ had been fruitless.—B. **Judgment seat** = elevated above the spot which the spectators occupied, and before the palace (John 19:13).—C. **His wife sent, etc.** Tradition has assigned to her the name of Claudia Procula. Besides various men of heathen birth, who are mentioned in the Acts of the Apostles as having been influenced by revealed truth, "devout women" (comp. Acts 17:4), that is, pagan females who adopted the Jewish faith, are also mentioned (Acts 13:50). Pilate's wife, who had accompanied him when he received his appointment, like the woman of Canaan, may (15:22) have been, at an earlier period, deeply impressed by "the fame" of Jesus (4:24; 9:26), which reached all classes (14:1). She had doubtless been alarmed during that eventful night by the tumult, when Pilate sent forth the troop of soldiers (26:47, B.). Towards morning ("this day;" the civil day of the Romans began like our own at midnight), during her troubled slumbers, the painful **dream** occurred. An unusual oppression weighed on her soul, in consequence of which she conveyed a warning message to Pilate. Matthew gives no intimation whether the dream resembled, on the one hand, those which in ordinary cases external sounds or an uneasy mind may produce, or, on the other, those which God sent to Pharaoh (Gen. 41:1, ff.) or Nebuchadnezzar (Dan. 2:1; see above, 1:20, C.); when we refer to 1:20; 2:12, 19, 22, the latter origin seems to be indicated.—**That righteous one** (1:19, B., as in Acts 3:14, not *man,* which word does not occur in the original) is a phrase implying that Pilate's wife, either from previous knowledge or through the extraordinary dream, had obtained good evidence of the Lord's holy character. Providence furnishes Pilate in this testimony of his wife with an additional opportunity to adhere to an equitable and righteous course of action; and the circumstance that, in ver. 24, he uses his wife's expression, "that just one," shows that her message had made an impression on him.—**Have thou nothing to do.** For the same phrase, see 8:29, B.; here it expresses the desire of Pilate's wife that he should refrain from exercising any direct official authority in the case of "that righteous one," which would involve the condemnation of the latter; she desired that he would dismiss the prisoner at once.—**Saying** = through her messenger (8:5, C.).

20 Now the chief priests and the elders persuaded the multitudes that they should ask for Barabbas, and destroy Jesus.

The priests appear to have suspected Pilate's intentions (ver. 17, B.); when dealing with prejudiced countrymen or Jews, they easily succeeded in thwarting the hated pagan's design, while he was still engaged with his wife's messenger. Previously, the Lord's enemies had feared that His popularity would interfere with their murderous designs (26:5). But now when the fickle multitude saw the Lord as a prisoner and apparently helpless, they at once abandon Him, cast Him off, and become the willing instruments of their artful and malignant rulers. The hosannas which welcomed Him who restored Lazarus to life (21:9, C.) are converted into shouts of execration (ver. 22), addressed to a condemned and manacled prisoner.—**Ask** = *ask for, desire*, as in 20:20; 27:28; Luke 1:63; Acts 3:14.

21 But the governor answered and said unto them, Whether of the twain will ye that I release unto you? And they said, Barabbas.

The governor ... said = repeating his former proposition (Luke 23:20, 22), having been rendered still more anxious by his wife's extraordinary message.—**Whether of the twain** = which of the two (5:41, B.; 21:31, A.).

22 Pilate saith unto them, What shall I do then with Jesus which is called Christ? They all say, Let him be crucified.

A. Pilate saith = appeals to their natural sense of justice, implying: What do you honestly believe that this accused person deserves? The popular excitement had now reached such a height that, as in many similar cases, the voice of passion silenced the dictates of reason and justice (comp. Acts 21:35, 36; 22:22, 23).—**B. Let him be crucified.** Crucifixion was a mode of inflicting capital punishment not known to the Jewish law. The latter directed that death should be inflicted with the sword or by stoning. Barabbas, as an outlaw, had been condemned by the Romans to death on the cross. The Lord's enemies eagerly take advantage of this circumstance, and say: Release Barabbas and transfer his punishment to the other (comp. John 18:31, 32, with Matt. 20:19 and John 12:32, 33). Crucifixion was practised by the ancient Persians, Assyrians, Egyptians, Carthaginians, etc. The Romans did not inflict it on a citizen, but only on slaves and outlaws, such as counterfeiters of coin, insurgents, pirates, etc. Hence when Paul preached a *crucified* Christ, Jews and Greeks heard him with ignorant contempt (1 Cor. 1:23; Gal. 5:11). If the delinquent survived the scourging with thongs which usually preceded it (ver. 26, B.), he was compelled, as an additional mark of degradation, to carry the cross to the place of execution (ver. 32), although this circumstance may not have occurred in every case. When he was affixed to the cross, which was usually done after the cross itself had been planted in the earth, he was securely tied, and nails were driven through his hands and feet (see Ps. 22:16, and comp. Luke 24:39, 40); the weight of the body was partially sustained by a slight projection in the middle of the upright beam, somewhat resembling a seat. The sufferer, while he was suspended, almost in a nude state, on the cross, endured unspeakable torment arising from the unnatural and rigid position of the body, the laceration of the numerous nerves of the hands and feet, the violent inflammation and swelling of the wounded limbs, which produced an intolerable thirst, and from the continual pressure of the weight of the limbs on the lacerated parts. The impeded circulation of the blood created, besides, agonizing pains in the head, a horrible oppression on the chest, and a feeling of anxiety and distress which no language can adequately describe. All these pangs continually increased in intensity; sometimes the sufferer lived three days in the midst of these torments. A liberal and humane interpretation of Prov. 31:6 had introduced among the Jews the practice of giving to prisoners on their way to their execution a stupefying drink (ver. 34), in order to produce a partial unconsciousness of pain. The corpse was usually suffered by the Romans to remain on the cross until it decayed or was consumed by birds of prey. Among the Jews, however, the bones of the limbs of the sufferer were usually broken, and other wounds inflicted, for the purpose of hastening his death and removal from the cross.

It was this awful punishment which the malice of the Lord's enemies desired to inflict. Divine Providence permitted the event to occur, inasmuch as such a mode of execution, while inexpressibly degrading and painful, did not, like the ordinary mode of beheading, stabbing or stoning, actually produce a fracture of any portion of the body (ver. 56, C.). The original form of the cross, which was constructed of two beams, resembled the letter T; the one employed in the case of the Saviour, as the position of the inscription shows (ver. 37), resembled the printer's obelisk ( ), and is called the Latin cross; the Greek cross resembled the mathematical sign of addition (+); the St. Andrew's cross, the mathematical sign of multiplication (×), or the letter X; St. Peter's cross is an inverted obelisk ().

²³ And he said, Why, what evil hath he done? But they cried out exceedingly, saying, Let him be crucified.

The meaning is: I cannot consent, or, It is not just, *for what evil, etc.?* The Lord Himself had once asked the same question (John 8:46). Pilate's hesitation, which led the infuriated multitude to apprehend that their victim would escape, extorts still wilder shouts of hatred and revenge. At the same time, all parties, Judas, Pilate, the Jewish leaders and the multitude, confess by words or by an expressive silence that not the slightest blemish can be found in the character and conduct of the accused.

²⁴ So when Pilate saw that he prevailed nothing, but rather that a tumult was arising, he took water, and washed his hands before the multitude, saying, I am innocent of the blood of this righteous man: see ye *to it*.

A. When Pilate ... nothing = found that his repeated remonstrances ("the third time," Luke 23:22) made no impression. At this stage in the proceedings a new fear had seized Pilate; the name "Son of God," which had occurred in the charges against the Lord (John 19:7, 8), combined with his wife's singular dream, led him to apprehend that Jesus might possibly be one of his own heathen deities. But the Jews, who well knew the jealous and vindictive cruelty with which Tiberius, the Roman emperor, crushed all who threatened his authority, now tumultuously exclaim: "If thou let this man go, thou art not Cæsar's friend" (John 19:12) = if thou dost release him, thy own life will be forfeited, for we shall accuse thee before the Roman emperor ("Cæsar," 16:13, B.), and accomplish thy ruin. This argument prevailed! As the repentance of Judas was not an evangelical repentance, but fear, remorse and despair (ver. 3), so Pilate's views of Christ were not equivalent to an evangelical faith, but were more allied to superstition and heathenish opinions than to an enlightened conception of the Saviour's person; hence his convictions of the Lord's innocence and high character yielded to his own worldly lusts and selfishness.—**B. He took ... hands.** Among the symbolical actions (10:14, C.; 18:2, B.) which were known to the Jews, and, in some instances, to other ancient nations, the act of washing the hands indicated that the person who performed it denied all participation in the guilt which others contracted by the crime (see Deut. 21:6; Ps. 26:6). Pilate's reluctant consent to the execution of the Lord had been extorted from his fears; he here conforms to the significant practice of the Jews which he well knew, and which certain analogous pagan lustrations rendered intelligible to him, for the purpose of intimating to them that they alone should bear the guilt of the act. Nevertheless, the water could as little relieve his conscience from a sense of guilt, or cleanse his soul, as the "blood of bulls and goats" of itself could cleanse from sin (Hebr. 9:9, 14; 10:1, 2).—**C. I am innocent, etc.** = free from the guilt contracted by the crime—entirely innocent (see 2 Sam. 3:28; Acts 20:26). Cain, the murderer, before Pilate's day, had also declared his innocence (Gen. 4:9).—**See ye, etc.** = I cast the whole responsibility on you (ver. 4, B.).

^{25} And all the people answered, and said, His blood *be* on us, and on our children.

In the madness and fury of the moment, the entire multitude, utterly regardless of the awful import and effect of their defiance of the Most High, promptly accede to Pilate's terms, and assume the whole crushing guilt of the deed (ver. 24, B.).—**His blood be, etc.** = let the punishment, if there be any inflicted, come on us and our nation (see ann. to 23:35, B., C.). And that blood did come in a fearful manner on them, even according to the words: "Let thy wrathful anger take hold of them" (Ps. 69:24, and see Ps. 109:17). The predictions of the Lord in ch. 24, referring to the destruction of Jerusalem and its horrors, were all fulfilled. Their **children** = descendants to this day, still seem to bend under the grievous weight of this imprecation.

^{26} Then released he unto them Barabbas. But Jesus he scourged and delivered to be crucified.

A. Released—Barabbas. Pilate, who was deeply mortified that the despised Jews had sufficient power to defeat his purpose of liberating the accused Jesus, sullenly released the notorious criminal; he permitted Jewish turbulence and malice to tarnish the majesty of the Roman law by the execution of an innocent victim. He partially vented his spleen when he placed the inscription on the cross (see ver.

37 and ver. 38, ann.).—**B. But Jesus he scourged.** The **scourging,** which, among the Romans, preceded crucifixion (ver. 22, B.), was distinguished by its excessive barbarity from the Jewish mode of inflicting the punishment (10:17, C.), and was not applied in the case of a Roman citizen (Acts 22:25). The Roman scourge was made of leathern thongs fastened at one end to a wooden handle, and armed at the other with pieces of metal, in order to increase the severity of the punishment. The offender, bending over a low pillar or block, to which he was tied, exposed his entire back to the blows; these were inflicted without measure until large portions of flesh were torn away; the sufferer sometimes fainted and even died before the executioner withheld his arm. In the present case, the earlier proposition of Pilate (Luke 23:16, "chastise" = beat, scourge), and his subsequent appeal, in John 19:1, 4, 5, seem to indicate that he may have entertained a lingering hope that the ferocity of the Jews would be appeased on seeing the bleeding, fainting victim, and would consent to spare his life. The Jewish thirst for blood prevailed, and Pilate, completely subdued, **delivered him** = yielded Him up (17:22) to the executioners.

²⁷ Then the soldiers of the governor took Jesus into the palace, and gathered unto him the whole band.

The palace, literally the *prætorium*. [First meaning the headquarters of the commander-in-chief of a Roman camp, and then the residence of a Roman procurator.] The place here described afforded room for the whole troop, and, at the same time, freed the latter from the presence of the Jews. The conduct of Pilate in permitting the gross indignities now offered to Jesus shows that while his conscience had been alarmed and his fears awakened previously (ver. 18, 19, 24), no pure and elevated feelings dwelt in his heart.

^{28, 29} And they stripped him, and put on him a scarlet robe.—And they planted a crown of thorns, and put it upon his head, and a reed in his right hand: and they kneeled down before him, and mocked him, saying, Hail, King of the Jews!

The Lord had been falsely accused of aiming at kingly power (ver. 11). Herod, without inquiring into the truth of the charge, had basely and unjustly exposed this claim to derision (Luke 23:11). These Roman soldiers, whose coarse manners had taught them to enjoy sport of such a brutal character, repeated Herod's pitiful jest. The **scarlet** or "purple" (John 19:2) robe represented in mockery the costly apparel worn by kings, and also by Roman generals of armies. (The Greek terms for colors are in many cases very indefinite; thus, one of these words, translated "purple," is applied both to any dark and to very light shades of red.) The **crown of thorns** (possibly the *naba* of the Arabs, a very common plant with pliant branches which were covered with small and sharp spines), while it in mockery represented a royal crown, was also intended to inflict pain; the frail **reed** (11:7, A.) was a mockery of a royal sceptre, the badge of power (Esth. 4:11); and when they **kneeled down,** they offered the Lord in derision the homage rendered to an oriental monarch (2:2, D.—Hail, etc., 26:49, B.).

³⁰ And they spat upon him, and took the reed, and smote him on the head.

The scenes described in 26:67 are here repeated; the additional cruelty is mentioned that His head was beaten with the reed, in order that the thorns might inflict new pangs.

³¹ And when they had mocked him, they took off from him

the robe, and put on him his garments, and led him away to crucify *him*.

These savage men are at length satiated, and their coarse and brutal jest begins to weary them. Roman soldiers of an earlier age would have disdained to be guilty of the cowardly act of abusing a solitary, bleeding and unresisting victim.

³² And as they came out, they found a man of Cyrene, Simon by name: him they compelled to go with them, that he might bear his cross.

A. Came out = of the city, within the walls of which the execution of criminals was not permitted (see 21:39, B.).—**B. Cyrene** = a large city in Libya (Africa), at a short distance from the southern shore of the Mediterranean Sea. So many of the Jews of this city (who constituted at one time one-fourth of the population) came to Jerusalem, that they occupied a synagogue of their own (Acts 2:10; 6:9); many of them became Christians (Acts 11:20).—**C. Simon by name.** The unmerciful treatment which the Lord had received during the whole preceding night and the scourging which succeeded had probably so completely exhausted Him, that He tottered under the weight of the cross (John 19:17). The soldiers, perceiving a stranger advancing towards them with the intention of entering the city ("coming out of the country" = the fields near the city, Luke 23:26), "laid hold upon" him, possibly instigated by the accompanying Jews, who may have recognized a disciple of the Lord in him, and placed the cross on him. That act resembled, as the original word for **compelled** (5:41, A.) implies, a military requisition or impressment. Afterwards, or at least on the way to Golgotha, the scene occurred which is described in Luke 23:27–31. The mention of the names of Simon's sons in Mark 15:21 (probably eminent members of the Church at a somewhat later period) has led some to suppose that the mother of Rufus, whom Paul regarded with filial love (Rom. 16:13), and Rufus himself, were members of this Simon's family.

33 And when they were come unto a place called Golgotha, that is to say, the place of a skull,

Golgotha. The deep interest attaching to this spot has led to the presentation of its name in four languages: Hebrew, or rather Chaldee (Aramaic), *Golgotha* (John 19:17); Greek, *kranion* (Luke 23:33), for which the translators (see margin of the English Bible) employ a form constructed from the Latin, *calvaria,* namely, *Calvary;* the English term is *skull,* and so occurs as the translation of the Hebrew word *Gulgolct* in 2 Kings 9:35.—**A place of a skull** = a spot called *The Skull.* It was possibly a knoll or skull-shaped eminence, or contained a rock resembling a human skull in shape, but the site has not been positively ascertained, neither does sufficient authority exist for terming it a *mount* or mountain. Robinson says (Bibl. Res. I. 417): "I am led irresistibly to the conclusion that the Golgotha and the tomb now shown in the church of the Holy Sepulchre, are not upon the real places of the crucifixion and resurrection of our Lord." This impression was deepened at his second visit in 1852 (III. 254–263).

34 They gave him wine to drink mingled with gall: and when he had tasted it, he would not drink.

A. Wine ... gall. The cheap acid or sour wine of the country is meant, usually medicated or drugged (hence "mingled with myrrh," Mark 15:23), when given in cases like the present (see above, ver. 22, B.). The infusion of **gall** in this particular case may have proceeded from the indescribably malevolent feelings of one of the by-standers, who desired to inflict an additional pang (see Ps. 69:21).—**B. He ... drink.** This circumstance, which is mentioned also in Mark 15:23, without reference to the gall, indicates that our Lord was not willing to be bereft of consciousness and the sense of pain in His last moments by the stupefying mixture: He afterwards received the unmixed wine (ver. 48; John 19:30), which relieved His thirst.

³⁵ And when they had crucified him, they parted his garments among them, casting lots.

A. Crucified him (see ver. 22, B.). "Then said Jesus, Father forgive them, etc." (Luke 23:34).—**B. Parted his garments.** The Roman law granted the apparel of a criminal to his executioners as a perquisite (see the prediction in Ps. 22:18).—**His garments** (= clothes), with the exception of one article, were cut asunder at the seams, in order to allow a more even distribution of the materials. The details are given in John 19:23, 24.—**C. Casting lots** = "what every man should take" (Mark 15:24); the Roman watch, as in this case, usually consisted of a quaternion = four men (Acts 12:4), relieved every three hours. They cast lots specially for the coat, as no one had direct claims to it; these rude pagans, in one sense, engaged in a "game of chance."

³⁶ And they sat and watched him there.

Watched = that none of the friends of the sufferer might remove Him from the cross.

³⁷ And set up over his head his accusation written, This is Jesus the King of the Jews.

A. Set up ... accusation = according to Pilate's directions (John 19:19). A tablet was frequently affixed to the top of the cross, on which was written a "title" (John 19:19), that is, a statement of the offence (**accusation**) for which the individual suffered.—**B. This is Jesus** ("*of Nazareth,*" John 19:19), etc. This inscription, and the stern refusal to change it (John 19:22), together with the fact stated in ver. 38, below, strikingly exhibit the exasperation of Pilate against the Jews, proceeding not primarily from his disgust at their treatment of One whom he regarded as innocent, but rather from the personal affront offered to him by their artful mode of compelling him, the proud Roman, and their superior in rank, to submit to their will (ver. 24, A., and 26, A.). In place of simply stating the offence implied in John 19:12, he chose the present inscription, with slight variations in the three languages (Luke 23:38), both for the purpose of appearing in the Roman emperor's eyes as the conqueror of an usurper, and also of mortifying the pride of the Jews. For, when he placed One whom he represented as their "king" in such a degrading position, he heaped disgrace on the whole nation, particularly as the three languages spoken by the Jews, by strangers or Greeks, and by Romans were all employed (John 19:20).

38 Then are there crucified with him two robbers; one on the right hand, and one on the left.

Two robbers. Possibly two of the associates of Barabbas in his crimes, who are mentioned in Mark 15:7, and who had been guilty of rapine and bloodshed during one of the many insurrections of the day; they cannot have been Roman citizens (ver. 22, B.). The position which Pilate assigned to these two Jewish criminals on the right and the left of the "King of the Jews,' *after* ("then") the Lord had first been nailed to the cross, and the simultaneous execution itself, were circumstances exceedingly unwelcome to the Jews. The

"King of the Jews," elevated above the multitude, is attended by representatives of the nation at his right and left hands (20:20, B.); the whole scene, like the inscription (ver. 37, B.), was designed by Pilate to be a bitter mockery at the actual bondage of the Jews. In John 8:33 they had foolishly disowned the government that held them in bondage, and nothing but the superior power of their bitter personal hatred of Christ extorted from them unconsciously the humiliating confession: "We (the children of Abraham) have no king but (the pagan Roman emperor) Cæsar" (John 19:15). Mark refers in 15:28 to the fulfilment of Isai. 53:12; the Lord Himself had previously announced to His disciples that this prophecy would be fulfilled in His case (Luke 22:37).

39 And they that passed by railed on him, wagging their heads,

A. They ... by = strangers and citizens, all being unoccupied during the festival. **Reviled,** lit.*blasphemed* (see 9:3, C.).—**B. Wagging** (= shaking) **their heads.** This gesture of derision (foretold in Ps. 22:7) was equivalent among the Jews to the offer of a grievous insult (2 Kings 19:21; Job 16:4; Ps. 109:25; Isai. 37:22).

40 And saying, Thou that destroyest the temple, and buildest it in three days, save thyself. If thou art the Son of God, come down from the cross.

A. Saying ... days. The allusion is to the slanderous charge mentioned in 26:61.—**Save thyself** (see ver. 42).—**B. If thou art, etc.** = others of the multitude said: "If thou claimest to be, etc.," alluding to the words in 26:63, 64.—**Come down etc.** = prove it by freeing Thyself. Is not the voice of the arch-enemy, who once said, "Cast thyself down, etc." (4:6), again heard in these words of indescribable malignity?

⁴¹ In like manner also the chief priests mocking *him*, with the scribes and elders, said,

These, the highest dignitaries of the Jews, are betrayed by their wicked hearts into the commission of acts so vile and brutal, and really so blasphemous, that we might have expected even the dregs of the populace to recoil in horror from such baseness and impiety.

⁴² He saved others; himself he cannot save. He is the King of Israel; let him now come down from the cross, and we will believe on him.

A. He saved ... cannot save. The original word **to save** is sometimes employed in the case of a miracle, as in 9:21, 22; Mark 6:56, and then translated: *to make whole.* The sense is: He delivered others from danger, sickness and death by divine power, as His adherents allege, but those accounts are mere fabrications, for He cannot rescue even Himself from death. There is, possibly, a profane allusion, intended to be an additional mockery, to the name Jesus (see 1:1, B.). As all was said in scorn (ver. 41), some interpreters propose to give an interrogative form to the words, which the original will allow, thus: "He saved others? Himself he cannot save?" The sarcastic allusion then is to His present helplessness as an evidence that He always was a mere pretender. These malignant and impious men forget that the omission to perform an act does not prove an inability to perform it, else the divine omission to prevent various deeds of Satan, such as the original temptation (Gen., ch. 3; 2 Cor. 11:3), or his present control of the Jews, would prove that God was inferior in power to Satan.—**B. He is the king, etc.** = they make this profession, but even the greater miracle of the resurrection did not expel the venom from their hearts, and conduct them to faith (28:11, ff.; Acts 5:28; Luke 16:31 (see ann. to 12:39, B.).

⁴³ He trusted on God; let him deliver him now, if he desireth him: for he said, I am the Son of God.

A. He trusted on God = always professed to be obedient to God and full of trust in His love. Of that trust various illustrations occur in the Lord's words in John, ch. 5, 6. His enemies, in their blindness, are not aware of the glorious tribute which they here really offer to the uniform holiness of the Saviour's words and conduct, neither do they remember that they are at the moment literally fulfilling the prediction in Ps. 22:8.—**B. If he desireth him** = if He, God, really delights in Him (see Ps. 22:8, English Bible, margin); so, with the insertion of a negative, the words, "thou wouldest not," are equivalent to "thou hast had no pleasure," in Hebr. 10:5, 6. The spirit in which these words are uttered is one of impiety and blasphemy.

⁴⁴ And the robbers also, that were crucified with him, cast upon him the same reproach.

As Matthew is hastening to the close of his narrative, in which he designs to give special prominence to the Lord Himself, he omits the case of the penitent malefactor described in Luke 23:39–43. It is, indeed, possible that the latter may at first have united with the other malefactor in reviling the Lord, and, struck by His holy bearing, have been convinced of His innocence and his own iniquity; so heathen persecutors in later ages are occasionally said to have become believers on seeing the faith of expiring martyrs. Still, the circumstances do not render it probable. Matthew rather seems to use the plural number, **thieves**, in place of *thief*, according to the mode described above (21:5, F.). So Mark in

7:17 ascribes Peter's question (Matt. 15:15) to the "disciples" generally. At this point, or somewhat later, the affecting incident related in John 19:25–27 probably occurred.

⁴⁵ Now from the sixth hour there was darkness over all the land until the ninth hour.

A. Sixth hour. The Lord had been crucified (= affixed to the cross) at the "third hour" (Mark 15:25), according to the Jewish computation of the hours (Matt. 20:3, B.) = nine o'clock in the morning. The **sixth hour** was our twelve o'clock or noon, the **ninth** our three o'clock P. M. When, in John 19:14, the Saviour is represented as standing before Pilate, previously to the crucifixion, "about the sixth hour," that evangelist, who wrote long after Matthew, and under different circumstances, conforms to the mode of computing the hours adopted by the Romans. Now, they counted the hours (after the close of the Punic wars, b. c. 147) from midnight to midnight (forming the civil day of 24 hours). The "sixth hour" in the Gospel of John is, accordingly, also our six o'clock (comp. John 1:39), where the Roman and modern ten o'clock a. m., rather than the Jewish *tenth* hour or four o'clock p. m., is meant; so, too, John 4:6, 52.—**B. There was darkness.** "The sun was darkened" (Luke 23:45) during three hours. The passover was always celebrated at the time of. the full moon (see 26:2, B., § 2, and 26:46), when the moon is opposite to the sun; an ordinary eclipse of the sun (occasioned by the intervention of the moon between it and the earth) cannot then occur. Moreover, no such eclipse continues three entire hours. Hence this darkness, like the other signs mentioned in ver. 51, was extraordinary and miraculous; the God of nature most forcibly called the attention of men to the solemnity of the hour in which "the

Lord of glory" (1 Cor. 2:8) suffered shame and death. The darkness likewise reminded men of that "thick darkness in all the land of Egypt" which preceded a great deliverance of the people of God, but portended the ruin of God's enemies, whose place the Jews now assumed (Exod. 10:22).—**Over the land** = probably *Judæa,* as the same term is understood in Luke 4:25; 21:21 and 23, while in Luke 23:44 and James 5:17 the same word is translated "earth" (comp. 5:5, B.).

⁴⁶ And about the ninth hour Jesus cried with a loud voice, saying, Eli, Eli, lama sabachthani? that is, My God, my God, why hast thou forsaken me?

A. With a loud voice = indicating the intensity of His feelings [and the fact that His strength was not exhausted].—**B. Eli, Eli, etc.** In several instances (e. g. Mark 5:41; 7:34) the evangelists have preserved the identical Aramæan (Syro-Chaldaic) words of the Lord. This vernacular language of the Jewish people differed somewhat from the ancient Hebrew in pronunciation and other features. The first four Hebrew words of Ps. 22 are given by Matthew in letters of the Greek alphabet; he subjoins the translation after the words: *that is to say.* The difference in Mark 15:34, *Eloi,* arises from a difference in the Syriac pronunciation. That whole Psalm (see above, ver. 35, 39) is a prediction of the Redeemer's sufferings. The language in John 8:29; 16:32, as well as in John 13:1, 3, the peaceful and confiding words of the expiring Saviour in Luke 23:46 (quoted from Ps. 31:5), and the very term here employed: My *God,* forbid us to believe that the Lord lamented that He was abandoned and cast off by His Father in that awful moment; he who proves by such an earnest prayer that *he* has not forsaken God, is surely not himself forsaken. The believer now often quotes words of the Psalms in seasons of sorrow (like these: "All thy waves and thy billows are gone over me," Ps. 42:7), when a strict literal application is not intended. There is, further, no plain indication that the "agony" experienced in Gethsemane (26:37, C.) had returned; moreover, the Lord had just declared that the gate of paradise was open for Him (Luke 23:43). It would then seem that He was not at that moment uttering the language of despair; He appears, during these three hours of darkness, while awe and dread had produced silence around Him, to have been occupied with reflections (John 19:28) on the twenty-second Psalm. The afflictions there predicted had come upon Him (ver. 6–8, 12, 13, 16–18); at the same time cheering words of submission, of faith and of joyful, animating hope occur in that Psalm, especially from ver. 22 to the end; e. g. ver. 24: "neither hath he (the Lord) hid his face from him (the afflicted one)." All these sentiments of sorrow and distress, of faith and joy in God, arise successively in the sufferer's soul; and now, "knowing that all things were now accomplished" (John 19:28), He attests before heaven and earth, by repeating the introductory words, that all the predictions and promises of the old covenant, referring to His atoning work, have been literally fulfilled, and that His work is "finished" (John 19:30). His very last words (Luke 23:46) are a quotation from Ps. 31:5.

⁴⁷ And some of them that stood there, when they heard it, said, This *man* calleth Elijah.

Elijah signifies: *my God is Jehovah* (the latter holy name appears in its abbreviated form as *Jah*, which is found in Ps. 68:4). The first two syllables of the name (namely, *Eli-*) coincide with the first words of the Psalm just quoted by the

Lord, and hence some of the bystanders, possibly foreign Jews to whom the Greek language was more familiar than the Aramæan, supposed that the well-known name of the prophet had been mentioned, and seriously thought that the Lord referred to him. It was generally believed by the Jews at that time that Elias would really return to the world as the harbinger of the Messiah (see ann. to 17:10). Now, when we consider that several hours had already elapsed since the Lord had been affixed to the cross, during which the exultation of His enemies had subsided, and that the preternatural "darkness" had deeply impressed and alarmed the Jews, and inspired them as well as the centurion with "fear" (ver. 54), it does not seem probable that those bystanders (who, moreover, professed to revere the letter of the Scriptures and the divine name itself) would jest in a spirit of levity, and pretend to find a play upon words here.

⁴⁸ And straightway one of them ran, and took a sponge, and filled *it* with vinegar, and put *it* on a reed, and gave him to drink.

The Lord had said: "I thirst" (John 19:28). One of the spectators, deeply moved by all that he beheld, and, possibly, governed by a humane impulse, performed the act here described.—The **vinegar** was the acid wine of the country mixed with water, which the soldiers, who used it as an ordinary beverage, had brought with them (John 19:29; comp. Numb. 6:3; Ruth 2:14). The **sponge**, which, under the circumstances, suited better than a cup, was attached to a hyssop stalk or stem that was at hand; the latter was of sufficient length, although the plant is not large, as the feet of a person suspended on a cross were not elevated far above the ground.

⁴⁹ And the rest said, Let be, let us see whether Elijah cometh to save him.

The single Greek word, translated **Let be,** is, probably, not to be understood here in the chiding sense of "Hold!" or "Forbear!" but was rather addressed to others, in the sense of "Come! Well!" The sense is: The others, doubting, fearing, and yet disposed to defy their fears, said to each other, with the view of stifling their rising apprehensions: We will see = we do not believe that Elijah, etc.

⁵⁰ And Jesus cried again with a loud voice, and yielded up the ghost.

A. Cried again (ver. 46) ... **voice** = exclaimed in loud and emphatic tones: "It is finished" (John 19:30); "Father, into thy hands, etc." (Luke 23:46; comp. the same term "to cry," as descriptive of a powerful emotion expressing itself in words, in 9:27; Rom. 8:15; Rev. 6:10). The "Seven Words" of Christ, uttered on the cross, occurred in the following order: Luke 23:34; Luke 23:43; John 19:26 and ver. 27; Matt. 27:46, or Mark 15:34; John 19:28; John 19:30; Luke 23:46.—**B. Yielded up the ghost** = his soul. The word **ghost** (see 1:18, D.) originally signified *breath, wind* (2 Thess. 2:8); it was then employed in the sense of *spirit* (= incorporeal, immaterial, Luke 24:39, as contradistinguished, for instance, from the material body); thus the terms *Holy Ghost* and *Holy Spirit* (Luke 11:13; 12:12) are precisely the same in meaning, as they are identical in the Greek. Like the original word in the present text, and in John 19:30, the word **ghost** (= spirit), in addition to other meanings, was also employed as a name for the human soul or spirit; it occurs in this sense here as elsewhere (James 2:26). So a corresponding Hebrew word in Job 11:20 may be translated *ghost* as in the text, or *breath* as in the margin of the English Bible, or the whole may read: "Their hope shall be as the breathing out of the soul." The analogous Greek phrase occurs in Mark 15:37 and Luke 23:46, and may be translated in both passages as here, literally: *breathed forth,* namely, the spirit or soul. The English word *expire* also simply means originally, *to breathe out.* The sacred writers, finding no terms in human language that could adequately describe the vastness and solemnity of this event—*the death of Christ*—here observe an expressive silence.

⁵¹ And, behold, the vail of the temple was rent in twain from the top to the bottom; and the earth did quake, and the rocks were rent:

A. Vail of the temple. This vail (for which see Exod. 26:31; Lev. 16:2; 2 Chron. 3:14) was suspended before the "Holy of Holies," or Holiest of all (Hebr. 9:3, 7), containing the ark of the covenant, which none could enter except the high priest, and he only on the day of atonement (Exod. 30:10; Lev. 16:2, 12), "the Holy Ghost this signifying, that, etc." (Hebr. 9:8). Hence, the rending of the entire vail, and the exposure of the interior, now signified that under the new covenant we have "boldness to enter, etc." (Hebr. 10:19). The believer now approaches the presence of God, through Christ his advocate (1 John 2:1), without the intervention of earthly priests and the sacrifice of animals. Very possibly this wonderful event influenced some of the priests in the city who afterwards became disciples (Acts 6:7).—**B. The earth, etc.** This earthquake, like the darkness mentioned in ver. 45, was preternatural = a miracle designed to attest the momentous character of the event that had occurred. All these indications of the special attention of the Most

High to the passing scene doubtless tended to strengthen the disciples and other believers whom the awful manner in which their Master seemed to perish had overwhelmed with grief.

⁵², ⁵³ And the tombs were opened; and many bodies of the saint that had fallen asleep were raised,—And coming forth out of the tombs after his resurrection, they entered into the holy city, and appeared unto many.

A. And the ... opened. A deep darkness had for ages covered the grave viewed as the portal to the eternal world (see 11:23, B.). That darkness was dispelled by "our Saviour Jesus Christ, who hath abolished death, and hath brought life and immortality to light through the Gospel" (2 Tim. 1:10). This distinguishing feature of the Gospel, and also the glorious work of Christ, who "through death" destroyed "him that had the power of death, that is, the devil" (Hebr. 2:14), are strikingly illustrated by the actual opening without human agency of graves in the vicinity of the city. At that moment the work of the "quickening" (= life-giving, John 5:21; 1 Cor. 15:45) Saviour was "finished" (John 19:30).—**B. Saints** = holy persons. The original word is often translated "holy" (e. g. 4:5; 7:6; 25:31, and throughout the N. T.). When the Church, the "body of Christ" (Eph. 1:22, 23) was organized, it was assumed that all who were members of it were now consecrated to God, purified and sanctified by the Holy Spirit (Rev. 6:2–6); they were, accordingly, like the prophets (Acts 3:21) called *the holy ones = saints* (comp. Acts 9:1, 2, with ver. 13, 14, 32, 41, of the same chapter), in contradistinction from unconverted Jews and Gentiles. In such a sense (= members of the church of Christ, true believers, consecrated to God and His service), the word very frequently occurs in the Epistles (e. g. Rom. 1:7; 15:26; 16:2, 15). In an analogous sense (= persons who had consecrated themselves to God and His service), the word may occur here in reference to devout persons who had lived under the old covenant. Still, it is possible that these individuals were believers who had recently died, like Simeon, Anna, the shepherds, etc. (Luke, ch. 2), and who appeared to their surviving friends.—C. **Fallen asleep** = had died (comp. Dan. 12:2; John 11:11; Acts 7:60; 1 Thess. 4:13, 14). The Greek word has furnished us with the term *cemetery*, lit.*sleeping-place*.—D. **After his resurrection, etc.** The graves were opened by the earthquake at the moment of the Saviour's death; the next event was His own resurrection, as "the first-fruits (earliest, first) of them that slept" (1 Cor. 15:20). Then only ("after, etc.") these opened graves sent forth their tenants. The circumstance that the latter **appeared unto many** is here revealed; but divine wisdom has withheld from us not only the knowledge of their names, but also the precise purpose of their appearance, except that we may easily judge that they furnished additional evidence of the Lord's divine mission. It appears from 1 Peter 3:19; 4:6, and possibly from Eph. 4:9; Col. 2:15, that the Saviour Himself, probably after His resurrection on the third day, and before He appeared to any of His disciples, visited the world of the dead; His proceedings are not, however, further revealed, and human wisdom, unaided by further revelations, which have been withheld, cannot explain the mystery.—**Holy city** (see 4:5, C.).—**Appeared unto** many = as Christ Himself did, "not to all the people, etc." (Acts 10:41).

54 Now the centurion, and they that were with him, watching Jesus, when they saw the earthquake, and those things

that were done, feared exceedingly, saying, Truly this was the Son of God.

A. The centurion (see 8:5, B.). This officer doubtless had superintended the execution in the present case, and commanded the watch mentioned in ver. 36.—**B. Those ... done** = the darkness (ver. 45), but specially the utterance by the expiring Lord (Mark 15:39) of words which were so full of sublime peace and hope (ver. 50, A.).—**They feared exceedingly** = they felt, when the awful signs in nature occurred, that here no malefactor had died, but that *they themselves* were the true criminals; others, moved with fear, "smote their breasts" (Luke 23:48) and hastened away from the spot.—**C. Truly ... Son of God** = divine (see also Luke 23:47, and comp. Acts 14:11). This blind heathen and his attendants, aware of the charges of the Lord's enemies (John 19:7), and deeply moved by the signs which they saw, now confessed that the Lord was innocent, holy and divine.

55 And many women were there beholding from afar, which had followed Jesus from Galilee, ministering unto him.

A. And many ... afar off = including certain believing *men,* as the form of the Greek word translated "acquaintance" in Luke 23:49 shows. This group is peculiarly interesting; these devout believers, repelled from the neighborhood of the cross by rude soldiers, are still so full of devotion and love, that, anxious to testify their fidelity to their dying Lord, they can, by the power of faith and love, endure to witness the heartrending spectacle.—**B. From Galilee ... him** (see Mark 15:41; Luke 8:2, 3). The vast spiritual blessings which He had conferred on those individuals had won all their faith and love, and they consecrated themselves wholly to His service.—**Ministering** (see 4:11, B.).

⁵⁶ Among whom was Mary Magdalene, and Mary the mother of James and Joses, and the mother of Zebedee's children.

A. Mary (lit. *the*) **Magdalene.** The latter appellation, annexed to Mary's name, in order to distinguish her from other Marys, such as the sister of Lazarus, simply indicates by its termination that she was a native or resident of the town of Magdala, mentioned in 15:39. (So the geographical appellation in Mark 1:24; 14:67; Luke 4:34, in the original is *Nazarene*.) The miracle of grace which the Lord performed for her (Mark 16:9) is mentioned by Luke, ch. 8:2, soon after describing (in 7:37, ff.) the devout act of the "woman who was a sinner." Hence some interpreters suppose that woman to be this Mary. Her deep devotion to her deliverer, manifested at the cross, at the burial, and after the resurrection of the Lord, has secured for her an eminent position in the concluding remarks of the four evangelists. Of the earlier and later history of this highly favored woman, authentic history has preserved no details.—**B. Mary ... Joses,** the wife of Alpheus = Clopas (John 19:25, margin, and see 13:55, C.).—**C. The mother, etc.** = Salome (Mark 15:40), the wife of Zebedee (see 20:20, B.). These devoted adherents suffered an additional pang when a soldier pierced the Lord's side with a spear (John 19:34), inflicting a ghastly and very large wound (John 20:27). Still, not "a bone was broken" (John 19:32–37; see Exod. 12:46; Numb. 9:12; Ps. 34:20); hence, while the Lord "poured out his soul unto death" (Isai. 53:12), His body was not "broken" = subjected to mutilations or fractures (see 26:26, D., and 27:22, B.).

⁵⁷ And when even was come, there came a rich man

from Arimathea, named Joseph, who also himself was Jesus' disciple:

A. Even = Friday, somewhat before sunset. The bodies of the crucified usually remained for some time in their exposed condition (ver. 22, B.); Jewish usages, however, founded on Deut. 21:23, and enforced in this case by the approach of the great passover Sabbath, would not allow the corpse to remain on the cross (see John 19:31–37).—**B. There came** = probably to Golgotha, while the soldiers took the body down from the cross, and before they had disposed of it.—**C. A rich man, etc.** (see the full description of Joseph in Mark 15:43; Luke 23:50, 51). The statement that he was **rich** alludes to Isai. 53:9 = he was able, in accordance with the prophecy, to furnish a fitting grave (ver. 60) for the Lord. He had been a timid "disciple" (John 19:38), but now nobly redeemed his character when the lifeless body of the Lord most of all needed the honors usually rendered to the dead; he cast off all fear, and "boldly" came forward (Mark 15:43). Nicodemus, the former visitor of the Lord (John 3:1, 2), now exhibits equal fearlessness and faith (John 19:39). Both had previously yielded too much to personal fears, but the scenes which occurred at the crucifixion (ver. 54) had shown them so plainly the presence of God, that they cast off all fear of man.—**Arimathea**, supposed by some to be identical with Samuel's birthplace (1 Sam. 1:1, 19), among whom is von Raumer; others identify it with Ramah (Ramleh) in the plain of Sharon, about three miles from Lydda, which "was nigh to Joppa" (Acts 9:38), and thirty miles northwest of Jerusalem. Luke's remark in 23:51, that Arimathea was "a city of the Jews," possibly refers to the grant of the three districts of Apherima, Lydda and Ramatha to the Jews about

b. c. 145 (Jos. Ant. 13, 4, 9). Ramah, mentioned in 2:18, and identified by some writers with Samuel's birthplace, is by others regarded as a different place. As the name *Ramah*, signifying *height, high place,* occurs in the Scriptures as that of several different spots, interpreters have not yet been able to distinguish each one from the rest with entire precision. Robinson inclines to the opinion that Samuel's birthplace and Arimathea are identical; he thinks that Ramleh and Arimathea were two different places, but is satisfied that the ancient site of Arimathea cannot now be positively identified (Bibl. Res. II. 239–241; III. 141).

⁵⁸ This man went to Pilate, and asked for the body of Jesus. Then Pilate commanded it to be given up.

A. Went to Pilate = from the place of crucifixion, before the ultimate disposition of the body was determined.—**B. Asked, etc.** Pilate might have, as in similar cases, claimed a gratuity in money for the favor; however, he still remembered the uneasiness which he had experienced in the morning (ver. 19, 24), and his apprehensions appear to have returned when he received the centurion's report (Mark 15:44, 45). He gladly offered the only atonement for his unjust and cruel conduct which the circumstances allowed.—**Begged** = *asked, desired,* as the word is else, where almost uniformly translated, as in 14:7; 20:20.

⁵⁹ And Joseph took the body, and wrapped it in a clean linen cloth,

The hour of the day was late, and the Sabbath was at hand (Luke 23:54 = Friday evening at sunset), when no work was permitted (Luke 23:56). As the process of embalming the body was deferred by Joseph and Nicodemus (who did not expect the resurrection) until the close of the Sabbath, they hastily "wound" the body in "linen clothes" (John 19:40), that is, strips or bandages of "clean," namely, *new* linen placed around the body; they also deposited the "spices" around it (John 19:39, 40). It was their intention to complete the embalming after the close of the Sabbath. The Greek name for **linen cloth** indicates an article of elaborate finish and great value.

⁶⁰ And laid it in his own new tomb, which he had hewn out in the rock: and he rolled a great stone to the door of the tomb, and departed.

A. And laid ... rock.—New = "wherein never man before was laid" (Luke 23:53; John 19:41), consequently *clean* in the Jewish sense = not yet defiled by the presence of a corpse (22:27, A.).—**His own** = intended as a burial-place for himself and his family. It appears from John 19:41 to have been constructed in a garden which Joseph owned in the vicinity of Golgotha (comp. 2 Kings 21:26). Such depositories were often natural cavities (Gen. 23:17), or were hewn out of the rocks (8:28, C.; Isai. 22:16).—**B. Rolled etc.** The mode of burial among the ancient Jews varied in some respects with the circumstances. Wealthy persons like Joseph (ver. 57) constructed extensive tombs, consisting of chambers and passages, with niches or recesses; his own admitted several persons (Mark 16:5; Luke 24:3). A low entrance or door conducted to the interior. In such cases the corpse was not lowered as when one is deposited in a modern grave, but was carried into the vault, which was entered by a horizontal avenue. Such was the burial-place of Asa (2 Chron. 16:14). In a tomb of this kind, the entrance to which was on the side of a hill, the body of Jesus was "laid" (John 19:42) = *placed, put*. The door or opening was perpendicular, and not flat or horizontal like the mouth of a modern grave; hence the stone was rolled *to* ("unto" Mark 15:46) the door. John accordingly "stooped down" = bent *forward* (not *over*), in order to look in through the low entrance, while Peter went *into* (not *down into*) the sepulchre; Mary stood on the outside (John 20:5, 6, 11). Robinson says: "The numerous sepulchres which skirt the valleys on the north, east and south of Jerusalem, exhibit for the most part one general mode of construction. A doorway in the perpendicular face of the rock, usually small and without ornament, leads to one or more small chambers excavated from the rock, and commonly upon the same level with the door. Very rarely are the chambers lower than the doors" (Bibl. Res. I. 352). "The numerous sepulchral chambers around Jerusalem are all excavated horizontally in the natural or artificial face of the rock, with the exception of the tombs of the prophets, which differ from this as well as from all others. The entrance is always at the side, and never above" (Bibl. Res. III. 181).

61 And Mary Magdalene was there, and the other Mary, sitting over against the sepulchre.

These two Marys are mentioned in ver. 56. The scene presented by these devout and faithful women, sitting at that late hour in that spot, in loneliness and unspeakable grief, unable to abandon the remains of their adored Master, and yet without well-defined hopes of His resurrection (16:21, B.), is deeply affecting.

62 Now on the morrow, which is the day after the Preparation, the chief priests and Pharisees were gathered together unto Pilate,

A. The next day = the Sabbath day, probably Friday evening after sunset, when the Sabbath began. Our own

Saturday, beginning at midnight, therefore commences several hours after the Jewish Sabbath.—**B. The day of Preparation** = Friday (see 26:2, B., § 5) = the ever memorable day of the Lord's crucifixion.—**C. The chief priests, etc.** = unable to find repose, even after the successful commission of the bloody deed; a guilty conscience gave additional poignancy to their fears; hence they violate by this *business transaction* their own rules respecting the sanctity of their Sabbath.

⁶³ Saying, Sir, we remember that that deceiver said, while he was yet alive, After three days I will rise again.

A. That deceiver = who claimed to be the Messiah and Son of God (26:63; John 7:12). The same appellation was given to the Lord's followers (2 Cor. 6:8).—**Sir** (8:2, C.).—**B. Said, while, etc.** The Lord had repeatedly predicted His resurrection on the third day, both in the presence of His disciples (16:21, F.), and also in public (12:39, 40). One of these occasions, described in John 2:19–21, had been vividly recalled to their memory (26:61).

⁶⁴ Command therefore that the sepulchre be made sure until the third day, lest haply his disciples come and steal him away, and say unto the people, He is risen from the dead: and the last error shall be worse than the first.

A. Be made sure = be secured; the same word is rendered "made fast" in Acts 16:24.—**B. Lest his disciples ... dead.** They seem to fear that the words of the Lord respecting His resurrection will be verified, but they hide their fears by the weak device of alleging that the timid and scattered disciples might undertake the hazardous work of removing and concealing the body, and then publishing that their Master had risen from the grave.—**C. The last error** =

deception, fraud, that is, the *pretended* resurrection of the Lord. They speak as if the accuracy of their opinions were undoubted.—**D. The first** = error or fraud; they here refer to the Lord's claim that He is the Messiah, which they wickedly term an imposture.—**Worse** = for the public order and peace. The whole phraseology is of the nature of a proverb (see ann. to 12:43–45, A.).

⁶⁵ Pilate said unto them, Ye have a guard: go your way, make *it* as sure as ye can.

A. Pilate said. His ready compliance with their request shows that while, as a heathen, he would at another time have "mocked" on hearing that any one should really believe in the possibility of the resurrection of the dead (Acts 17:32), his own personal fears had not yet passed away (see ver. 58, B.).—**B. Ye have a watch** = a guard. This detachment of soldiers appears from 28:12, 14, to have been taken from Pilate's own men, and cannot therefore refer to the temple-guard mentioned in ann. to 26:47, B. The latter, besides, consisted of Jews, who would have violated the law of the Sabbath by performing the service—an additional reason of the Jews for requesting a guard consisting of heathen. The original may accordingly be so understood, that Pilate at once issued orders to a company of men, and then, turning to the Jews, said: Now ye have the guard, go at once, etc.—**C. As ye can,** lit. *as ye know how* = in the most effectual manner known to you. Pilate, himself much alarmed, eagerly assents to the proposition, and urges them to act without delay.

⁶⁶ So they went, and made the sepulchre sure, sealing the stone, the guard being with them.

A. So ... stone. The stone placed at the door by Joseph (ver. 60) was not disturbed; it was **sealed,** as, probably, in the case mentioned in Dan. 6:17, by stretching a cord over it, and fastening the ends by means of wax or any other adhesive substance, like sealing-clay, to the rock which formed the edge of the opening; the wax or clay received the impress of a private seal, and thus its condition at any time would indicate whether the vault had been secretly entered, or had remained undisturbed.

13

Matthew 28

¹ Now late on the sabbath day, as it began to dawn toward the first *day* of the week, came Mary Magdalene and the other Mary to see the sepulchre.

   A. In the ... sabbath = late, or, some time after the close of the Sabbath; the precise time is not stated; the circumstance occurred several hours after sunset of Saturday evening, which coincided with the end of the Sabbath; hence Mark says: "When the sabbath was past" (16:1).—**B. As it ... week** = "very early in the morning" (Mark, Luke), "when it was yet dark" (John 20:1). A comparison of the accounts of the four evangelists furnishes the following results:—Before the sun had risen on the **first day of the week** (= Sunday), **Mary Magdalene, the other Mary** (see 27:56, 61), Salome (Mark 16:1), Joanna and other women (Luke 24:10) proceeded to the grave, in order to complete the process of anointing the body, which had been interrupted on the previous Friday evening (see above, 27:59). Mary Magdalene appears, as John soon afterwards did (John 20:3, 4), to have hastened onward alone, when it was yet dark (John 20:1); to her the Lord "appeared first" (Mark 16:9; John 20:11, ff.). Afterwards the other women "came unto the sepulchre at the rising of the sun" (Mark 16:2: Luke 24:1).—**To see the sepulchre** = for the purpose of anointing the body (Mark 16:1).

² And, behold, there was a great earthquake: for an angel of the Lord descended from heaven, and came and rolled away the stone, and sat upon it.

A. And, behold. In order to explain the circumstance that the stone no longer obstructed the entrance (Mark 16:3), Matthew here supplies the history of the events which occurred during the earlier part of the night, that is, after the first day of the week had commenced, or during the interval between the close of the Sabbath and the arrival of the women at the grave. The eventful "third day" (16:21, F.) after the crucifixion had commenced on Saturday evening at sunset; the *second* day extended from Friday evening to Saturday evening. The *first* day of the three, or the day of the crucifixion, was Friday, in the afternoon of which the Lord had been buried (27:57, A.; see 12:40, A., and 26:2, B., § 5). The stone was rolled away, not for the purpose of removing an obstruction to the passage of the Saviour, to whose glorified body well secured doors offered no hindrance (John 20:19, 26), but of exhibiting to His followers the *empty* grave.—**B. A great earthquake.** This concussion of the earth marked the advent of the angel.—**C. An angel** = not a human being, although in appearance "a young man," Mark 16:5. ("Let all the angels of God worship Him" = the Son, Hebr. 1:6.)—**D. And came, etc.** This event took place before the arrival of the women at the grave (Mark 16:4). The solemn scenes which now occurred, the raising of the Lord's body (2 Cor. 4:14), and His own acts immediately afterwards, are not here further unfolded by the sacred writer; neither is the place revealed where the Lord abode during the succeeding forty days.

³ His appearance was as lightning, and his raiment white as snow:

A. Appearance. The Greek term, like the corresponding Hebrew (Exod. 24:17, *sight;* Ezek. 1:16, 28; Dan. 10:18, *appearance*), strictly means *aspect, appearance, form, looks,* alluding to the brightness or splendor of the angel's appearance. Matthew compares the latter to the vividness or brightness of the lightning.—**B. His raiment, etc.** The original term in Luke 24:4, "shining (lit. *lightning-like*) garments," explains the meaning of the **white** raiment = brilliant, shining appearance of the angel's garments (see ann. to 17:2).

⁴ And for fear of him the watchers did quake, and became as dead *men.*

A. The watchers = the guard mentioned in 27:65, B.—**B. Did shake, etc.** The terror inspired by the earthquake and the appearance of the angel during the night overwhelmed the keepers, and they fainted or lost all consciousness = "became as dead men."

⁵ And the angel answered and said unto the women, Fear not ye: for I know that ye seek Jesus, which hath been crucified.

A. Answered and said = addressed the women before they spoke (see 11:25, C.); or, more precisely, he responded appropriately to the terror which they manifested. Matthew here resumes the direct narrative from ver. 1. It appears from Mark 16:5, that after the keepers had fainted on seeing the angel, the latter entered the sepulchre (see 27:60, B.); afterwards the women followed. The other angel, who was also seen (Luke 24:4), remained silent, and Matthew, who describes the speaker alone, accordingly does not mention the other (comp. 8:28, B.).—**B. Fear not ye, etc.** = yield not, like the keepers, to your terror. They are not servants of the Lord, but ye know, love and revere Jesus, and have therefore no reason to be affrighted (Mark 16:5). I know that your purpose in coming hither is to perform an act of reverence and devotion.—**Jesus ... crucified,** lit. Jesus, the Crucified One = ye were not ashamed of Him even when He appeared as the Nazarene (Mark 16:6 and Matt. 2:23, C.). Paul afterwards, with fuller knowledge than these women possessed, even *gloried* in the cross of Christ (Gal. 6:14).

⁶ He is not here: for he is risen, even as he said. Come, see the place where the Lord lay.

The women are not yet prepared to understand and believe the fact of the Lord's resurrection. The angel recalls to their minds the Lord's own repeated predictions of the event (16:21, F.), and desires them to approach nearer and view the vacant spot or cavity which the body had occupied, as an evidence that He lived again (comp. Luke 24:5–7).—**The Lord** = of the angels as well as of human beings (Phil. 2:10).

⁷ And go quickly, and tell his disciples, He is risen from the dead; and, lo, he goeth before you into Galilee; there shall ye see him: lo, I have told you.

The disciples, who could not originally understand the Lord's predictions respecting His death and resurrection (Mark 9:31, 32), are not even yet sufficiently strong in faith, in order to believe the statement previously made by the Lord (see Luke 24:9–11). The angel is now commissioned to send to the disciples the message that the event had really occurred; he repeats the promise which the Lord Himself had made in 26:32.—**There shall ye see him.** These words the women are directed to repeat to the disciples (see ver. 10, below). Divine pity sustains the fainting disciples in this hour of trial (Mark 16:10); that same pity remembered specially the weeping and penitent Peter (Mark 16:7).—**He goeth before you** = He will there be found by you.—**Lo** (2:9, B.).—**I have told you** = tell the disciples, when they hesitate to believe you (Luke 24:11), that an angel from heaven had revealed the fact.

⁸ And they departed quickly from the tomb with fear and great joy; and ran to bring his disciples word.

Before the women had fully recovered from the "fear" which the unexpected appearance of the angels had inspired, they receive, to their "great joy," unquestionable evidence of the Lord's resurrection. In this state of mind they hastened ("did run") to the spot where the disciples were assembled, without pausing to communicate the wonderful intelligence to any one whom they encountered on the way (Mark 16:8).

⁹ And, behold, Jesus met them, saying, All hail. And they came and took hold of his feet, and worshipped him.

A. And as they went. Their faith in the angel's words is rewarded before they reach the appointed spot, by the appearance of the Lord Himself, who graciously addresses them.—**All hail.** The Greek term, which occurs also in 26:49, B. (which see), is here employed (without the word "all," which the English phrase often supplies) as a most kind and friendly salutation.—**B. Took hold ... feet.** Compare the conduct of the woman of Shunem (2 Kings 4:27). These devout women, in their rapture at finding the Lord whom they **worshipped** (2:2, D.), yielded unconsciously to their fear of again losing Him, and instinctively clasp His feet with their hands, as if they wished to retain Him forever. A similar movement, from a similar impulse, seems to have been made by Mary Magdalene (John 20:17).

¹⁰ Then saith Jesus unto them, Fear not: go tell my brethren, that they depart into Galilee, and there shall they see me.

A. Then said Jesus = to the women who still trembled on seeing one that had been dead now living and moving before them, and who were, nevertheless, filled with joy. The wonderful events which here so rapidly occurred will easily account for their conflicting emotions.—**B. Tell my brethren.** The Lord had previously called His disciples "friends" (John 15:15). Here, as in 12:49, 50, with overflowing love, and in view of their sanctification and adoption as the children of God (Rom. 8:14–17; 1 John 3:2), as well as for the purpose of indicating that He retains His human nature, even in His glorified state, He condescends to call them **brethren** (Hebr. 2:11). The same gracious message is also given to Mary Magdalene (John 20:17), and here a renewed invitation is sent to meet Him in Galilee (26:32).

¹¹ Now, while they were going, behold, some of the guard came into the city, and told unto the chief priests all the things that were come to pass.

A. Now ... going. The keepers, after recovering from their terror, and finding the grave open, had withdrawn from the spot, probably before the arrival of the women. Hence, at nearly the same time, tidings of the Lord's resurrection are brought both to His friends and to His enemies.—**B. Some of the guard** (27:65) = the officers, or, possibly, the boldest of their number.—**C. Told, etc.** The keepers were seriously embarrassed. A Roman sentinel who deserted his post, or slept during his watch, was exposed to the most severe military punishment (comp. the case in Acts 12:19). These keepers, however, had been temporarily transferred to the service of the chief priests (27:62–66); to the latter, accordingly, some of their number report the wonderful events which had occurred during the night, and which they represent as a sufficient excuse for the failure of their mission. They doubtless understood the position of affairs, and hoped to make a satisfactory arrangement with their employers.

¹² And when they were assembled with the elders, and had taken counsel, they gave large money unto the soldiers,

When they = the chief priests just mentioned. A meeting of the council is held at once, and the difficulties of the case are considered. On the one hand, the testimony of the keepers is clear, consistent with the whole history, character and words of Jesus, and incapable of being contradicted. On the other hand, if the facts be made known publicly, the chief priests can look for no other result than their own ruin (comp. Acts 4:2; 5:28). Consequently they are in the power of the keepers, and hence we hear of no rebukes or menaces addressed to the latter. They finally determine to bribe the soldiers and conceal all the facts from the public; the circumstances admitted of no rational method of accounting for the disappearance of the body except a statement of the truth, and they accordingly can assign only an improbable and insufficient reason.—**B. Gave large, etc.** The word rendered **large** is translated variously: *much* (Luke 7:12; Acts 5:37); *many* (Luke 8:32; 23:9); *enough* (Luke 22:38); it indicates here that a sufficiently large sum of money was paid to the soldiers, both to satisfy their cupidity, and also to induce them to expose themselves to the infamy of sleeping on their post. The amount was evidently far more than the pitiful sum paid to Judas (26:15).

¹³ Saying, Say ye, His disciples came by night, and stole him away while we slept.

That the body of the Lord had disappeared from the grave was unquestionable; His enemies, who are resolved to conceal the truth, can devise no explanation which will satisfactorily account for the event without involving the keepers in some danger. The explanation which they finally determine to give is an obvious absurdity. For if the keepers were asleep, how could they know *who* had stolen the body? But if they did know, why did they not endeavor to recover the body from the guilty persons?

¹⁴ And if this come to the governor's ears, we will persuade him, and rid you of care.

Possibly they assure the watch that Pilate would not closely investigate the matter, inasmuch as the soldiers had been temporarily released from his immediate service. But if—they continue, in their appeal to the keepers—he should hear ("come ... ears") that you are reported to have slept at your post, or should subject you to an examination, we will **persuade** him = we will induce him to overlook the matter by alleging that we, your immediate employers, are satisfied with your conduct. Possibly they imply that they will bribe Pilate also, whose venal character was well known. Thus—they conclude—we will **rid you of care** = make you free from anxiety. The same Greek term is translated in 1 Cor. 7:32, "without carefulness." The whole circumstance of bargaining with the keepers was excessively mortifying to the pride of the Jews.

¹⁵ So they took the money, and did as they were taught: and this saying was spread abroad among the Jews and

continueth until this day.

A. So they took ... taught. The keepers, in consideration of the large amount of the bribe, consented to follow the plan which they were "taught" to adopt, submitting to the disgrace and danger, in view of their pecuniary gains.—**B. And this saying** = this unfounded statement or story that the Lord's disciples had secretly stolen and hidden His body.—**C. Was spread abroad.** This slander was so successfully propagated among the unbelieving Jews by the Lord's enemies, that long after the time of the evangelist it was repeated by Jewish writers. But the all-seeing God knew the truth! His inspired servant has here communicated it to the world.—**D. Until this day** = the time when Matthew wrote the present narrative (27:8).

¹⁶ But the eleven disciples went into Galilee, unto the mountain where Jesus had appointed them.

A. But. Matthew simply states the fact without specifying the time. To the apostles Christ "showed himself alive after his passion (= suffering, Matt. 26:1) by many infallible proofs, being seen of them forty days" (Acts 1:3). When He occasionally appeared during this period He addressed to them many impressive words, which the evangelists record. Matthew here selects that appearance of the Lord with which the institution of the sacrament of Holy Baptism was connected. Inasmuch as, according to Luke 24:50, 51; Acts 1:12, the Lord's ascension occurred at or near Bethany, on the Mount of Olives (see 21:17), whereas the words here recorded were spoken in Galilee, it is obvious that the present appearance of the Lord occurred before the day of His ascension.—**B. The eleven, etc.** (see 26:32). It is probably this appearance of the Lord to which Paul refers in 1 Cor.

15:6, when "above five hundred brethren at once" saw Him. In that passage the apostle, omitting the several appearances which the women witnessed, specifies those only which were beheld by one or more of the eleven. The latter may be supposed to have gathered together on the occasion the Galilean believers, who were numerous; in Jerusalem "the number of names together were about a hundred and twenty" (Acts 1:15).

¹⁷ And when they saw him, they worshipped him: but some doubted.

A. When they = the assembled multitude.—**Worshipped** (ver. 9, B., above).—**B. But some doubted.** The original word (see above, 14:31, C.) here indicates a hesitation on the part of some to obey the first impulse and unite in the worship of the Saviour. The eleven cannot be meant, for they had, very soon after the resurrection, seen the risen Lord (comp. John 20:20). Those who "doubted" (namely, whether He who now appeared was really Jesus of Nazareth) were, accordingly, some of the five hundred mentioned above (ver. 16, B.) Even the eleven themselves could not believe the tidings when first brought by the women (Luke 24:11; John 20:25), with which unbelief the Lord upbraided them (Mark 16:14). When they afterwards saw Him themselves, they were at first "affrighted, and supposed that they had seen a spirit" (Luke 24:37); then, after they received proofs of His bodily appearance, they "believed not for joy" (Luke 24:41) = the transition from the deepest grief, hopelessness and terror to the most exalted joy, overpowered them. Such varying emotions may have controlled "some" of the five hundred; while fear had seized them, joy and hope dawned in their souls, and they **doubted** = experienced in their souls a conflict of opposite emotions.

¹⁸ And Jesus came to them and spake, saying, All authority hath been given unto me in heaven and on earth.

A. Came = drew near unto, *approached,* as the original implies; when He was first seen, He was still at a certain distance from them; He came near in order to convince them of the reality of His presence.—**B. All authority, etc.** (comp. for the sense 11:27, B., where the same emphatic term **all** occurs, and see Dan. 7:14).—**In heaven and** (*upon*) **earth** = so "that he might fill all things" (Eph. 4:10), namely, He, the God-Man, is henceforth to reign in glory, both as the eternal Son of God, and as the Son of man, His human nature being raised to a participation of the glory of His divine nature (see 26:64, C.).

¹⁹ Go ye therefore, and make disciples of all the nations, baptizing them in the name of the Father, and of the Son, and of the Holy Ghost:

A. Therefore = since I, your Lord and King, in the fulness of My power, give you such a commission and such authority. The Lord, in the brief but comprehensive words of this verse, first prescribes the missionary duties of the Church; secondly, institutes Baptism; and, thirdly, proclaims the doctrine of the Trinity.—**B. Make disciples.** The construction in the Greek (the employment of the participles "baptizing," "teaching") shows that the mode of "making disciples," as far as human instrumentality is employed by the Lord, consists in the two acts of, first, "baptizing," and, secondly, of "teaching" (ver. 20), so that, according to the order of the words adopted by the Saviour, and doubtless in view of Infant Baptism, the individual is first *baptized,* then *taught* (receiving the engrafted word, James

1:21), and so made a disciple. Alford says: "The process of ordinary discipleship is *from baptism to instruction*—i. e. is *admission in infancy to the covenant,* and *growing up into an observing of all things,* etc.—the *exception* being, what circumstances rendered so frequent in the early Church, *instruction before baptism* in the case of *adults*." In the age of the apostles, when none but unbaptized adults were addressed, the former first preached, and then "made disciples" (as the word translated "taught" in Acts 14:21 properly implies) by baptizing and further instructing those hearers who yielded to the power of the truth (comp. the cases in Acts 8:12; 19:1–8). The Lord's words in the present verse, however, refer to the Church in its subsequent, fully organized and established form; it is His purpose that infants should be regularly introduced into it by the sacrament of Baptism (see 19:14, B.). To this right and title to admission into the Church, and to the blessings of baptism, so graciously given to children, Peter refers, when, after offering baptism to his penitent hearers, he adds: "The promise is unto you, and to your children, etc." (Acts 2:39). The reception of infants into the old covenant is strictly enjoined in the O. T., and circumcision was instituted at a very early period as the initiatory rite (Gen. 17:9–14). When baptism was substituted by the Saviour for circumcision, as we learn from Col. 2:11, 12, it was not the purpose of Him who said of little children, "Of such is the kingdom of heaven" (see 19:14, B.), to abridge the privileges enjoyed by infants under the old covenant, but much rather to enlarge them under the new and better covenant. Hence baptism is here mentioned as the first act in the process of "making disciples," and is followed by that of "teaching" (ver. 20).—**C. All the nations** = all other nations as well as the Jews, who are now no longer God's peculiar people (Rom., ch. 11). These emphatic words, "all the nations," admit of no restriction. The Gospel with all its blessings is designed for all men without exception; every individual who does not wilfully reject the Gospel terms (Acts 20:21) here receives a right to be admitted into the Church = "all the world"—"every creature" (Mark 16:15). Nations consist of adults and children; consequently, all these receive the privilege of entering the Church by Holy Baptism, and of being thus placed under its life-giving influence. See the next ann. D. "God so loved the world, etc." (John 3:16).—**D. Baptizing.** The holy sacrament of Christian Baptism is in its whole character different from John's baptism (see 3:6, A.). The former is here set forth, *first*, as a universal institution, embracing even the youngest children, for whom the Lord as little here forgets to provide, as when He said to Peter: "Feed my lambs" (John 20:15; Acts 2:39); *secondly*, as a permanent usage of the Church; and, *thirdly*, as a means of grace. In respect to its efficacy as a means of grace, the Lord Himself, referring prophetically to the present institution of the rite, speaks of the baptized person as one "born of water" (John 3:5); subsequently Paul calls it "the washing of regeneration" (Tit. 3:5). Its saving efficacy, conveyed through faith, is abundantly proved by passages like Mark 16:16; Acts 2:38; 22:16; 1 Peter 3:21; Eph. 5:26. (On the mode of baptism, see 3:6, B.) When Paul in 1 Cor. 7:14 declares that the children of a believing father or mother are "holy," he must refer to the influence of baptism which had been administered to them, even as in 1 Cor. 6:11 and Eph. 5:26 he connects sanctification with baptism. The appeal which he makes to children in Eph. 6:1 assumes that they have already been baptized.—**E. In the name of.** To baptize *in* the name of the Father, etc., here implies not only that the act is performed by divine authority (see 7:22, E.), but also that as John's baptism was "unto repentance" = a confession of sins that should be repented of (see 3:11, A.), so the baptism *unto* the Father, etc. (as the word is in the original, or *into,* as rendered in Rom. 6:3; Gal. 3:27), is, further, equivalent to a confession of faith in the Triune God. The whole act, moreover, is the consecration of the individual to God; he had been "by nature a child of wrath" (Eph. 2:3), but is now in Christ "made nigh" (Eph. 2:13), grafted into the Church (1 Cor. 12:13), and consecrated to God forever. Hence Paul, who says only figuratively that the Jews had been baptized "unto Moses" (1 Cor. 10:2), absolutely denies in 1 Cor. 1:13 that in the case of Christian baptism any one can be baptized literally in (unto) the name of a human being. This holy rite is designed to connect the baptized person intimately with the Triune God, the fountain of life, as the branch is connected with the vine (John 15:4). We were—says Paul in Rom. 6:3—baptized into Christ's death = admitted into union with Him and full participation in all the benefits of His death. At the same time, even as in the cases mentioned in 2 Kings 5:14; John 9:7, so in Holy Baptism, "it is," as Luther says, "not the water that produces these effects, but the Word of God [the divine command in Matt. 28:19 and promise in Mark 16:16] which accompanies and is connected with the water, and our faith which relies on the Word of God connected with the water."—**F. The Father ... Ghost.** The doctrine of the Trinity, which is fully set forth in the writings of the apostles, is here announced by the Saviour. Each of the Three Persons is distinct in name and operations, each Person is God, and yet the Three Persons are only one God: hence the Lord does not say: in the *names*, as of many, but as of one = in the name (see 3:17, B.).

[20] Teaching them to observe all things whatsoever I commanded you: and, lo, I am with you alway, even unto the end of the world. Amen.

A. Teaching. The sense of this word may be gathered from many other passages in which it occurs; for instance, 4:23; 5:19; 9:35; 15:9; it is usually applied specially to the act of conveying instructions orally, or by word of mouth, while the word similarly translated in the foregoing verse (19, B.) includes other official acts of ecclesiastical teachers.—**Them** = the individuals constituting the "nations."—**B. To observe ... commanded you.** The word translated **to observe**, besides the general meaning, *to obey* or fulfil *precepts* or commandments, also indicates the *duty* of receiving divine truth with faith, as passages like John 8:51; 14:24; 17:6; 2 Tim 4:7; Rev. 22:9, abundantly show. Hence "all the things" which the Lord Jesus **commanded** (= enjoined upon, or prescribed) include the doctrines as well as the duties of our holy religion; both are to be conscientiously and faithfully maintained.—**All things** = forbidding the slightest change in any of the doctrines and duties of religion. The grace conferred, first, in Holy Baptism, then through the Word (religious instruction, Scriptures), and, lastly, in the Holy Communion (as the three divinely-appointed means of grace given to the Church, through all of which the Holy Spirit operates on man), conveys the needed wisdom and strength to "observe all things, etc.":—**C. Lo.** Once more the Lord employs this word, in order to direct attention specially to the words that follow (see 1:20, B.).—**D. I am ... world.**

That **end of the world** of which the Lord here speaks (see 24:3, E.) is the period described in 2 Peter 3:7–10, when the "day of judgment," or "the day of the Lord," shall have come, and when "the earth and the works that are therein shall be burned up." The first disciples, to whom these words were addressed, closed their lives long before it was possible for them to visit all nations themselves: nevertheless, the Lord says: "I am with you alway." He, therefore, evidently designs to extend the promise to those who succeeded the original preachers of the Gospel in the divinely-instituted office of the ministry. These succeeding heralds of the cross appointed or ordained other teacphers, and the latter again transmitted the office in their turn to others (see 1 Tim. 3:1, ff.; 5:22; Tit. 1:5). Hence, the Lord Jesus will abide with all His believing people = the Church, while the earth endures.—**Alway,** lit. *all the days* = perpetually (comp. Ps. 72:5); in Gen. 8:22 the Hebrew (see margin of Engl. Bible) is: "Unto all the days of the earth" = while the earth remaineth; afterwards, "we shall ever be with the Lord" (1 Thess. 4:17). Christ is with His servants in the fulness of His grace and power (Gen. 39:2; 2 Cor. 12:9), and with the gifts of the Holy Spirit (comp. Matt. 18:20, C., and John 14:16, 20, 23).—**I am with you** = "in the fullest sense; not the *Divine Presence as distinguished from the Humanity* of Christ. His Humanity is with us likewise."—Alford. The possession by the latter of the divine attributes is here implied (see ver. 18, B.).—**E. Amen** (see 5:18, A.).

Appendix

EXCURSUS I

Kingdom, *of heaven—of God—of Christ—of the Father.* § 1. The word *kingdom* sometimes stands alone; Matthew generally introduces the phrase: *kingdom of heaven,* while Mark, Luke (both in his gospel and in the Acts), John in his gospel, and Paul in his epistles, employ that of *kingdom of God.* The fundamental idea expressed by all these terms, wherever they occur, is that of *the divine authority, as exclusively and cheerfully acknowledged by intelligent creatures;* such an acknowledgment establishes a state of security and of holy joy in consequence of the communion with the blessed God to which it conducts.

§ 2. The Jews had long been familiar with the conception of God as their king, in the sense of *Supreme Ruler* (1 Sam. 12:12), to which relation of God to the Jewish people the term *Theocracy* alludes = a government administered immediately or directly by God Himself; the term appears to have been introduced by Josephus, c. Ap. II. 16 (17). The prophets also represent God as the king or ruler of all the nations of the world: they then teach not only that He in reality possesses all dominion and power, but also that when his authority shall be generally understood and *recognized* at a future time (namely, after the Messiah has appeared), He will, in the fullest sense, be the king over all (Isai. 2:1–4); then will "the kingdoms of this world become the kingdoms of our Lord, and of His Christ" (Rev. 11:15). This point is distinctly stated in Dan. 2:44: "The God of heaven shall set up a kingdom which shall never be destroyed." Daniel proceeds to explain in ch. 7:14, 27, that this kingdom is that of the Messiah = of Christ. The same truth is elsewhere taught (Ps. 2:6; Jer. 23:5; Mic. ch. 4; Zech. 14:9; Ezek. 37:24).

§ 3. An earthly kingdom (as Lisco remarks in his work on the Parables, in his Introduction, § 6), presents four distinguishing features:—(1) A ruler or head; (2) Subjects, members of the state; (3) A leading policy or general system or spirit of government; (4) A distinctly defined and prescribed system of laws. These particulars, in such a combination, furnish an image of God's kingdom. (1) He is the Supreme Ruler; (2) His intelligent creatures, angels and men, viewed as subjects, constitute the noblest part of His kingdom; (3) That kingdom *comes* (Matt. 6:10), or is erected and established in proportion as the divine authority becomes known and is acknowledged and duly obeyed; for its leading object or general purpose, namely, the glory of God revealed in the happiness of His creatures, is then manifested or realized. (4) Its great principle of law is love (Matt. 22:37–40; Rom. 13:8, 10) not only in this world, but also in the eternal world (1 Cor. 13:8); and *that* law is set forth in the Holy Scriptures. Now this kingdom, in which love is the eternal law, is made perfect and complete, when the divine will meets with no further opposition, but is obeyed heartily, exclusively, completely, and forever, that is to say, when sin and death are completely overcome, and salvation and eternal blessedness constitute the portion or condition of the members of the kingdom.

§ 4. This kingdom is called, first, the kingdom *of God,* or, *of the Father;* the term indicates its general nature, its origin, etc; secondly, the kingdom *of Christ,* its immediate Head (Eph. 1:20, 23), who is *one* with the Father (John 10:30; Phil. 2:9–11; Hebr. 1:6); thirdly, the kingdom *of heaven,* in order to indicate its divine character, or its spiritual nature (John 18:36, 37) as distinct from a perishable world, and also to express its purity, holiness, eternity, etc.; fourthly, *the kingdom,* to indicate that it alone exists legitimately, truly, and eternally.

§ 5. As God, the Creator, who is almighty and omnipresent, can enforce His will in all places, His kingdom, in the widest sense, "ruleth over all" (Ps. 103:19), that is, over all space, over all creation, over heaven, earth, and hell. So, too, God is the Father of all (Mal. 2:10), inasmuch as He gave life to all men; still He is called *Father* in a special sense, as when we say: "Our Father," in the Lord's Prayer, referring pre-eminently to our adoption through Christ as His children by faith (Rom. 8:15). In the same restricted sense, "the kingdom of God "is a phrase not so much including the entire widely extended dominion of God, as rather, indicating *that* portion of it in which he is gladly recognized as the Lord, sincerely revered and worshipped, and ardently loved. In this sense the prophet Obadiah (ver. 21) says: "The kingdom shall be the Lord's." We may therefore say, that "the kingdom of God "is a phrase implying the existence of an intimate and happy communion between God's intelligent creatures and Himself, in whatever part of His empire those creatures may be found. The term can also designate, or be the name of, any

APPENDIX

institution which God may be pleased to devise and grant for the purpose of restoring that union between Himself and men, which sin had destroyed.

§ 6. The subjects or members of the kingdom of God are, first, the holy angels, who love, obey, and adore God; secondly, believers on earth, who, having received Christ in faith, are governed willingly and exclusively by the divine will, and in this sense, the kingdom of God is the Gospel kingdom (Matt. 6:33; 21:43; Acts 1:3); thirdly, "the spirits of just men made perfect" (Hebr. 12:23), that is, the redeemed in heaven, deceased "saints," who will accompany the Lord at His final coming to judgment (1 Thess. 3:13). For by all these the authority of God is recognized and truly revered, and they are happy in their communion with God.

§ 7. Now as the distinguishing features of the true subjects of the kingdom are, for instance, knowledge, love, obedience (see Rom. 14:17), this kingdom is not of a material, earthly character (John 18:36), but from its very nature belongs to the spiritual world; in this respect it is *invisible* (Luke 17:21; 1 Cor. 4:20). Nevertheless, in as far as true believers, while they are renewed and sanctified by the divine Spirit (Col. 1:13; Matt. 13:38), although no longer *of the* world, are still *in* the world, according to 1 John 4:5, 17, as an institution designed to bless and save men, is also in the world and among men, and is capable of being a *visible* kingdom.—The kingdom of God, if we may employ as an image, an earthly kingdom which has been enlarged by the recovery of a long-lost province, extended anew its borders when this world, long alienated from its God, was reclaimed by Christ, or will extend them when this world, by a renovating and sanctifying process, shall be fully annexed to those portions of the kingdom which remained faithful to the great King.

§ 8. Those who repent and believe are required to confess Christ before men (Matt. 10:32, 33), and by all possible means sustain the great instrumentality by which men are turned to God and maintained in the faith, namely, the preaching of the word (Mark 16:15; Acts 26:17, 18; Hebr. 10:25). Further, they are uniformly required to be baptized and to commemorate the Lord's death in the Holy Supper, of which the Acts and the Epistles furnish numerous illustrations. Their union on earth as disciples of Christ, constituting an organized society, resulted in the establishment of the visible kingdom of Christ on the day of Pentecost (see Acts 2:47; 8:1; 15:22; 1 Cor. 14:4). This *Church*, consisting of the true disciples of Christ, is termed the "body" of Christ, He being the head (Eph. 1:22, 23; 5:25–27; Col. 1:18, 24). Thus the Church "is the congregation of all believers, among whom the Gospel is preached in its purity, and the holy sacraments are administered according to the Gospel." Hence the Church of Christ is frequently called *the kingdom of God,* especially in the Parables (Matt. 5:19; 13:24, 31, 33, 47), since in it, through the means of grace (by which the Divine Spirit operates on the individual), the communion between God and man is restored; it is the divinely appointed medium through which men are conducted to heaven, wherefore it is called "the pillar and ground of the truth" (1 Tim. 3:15, 16). Now when the Church, thus viewed as the kingdom of God, is mentioned in reference to its purity, holiness, etc., the invisible Church is meant (see above, § 7); at other times, its visible organization, or its living members are specially the objects to which reference is made, and then the visible Church is meant.

§ 9. Now, this material world will come to an end (2 Pet. 3:10, 11), but the people of God will forever occupy the mansions in heaven which Christ has prepared for them (John 14:2). Then the kingdom of God, which at present counts human beings on earth among its members, will consist solely of inhabitants of heaven (as far as we have disclosures in the Scriptures), that is, the holy angels and the redeemed; all these will enjoy eternal bliss and glory in the presence of God. In this special sense the "kingdom" is sometimes mentioned in the N. T. (Matt. 25:34; Acts 14:22; 1 Cor. 15:50; 2 Tim. 4:18; Hebr. 12:28; James 2:5).

§ 10. The term: *Kingdom of*, etc. (while the fundamental idea of communion with God, flowing from a cheerful recognition of His authority is retained), is specially the kingdom of Christ, that is to say, it proclaims His atoning and redeeming work, commenced on earth and developed in its whole glorious extent in eternity. It may be defined, according to the connection in which it occurs, and the peculiar aspect in which it is viewed, in the following different modes, of which the parables of the Lord Jesus furnish many illustrations:—

(a) In its general sense, as shown above, it embraces angels and men, who love and obey God as their king, and it includes time and eternity (Luke 1:33).

(b) In a restricted sense, including human beings only, it designates living and departed saints, believers on earth and saints in heaven. All these form one kingdom, having one King whom they love and obey, or are governed by one Law—Love—which prompts to obedience. A distinction is sometimes made between the Messiah's kingdom of grace on earth (Matt. 19:23), and the kingdom of glory in the eternal world (2 Tim. 4:18).

(c) Sometimes, in reference to earthly relations, the Church (16:18, D.) is meant in a special sense, viewed as the divinely appointed means for establishing a communion between men and God, including the old covenant which prepared the way for the new and better covenant (20:1, B.).—In some cases the visible Church in its whole extent is meant (Matt. 13:3, 19, 24, 31, 41, 47), consisting of all who confess Christ on earth, independently of their internal or spiritual state, and viewed only as Christians in distinction from Jews and Gentiles, infidels, etc. Thus, in Matt. 22:2–14, the "kingdom of heaven" (ver. 2) includes the man who had not on a wedding-garment (ver. 11; Col. 4:11). In other cases, the invisible Church, consisting of true believers alone, is specified; these alone constitute the true Church (Acts 1:3; 8:12), while many hypocrites and impenitent sinners are connected with the visible Church (comp. Matt 13:24 ff. with ver. 38, and see Matt. 5:20; 6:33; 11:11; 13:33; Luke 9:62; Col. 1:13; Rom. 14:17).

(d) The future state of the redeemed exclusively, as they exist in heaven, is sometimes meant. In such cases the Church is viewed in its eternal and heavenly fruits or results as the true realization, development, and completion of the kingdom of God. That kingdom, therefore, in this aspect, begins on earth, but is revealed in its bliss and glory only in the eternal world (Matt. 5:3, 10; 7:21; 8:11; 13:43; 25:1, 34; 26:29; Acts 14:22; 1 Cor. 6:9, 10; 15:50; Gal. 5:21; Eph. 5:5; 2 Tim. 4:18; James 2:5; 2 Pet. 1:11.)—The whole phrase, therefore, while the one fundamental conception stated above is always expressed by it, adapts itself to the various changes which necessarily occur in the spiritual state of a fallen creature like man, who must pass from spiritual death to spiritual life, and be transferred at last from this fleeting world to one that is eternal, before all the gracious purposes of God are fully attained.

EXCURSUS II

Demoniacs. The Greek word *demon* (*daimon, daimonion,* which the Greeks applied to any of their imaginary propitious or unpropitious gods or beings belonging to the invisible world) in the N. T. designates one of the evil spirits or fallen angels (Matt. 25:41; Eph. 6:11, 12; 2 Pet. 2:4) who, with their head, Satan (Mark 1:13), "the God of this world" (John 12:31; 2 Cor. 4:4; 1 Pet. 5:8), constitute a kingdom (Matt. 12:26), and produce all the moral and physical evils in the world (John 8:44; 1 John 3:8, 12). The fall of man (Gen. ch. 3; 2 Cor. 11:3; Rev. 12:9) was equivalent to his separation from God, the only source of bodily and spiritual life, health and happiness. Hence, not only was his moral nature thereby depraved, but his body became subject to sickness and death (Rom. 5:12 ff.). Even inanimate nature shared in the consequences of the curse of God which followed Adam's fall (Gen. 3:17; Rom. 8:20, 21). Thus man became exposed in his spiritual affairs to the assaults and dominion of Satan, and his bodily frame also shared in this awful result of sin. With regard to the *demoniacs,* that is, "persons possessed by demons" = by unclean or evil spirits, many points are not revealed to us; indeed, even in cases in which no direct agency of such beings occurs, as in dreams, madness, etc., the reciprocal action or the reaction of the body and the mind, and the peculiar movements of the soul and its faculties, present mysteries, which no one can, from the nature of the subject, fully unfold. Thus, among the demoniacs mentioned in the N. T., we find persons of both sexes, of various ages and conditions, etc.;—for instance, a young female (Matt. 15:22), a boy or child (Matt. 17:18), two men (Matt. 8:28). Some, as in these last two cases, indicate extreme mental derangement: but the woman mentioned in Luke 13:11, 16, appears to have suffered from "the spirit of infirmity" or "Satan" only in her bodily organization. We cannot, for want of revealed facts, which we do not possess, decide whether such individuals had been more guilty of gross vice than others, or whether other causes produced such startling results. Neither can we explain all the incidents, the purposes of the demons, their immediate subsequent history, etc., to which the case in Matt. 8:28 ff. directs attention; nor can we always declare positively whether the words proceeding from the mouth of a demoniac were uttered with a consciousness of his personal identity (Matt. 8:29), or whether, while he himself was unconscious (as when persons speak in their sleep), the words and thoughts proceeded from the indwelling evil spirit (Mark 5:9; Luke 4:34; 9:39; Acts 16:16 ff.).—The following truths, on the other hand, are deduced with certainty from the N. T. The cases of the demoniacs were not simply those of ordinary diseases, epilepsy, etc., as the language and deportment of Christ and of the evangelists demonstrate (Matt. 9:32; 17:21; Mark 1:25; 9:25; Luke 4:35; and see Acts 10:38; 16:18). Satan and his angels do exercise a certain degree of power in the world over the souls of men when not shielded by divine grace (John 13:2, 27; Acts 5:3; 2 Cor. 4:4; Eph. 2:2; 2 Tim. 2:26) over their bodily nature (Matt. 17:15; Luke 13:16; Acts 5:16; 10:38; 1 Cor. 5:5), and also over other objects;

APPENDIX

see ann. to 8:26, C.). Divine wisdom tolerates these and other evils for holy purposes; but this pernicious influence of Satan is already so greatly abridged (Luke 10:18; Acts 26:18; Rom. 16:20) that it ceases to be formidable to those who seek divine aid (James 4:7; Eph. 6:10 ff.; Col. 1:13; 1 Pet. 5:9). When the gracious plans of God shall have reached their consummation, Satan's whole power to harm God's creatures will be abolished entirely and forever (Hebr. 2:14; 1 John 3:8; 2 Thess. 2:8; Rev. 20:10, 14).

www.ingramcontent.com/pod-product-compliance
Lightning Source LLC
Chambersburg PA
CBHW070135100426
42743CB00013B/2706